# NEW TRENDS IN 20TH CENTURY DRAMA

# New Trends in 2oth Century Drama

A Survey since Ibsen and Shaw

by

## Frederick Lumley

New York
OXFORD UNIVERSITY PRESS
1972

NEW TRENDS IN 20TH CENTURY DRAMA *is a fourth edition
of* TRENDS IN 20TH CENTURY DRAMA, *first published in
1956; second edition, published in 1960; Third
edition, 1967, reprinted 1969. Fourth New edition 1972*

© Frederick Lumley 1967, 1972
Library of Congress Catalogue Card No. 67-14436


MADE AND PRINTED IN GREAT BRITAIN BY
C. TINLING AND COMPANY LIMITED
LONDON AND PRESCOT

# CONTENTS

# ILLUSTRATIONS

# PREFACE TO THE 1972 REVISED EDITION

TRENDS in the theatre seem to bring with them their own passing of generations. Even in the last five years, since my previous edition, the new theories of Grotowski have taken root, as have Peter Brook's own free style experiments in group collaboration, not to mention the influence of the tribal liberation of *Hair*: the continued existence of playwrights seems threatened. Nothing, however, is so new that it has not appeared before; the indecent *phallus*, the emblem of fertility, was prominently displayed in the attic comedies of Aristophanes; the *Commedia dell'Arte* relied on improvisation and abolished text long before the age of Marshall McLuhan.

In this edition I have had the opportunity of reading Jean-Paul Sartre's first play, *Bariona*, which the author has at last published, and which is discussed in chapter ten. Among new plays by established playwrights figure the names of Edward Albee, Jean Anouilh, Max Frisch, Christopher Fry, Arthur Kopit, Arthur Miller, John Osborne, Harold Pinter, James Saunders and Sir Terence Rattigan. New names included for the first time are Peter Luke, the late Joe Orton, Günter Grass, Tom Stoppard, and the late Yukio Mishima. Finally I feel I can no longer remain silent about the "theatre of panic" of Fernando Arrabal.

I have re-arranged the order of playwrights in chapters 18-21 to enable the reader to find individual works more quickly. I hope this new edition will continue to serve enthusiasts of the modern theatre, both as a companion to the works discussed and provide personal views passionate enough to provoke disagreement and debate.

Frederick Lumley
January 1972

# INTRODUCTION

AT the outset it would be useful to outline as it were our terms of reference; titles of theatre books remain elusive and open to misinterpretation. In the decade since the original edition of *Trends in Twentieth Century Drama* first appeared in 1956, dramatic horizons have expanded; it is clear that the time has now come for a major reassessment to take into account the many new playwrights on both sides of the Atlantic, as well as in Europe, and the influence of the older generation of dramatists—included in the original volume—on the younger playwrights. Arthur Miller has remarked how difficult it is to orient ourselves in the snake-pit in which we live; in the theatre a sense of direction and perspective are more than ever essential. I have in this respect remained close to my original aims, and though numerous works have now been published on the modern theatre, nearly all of them are in closed compartments. We have interesting studies of the new English dramatists, or well documented accounts of the fringe theatre, like the Theatre of Dissent, or Theatre of the Absurd, but little has been done to consider the works of important and different dramatists like Osborne, Pinter, Wesker, Arden and Shaffer, to name some of the English school, with American and Continental figures such as Albee, Dürrenmatt, Frisch and Peter Weiss. It is indeed an anomaly that in the age of communications where everything happens simultaneously throughout the world, so little effort has been made to see the whole; we seem almost to have entered a period of new isolationism, not of continents, but each in his intellectual ghetto.

By 1956 I complained that it was no longer 'fashionable' to use the word 'theatre' by itself; some sort of appendage was necessary by way of explanation: 'experimental', 'art', 'proletarian', 'naturalistic', 'mystical', 'box office' and others. Since then we have many new labels to add: 'Theatre of Cruelty' (borrowed from Artaud), 'Theatre of

Embarrassment', 'Theatre of the Absurd', 'Anti-Theatre', to name a few. Good plays and good theatre are no longer accepted as critical currency. Yet in spite of this, if we consider drama as an art, labels are completely immaterial. Perspectives are the only standards we can assert in seeking to understand a playwright's aims and influences within the living traditions of the drama. This is an age where the director has become all powerful, as we have been forcefully reminded by Professor Allardyce Nicoll, whose book *The Theatre and Dramatic Theory* (1962) sounds like the voice of sanity from the wilderness. Professor Nicoll remarks that in the Elizabethan theatre there was no conflict between the dramatists and actors, and little distinction between 'theatrical' and 'dramatic' objectives. Then came the *éminence grise* of the modern theatre, the director. "Numerous persons concerned with the theatre today" Professor Nicoll writes, "most of them sincerely eager to further the interests of the stage, illogically muddle together the drama as an art to be cultivated for its own particular sake and their own predilection for plays of a special kind." This striving to serve "two masters" can only end in confusion. It can also carry us beyond the boundaries of the drama, for Professor Nicoll reminds us that a very considerable area of theatrical endeavour—he lists opera, ballet, the *commedia dell'arte* and mime as examples—have nothing to do with the drama proper. We shall examine in the next chapter some of the theories of the drama; suffice it to remark here that nothing is ever so new as it seems revolutionary at the time; in the end all theories return us inevitably to the fundamentals of the drama, or alternatively leave us outside the dramatic experience.

Who then are the new playwrights; who are the masters and who the disciples? It should be noted that although 1956 marked the turning point for the new British drama, in some countries the year was quite uneventful. By 1956 Paris playgoing, together with the sense of *malaise* which the Algerian war and the crumbling of the Fourth Republic brought to France at that time, was in full decline, with most of the experimental left-bank theatres already forced to close. However, 1956 can serve as a landmark for the modern drama, the new stirrings in Germany, the death of Brecht, the arrival in German Switzerland of Friedrich Dürrenmatt and Max Frisch as important new dramatists. 1956 also saw the arrival in London of the Berliner Ensemble, which was to have such a profound impact on the British theatre and theatre-going public. On the other hand if everything seemed to happen of a sudden in 1956, it will be found that most of the groundwork had been done, the theories published if not performed, in the period between the two world wars.

It is not our intention to survey the whole field of the modern drama which emerged in the closing decades of the nineteenth century—and what critic worth his *métier* has not had his say on the giants of the period: Ibsen, Strindberg, Shaw, Tchekhov, Synge?—but to assess the importance of those who appeared as I have suggested, since Ibsen and Shaw. The theatre of Ibsen and Shaw, I believe, belongs to another age; the social-purpose plays of Ibsen, the buoyant cocksureness of Shaw seem no longer to express an age in transition, where everything is uncertain and dominated by an *inquiétude,* and a blind groping for a way of life in a civilisation where crisis has become normality. If in the decades prior to 1956 the English theatre was in the doldrums, this was partly caused through the negative influence of Shaw and "the very wrong influence", as Mr. Ronald Peacock has observed in his book *The Poet in the Theatre,* of the social-purpose plays of Ibsen. The 'deceptive' skill of Ibsen is only matched by the 'deceptive' skill of Shaw. Both writers could have no imitators and both were to encourage hundreds of would-be imitators. Alas, none of their disciples had the mental genius of their masters. It is paradoxical that Ibsen and Shaw won so complete a victory for the play of ideas that, in the years which followed, imagination gave way to facts, and with lesser writers the English theatre became frigid and passionless. By 1921 Gordon Craig was complaining that the English theatre had neither drama nor art. Instead of a theatre of imagination for which he appealed, each succeeding decade confirmed that English playwrights had become servile to mediocrity and gentility; emotions were as damp as a London smog. Only the actors, as always in Britain, were second to none. The playwrights following Shaw seemed to have learned their craft from William Archer's textbook; only Noël Coward and James Bridie seem to stand apart; Coward indeed has already entered the repertory of the National Theatre and I hope one day a place will be found for Bridie—even if he never wrote a masterpiece. When we consider the other names, who cares today about the work or survival of playwrights like C. K. Munro, Clemence Dane, Clifford Bax, A. A. Milne, R. C. Sherriff, John Galsworthy, Emlyn Williams, John Drinkwater, or Charles Morgan? Even Somerset Maugham had himself deserted the theatre before the theatre deserted him.

These decades with the accent on escapism are a far cry from the theatre that matters; yet all was not frivolous, and on the continent Pirandello was experimenting with the aesthetics of the drama and may be considered as the father of the modernist movement. In his exploration of the planes of illusion and reality Pirandello had challenged the principles of the naturalistic school; in his introspective cerebral drama where intellect and emotions seem allied to a profound and genuine discovery of the human condition, we are reminded of the voice of Aristotle: "No great genius was ever without some mixture of madness, nor can anything grand or superior to the voice of common mortals be spoken except by the agitated soul." The way was open for the anti-naturalistic theatre, with the examples we find in Giraudoux, Lorca, Anouilh and Tennessee Williams. The challenge of naturalism in Germany took the form of either Expressionism or its derivative, the Epic Theatre originally conceived by Büchner and rediscovered by Piscator and Brecht. The European theories of the drama are responsible for the masters of the modern movement; without them the British drama would have known no 1956, while the American drama was still too young and in need of European stimulae before discovering its true identity.

Each decade assumes its own tempo; the Thirties opened with the breakdown of an economic system and closed with the prospect of Nazism conquering the world. Even the optimism of a dramatist like Giraudoux disappeared as France was overrun, but the British theatre refused to succumb; it preserved an atmosphere of jocular irrelevance right up to 1956 and Suez. Long before then the European theatre had surrendered to a profound pessimism; the dramatist had become a kind of lay analyst, with the theatre in a state of nervous depression.

The playwrights I am not particularly tolerant with in this survey are those who choose the narrowest horizons, who see and depict life only in the grotesque phase of its sordidness, who distort it unsparingly so that the humanity of the great dramatists of the past is no longer recognisable, where characters are neither life-size nor exceptional beings, but puppets. Our new 'masters' have dug an unbridgeable ditch. "Pessimism" Arnold Bennett once remarked, "when you get used to it is just as agreeable as optimism. Indeed, I think it must be more agreeable, must have more real savour, than optimism—from the way in which pessimists abandon themselves to it." I am against the fashionable cult of pessimism (which is such a powerful and negative force at the present time), not genuine pessimism. The false pessimism threatens to destroy the humanistic framework so essential for the concept of tragedy. And I do not agree with Mr George Steiner's thesis that tragedy is dead.

This book does not claim to be a history of the contemporary drama nor even to offer an account of the stage during the last half century. We are not here recording performances seen, such as dramatic critics delight in compiling from their notices written in the heat of the event, and often with such little objectivity. Still less are we interested in the sophisticated triangular concoction, the sentimental musical, or the slick who-dunnit; we are not concerned with the theatre as light entertainment and as relaxation. This study is about the theatre judged as an art, a living theatre continuing the great tradition of dramatic literature. For we shall judge a dramatist both by the literary and dramatic quality of his work, remembering C. E. Montague's remarks that the two terms can be complementary, and are not necessarily opposed: "if one's conception of literary quality and dramatic quality be confused and shallow, the distinction is a gaping one. If by literary quality you mean bookishness, and by dramatic quality you mean staginess, the antithesis between them may be striking. But in proportion as one examines and defines more exactly one's own conception of literary excellence on the one side and of dramatic excellence on the other, one finds the assumed contrast and antagonism to be fading away into nothing".

Our playwrights then are selected, not according to box-office tabulation, nor for their political messages, or because they are out for a shock or a gimmick, but for their ability to make the theatre live as an art. We may agree to differ on the selection, on enthusiasms and regrets; at least the choice cannot be ignored. Nor do they belong to any one style, school or nation. Our dramatists, whatever their conception of the world and however outrageously provocative they may be, view life as a contest of dramatic forces to be resolved according to an attitude of mind. I do not propose to discuss dramatists in the way histories of the drama invariably do, with an impartiality which imparts nothing. Should I be accused of being partial there is always the defence offered, I think it was, by Lord Hewitt, when he declared that the only impartiality of which the human mind is capable comes from understanding neither side of the case. My partiality is the result of an attitude of mind, a desire to identify what we see in the theatre with a philosophy of life which is neither excessive nor distorted. In judging a play I shall also apply Baudelaire's critique: "In order to be fair, that's to say in order to fulfil its purpose, criticism must be partial, passionate, political, in other words, strong in an exclusive viewpoint, but a viewpoint which unfolds the widest horizons."

There is no place in this book for the Soviet theatre, since both the commissars and the dictates of socialist realism take over from purely aesthetic considerations, and art cannot prosper when subjected to reprobate intentions. Except for Afinogenov's *Distant Point* (and under Stalinism Afinogenov was himself in disgrace for many years when he might have been creatively productive) the Soviet drama since Gorky is at a lower ebb than the tritest offerings of Broadway or the West End, which do, after all, aim at entertainment. It is a far cry from the proud days of Tchekhov, the old Moscow Arts Theatre and Stanislavsky. There was a glimmering of hope for the Russian theatre in the post-Stalinist "thaw", when grievances were given a temporary hearing. Rigid censorship was soon resumed. Pasternak dared to use art creatively, and his offence was all the greater not because he was against communism, but above it. The continuing trials of Soviet writers does not suggest that freedom of expression is likely in the foreseeable future.

Our view, then, is of world theatre. The theatre is an international art, yet it is especially noticeable in the modern theatre that the best dramatists are those who are intensely national; it is·as if plays, through their nationality, attract international recognition. Even if no mention were made of a writer's nationality in this book, there would never be a moment's hesitation as to which nation he belonged. No one could be more Spanish than Lorca, French than Claudel, Giraudoux, Anouilh; Italian than Pirandello; more American than Tennessee Williams or Miller, or more English than Osborne, Pinter or Arden. Our dramatists epitomise their national temperament even when dealing with themes of universal application.

A survey of the theatre since Ibsen and Shaw proves that in spite of the excesses of the box office and the growing eclipse of the individual in society, good theatre is neither dead nor dying; on the other hand there is no cause for complacency. The important masters of the period —Pirandello, Giraudoux, Claudel, Lorca, O'Neill are dead. Yet the young dramatist today has greater possibilities to experiment than those immediately in the shadow of Ibsen and Shaw. If the theatre is to survive, it must do so at the hands of the artist and poet, not through the reforming zeal of political or religious missionaries. It must appeal to audiences through sensitivity, enabling them to identify the world through the expressiveness and inspiration of poetic vision, or, if you prefer, poetic reality. The drama is not for any class or artistic clique; it is for the public, though it will inevitably appeal to its audience at different levels.

In considering the place of drama in society we have to ask ourselves the question, not whether the theatre is mortal, but how the theatre can survive. It is not sufficient for a playwright to believe in the art of the drama, he must also find his audience. It is seldom realised how few theatre-going centres there are, and what a minority public they attract. In recent years the number of theatres in the provinces, and on 'the Road' in the States, has been dwindling; even the commercial playhouses of the three main theatre-going capitals have been experiencing the customary crisis. I believe however there is now a current trend which is going to reverse the process; new provincial municipal theatres are replacing the old weekly repertory theatre with its stale triangular drawing-room comedies; the new repertory, while not generally as adventurous as it would be freed from the control of town treasurers, at least can pursue a middle course of a museum repertory of the best plays from the past and present, with very occasionally an experiment. The trend for municipal theatres was already well established in Western Germany, and in France the success of the dramatic centres has been given a new lease of life in Malraux's plan to attach *Maisons de la Culture* to them, and lure talent away from Paris through government subsidies. In the States the various foundations ensure that the public in the different States is not denied a living theatre where a professional organisation already exists. The changing means of communication will probably result in London, Broadway and Paris having less influence than in the past, and henceforth it will be more difficult for the type of *avant-garde* play of very minor appeal and *snobisme* to find an outlet in this new concept of theatre. The commercial theatres of London, Broadway and Paris will continue, but fewer in number. The hopes of the dramatist of promise will be the prestige of a limited number of performances in a repertory of a state or municipal playhouse. Perhaps the time has come not only for subsidised theatre, but as Peter Brook has suggested, a subsidised audience, to make playgoing a necessary part of everyday life.

In this short introduction I have given a sufficient outline of some of the problems with which we shall be concerned, and the approach which will be made in the following chapters. I do not claim that the views reached in either the individual studies of dramatists or the book as a whole will be in any way original; but at least it was Goethe who said that you do not forfeit your originality because you recognise a truth which has already been recognised by others. The new reappraisal of playwrights and their relation to the modern theatre will, I hope, lead to a better understanding of contemporary trends.

# ONE

# THE DRAMA SINCE IBSEN AND SHAW

"Human life is reduced to real suffering, to hell, only when two ages, two cultures and religions overlap ... Now there are times when a whole generation is caught in this way between two ages, between two modes of life, and thus loses the feeling for itself, for the self-evident, for all morals, for being safe and innocent."

HERMANN HESSE: *Steppenwolf*

WE must agree with Hermann Hesse that a man from the Middle Ages would detest the whole mode of our present-day life as something far more horrible and cruel; indeed like the wolf from the steppes our generation has lost its way, strayed into the town and the life of the herd. The drama since Ibsen and Shaw seems like Steppenwolf to have gone "through hell from one end to the other" without having found any sense of belonging or identity. The dramatist finds it difficult to give expression to our times because in doing so he expresses his own confusion and uncertainties. There is the drastic alternative, to change the world, and to begin with an assault on the aesthetics of the drama. The European theories of the modern drama have taken three directions; first an effort has been made to escape the frontiers of the drama through mysticism and spectacle (of which Reinhardt's productions in the Berlin of the Twenties come as the obvious example). There has secondly been the theories of Epic Theatre, again dating from the Germany of the Twenties, and in which Brecht has played a predominant role, which seeks to eliminate emotion, participation and identification, and make the audience think and reflect instead of feel. Yet a third direction has been taken by the so-called Theatre of Cruelty, originally devised by Artaud as, to quote Peter Brook's pamphlet for the Royal Shakespeare Company's four week Experimental Season at LAMDA, "a collage, a form of surrealist revue composed of shots in the dark, shots at distant targets". In the Fifties the French left-bank theatres presented us with a no-man's-land where the characters acted like puppets reciting questions to which the answer was silence. It is doubtful whether pushed to their logical conclusion any of these methods may claim to remain within the frontiers of the drama; on the other hand in spite of their intentions the first two methods used in moderation can return us ultimately to the fundamentals of the drama, while a combination of the second and third forms, the Brechtian Epic with the Theatre of Cruelty, has given us one impressive work which is a challenge for any director, the *Marat-Sade* play by Peter Weiss, which we shall discuss in a later chapter.

Why do we go to the theatre? Why do playwrights exist and for whom do they write? Such questions have been debated through the centuries. In the Elizabethan era reasons were advanced why society should not go to the theatre, and why poets should not write plays; the drama was aesthetically condemned by Sir Philip Sidney and morally attacked by the puritans. The contemporary drama during the first half of the twentieth century ceased to be taken seriously by the public, although even before the first world war theorists such as Edward Gordon Craig (whose book *The Art of the Theatre* was published in 1905) the static naturalism of the current dramatic form. It was almost like Nietzsche's famous differentiation between the prophets who seek to change the course of the world and the public who follow the actors, unaware of what is happening. In the inter-war years the theories which have so influenced the modern theatre were formulated; the names of Gordon Craig, Max Reinhardt, Jacques Copeau, Henri Ghéon, Antonin Artaud, Erwin Piscator and Bert Brecht—to name a few—emerged. Yet the public continued to regard playgoing, to use Agate's description, as a 'diversion'. Play-wrights were the servants of their public; this was no time for those who believed that a play had first to be judged as an art, and that the artistic criterion did not bend to the demands of the caterers. Pirandello was not only not understood; he was hardly admitted. 'The box-office never lies' might have been an American adage, but the London theatre managements were the first to follow it. Time and again the argument was raised: did not Shakespeare write for the commercial theatre and please his public? — a glorious example of the dangers of simplification and wishful thinking. Were the commercial pundits quite the same in Elizabethan times? And even if we could equate the denominators of public taste then and now, are we so certain that Shakespeare would have served his public at any price? Might he not have left the theatre for, say, the novel? Was it not a later generation which substituted a happy ending for *King Lear*?

Until the storming of the Royal Court in 1956 and the all round shake-up of the drawing-room complacency of the British theatre, the critics of the Anglo-Saxon world had given little lead to the problems of contemporary drama and life. With the exception of George Jean Nathan, Eric Bentley, John Gassner, Barret H. Clark and a few other American critics, the theatre had been taken for granted. If Hollywood provided the dream factory, the theatre box-office was like a cocktail bar where you could stick to your tried favourites. It was in Europe where the new theories were being formulated, in France, Germany and Italy. And although Gordon Craig was an Englishman, his shabby treatment by his native country forced him to reside in Italy and France and he became truly a European. Craig pleaded for a unity of production in order to make a theatrical achievement possible; above all he demanded imagination. In *The Theatre Advancing* (1921) he explained that imagination was "far more rapid than the inventions of modern science, far more powerful than anything in the world, it can pierce all that is material, no matter how dense; it leaps all divisions, no matter how wide. While it is the one thing needful today, it is the one thing disregarded". But his theories and his advice went largely unheeded, when not rebuked, like all prophets in their own country; he was however, to have a profound influence on the Continent, stimulating Max Reinhardt and Jacques Copeau in their early work. We shall not examine here the theories of Craig, which cannot be described satisfactorily in a short account and which do not in any case come within the scope of this book. Having paid this tribute to him for his pioneering work, for his courage in shaking up theatrical imagination, it is the French theories of the drama we shall consider.

There is, of course, no one dominating theory in French discussions of the theatre, but several diverging viewpoints. They all belong, however, to the anti-naturalist camp, and are concerned with the participation and communion between actors and audience in the theatre. They vary from the extreme vision, the dream of Copeau for a mass audience and spectacle, linked with the view that "there will only be a new theatre on the day when the audience will be able to whisper the words of the actor at the same time and with the same spirit as he", to the idea expressed by Georges Jamati that "a theatrical play must establish a union between our inner self and that of the author, his interpreters and his characters". This latter view has approximations to George Jean Nathan's belief that "one does not go to the theatre to see life and nature; one goes to see the particular way in which life and nature happen to look to a cultivated, imaginative and entertaining man who happens, in turn, to be a playwright".

The French theories, involving as they do to some extent the conception of magic and the importance of collective communion, have been vigorously challenged by Eric Bentley in an article in *Theatre Arts* (March, 1950)* — the French 'highbrow' theatre, which from Gaston Baty onwards becomes "a theatre of dreams, a consensus of opinion unfavourable to Naturalism and all realism, favourable to magic and other-worldly vision". Bentley pins down the word 'magic' and suggests that this may be interpreted on religious grounds and in fact is so interpreted, rather than on the aesthetic 'as if' contact. The theatre thus becomes associated with the concept 'more than a theatre', the existence of the supernatural, and Bentley goes on to assert that these mystical theories of the theatre have been fostered "by the modern flight from freedom, from decisions, and from the self". In creating a force which unites the audience as if in a dream, the theatre is in danger of a crime politically known as totalitarianism. From this stage a play can by-pass dramatic art and lead straight into a religious — or political — communion. Bentley attacks the idea of a theatre being more than a theatre under three headings, an historical heresy, a psychological perversion, and political fascism. He claims on the first accusation that the supporters of a mystical theatre demand that the theatre return to its origins and be in essence religious. On the second crime he likens the audience to "Hitler's storm troopers wildly losing their separate existence in a celebration of the Volk". All this leads to his third assumption that the audience would consist of individuals with identical opinions, which would, in practice, reduce it to either a Christian or a Marxist gathering.

If we consider Bentley's case objectively, we have to admit there is an element of fanaticism in the theories of some of the theorists, notably Copeau, Henri Ghéon, and Antonin Artaud, if pursued beyond the boundaries of the play. But Bentley so states his case against the whole current of modern French drama, linking Claudel with his argument, dismissing Giraudoux, that we get the impression that the entire state of the anti-naturalist theatre in France should be viewed

* Reprinted in *In Search of Theatre*.

with suspicion. The reaction against magic has led to Brecht's concept of 'alienation', which Bentley was among the first to bring to the notice of the Anglo-Saxon world and which we shall discuss in a later chapter. Brecht sought to end the "temporary half faith" between the audience and the play by reminding them that their function at all times was to think and reflect, not participate; they had to substitute reason for emotions. The theatrical illusion was taboo, Brecht ideally wanted a "smoker's theatre", where the audience could wander round like in a cafe while the actors were performing, and remain unmoved by their performance. Again pushed to its logical conclusion we have escaped the frontiers of the play.

The impact of Brecht has been as great on modern playwrights as different as, say, Max Frisch is from John Arden; the impact of the anti-naturalistic theories has been equally important, affecting playwrights from Lorca to Anouilh and Tennessee Williams. Yet in both theories we are returned to the fundamental concepts of the drama that emotions do matter, and that feeling and intelligence make up the complete whole. Professor Nicoll has reminded us in *The Theatre and Dramatic Theory* that "A thing which is forgotten by most of those who today are illogically seeking to impose Brecht's concepts on our stage is that even he, towards the close of his career, was forced by the theatre's innate power to admit that, when all had been said, the emotions could not be renounced and that the playhouse has to be regarded as 'a place of entertainment'." It seems that alienation can be used effectively, and within limits, if the character is sufficiently dramatic (as for example Mother Courage) and the personal vision absolute. Brecht was able in his best plays to achieve this; with a young dramatist like John Arden it is difficult to assume a standpoint like that of Brecht; his play *Serjeant Musgrave's Dance* seems to me to fail because the character of the Serjeant is not sufficiently powerful for us to be moved, and Arden has not a powerful poetic vision to overcome confusion; strangely enough his best play *Armstrong's Last Goodnight* succeeds for old-fashioned reasons, for we share an emotional interest in Armstrong, and the border ballads come naturally into the rhythm of the structure, without any 'alienating' effects. It may be stated that a dramatist must have a philosophy of life and through his personal vision he should reveal something to us of which we were not previously aware.

Just as Bentley was against a religious play becoming a mechanical chant, so we must beware of Epic Theatre becoming a purely political manifestation. Politics is not, and never can be, a substitute for the art of the drama. The creative elements of *mise-en-scène* on the other hand have a right to be exploited as an art, either by the anti-naturalists or the Epic followers. Likewise there is no reason why emotions should be controlled in the anti-naturalist theatre with the puritanical intellectuality which Epic Theatre demands, and on which Bentley insists. Critics who support Epic Theatre must allow a religious conception of theatre as well which establishes an equilibrium between the forces of magic and those of sensibility and intelligence. Even when our mind is grasping the infinite, when we are sharing communion with our neighbours and the actors, we do so because we have gone to the theatre with a desire to believe in make-believe, and know we can at any time see it as it really is, or judge it afterwards as such. If we are unwilling to surrender our individuality on such occasions we surely miss the supreme moments of theatre; we live a play through communion; we judge it afterwards by intelligence. If a play is only to be judged as intellectual dialogue, far better read the play. For a performance is to be felt, not thought.

If certain theorists have longed for a return to ceremonial spectacle, to mass-crowds rather than a play-going public, this has not achieved any importance, any more than a pageant is important. On the other hand there has been a revival of drama in France which evokes miracles and calls in the aid of dreams and imagination. In many instances the plays are religious, but they do not fall victim to the accusations raised by Bentley. In the first place the return to religion in France has not been a return to medieval mystery plays or the liturgy as practised by the Church. Religious drama has not sought the origins of the theatre, but has remained modern, secular and free. The audience does not worship. Even in Claudel, as critics have pointed out, the Pope is not always right, though the office of the Pope is of course respected. It is the idea that though one may criticise the President of the United States as President, one does not criticise the institution of 'the President'.

The anti-naturalist theatre seeks a means of creating poetic reality by extending the dramatic horizons by calling on the creative resources of the theatre. But this 'magical approach' is done inside, not outside, the auditorium. In other words, the audience inside the theatre *do* accept the 'rules of the game' as Henri Gouhier puts it, the belief in 'as if'; communion is made at this level, and not at the level of what the audience or, indeed, the author think as individuals in the street. Thus it is possible for an atheist to accept a Christian play because he has accepted the principle of collaboration voluntarily. But it goes beyond this. The play does not preach; it presents a dramatic conflict. We are not interested in the mere existence of a character; we do not accept Macbeth or Hamlet as individuals, but as part of a dramatic conflict which is given meaning when an appeal is made to life values and the play is given a religious or philosophical significance. Again in the words of Gouhier, we are willing to believe in the intervention of destiny, we are willing to accept the appearance of ghosts or the realisation of miracles, even though as individuals in the street we would no more believe in ghosts than in flying saucers.

Thus the audience is not composed of individuals who hold unanimous viewpoints; on the other hand an audience must not be antagonistic or hostile to the general outlook of the play. Should an individual feel so strongly on a certain subject that he cannot surrender his beliefs, if the 'as if' contact gives way to animosity, if there is no longer any sympathy between him and what is happening on the stage, he will no longer be able to share communion. Should this be the reaction of the audience as a whole, collective participation will give way to individual feelings and the audience will act as so many individuals. Ask any actor what that experience would mean.

But supposing we have an audience which, though far from sharing identical opinions, has more or less a similar outlook on life, the same hopes and fears, and if not a common aspiration at any rate the same vision of the world. As M. Georges Jamati has observed in *Théâtre et la vie intérieure,* the greatest periods of drama are those where there is such agreement between people. It is then that "the great dramatist gives expression to hopes which are in the air, he draws them, models them, portrays them. It is at that moment that genius reveals itself, like the voice of collective sentiment".

This is no longer the case to-day. The new means of mass communication have extended our vision of the world on the one hand and diminished it at the same time. All things are possible, immediate, instant. In the end we have all shades of religious denominations and political concepts from revolutionaries to reactionaries as well as those who disbelieve in our audience. We are agreed on nothing, it is only the vision of the dramatist which counts. Any theory of the drama ultimately returns us to base; this base has nothing to do with the age in which we live. We have to conceive art as out of time and a creator's vision as relative as well as revealing. It seems to me that the theatre can only live through personal discovery, and that discovery by the public will only be worth while if the theatre discovers the beauty of poetry — in the widest sense, poetic vision — and the power of imagination. The only theatre that can live is one which is not afraid of life, which does not offer escape from moral responsibilities. Man cannot escape from thinking, as Sir Thomas Browne expressed it, "of things long past and long to come; acquaint thyself with the choragium of the Stars and consider the vast expanse beyond them. Let intellectual tubes give thee a glance of things which visive Organs reach not. Have a glimpse of incomprehensibles and Thoughts of things which Thoughts but tenderly touch". The theatre, through the communion between audience and actor, is in a position to make man experience the supreme moments of life, the heights of human achievements; it can plunge him into the depths of despair and rescue him, it can throw his prejudices into confusion and produce in him a state of enlightenment. The theatre in the transient world between two ages in which we live may react like a sleepwalker unsure of its directions, aware that there is no turning back, but afraid of the new. As such it is more than ever an integral part of man's expression, and like man, will survive.

# FROM PIRANDELLO TO GIRAUDOUX

OUR first study, that of Luigi Pirandello, may seem at a cursory glance in direct opposition to the French theories of the drama and the anti-naturalist school, and that his *teatro dello specchio* (theatre of the mirror), with its emphasis on the drama of the intellect rather than of passions, would firmly establish the claims of the naturalist over the anti-naturalist camps. Exactly the opposite has taken place. Pirandello's exploration through the mask and face technique, with its different planes of illusion and reality, has led directly into the anti-naturalistic camp. It was Jean Giraudoux who was to adopt a theatre of contrasts to explore an imaginary universe which has similarities with our own, only it reflects to an imperfect world the mirror of the ideal. The anti-naturalist trend was to extend further to writers such as Jean Anouilh, and also to the existentialist school. It is as if Pirandello, himself discarding the limitations of naturalism, discovered in his cerebral drama the field of magical illusion, but, bound to the torments of this world, he never attempted exploration. Perhaps the differences between Pirandello and the anti-naturalists who followed him are not so striking as are the similarities. In the modern theatre, whether in the *teatro dello specchio* style, or the dream world of Giraudoux, or the nostalgic vision of Anouilh, the modern dramatist wishes to intervene directly in our life and thoughts. As such, playgoing becomes an integral part of our existence.

TWO

# THE MASK AND FACE OF LUIGI PIRANDELLO

"No man can justly censure or condemn another, because indeed no man truly knows another."

SIR THOMAS BROWNE

"What do we really know of other people? Who they are . . . how they are . . . what they do . . . why they do it . . ."

PIRANDELLO, *Così E (se vi pare)*

HE who has been born a character, Pirandello tells us, can alone afford to laugh at death, for his being does not change from day to day. Those characters, interviewed by their creator (so the story goes) on Sunday mornings, including the six who were discarded, live on and suffer within the 'immutable bounds' of their creation, the struggle between objective truth and subjective logic, the absolute and the relative, the real and the illusory, the mask and the face. What is important to remember at the outset is that these characters are a mirror not to the world, nor to any literary fashion, but to Pirandello's own life; they are his apology for and justification of his profound pessimism.

For Pirandello is a dominant pessimist; everything is purely transitory, reality only exists at a given moment of time, the flash of a camera or a gun. Nothing will stem the tide of physical destruction, the heart beats a slow funeral march which makes our hopes of to-morrow the lost chances of yesterday. Again and again Pirandello expounds the motivation for his pessimism in his plays, until the drama of action becomes a scientific investigation of the human mind, or cerebral theatre. The audience is asked to give attention to the complexities of inner contradiction, to follow involved explanations which are so seductive that the critic is apt to become exponent, and merely quote rather than comment. It is always easier to accept the resignation of pessimists rather than search for your own judgment, for there is a vogue and school for pessimism to-day which may offer a facile solution, but fails to convince. Pirandello, on the other hand, is one of the few modern writers whose pessimism does convince; his pessimism, however, does not spring from a surfeit of hate, or from the fact that this is the worst of possible worlds; it is because his eyes sadden at seeing so much that is beautiful and yet so irrelevant to the human façade, with its bruises and scars. There is no doubt that Pirandello would, alas, second Schopenhauer's belief that if you knocked at the graves of the dead and offered them a return to life, they would shake their heads. No one would expect Pirandello to wish his life over again.

More than any other modern writer, Pirandello's work can only be appreciated fully as a parallel to his life. He was born at Girgenti in Sicily in 1867, seven years after the union of Sicily with Italy. His father Stefano, a rich owner of sulphur mines on the island, was a violent figure who defied even the powerful Mafia. His mother was a docile and long-suffering wife who accepted her cruel life after being abandoned by her husband for another woman. The silent suffering of his mother must have affected Pirandello's own behaviour in his pitiful marriage. The whole environment of Sicily, an island which had scarcely emerged from the Middle Ages, the contrasts between rich and poor, the chiaroscuro of the landscape, the balance between life and death — whether by starvation, disease, childbirth, or the Mafia — must have permanently moulded the outlook of the young Pirandello. His whole theatre is a theatre of contrasts.

After studying at Palermo, Pirandello was sent when he was eighteen to the University of Rome, but a clash with some of the professors (Pirandello had inherited his father's independence) over teaching methods made it advisable for him to leave, and he took his doctor's degree instead at Bonn in Germany. Already he had started writing poems and short stories about Sicilian life, and on his return from Germany he decided to devote his life to writing fiction. He lived among a group of other young writers and artists, and became a fierce opponent of D'Annunzio and the school which was in fashion in Italy at that time. Because of this his name remained unknown, and none of his work found publication for several years.

In 1894 Pirandello's father arranged a marriage for him with the daughter of his business partner. Although he had never met the girl, Antonietta Portulano, they were married and they settled in Rome on an allowance given by Pirandello's father. For a few years life was uneventful, and three children were born of the marriage. Then in 1904 came disaster. The family fortunes were lost, and this coincided with the mental collapse of his wife. Her form of madness took the shape of unreasonable jealousy, and even though Pirandello stayed at home in his free hours (he had been forced to take a school-teacher's post) she continued to hurl abuse at him and make accusations of unfaithfulness. His life became so much a prison that he began to see in his mind another character, the one described by his wife, and so the world between madness and reality, and reality and illusion came into existence. Pirandello stayed by her side, although his mind acted as a dam to the torrent of her fury, and was powerless against the irrationality of her accusations. Life became a daily torture, in which the only outlet he could escape to was in his writing. Isolated from his friends, isolated mentally from his wife, he flung himself into a frenzy of activity, where the depth of his tragedy was reflected. The 1914-1918 war added to his difficulties and his wife's illness. Their elder son was taken a prisoner of war, their younger was ill in a military camp, and their daughter tried to commit suicide. In 1918 relief came with the death of his wife.

It was during the war that Pirandello had turned to the theatre, and from 1918 onwards he devoted himself to a prodigious output of plays. Fame came slowly in its wake, until in 1921 he became a world celebrity with the production of *Six Characters in Search of an Author*. In 1925 his elder son founded an arts theatre in Rome, and asked his father to become artistic director. Pirandello accepted, and invested a considerable fortune in the project. He hoped that Rome would be able to assume the leadership in modern drama, and had the theatre succeeded, there is every reason to believe that a vigorous school would have been founded. But with its financial failure Pirandello was again a poor man, and felt little inclination to stay on in Italy. Instead he travelled, directing his plays all over the world — it mattered little to him whether it was London, Paris, Prague, Berlin, Vienna, Budapest, New York or South America. In 1934 he received the Nobel Prize. He then returned to Rome, where the final tragedy overtook him on 19 December, 1936.

It is hard to draw a dividing line between the real and illusory worlds of Pirandello; certainly the illusory never surpasses the horror of the real. Pirandello does not seek escape from his suffering in some false dream world, nor does he remain a victim of human misery; rather it may be said that he attempts to transplant his purgatory to the level of tragedy. His theatre does not lend itself to a label. He has been accused of absenting himself from life, of deserting naturalism for the abstract mosaic of cerebral drama; he has been accused of being too much a naturalist with the failings of a naturalist, not having the powers of poetry and imagination to prove his thesis wrong; he has been dismissed as a trick-comedy writer; still others have branded him with the decadent Twenties. It is Pirandello himself in a truly Shavian manner who makes the director in *Six Characters* say of his work; "Ridiculous, do you call it? What can I do if no good plays come from France and we are reduced to put on the stage plays by Pirandello which require a 'highbrow' to understand them, and never satisfy either the actors, the critics, or the public?"

Although his pessimism is unquenchable, his plays do not exploit pessimism. There is a mask over life, and this mask often causes wild hilarity. The more you laugh, the deeper the tragedy. It is through laughter, irony, inconsistencies between the mask and the face, that Pirandello unfolds his drama. His technical skill is unfailing, his dialogue, so tense and abrupt, ideal for his purpose. His characters are not lovable, Pirandello has not a great love for people. They are ordinary individuals, good and bad. Like the Six Characters, some are fully drawn, others merely suggested. Often the dialectics of the problem prevent their appearing to us until the mask is withdrawn and they suddenly emerge as individuals — for Pirandello is a great individualist.

He has a philosophy, but he does not insist. This is how he sees life, but for every individual truth is something different. He believes in the triumph of pessimism, it is instinctive in his nature, his honesty, that his characters suffer and do not rise above their immediate anxiety. But then truth is what each of us makes of it. "We believe ourselves one person," he tells us, "but it is true to say that we are many persons, many according to the possibilities of being which exist within us. We are one for this and another for that person — always diverse and yet filled with the illusion that our personality is always the same for all." There is something reminiscent here of Strindberg's views on naturalistic drama, where incidents in life are caused by a whole series of motives, and the spectator merely selects the one "his own intellect finds the easiest to grasp, or the one which brings most credit to his powers of discernment." But Pirandello's method extends in quite a different context the Strindbergian point of departure. Strindberg's 'incidents' become for Pirandello 'abstractions', and the idea of resolving inner contradictions through dialectical reasoning bears little relation to what Strindberg attempted in his 'naturalistic tragedy'.

Pirandello, however, started out in the tradition of naturalism, and gradually deserted it when his experiments led him to choose the introspective drama of the individual in its place, or the *teatro dello specchio* (theatre of the mirror) as he called it. If some of his characters are naturalistically conceived, in that they accept the ordinary conventions of life and conform to a *modus vivendi*, other characters aspire to eccentricity; they belong not to the naturalistic theatre, but to the theatre of the grotesque. Essentially Pirandello's characters are puppets answering to the workings of his mind. The production must therefore be stylised, in the Italian *commedia dell' arte* tradition, and it is worth remembering that Pirandello collected his plays under the title *Maschere Nude* ("naked masks") and not "faces". To interpret these masks the actor must both work within the tradition and have the ability of turning passions into a drama of the intellect.

No solutions are posed, the question mark is never answered. In *Right You Are (If You Think You Are)* all the different explanations, although each is contradictory, may be taken as correct, since truth is what you make it. It is as if Pirandello says, "Please leave us all in peace", a reassertion of the rights of the individual against the interference of others. Those who imagine Pirandello to be some kind of theatrical psychoanalyst and disciple of Freud have completely misunderstood the premise of his theatre. To be left alone in uncertainty, in the knowledge that everything is uncertain and insecure, aware that our mechanism is running down — again we must return to his pessimism, which is always in spate. The crying need is for a certainty, a faith which would give him courage to face his pessimism, but God, to Pirandello, is negative, he is powerless and cannot rescue suffering humanity. Pirandello sees the frailty of man like Claudel, only without the latter's religious security. For Pirandello, life is a "second of illumination" and all is over. His religious play *Lazzaro* is not on the level of his better work, although he has taken for the theme that of a scientist who brings back to life a dead man. The religious discussions are vague and conventional, and Pirandello soon prefers to turn to the idealisation of healthy farming life with its honest labour and unsophisticated pleasures. Life after death is also the theme of *The Life I Gave You (La Vita che ti diedi)* when Donn'Anna refuses to believe her

Luigi Pirandello

Jean Giraudoux

T. S. Eliot

Paul Claudel

son is dead: "Not even you can tell me that my child is dead", she insists. "You say that God took him back with Him . . . Don't you feel that God is not there as long as he wishes to abide here, in me, in us; not only for ourselves but also that all those who have gone away may continue to live?" And later on she explains: "God wants my son to continue to live. Not of course the life that He gave him here, but that which I have always given him! This cannot be taken away from him as long as life endures in me." Death can be conquered by an illusion, but this is a poor substitute for the 'eternal' lives of the characters a soul may create. Perhaps for Pirandello religious belief, like other truths, varies according to the concealed consciousness of the individual; but we feel the fear of Pirandello's own isolation.

Yes, Pirandello suffers from obsessions, his plays are exaggerations, sometimes over-subtle and always variations (but what brilliant variations!) on a repetitive theme. Nevertheless, the position Pirandello occupies at the cross-roads of modern drama and the influence his works have had on younger writers place him in importance as one of the giants of the modern theatre. While he was still writing, the idea of different planes of reality had, consciously or subconsciously, been taken by Jean Giraudoux as the style so admirably suited to his anti-naturalistic interpretation of life. For Giraudoux (whose work we shall consider in detail in the next chapter) chose to set his plays in an imaginary framework, but one full of significance, presenting a symbolic picture, a fantasy and dream world which has similarities to our own — only with a difference, that it is a world that might have been if mankind had but remembered the meaning of those human virtues of love, hope, forgiveness and understanding. It is a world which still can be if we have faith in man. Giraudoux had faith in man, and his optimism (not a facile optimism, but balanced realism) might almost have been written in reply to the pessimism of Pirandello. It is the philosophy that this writer, at any rate, would prefer to accept, but oh how hard it is to counteract the overwhelming power of Pirandello!

More recently we find the influence of Pirandello very markedly in the plays of Jean Anouilh, and also in the works of the existentialists, both the Christian and atheistic branches. In Anouilh, both in the *pièces roses* and the more recent savage farces where their mask-like characters turn ridicule to pathos, the mood of Pirandello is often caught in a less intellectual and profound way. *Léocadia* ("Time Remembered" in London production), for example, with its theme of the image of an illusory past, recalls immediately Pirandello's *As You*

B

*Desire Me.* A list of all the writers who have followed in Pirandello's wake would lead to tabulation — they range from Ugo Betti in Italy, Priestley in England, to Thornton Wilder and Tennessee Williams in the United States. The chances are that the list will continue to grow year by year, for Pirandello revealed the loneliness of the individual who does not want to be one of a crowd, the slave of the superman (against whom Pirandello had rebelled in his youth) whether he be in the uniform of the commissar, the fascist dictator, or the managerial revolutionary of James Burnham.

Pirandello has emerged as a figure who has given new life to the theatre at a time when the sources of naturalism had ceased to excite; whether the new direction of the drama will again turn full circle and return to naturalism, time alone will tell. The French theatre is always happiest when it turns its back on naturalism. The American drama, the youngest drama, has still to come to maturity. But it is interesting to note that one of its leading playwrights, Tennessee Williams, stated recently that he considered Giraudoux the most important modern dramatist, while any observer can see he has studied his Pirandello very carefully. What could be closer to Pirandello than the following example, the opening lines of *The Glass Menagerie,* written twenty-four years after *Six Characters?*

> Yes, I have tricks in my pocket, I have things up my sleeve. But I am the opposite of the stage magician. He gives you illusion that has the appearance of truth. I give you the truth in the pleasant disguise of illusion.

Pirandello's mask continues to be borrowed. To tell the truth, he never had need of it, because what is unique in Pirandello's own personality is that there is no difference between his mask and his face. *Ecce homo!*

★

The early plays of Pirandello are merely sketches with a Sicilian setting, dramatised from his short stories. The first work worth considering is also an adaptation of an earlier story, *Pensarci, Giacomino* ("Think of It, Giacomino"), where we hear the familiar themes of Pirandello's future work as if in a kind of overture. The story concerns an old schoolmaster, Professor Toti, who instead of retiring and receiving his pension decides to stay on teaching, marry a young wife, and thus force the government to pay her the pension when he dies; in this way he will cost the government a lot of money, do the girl a good turn, and give himself a few years of happiness. He regards it purely as a charitable deed. The girl he marries is Lillina, who is expecting a child through her affair with Giacomino. Toti has no intention of interfering, rather he encourages the lovers. Everywhere the neighbours say the situation is scandalous, but Toti is only concerned with keeping Giacomino beside Lillina, and seeing that he does not marry someone else before his own death. If everyone is happy, let the scandal-mongers mind their own business.

The next play, *Right You Are (If You Think You Are)*, written in 1916, is one of the most important of Pirandello's works. As in *Think of It, Giacomino*, the message seems to be live and let live. It is a tragedy, a revolt against wanton interference by others with what we wish to keep to ourselves, our hidden truths. What, then, is the tragic situation in the play? The answer is that we don't know. A certain Signor Ponza has newly arrived in a town with his wife, and taken a small room in the attic of a building. Next door, in a luxurious apartment, lives Signor Ponza's mother-in-law, Signora Frola. The mystery arises when Signor Ponza tells us that his wife is his second marriage, he having lost his first wife in an earthquake some time ago; Signora Frola, on the other hand, claims that her daughter is not dead, but that Signor Ponza refuses to let her see her. Daily she makes the journey to Signor Ponza's flat and, refused admission, she contents herself by gazing at her daughter's silhouette. This scandalous situation sets the whole town talking, and curiosity mounts as strangers turn detectives. Both Signor Ponza and Signora Frola accuse each other of madness. Signora Frola admits that for a year her daughter went to a sanatorium, and on her return Signor Ponza refused to recognise her as his wife, and insisted on going through the wedding ceremony again. Ponza then admits to pretending madness in order that Signora Frola should keep her illusions. At this stage the *raisonneur* of the play, Laudisi, turns ironically to the assembly and exclaims, "There you are, ladies and gentlemen, the truth is discovered." The only thing to do, people decide, is to ask Signora Ponza herself. And here is her answer:

SIGNORA PONZA    And what can you want of me now, after all this, ladies and gentlemen? In our lives, as you see, there is something which must remain concealed.

|  | Otherwise the remedy which our love for each other has found cannot prevail. |
|---|---|
| PREFECT | (*with tears in his eyes*) We surely are anxious to respect your sorrow, madam, but we must know, and we want you to tell . . . |
| SIGNORA PONZA | What? The truth? The truth is simply this. I am the daughter of Signora Frola, and I am the second wife of Signor Ponza. Yes, and — for myself, I am nobody, I am nobody . . . |
| PREFECT | Ah, but no, madam, for yourself . . . you must be . . . either the one or the other. |
| SIGNORA PONZA | Not at all, not at all, sir! No, for myself I am . . . whoever you choose to have me. |

In *Il Piacere dell' Onestà* ("The Pleasure of Respectability"), written the following year, the mask breaks down before the force of life. The Marquis Fabio Collo, separated from his wife, meets an attractive society girl Agata Renni and seduces her. To avoid scandal and save appearances, the Marquis and Agata's mother decide that a legal husband must be found for Agata, but a husband for form's sake only, merely to protect honour. They call upon the services of Angelo Baldovino, an impoverished intellectual, who accepts the rôle. Baldovino, however, has no intention of being made use of and demands that, in playing his part as husband, Agata should play hers as wife, and, since honour must be respected, cease her affair with Fabio. Fabio, desperate to get rid of Baldovino, plans a ruse whereby Baldovino will appear to have misappropriated money, but Baldovino avoids the trap. He can no longer carry on playing his part of being a puppet husband, for he has genuinely fallen in love with Agata. He, therefore, having proved his innocence, asks Fabio to ruin him and he will go away. This is no longer convenient for the others, since honour must still be protected. Baldovino is determined to go, when Agata, who had gradually come to think of Baldovino as her husband, tells him that she will go with him. Now that he can drop the mask and be her husband, Baldovino consents to stay.

In *The Pleasure of Respectability* there is quite a social satire to be found in the poor intellectual who does not sell his honour, whereas the rich believe that honour can be bought and does not need to be practised. Honour is also the theme of *Il Giuoco delle Parti* ("The Game as He Played It"), but viewed from a different angle. This time the husband, Leone Galla, has resigned himself to the behaviour of his unfaithful wife, Silia, whose sensuous nature delights in tormenting her many lovers. Silia's latest lover is Guido, but what infuriates her is that Leone could not care less. Silia asks Guido whether they cannot think of a way to kill Leone. Chance offers them an opportunity when she invites passing revellers into the house and sends her servant to tell the neighbours that she has been assaulted. Guido hides in the next room. Leone, for his honour, will have to fight a duel, and the man chosen for the insult is a renowned swordsman. Leone calmly agrees, and takes Guido for his second. But now the tables are turned: on the day of the duel Leone tells Guido that he has done the challenging; Guido, to all intents the real husband, must do the fighting, especially as he had been in the house when the insult happened. No match for Leone's cerebral logic, Guido fights and is killed.

There is intense bitterness and irony in Pirandello's next play *L'Uomo, la Bestia e la Virtù* ("Man, Beast and Virtue"); it is both his most naturalistic, most aggressive and perhaps his least appealing play. The plot involves a teacher, Signor Paolino, who is horrified by the hypocrisy of people and the stupidity of his pupils. The mother of one of his pupils, Signora Perrella, is his mistress and she is going to have a baby. Her husband, a sea captain, brutal, selfish, intolerant, only comes home for a day between long voyages, and then never looks at his wife. If only he would make love to her on his next visit, Signora Perrella's virtue would be saved, but she knows that this is impossible. At last Paolino finds a way to save her by asking the chemist, a man he had previously denounced as a hypocrite, to make a love potion to place inside a cake the captain would eat. The trick works and her reputation is saved. The Machiavellian world leaves an unpleasant impression, when virtue, in order to be saved, requires that Paolino, the man who has placed virtue in danger, should further through a trick see his loved one made virtuous again in the arms of the beast.

Pirandello then turned to the *teatro dello specchio*, and in *Tutto per bene* ("All for the Best") he has drawn in the character of Martino Lori a disillusioned, tragic figure we shall not easily forget. For Lori, who for years had worshipped the memory of his wife and had given all his love on earth to his only daughter, suddenly has the truth revealed to him so that all his hopes, illusions, the meaning of life itself are shattered. One look in the mirror and he sees his past as others have seen it, he sees that his life has been a mockery.

The play centres on the big scene, the *coup de théâtre* which was so important to playwrights of the old school, in this case between Lori and his daughter Palma. Palma enters the drawing-room where Lori is sitting in the dark, and mistakes him for Senator Manfroni, a rich man who has taken a fatherly interest in her which has gone to the extent of arranging a good marriage for her and giving her a handsome dowry. Lori has never questioned his motives, but sometimes feels the way his daughter cruelly dismisses him and transfers her affection to the senator. Palma calls out "father" and then seeing Lori, immediately shrinks away from him. When Lori asks her why she behaves like this, she tells him outright that she is tired of his 'acting' the part of her father. For of course Manfroni is her real father. Everyone else except Lori already knew this, and believed that Lori was merely acting the part (and greatly over-acting) of his devotion to his wife's memory, to the extent of going daily, in all weathers, to the cemetery to put flowers on her grave; always, in other words, acting false grief. At the moment of truth, Lori finds life unbearable. He thinks of revenge, but there is nothing that he can do that would not make things look even more ridiculous. He must go on acting the part, only with the mask off. His only consolation is that Palma, who had previously scorned his affection, now feels truly sorry for him and lends him her sympathy. Perhaps it is "all for the best".

The next play from Pirandello was his famous *Sei Personaggi in Cerca d'Autore* ("Six Characters in Search of an Author") where, at the height of his powers, he examines the very essentials of dramatic creation, the theatre, and life. The play, a most profound study, can be judged on several planes, from the satirical comment it has to make on the artificiality of theatrical production to a metaphysical enquiry into the nature of aesthetics. Perfect art can never be perfect reality; rather, the more perfect the illusion the more removed it is from reality. Neither the humdrum reality of every-day life, nor the slick professional interpretation of fiction can be accepted. The only fusion between reality and art would lie in Pirandello's own imagination, and it is for this purpose that he creates his own six characters. They correspond neither to the real nor to the theatrical delusion, for they are the instruments of creative inspiration. Already in a short story entitled "The Tragedy of a Character" he had developed his thesis for the play. "Nature", he tells us, "uses the instrument of human fantasy in order to follow her high creative purpose. A character in a play comes to life just as a tree, as a stone, as water, as a butterfly, as a woman." The "six characters" are a direct result of the human fantasy translating life in terms of art. Pirandello reveals the intense suffering of their creation compared with the stock romantic figures they become when actors take over. How admirably has Pirandello made this a drama both of passion and of intellect! The plot of the play is conveyed in the title, a play of characters where each character, consumed by the passion of his own consciousness, is driven to confession, by acting his own shame and tragedy on the stage.

The stage is not set for a play. The audience, on entering the theatre, see the theatre in its raw essentials, stage, footlights, props at sixes and sevens, stage hands and carpenters at work . . . the theatre without its greasepaint or glamour. Actors arrive in small groups, then the producer and finally the leading lady. The cast, thus assembled, start rehearsing Pirandello's *Il Giuoco delle Parti*, which seems to be giving them great trouble. A theatre usherette enters followed by the Six Characters. In his stage directions, Pirandello emphasises: "The characters must not appear as phantoms, but as created realities, immutable creatures of fantasy. They are more real and consistent than the voluble actors."

The Characters consist of the father (who also acts as the spokesman for the others), a man about fifty; the mother, appearing crushed beneath "an intolerable weight of shame and sorrow"; the step-daughter, aged eighteen, attractive, vivacious and impudent in manner; a gawkish younger brother of fourteen; a little girl about four; and the son, a taciturn youth of twenty-two who stands aloof from the rest and wishes to take no part in the proceedings. Evidently he is the character the author has not conceived very clearly in his mind. All the characters are dressed in black (except the baby girl, who wears a black sash over a white dress); the mother wears a heavy veil and never raises her eyes from the ground.

The producer, angry that his rehearsal should be interrupted, asks them what they want. The father replies they are looking for an author, any author. "But there's no author here, because we aren't rehearsing a new play", the producer replies. At this the step-daughter pushes her way forward and exclaims: "All the better, all the better. Let your new play be in us." The producer asks them if they are playing a practical joke, but has to believe the father's answer that they carry in them "a heart-rending drama" — "which could be your fortune", the step-daughter adds. "Where is your script?" the producer enquires. "The drama", the reply comes, "is in us, and we are impatient to represent it: our inner passion drives us to this." The characters plead that instinct makes them desire to live, if not for eternity, at least for their hour upon the stage. So the producer is persuaded; after all, their drama could not be worse than the one they are rehearsing. He orders a short-hand writer to take down their dialogue and instructs his actors to pay attention so that they should interpret the scene after the characters have acted it.

The story of the Six Characters is a drama of a divided family, tormented by the shame which has befallen them. The play within the play seizes us with its reality, until we forget the actors sitting on the stage like an Elizabethan audience. The father is a highly intelligent man who has married a woman of the people, kindly and homely, but unable to rise to her partner's intellect. She found sympathy with her husband's secretary, and when the father discovered this, he sent her away with her lover, keeping for himself their only son. Living with the secretary, the mother had three illegitimate children, the step-daughter, the boy of fourteen and the little girl aged four. The father, after he had sent his wife away, felt as lonely as he had in her company; only no longer did their son, her son, mean so much to him. But the years passed. During this time, following the death of the secretary, the mother had to bring up her three children in bitter poverty. Having to start work, she found sewing to do for Madame Pace, a fashionable establishment. The step-daughter, no longer a child but aged eighteen, used to visit Madame Pace's establishment with this work for her mother; but there was also another sort of establishment at Madame Pace's, it was the same sort of house as Madame Tellier's. It was there one night that the step-daughter met the father, and, not recognising each other, she was about to give her body to him when the scream of the mother saved them from disgrace. The father, to make amends, took the family under his protection where they are living out the complicated pattern of their shame; ahead lies a tragic despair. The mother has been completely crushed by the event, and her only happiness is denied her, because her legitimate son refuses to hear her tragedy or have anything to do with them. He suffers the same unhappy solitude as his father; the father complains bitterly that one moment of weakness has turned him into a character which is not him; the step-daughter, however, sees only the sensual, hypocritical old man in the father, and she also turns her hatred on his son, for his secrecy. There remain the little girl and the adolescent boy. One day, while playing in the garden the little girl drowns in a pond, and the boy, who can stand life no longer, draws a revolver and shoots himself. Reality reaches a parallel with the event (only slightly dramatised) of what happened in Pirandello's own family. The characters arrange the stage so as to resemble as closely as possible reality. Both the father and step-daughter remonstrate against the type acting of the actors who interpret their scene, but the producer defends his actors:

> You're not going to pretend that you can act? Do you suppose the spirit of the piece is in you? . . . Not at all, your soul or whatever you like to call it takes shape here. The actors give body and form to it, voice and gesture. And my actors — I may tell you — have given expression to much more lofty material than this little drama of yours, which may or may not hold up on the stage. But if it does, the merit of it, believe me, will be due to my actors.

They continue with their drama. The step-daughter wishes to live the scene of her shame by revealing the brutal truth. She will undo her dress and corset, and feel the repugnance, let the reality of the horror be seen. But the producer hastily reminds her that such things are not allowed on the stage. She finally agrees merely to have her arms bare, so that she can watch a vein throbbing which on that night reminded her of the sin she committed in the father's power. "Scream, mother, scream as you did then", she cries. The producer sees the dramatic curtain line.

And so the play is acted, until the final revolver shot brings the actors face to face with the reality of death.

| | |
|---|---|
| LEADING LADY | He is dead! Poor boy . . . dead, what a thing to happen. |
| LEADING ACTOR | Dead my foot. Just fiction. Quite unconvincing. |
| SOME ACTORS | Fiction? It's reality, reality. He *is* dead. |
| OTHER ACTORS | No, it's just the end, the end of the story. |
| THE FATHER | But what an end. Reality, reality, gentlemen, reality. |
| THE PRODUCER | Fiction, reality, to the devil with the lot. Lights, lights. I've never known such a happening. I've lost a whole day's rehearsal. |

The subject of dramatic illusion is also dealt with in *Ciascuno al suo Modo* ("Each in His Own Way"), where after each act two real characters in the audience, from whom the author took the idea of the play, are infuriated at seeing their own sad lives thus represented in the theatre. They interrupt the play when the woman leaps on to the stage and slaps the actress; confusion breaks out in the theatre and Pirandello tells us there is yet another act, but the play cannot go on any longer.

Also following up his ideas in *Six Characters*, Pirandello wrote *Questa sera si recita a soggetto* ("To-night We Improvise") in 1930, where again the playwright demonstrates his material. The contrasts are the same, the reality of the characters compared with the artifice of the stage conventions, and again the producer, inflated with his own importance, is the target of Pirandello's satire. The author expresses again some of his essential ideas, but, alas, the Six Characters are missing, and without characters of their intensity he is unable to keep the perfect balance between the dramatic and the intellectual which he achieved in *Six Characters*. This goes for many of Pirandello's less important works, which are always worth reading, and are never without those brilliant flashes of insight into the mind and the equally marked precision of his exposition; we shall only discuss one more of his plays, *Enrico IV*, which may be considered both as Pirandello's *chef-d'oeuvre*, and as the outstanding tragedy in the modern theatre — indeed, critics have called *Enrico IV* "a twentieth-century *Hamlet*".

*Enrico IV* is not, however, a tragedy in the classical sense, for as Giraudoux notes, tragedy and comedy are interwoven in the modern drama. The tragic vision, however, is that of a soul who relinquished the real world twenty years previously, when he became mad. On regaining his sanity, he finds that he can no longer return to take up his life where he left off. He is condemned to his solitude, his lunacy, his masquerade, his despair, "now, of necessity, for ever". It is a realisation of how life filters away while we breathe, and suggests that in madness alone can one find shelter for the omnipotent reality. In the character of Enrico IV — a giant who towers above Pirandello's other characters — we have a genuinely tragic creation, for whom "the time is out of joint", as it was for Hamlet, and whose tragedy also becomes a 'tragedy of reflection'. *Enrico IV* was not Pirandello's final work in the theatre, but in no other play did Pirandello give so poignantly his summing-up on life. It is as if through Enrico IV he is speaking to each of us, individually, his hidden thoughts.

We are in the Italian countryside of to-day, in a castle where everything appears as if it were an illusion of the eleventh century. All the courtiers wear the costumes of the eleventh century, except one who is dressed in French court costume of the fifteenth. He is the new courtier who, having applied for the job, learnt up all about Henry IV of France, instead of the Emperor Henry IV of Germany, some 400 years earlier. So he has to learn his part all over again. Such is the introduction we are given to this strange world; the action of the play, which started twenty years earlier, is already in a state of crisis when the curtain rises. Twenty years previously, we learn, a rich young Italian gentleman was disguised as Enrico IV for a pageant. He was riding with Matilde Spina, with whom he was in love, but who in turn was the lover of a mutual friend, Belcredi. During the procession Belcredi pricked Enrico's horse, which reared up and threw him head first. Enrico got up, and everybody thought he had had a lucky escape. But it soon became evident that Enrico was no longer acting; he believed he was indeed the Emperor. Instead of being sent to an asylum, being a wealthy man, his friends set him up in a castle, surrounded with courtiers groomed for their parts. So life passed, and after twelve years of madness Enrico regained his sanity. But here lies the tragedy: how could he take up his former life again? He became the grim observer of his own drama; he "preferred to stay mad, to live my madness with the most lucid consciousness and thus avenge myself of the brutality of a stone that struck my head . . . I filled this solitude, squalid and empty as it appeared to me when I opened my eyes, with the colour and splendour of that distant day of carnival".

The day comes when Matilde Spina returns, accompanied by Belcredi, her daughter Frida, Frida's fiancé, and a mental doctor, in the hope that they might still cure Enrico of his madness. There is a striking contrast in how the years have passed . . . how Matilde has aged from the portrait of her on the wall, made twenty years before, while Frida is exactly like her mother was then. Enrico appears; he also has aged, dyed his hair in a ridiculous fashion. He makes some uncomfortable remarks to his visitors on growing old, and then at the sight of his old enemy, Belcredi, he can no longer wear his mask.

The doctor (Pirandello dislikes the certainty of his scientific theories and pat answers) believes that Enrico is really mad, but Matilde believes that he is conscious of the mask he wears and wishes to be freed from it. The doctor has a plan, to confront him with Frida, instead of her mother Matilde, dress her as Matilde was dressed on the day, and place her beside the portrait. The doctor hopes the sudden confusion of seeing her will restore to his mind a conception of time and set it going once again "like a watch which has stopped at a certain hour". When Enrico does see Frida, terror seizes him; he believes that this is madness in reality — and then he understands the trick. Matilde and Belcredi try to persuade him to return with them but Enrico is not interested. Stung with fury — Frida is the girl he loved — he seizes her and as Belcredi rushes forward to take Frida from him, Enrico draws his sword and kills him. He can never now return to the world. The masquerade must continue, the mask must be worn . . . until death.

In *Enrico IV* we have Pirandello's most complete achievement, where man is alone in his solitude, where the life-force continues to reproduce humanity, but where age overtakes the individual and only illusions remain. There is much in Pirandello of the *théâtre de silence*; the unexpressed is often equal to what is actually said. It is a theatre of poetic vision, not of spoken poetry. A one-sided vision, but of genuine sincerity. It was the inconsistencies of life that troubled Pirandello, for he recognised that life must be consistent. "If life moved eternally it would never acquire consistency; if it acquired consistence, it would never move; and yet life must have both consistency and motion." Here, in Pirandello's own words, lies the mystery of life and a key to his theatre — as far as any key can be found to understand the 'own special world' of another human mind.

# THREE

# A DRAMATIST OF OPTIMISM: JEAN GIRAUDOUX

"Evidemment, la vie est ratée, mais c'est très, très bien, la vie."

*Electre*

THE inconsistencies of life were for Pirandello as impossible as the marble blocks Sisyphus had daily to roll up the hill in the world of shades; the world of Jean Giraudoux accepts their existence and resolves their contradiction by leading us into an imaginary universe where everything is made consistent. For the despair of uncertainty is substituted the hope of uncertainty; for the dialectics of cerebral theatre is substituted the spur of French logic. Giraudoux, like Cocteau's Orpheus, breaks the mirror of the *teatro dello specchio* to find the logical conclusion. We are in a theatre of contrasts more than ever, but logical imagination is substituted for nightmares; man rediscovers faith in his fellow-men, and the audience are reminded that though this is only fantasy, it is also only common sense. It is human to be foolish, but it is human also to have hope in the future, to believe that dreams may become reality. "Granted that life is a blunder, how very, very good life is", exclaims the gardener in *Electre*. "Granted", he continues, "that things never go well, that nothing ever turns out right, now and then you must confess that things turn out admirably . . . not for me . . . or rather, for me . . . ."

How far we are from the world of Pirandello! Life is not to be dreaded from day to day as the final tragedy approaches, it is to be lived fully as an adventure story culminating in the greatest adventure of all. When Giraudoux's most beautiful heroine is drawn towards the labyrinth of death and suicide, she is rescued by a humdrum citizen —

a French civil servant — who argues the case for life. For the road to death he offers her is the "slow, gradual, but certain" road of life. Life has its pattern, and confusion only enters when it is permitted. The vigorous rejection of naturalism by Giraudoux was something which Pirandello had hesitated to attempt, though the frontiers between illusion and a make-believe parallel of reality merely require for transition an attitude of mind. If Pirandello's experiments disturbed the very foundations of naturalism, Giraudoux's return to the opposite camp has been followed by all the important French contemporary dramatists, though strange bedfellows they make in any camp!

Before we consider the theatre of Giraudoux in detail, perhaps this is the place to give a brief outline of the state of the French drama and stage before and immediately after the first world war, and in particular pay homage to the work done by Jacques Copeau, Louis Jouvet, Charles Dullin, Gaston Baty, and Georges and Ludmilla Pitoëff, *metteurs en scène* who have transformed the French stage from one of its lowest ebbs for generations to its highest achievements since the great classical period of the seventeenth century.

The first decade of this century was not a happy one for the French theatre. The fervid activity in the European theatre generally — with London playgoers finally awakened from their nineteenth-century slumber (Ibsen had already knocked at their door) by Shaw's iconoclasm, Strindberg experimenting in his 'naturalistic tragedy', and Tchekhov presented by the Moscow Art Theatre — these events found little or no reflection on the Parisian stage during *la belle époque*. Any discussion, therefore, on the very significant renaissance of the French drama during the last thirty years must stress that prior to 1914 the French was the most closed and backward theatre in Europe, and that it is only comparatively recently that the French playgoer has taken his theatre seriously enough to expect plays which are his intellectual equal. To-day, indeed, one might well wonder whether certain plays do not make demands beyond the level of any average audience.

There is no denying that in the *théâtre d'amour* of Georges de Porto Riche, the *comédies de salon* of Henri Bernstein, or the superficial optimism of Alfred Capus and others, entertainment was to be had. But, for the most part, dramatists during *la belle époque* either had to content themselves with artificial trivialities or become disciples of Zola's new naturalism (Zola refused to recognise Strindberg as a disciple). Unfortunately, however much naturalism was to prosper in other countries, it has always been alien to the genius of the French character. Not even the great Antoine, who founded the *théâtre libre* in revolt against the conventions of *la belle époque*, was able to enforce naturalism as the alternative. His experiments had their utility in that they provoked men like Jacques Copeau to bring back the magic and imagination to the French theatre. Realism and naturalism was the wrong turning, the new drama in France lay in the discovery of the old traditions. As Jean Cocteau said of Antoine, "The Montgolfiers also had genius, but they retarded by a hundred years the progress of aviation" (the Montgolfier brothers experimented with the first air balloons at the end of the eighteenth century). Nor were the dramatists of the new school to become internationally known like other European naturalists; even the best of them, Henri Becque (far, far removed from the crudities of Zola), does not come across to-day without a certain monotone (very evident in a recent production of *La Parisienne* at the Comédie Française), while social documentary writers such as Eugène Brieux offer plain boredom. The truth is that naturalism does not find roots in the great and living tradition of French drama; the 'common-sense' dictates of naturalism forbid a logical conclusion, while the brilliance of so many French logical conclusions is that they discard the narrow horizon of common sense.

However stubbornly self-satisfied the French theatre may have been at the outbreak of the first world war, it could not shut its eyes completely to the work being done by men like Stanislavski at the Moscow Art Theatre, Adolphe Appia in Switzerland, or Edward Gordon Craig in England. In 1913 Jacques Copeau (1878–1949), a man of letters who had founded the *Nouvelle Revue Française*, put into practice a number of their ideas (and developed his own theories in their wake) when he formed his company at the Théâtre du Vieux-Colombier. Copeau saw the theatre in the hands of speculators and wished to return it into the hands of creative workers. He sought to harmonise all the elements of production, discipline his players and banish anything which might distract or deform the pure conception of the poetry and language of the play. His was the gift of a creative animation of the whole field of *mise en scène*. The theatre was not a copy or 'slice' of life, but an interpretation of an escape to the supreme moments of our being.

The war put a temporary end to Copeau's work, and the French theatre reached the limits of banality. With the peace, however, Paris was ready to assume the rôle of intellectual capital of the world. The time had come for little art theatres. Though Copeau closed his own theatre in 1924 and retired to the country, taking his actors with him, two young members of his company had already launched out on their own: Louis Jouvet and Charles Dullin; in 1921 Charles Dullin founded his company and moved the following year to the present Atelier Theatre in the Place Dancourt; in 1922 Jouvet found his home at the Comédie des Champs-Elysées. Jouvet may be said to have created there a modern theatre repertoire, while Dullin, after a few years, explained "My ideas on the theatre have changed a lot. They can be summed up in one sentence: when I began I wanted to make the Atelier a school for actors, to-day I would like to make it a school for authors."

Both Jouvet and Dullin believed in the anti-naturalistic theatre. For Jouvet the theatre was shrouded in mystery. Dullin attempted to create a 'Western style' of theatre as complete as the Eastern. He wished to find the sources and make the drama live again. His style was simple, but from it all elements of naturalism were banished. He placed special emphasis on music as an accompaniment to the acting, for, like rhythm, it accentuates the imagination of the play. In other words, Dullin sought a stylised theatre, which bourgeois naturalism had almost caused to disappear and which he recreated in a return to tradition and a return to poetry. The classics, consequently, always occupied the major part of Dullin's repertoire, but among modern dramatists he introduced Pirandello to France, produced Cocteau and Salacrou, and later the first play of Jean-Paul Sartre, *Les Mouches* (produced at the Théâtre de Sarah Bernhardt in 1943).

Among the other "animators of theatre" (to use Robert Brasillach's title of his excellent study of the French stage in the inter-war years) the names of Georges and Ludmilla Pitoëff and Gaston Baty must be mentioned, though an examination of their work would require a book in itself. Baty's theories were to respect the text, but to express the whole text so as to "translate what words alone cannot translate". Beyond the text commences "another zone, a zone of mystery, silence, what we call atmosphere, environment, climate . . ."

It is these names that have enabled the renaissance of the French drama to take place; it is only in the individual work of animators that any hope can be nursed for world drama. It is in the so-called art theatre, or *avant-garde*, that we find true theatre; neither commercial theatres (in to-day's unhappy economics) nor national theatres (with the experience of the greatest of all national theatres, the Comédie Française) can take their place. But these little theatres would be useless unless they were identified, as well as with producer and actors, with a dramatist. In the Paris theatres during the inter-war years you chose your theatre as you chose the book of your favourite poet. And when in 1928 Jouvet made his greatest discovery of all, when he presented the first play of Jean Giraudoux (then known only as a novelist), he made certain that Giraudoux would not be known merely as a dramatic author, but as a member of his company, turning out plays as required. Such was the beginning of a partnership broken only by the war and Giraudoux's death; the result was a victory for Jouvet and his players, for the little theatre, and for French drama. It may be said that with the plays of Giraudoux, and the subsequent discovery by the public of Claudel (whose works written before the first world war were known only by a small circle of admirers until the second), the French theatre has rediscovered its soul.

*

Jean Giraudoux was born at Bellac, a French country town in the department of Haute-Vienne, in 1882, and died on 31 January, 1944, the year of the liberation of the France he loved so dearly. By profession he was as much civil servant as writer, and spent most of his active life in government service. Somehow the two tasks never conflicted, though he did find himself in the paradoxical position of being head of the propaganda ministry in 1939, "Cassandre à la Propagande" as Aragon described the situation. After the fall of France he refused the position of French ambassador to Greece under the Vichy régime.

Giraudoux was always first in life, he never took second place in anything. At school he was naturally always at the top of his class, he was first in the Concours Général, in the Concours des Chancelleries, and, more surprising for a brilliant scholar, first in sports in university running. At the age of forty-six Giraudoux turned to the theatre, and with his first play he became the leading dramatist of his generation.

It was as if he had a mission to perform that Giraudoux saw the theatre. He explained his crusade thus: "The play is the only form of moral or artistic education of a nation. It is the only evening course available for adults and the aged, the only means whereby the most humble and least literate members of the public can find personal contact with the highest conflicts, and create for themselves an undenominational religion, a liturgy and its saints, sentiments and passions. Some people dream, but for those who do not dream there is the theatre."

In the realisation of his dream world Giraudoux found his magician in Jouvet, but it was not without the doubts of a mortal that Jouvet contemplated the manuscript of *Siegfried,* which Giraudoux had adapted from his novel *Siegfried et le Limousin.*

At first the play was considerably too long, and throughout re-hearsals Jouvet requested important cuts to be made, with which Giraudoux always did his best to comply. It was the language of the play, however, that most people feared, for here Giraudoux deliberately made no compromise. The dialogue of a novelist is written to be read, not spoken, and Giraudoux was a French novelist *par excellence.* Where-as the theatre so often requires the short, elliptical phrase, Giraudoux's style is complex, his sentences are loaded with subordinate clauses in which he allows his thoughts to wander far and wide throughout the domains of the universe. His is the magical language of poetry which, allied with his philosophical ideas and wit, is far removed from the conversation of every-day life.

The rôle of the writer in the theatre, Giraudoux believed, was to re-introduce style. He explained himself: "Our age no longer asks writers merely for books — every street corner is littered with them — what above all else it appeals for is language. The writer does not have, like the jester to some fortunate king, to search for scars and criticise in novels and plays, for after all, criticism can be as contemptible as flattery. Our age asks that the writer should reveal his mark of which he is the sole trustee — style. That is what we need to-day in the theatre." In Giraudoux the French theatre found a stylist with grace and nobility, of a quality with which perhaps only the language of Marivaux can be compared. Giraudoux is essentially polite theatre, the drama of the spoken word rather than action, of conflict through thought, never through histrionics. It is the recesses of the human mind that Giraudoux seeks to explore, and thus what problems he presents to any translator! How can one render a delicate prose style where every word has been carefully selected, into a relatively formless language like English? The answer is that most of his plays which have been presented in Britain and America have tended to be adaptations rather than translations, and have missed completely the poetry of the original.

Maurice Valency, who adapted *La Folle de Chaillot* for its Broadway production, has explained the translator's dilemma in an article in *Theatre Arts.* He points out the difference between importing a French play and a bottle of reliable French vintage. Not every play can change habitat without some adjustment. Mr. Valency believes that in cases where photographic accuracy is impossible, it is better for a translator to be himself creative and render an impressionistic version. Unfortunately there is a strong belief that Anglo-Saxon audiences will not listen to long-drawn-out speeches, and Valency laments that "the predominance of white over black in a page of typescript" is "very persuasive in managerial circles". The point is, in other words, that since the audience prefers short snappy dialogue, and it is the audience who pays the box-office, then it is the old story of the man who pays calling the tune. Whatever the flaws in the reasoning, managements do fall for it, and that is why a different Giraudoux is known in London and Broadway than in Paris.

There is yet another reason why the works of Giraudoux took a long time to reach London and Broadway, where the triumph of naturalism has so completely won the day. The theatre of Giraudoux is neither realistic nor is it altogether unrealistic. Intellect and imagination walk hand in hand, for the destination is not the never-never land of Barrie. In all Giraudoux's plays one can identify situations of real life, but they have a resemblance only; they are familiar, but there is a differentiation. If, for example, some of his characters make us think of Hitler and Mussolini, we know that they are not meant to represent Hitler and Mussolini. Giraudoux was too great an artist for that. What his plays have is a moral signification, and he selects those problems which have a capital importance for our own time and civilisation.

Giraudoux is an idealist, but he does not believe in miracles. He has confidence in man and prefers to leave him to search for his own solutions through debate and an appeal to the intellect. He does not believe that we live in the best of possible worlds, but he does not exclude the possibility that we could live in the best of possible worlds. His universe magnifies beauty, because he knows that it is an alternative to ugliness; the one would not exist without the other. Perhaps he remembers the verdict of Socrates — "Evils, Theodorus, can never pass away, for there must always remain something which is antagonistic to good." The antithesis of words, and the play on these words in the dialogue, is to be found throughout Giraudoux's plays. In *La Guerre de Troie n'aura pas lieu* the play is on the words 'guerre/paix'; in *Amphitryon* 38 the play is on the words 'jour/nuit'; it is on 'vie/mort' in *Intermezzo* and 'vice/vertu' in *Sodome et Gomorrhe*. In *La Folle de Chaillot*, Irma, the Parisian dishwasher, has a soliloquy in which she invokes the following examples: "I detest the ugly, I adore the beautiful"; "I detest the wicked, I adore kindness"; "I detest the evening, I adore the morning"; "I detest the devil, I adore God"; "I adore freedom, I detest slavery"; "I don't much like women, I adore men"; "I adore life, I detest death".

In his strange land of reality and make-believe, Giraudoux brings together both human beings and those who are not subject to human laws. Frequently the humans lack those human virtues of love, forgiveness, understanding which the non-human characters may display, but in the end these are only human failings which can be redressed. Many questions are asked which are as perplexing as the songs of the Sirens, but no definite answers are attempted. Young girls can retain their youth and beauty for eternity, or turn into the mad old hags of Chaillot, and we may live in a world where the mad old hags are the sane inhabitants. The only certainty is death and everlasting life, which, indeed, is the riddle of the universe.

Many modern writers have been moved, like Giraudoux, to ask what is the place of man in life, and although most have given more excessive interpretations than Giraudoux, none has been a greater humanist. Life is neither a tragedy nor a comedy. Laughter can follow tears and laughter can lead to tears. All the threads are interwoven in the modern theatre, as a character observes in *Siegfried*. This, then, is the point of departure for Giraudoux's study of life, where there are no borders between laughter and tears, no frontiers between dreams and reality, and where always we can see our vision of the ideal in terms of the real world.

It is very noticeable that in his first play Giraudoux expounds some of his essential ideas. The theme of *Siegfried*, which is both a psychological study of mental disintegration and at the same time a symbolic picture of Franco-German relations, haunted Giraudoux for many years, and formed material for a number of novels as well as his play. His approach has been widely commended. "There is no better introduction to the Franco-German problem," Louis Joxe affirms, "for it is not as a technician but as a man and less as a historian than as a psychologist that he [Giraudoux] succeeds."

The theme presents a remarkable situation. A French writer, Jacques Forestier, disappears on the battlefield, and everyone, including his friend Geneviève, assumes that he has been killed. In fact he has been struck with total amnesia, picked up by the Germans without any means of identification as to nationality, and taken to be German. He is re-educated by a nurse in all the German myths and culture. When the play opens he has risen to be a prominent political figure, a determined, vigorous leader who offers Germany hope and salvation from her moral and economic chaos. One German, however, suspects that "Siegfried" is French, and recognises in his writing and oratory the lyrical style which was precisely that of Forestier. He arranges for Geneviève and Robineau, a friend who knew him well, to come over from France and identify him. The discovery of his origin and the decision Siegfried must make forms the conflict of the play.

*Siegfried,* then, is a play of a struggle, a struggle in the mind of one man who admires France and is attracted by Germany, and is repelled by the faults of both countries. It is a struggle tormented by the prospect of war, and in his condemnation of fighting, dictatorship and military rule Giraudoux prepares the ground for ideas which he was to develop more fully in *La Guerre de Troie n'aura pas lieu.*

Siegfried chooses France, but he does not choose France as against the alternative of choosing Germany. Giraudoux preserves on the Franco-German struggle an optimism which, alas, though it was to be betrayed, is nevertheless still valid to-day. In the conflict between the two nations he finds less antagonism than parallelism, and if he condemns, it is the anonymous forces which prevent the two people living side by side in peace.

Consider the first meeting of two friends, Zelten, a German, and Robineau, a Frenchman, for the first time since the war:

ROBINEAU   . . . Well, what have you been up to these last twelve years, Zelten? You who so loved Springtime and music, joy and peace, what have you been up to?

ZELTEN   Waging war! War on thirty-five nations. Waging battle only on one . . . And what about you, old Goggles, the easy-going common man of the Royal and Imperial Libraries, tell me, my most dear friend, what have you been up to these last twelve years?

ROBINEAU   Waging war! On you . . .[1]

Neither of the characters is a principal in the play, yet this short scene must surely be one of the most touching in contemporary drama. Coming at the beginning of the play it makes the subsequent entry of Siegfried less dramatic, and if Giraudoux had been more of a technician he would certainly have reserved it for a more important stage or curtain in the play.

[1] See original on p. 405.

It is in the last act, set in the customs house on the Franco-German frontier, that Giraudoux makes Siegfried argue his decision to two German generals, who put the case for his staying in Germany. The customs house is itself symbolic, divided in two by a *ligne idéale*, the German half being well laid out, brightly painted, tidy and clean, centrally heated and, of course, thoroughly organised for customs procedure; the French side is shabby, untidy, offers neither comfort nor routine, and depends on the individual whims of the customs official as much as the room depends on an individual oil stove for heating. One should add that there is an aggressive Corsican official with cigarette behind the ear to put the finishing touches.

The German general, Ledinger, addresses Siegfried:

LEDINGER    Come back with us, my friend. You are unwell. You are losing weight. Come back.

SIEGFRIED    Yes, Ledinger, I have lost weight. But quite as great as that loss is the grandeur of the gift I have been bearing these recent nights. A convalescent in my condition is truly more in need of the most modest homeland. If one be cut off suddenly from Germany and given responsibility for France, the laws of equilibrium would have to be properly upset for him not to feel it. I may tell you that only the day before yesterday I had it in mind to disappear, to seek asylum in some third country, one I should have chosen as far as possible for its having no neighbours, no enemies, no monuments to the dead to unveil, no dead. A country without war in the past, without war in the future . . . But the more I hunted for it on the map the more I felt my attachment to nations which suffer and feel compassion — the more clearly I realised my mission.[1]

The tension mounts. The generals ask Siegfried if he cannot be persuaded to change his mind or, if not, whether they cannot announce that Siegfried has been killed in an accident. Thus he could become Forestier again, and the glory of Siegfried would be able to live for the German people. Siegfried refuses, and Ledinger asks him if he really prefers to live as it were under two shadows. The reply is:

[1] See original on p. 405.

SIEGFRIED    I shall live, simply that. Siegfried and Forestier will live side by side. I shall endeavour to bear becomingly the two names and the two destinies which happen to be mine. A human life is not a worm. Cutting it in two is not enough to let each part become a separate existence. Nor are there any sufferings so opposed, experiences so inimical, that they cannot fuse one day into a single life; for the heart of man remains the mightiest crucible of all. Before long maybe that faded memory, those homelands lost and found, that unawareness and awareness in which alike I suffer and delight, will make one coherent pattern, one single existence. That within one human soul, where the most contradictory virtues and vices cohabit, the word German and the word French should be the only ones unwilling to come to terms would surely be much too much. I, for one, am unwilling to dig trenches within my own being. I shall not enter France as the last prisoner let out of Germany's gaols. I shall enter as the first to benefit from a new learning or a new heart . . . Farewell. There is your engine whistling. Siegfried and Forestier bid you farewell.[1]

So Siegfried crosses the *ligne idéale*, to France, where only Geneviève remembers him. But we know that Siegfried will not resume the life of Jacques Forestier as if nothing had happened. Geneviève in the play now loves Siegfried as much as Jacques, and we feel that together they see before them the chance of a new life which could be the dawn of a new age.

*Siegfried* is not Giraudoux's masterpiece, but in no other play can we identify the author so closely with his leading character. If in its construction *Siegfried* is far from being a 'well-made' play, such as we expect from less gifted professional playwrights, it is because mere mechanics did not interest Giraudoux. It was through his style that Giraudoux was able to transform his characters into symbols of human destiny.

It is, however, by an author's second play that one judges a playwright, and *Siegfried*, after all, had been treated first as a novel. The test came eighteen months later, on 8 November, 1929, when Giraudoux produced *Amphitryon* 38 — so called because Giraudoux esti-

---

[1] See original on p. 405.

mated that thirty-seven writers had dealt with the same Greek legend before him in the theatre (it has been suggested that seventy-five would be just as good a guess). In *Amphitryon* 38 the course is set for a light-hearted adventure in the company of gods and men; the theme is the test of human fidelity; the story of Jupiter's plan to seduce the faithful Alcmena has an irresistible appeal. Once again style distinguishes the play and is itself sparkling with gaiety to suit the mood of Greek high spirits. In the background, however, we hear the rumbling and echoes of war — Giraudoux's ever-present obsession.

We are first introduced to two gods, Jupiter and Mercury, looking at the shadows of Alcmena and Amphitryon. From this amusing start we learn that Jupiter wishes to love Alcmena himself, and asks Mercury how he can obtain her consent. Jupiter explains it must be a human plan rather than a divine one, for he does not want to miss the finest moment in human love — her consent. The trouble is that Jupiter knows that Alcmena only loves her husband Amphitryon. Mercury replies that Jupiter must borrow the shape and form of Amphitryon, and that in order to remove Amphitryon from the scene they should make a war break out. Then Jupiter, in the guise of her husband, would be able to call on Alcmena pretending that he had slipped away from the army to pass the night secretly with his wife. Such is the human plan the gods adopt.

So no sooner has a trumpeter read a declaration of peace (peace is shortly to be defined as that period between two wars) than a giant warrior, no doubt symbolising war, announces that the Athenians have crossed the frontier. Everything goes according to plan; Amphitryon takes his leave of Alcmena, Jupiter assumes his form, knocks at the door, and is eventually admitted as Amphitryon.

A scene of high comedy follows in Act II. The following morning they wake up when the sun is already high in the sky.

JUPITER    What a divine night.

But Alcmena takes exception to the word 'divine'. She suggests 'perfect', 'charming', best of all 'agreeable'.

JUPITER    Then it was the most agreeable of all our nights, wasn't it, by far?

ALCMENA    That depends . . .

After considerable coquetry on this point Alcmena concedes:

> if you want an adjective for this night, my dear, I would say that it was conjugal. It had a feeling of security which bewildered me.

Soon Alcmena is having another argument which pricks Jupiter's pride, for it is none other than failing to show any interest or admiration in Jupiter himself. Jupiter cannot understand why she has no wish to be honoured, why she does not long to be able to walk through the air or over the water, to understand the meaning of other worlds (Alcmena replies that her neighbours have never interested her). As for being immortal, what is the good of that? Jupiter tells her she wouldn't die, but Alcmena only shudders at the prospect of eternal life. She believes it is treachery for a human to become immortal, and Jupiter has to acknowledge her stubborness by admitting to Mercury that she is the first being who is really human that he has ever met. He has much to tell Mercury:

> her life [Alcmena's] is a prism where the common inheritance of gods and men, courage, love, passion, spends itself in truly human qualities, steadfastness, gentleness, devotion, over which we have no control.

Of course he has fallen seriously in love with her, and announces that her future son would be his favourite son. Fresh complications have meanwhile arisen, for Mercury, according to the custom and thinking that Jupiter would like to spend another night with Alcmena, this time without disguise, has announced to the whole universe that Jupiter is to visit Alcmena to honour her with a son. When Mercury asks Jupiter what he now wants, Jupiter replies "that Alcmena should remain faithful to her husband and give herself to Jupiter".

But the meeting between Alcmena and Jupiter is not as Jupiter had anticipated. For Alcmena has her own proposition to make:

ALCMENA     You can taste love with others. But I would like to create between us a union both more fragrant and powerful; alone of all women I can offer it to you. I do.

JUPITER     And it is?

ALCMENA     Friendship.

JUPITER     Friendship! What is this word? Explain yourself. It's
            the first time I've heard it.

The situation is saved; all ends as Jupiter, Alcmena, Amphitryon and
the audience wish it to end. "He only wanted to test us," Alcmena tells
her husband.

It was with his third play *Judith*, which Jouvet produced in 1931,
that Giraudoux met his first theatre failure, a failure which came to him
as a double disappointment, since the play had undoubted literary
quality and the character of Judith, "la plus belle et la plus pure des
filles d'Israël", was his first complex feminine study.

Why, then, did the play fail? Giraudoux wrote afterwards in his
*L'Impromptu de Paris* that "le mot comprendre n'existe pas au théâtre",
but one cannot help thinking that Giraudoux was expecting too much
from his audience in asking them to follow the subtle psychological
transformations of Judith and at the same time to understand the rich
assortment of his many themes — first the war, then destiny, original
sin, relations between man and God, fatality, feminine pride, jealousy,
etc. . . . As far as the construction of the play goes *Judith* marks a
distinct improvement in Giraudoux's technique, and while following
the biblical story the author has made several changes to aid the dramatic intensity of the play.

The play opens with the news of a Jewish military defeat. The enemy
is at the gates, and it is decided that a Jewish woman should go and
offer herself to Holophernes, and by cunning kill him. Judith offers
herself, and sets out on her dangerous mission, while Jean, who is in
love with Judith, sends a prostitute, Suzanne, to try and reach Holophernes first.

Judith goes to satisfy her feminine instinct, and face to face with
Holophernes she knows she is betraying her God. Suzanne does not
succeed in her mission, because destiny has deemed otherwise. To
Holophernes Judith may be just another woman, but Judith, who has
only flirted with men up to now, has never known a man. "The duel
Judith-Holophernes has become that of a brown body and a fair one",
is Judith's summing-up.

The Jews are told of Judith's treachery, and Jean arrives at the camp
for vengeance, when he discovers in amazement that Judith has killed
Holophernes. The Jews interpret this as a sign that she has been faithful
to God and her country. In fact she had loved him and in a perverse

frenzy of love she had killed him. "Judith la putain", the guard mutters. But Judith suddenly accepts the decision of destiny, demands that the guard should be killed, and declares that "St. Judith is ready" for the triumphant procession.

With *Intermezzo* (produced 27 February, 1933) we are in the French countryside of our own time, in a little town where strange events are happening and where unknown spirits are said to be terrorising the population. For instance, in the monthly municipal lottery the first prize goes to the poorest person in the district instead of going as usual to the local millionaire, the young champion wins the motor-bicycle, no one votes in the local elections, and the inhabitants answer the census in such a truthful way as to bring blushes to the mayor's cheeks and make it impossible for him to return the questionnaires to headquarters. And all this because a ghost has come to haunt the town.

We would be wrong, however, to imagine that Giraudoux only meant the play to be a superficially amusing ghost story; there exists quite another level, where we can view life from two sides at the same time; there is the positive side, as depicted by the bureaucratic inspector, the bourgeois twin sisters, the controller of weights and measures, with his feet firmly planted on the ground but not incapable of poetic feeling and understanding; on the other side is the negative picture, the enemies of life, where the ghost hypnotises the imagination of the young and beautiful village schoolmistress Isabelle in search of the unknown and forbidden questions, which can be learnt only by being in love with death.

Once caught in this passionate labyrinth the living have great difficulty in rescuing Isabelle, but each of them tries in his own way. The controller, who is himself in love with Isabelle, tries to plead with her in the eloquence of a lover — almost with success. But Isabelle still cannot resist the ghost when he comes to keep his nightly rendezvous. There is nothing for it but that the controller should defeat the ghost by arguing the case for life. Isabelle is torn between two worlds, affected deeply by the controller's love for her, but tormented by the divine secret which, of course, the ghost will only disclose to her alone. Soon the ghost realises that she is not willing to leave her world for his, and withdrawing his offer he vanishes. Isabelle rushes after him and falls in a faint.

The inspector, the controller, the chemist each discusses how to bring her back to life. It is the little girls of the village school who understand perfectly the situation and solution. The chemist explains their remedy: "The only message, the only artificial circulation that we can practise in this case is to reconcile her sleeping consciousness with the noise of every-day life. It's not a matter of leading her back to herself, but to us." And so with the voluble chatter and idle gossip of the company, the choir of little girls' voices, Isabelle returns to life, the town returns to normal, and the millionaire wins the lottery as usual.

*Intermezzo* is a highly original play, a delightful meander in the realms of fantasy where Giraudoux could give full play to his imagination. One must add that it is an exceedingly difficult play to act. The first period of Giraudoux's writing came to an end with *Intermezzo* (even the title hints at this); in his next play he turned to his ever-present dread of war, which coincided with the ever-mounting tension in Europe at the coming to power of Hitler. *La Guerre de Troie n'aura pas lieu*, produced in 1935 (*Tiger at the Gates* in the Fry translation, London, 1955), is one of the greatest pacifist plays in literature. We are in Troy in 1935, for, with all the classical setting, we realise the fading hopes of the inter-war years — "The whole universe knows it, we're going to fight", as it is expressed in the second act. The opening dialogue explains the theme:

| | |
|---|---|
| ANDROMACHE | The Trojan war won't take place, Cassandra. |
| CASSANDRA | I'll wager you on that, Andromache. |
| ANDROMACHE | The Greek envoy is all right. We shall receive him cordially, wrap his dear little Helen up carefully, and give her back to him. |
| CASSANDRA | We shall receive him with insults. We shall not return Helen. And the Trojan war will be on. |
| ANDROMACHE | It would, if there wasn't a Hector. |

Hector is a general against war, a fighter turned pacifist; he believes battles stupid and senseless; but on his side there are those who believe any compromise would besmirch their country's honour and see in pacifism cowardice and betrayal. The war won't break out if Helen can be persuaded to return, and Helen has no desire to stay or go. She will do whatever people want her to do. The talks between Hector and Ulysses, the diplomatic representatives of the two sides, may seek a treaty to safeguard peace, but they cannot promise that their people will respect their policies. Chauvinism and primitive desires for vengeance are powerful instigators of war. And even Hector gives way to the momentary impulse when reasoning with Ulysses seems impossible: "Well, the die then is cast, Ulysses. Go away and fight. My hatred of war is only matched with the incontrollable desire to kill." Surely the most terrible words ever spoken by a pacifist.

*La Guerre de Troie* is a simply constructed, single-purpose play which moves rapidly towards its tragic fate. Giraudoux for the first time allows pessimism to influence him; he sees war as inevitable as long as some men (but not all) are what they are.

In *Electre*, presented 13 May, 1937, Giraudoux gives us his most complete work in the theatre, a tragedy following the classical design, with intensity and depth, written in a style which reaches the height of his poetic powers. It is a difficult play to read, and its long soliloquies make infinite demands on an audience and actors, but we are in a world where greatness is visible.

Once again Giraudoux goes to Greek mythology for his plot, and adapts it to suit his purpose. Orestes returns from exile to the palace of Agamemnon, his father, who is dead. He meets his sister Electra and learns that his mother Clytemnestra is the lover of King Aegisthus, who followed Agamemnon on the throne. Electra hates her mother, and when she has proof that she is Aegisthus's lover she at once suspects that her mother took part in the murder of her father. Her soul thirsts for the truth, it becomes an obsession. Orestes is the weaker, and finds it hard to understand the strength of Electra's bitterness. Once she has proof, it is Orestes who is to do the deed. Meanwhile the city has been attacked by the Corinthians; Aegisthus is the only person who can save the city. Electra no longer cares, she does not want the city saved by someone with stained hands. Orestes kills Aegisthus and his mother, and at last Electra is content. The city goes up in flames and falls to the enemy, but Electra has satisfied her intense egotism. "I have my conscience, I have Orestes, I have justice, I have everything", she exclaims. The Furies in the play warn her that she is now the guilty one, that she will never see Orestes again. Still Electra insists that she has done right, for out of the flames of destruction she sees the birth of a new city. She sees the dawn.

Giraudoux makes three innovations in the classical legend. First of all he introduces the Furies in the form of three little girls, the cheeky little schoolgirls of *Intermezzo* — they make fun of the palace gardener in front of a visitor with such impudent remarks as "if flowers are to smell sweet, gardeners must have a nasty odour". But there is a mystery about them; the gardener does not know where they have come from, and he can almost see them growing taller while he looks at them.

Then they know everything that has happened in the past (including many things no one else knows) and seem to know the future with equal certainty.

Throughout the action of the play the Furies grow until in the final scene they are adults, the same age and size as Electra. They act as a Greek Chorus, offering a malicious commentary on events and forecasting disaster. One can say that the play itself grows to full maturity along with the symbolic Furies.

There is also a second character introduced who acts as a Chorus, this time a beggar, who remains an obscure character and never reveals his identity to us. Thirdly, we have the character of the gardener, who is to marry Electra and so keep her out of harm's way (a plan of Aegisthus's). But Electra is herself disposed to marry the gardener, since she feels the need for a mother, and as the gardener says, he "was the only man, absolutely the only man who could be a kind of mother". The gardener is also a poet in his own way, and represents the qualities of joy and love. He therefore disappears from the play at the end of the first half, making a personal farewell 'lamento' to the audience.

For his next play, *Ondine*, presented on 27 April, 1939, Giraudoux was to return to Germany to borrow a fairy tale written by Frédéric de la Motte Fouqué, but the subject is also another aspect of that treated in *Intermezzo;* relations are broken between an individual soul in the shape of a young mermaid and the soul of the universe to which she belongs. A handsome German knight-errant, Hans von Wittenstein zu Wittenstein, meets Ondine in a fisherman's hut in the heart of a Rhineland forest. Hans is a singularly prosaic knight, with little imagination; Ondine, who does not share the same destiny as a mortal, is a portrait of youth, beauty, truth, innocence and fidelity. She immediately falls in love with the manly features of Hans, while Hans, although he is engaged to a Countess Bertha, is prepared to forget Bertha and marry Ondine. In obtaining permission from the King of the Ondines to marry Hans, however, Ondine has to make a bargain: should Hans ever be unfaithful to her he will die and Ondine, returning to the ondine universe, will forget all about him.

Hans is anxious to introduce his wife to Court life, and the pomposity of the Court scene enables Giraudoux to poke fun at human flattery, pride, jealousy, and so on — manners unknown and incomprehensible to Ondine. Here it is obvious that Ondine is a misfit. She knows immediately that she cannot hold Hans faithful. After a last attempt Ondine leaves him and in desperation spreads the rumour that she has been unfaithful first. The King of the Ondines knows the truth, and in vain Ondine pleads with him:

| | |
|---|---|
| KING OF THE ONDINES | The end draws near, Ondine. |
| ONDINE | Do not kill him. |
| KING | Our pact says we must. He's deceived you. |
| ONDINE | Yes, he's deceived me. Yes, I wanted to make you believe that I deceived him first. But do not judge the sentiments of men by our ondine standards. Often men who deceive love their wives. Often those who deceive are the most faithful . . . |

The King shakes his head and tells her she is talking almost like a woman. He is inexorable in his demands. Hans dies and Ondine no longer recognises him. "How I would have loved him", are her farewell words as she leaves behind Hans' dead body.

Ondine, I think, should be considered Giraudoux's achievement in the feminine ideal; he shows through Ondine, a woman who is more than a woman, the impossibility for men to understand perfection. What a misfortune it is to be merely human! In characters such as Ondine it is not Giraudoux's intention to make a psychological study of a woman; characters become rather symbols of virtues and vices, which act as masques, as in the drama of ancient Greece. There is, for example, little differentiation of character between Geneviève, Alcmena, Isabelle, Andromache and Ondine; we are introduced to the same young woman revealing Giraudoux's conception of fidelity in a world where love (in order to be faithful) is an essential condition.

Ondine, as we have noted, was produced in the spring of 1939. It was to be the last play of the Jouvet-Giraudoux partnership; within a few months Europe was at war, a year later France was under German occupation and it looked as though the whole free world was doomed. Giraudoux saw his hopes of an 'eternal friendship' between France and Germany shattered; Jouvet, forbidden, it is said, to play Giraudoux, left with his company for South America. When he returned to Paris after the liberation Giraudoux was dead.

It was perhaps inevitable that during the last period of his life Giraudoux should lose some of his former optimism; no sensitive writer could have remained uninfluenced by the times in which he lived. Three full-length plays were written before his death early in

1944; one notices a slightly different Giraudoux in all of them. In *Sodome et Gomorrhe*, presented in October, 1943, under the Nazi occupation, an apprehensive fear that the destruction of the world is at hand seizes the imagination of Giraudoux; in *La Folle de Chaillot*, presented by Jouvet in December, 1945, we notice an element of bitterness and a failing of theatrical force never evident in his earlier work; finally in his last play, *Pour Lucrèce*, presented by the company of Madeleine Renaud and Jean-Louis Barrault in October, 1953 (nearly ten years after the death of Giraudoux and two after that of Jouvet), the pervading note is despair for a purity which is to be found in this world only in a flash of lightning every ten years. The play was presented in London in 1958 under the title *Duel of Angels*.

There are many features to admire in all these plays; we recognise at once the unmistakable tones of the Giraudoux symphony, those idiosyncratic leaps into fantasy and poetry which are his genius and which, of all his contemporaries, he alone could accomplish. But somehow the symphony never reaches the world of *Intermezzo* or *Ondine* or the impeccable crescendo in *Electre*. Is the answer to be found in the absence of Jouvet? Giraudoux himself acknowledged his debt in these words: "The actor is not only an interpreter, he is an inspirer; he is the living mannequin through whom many authors quite naturally personify a vision which is still vague; and the great actor is a great inspirer."

The theme of *Sodome et Gomorrhe* is the relations between man, woman and destiny. The message of God is that he wishes man and woman to be united, to be a couple, an ideal couple, so that "you don't think either of the husband or the wife. He is there, she is there. That's all". But men, in their arrogance and stupidity, do not want this. They wish to have an exchange of man and woman, and this fatal misconception of the principle of love is the cause of all their misery.

Jean and Lia fail to stay united, and both retire to live with their own sex. Fire and destruction ravage the earth, but Jean keeps on pretending that all is well with the men, while Lia insists that all the women are happy. Thus the world is destroyed and humanity and civilisation reduced to ashes. It is alarming to think that the play, written before the use of the atom bomb, has grown in topicality — a justification, no doubt, for its excessive pessimism.

*La Folle de Chaillot* is an attack on another aspect of modern society, the unprincipled selfishness of exploiters against ordinary decent folk. The play is far from being a dull, doctrinaire, political satire. The

Eugene O'Neill

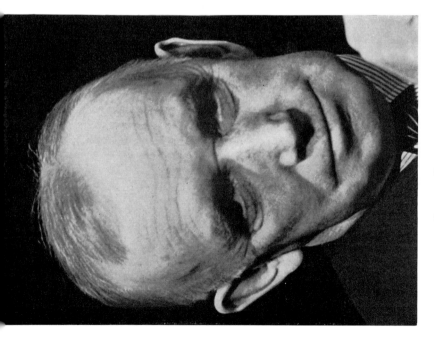

James Bridie

JEAN COCTEAU

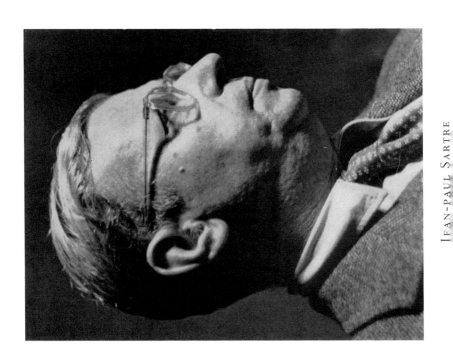

JEAN-PAUL SARTRE

Madwoman of Chaillot lives in a fantastic make-believe world of her own, and through her the harsh symbolic realism of the exploiters and their shady deals are contrasted with a dreamland where only such people as those who love honesty, beauty and the world are allowed.

The scene is the café, Chez Francis. The prospector tells a baron, whose name he wants for 'respectability' reasons on the board of his newly formed company, that he has discovered oil in the least prospected place in the world — in Paris. Because the authorities have refused him permission to drill for oil and destroy the centre of the city, he plans to blow up the city architect's office. But the young man they entrusted to throw the bomb fails in his duty (he tried to commit suicide instead); the Madwoman takes him under her protection and learns from him about the evil people who are everywhere in the modern world.

To the Madwoman the solution is simple. She sends the prospector a bottle of petrol with a letter saying she has found this liquid in her cellar and invites him (and all his friends) to call and inspect her discovery. This, as she anticipates, brings along all the evil men, as well as some representatives of the press (Giraudoux once worked in a government press office), and three of their mistresses. She shows them all down into her cellar, where a staircase vanishes mysteriously into the underworld and whence there is no return. When Irma, the café dishwasher, asks where they have all gone, the Madwoman tells her: "Vanished. They were wicked. The wicked evaporate." Though there may be no such sane conclusion, though we can no longer believe like the Madwoman that the good of course inherit the earth, in a simpler and less sophisticated world how the Madwoman would be praised for her logic!

*La Folle de Chaillot* is not altogether a satisfactory play. With *Pour Lucrèce*, Giraudoux's last play (he finished it in 1943 after *Sodome et Gomorrhe*), we have a more theatrically effective work, not without those inimitable flashes of the exceptional but flashes also of an irony and an unaccustomed bitterness. In taking the tragedy of Lucretia, wife of Tarquinius Collatinus, whose beauty and virtues inflamed the passion of Sextus and incited him to rape her (which led Lucretia to commit suicide), Giraudoux has made a number of important variations in his treatment — the theme is one of his favourites, the purity of love. First he transplants the action from Rome to a city with only a Roman heritage, Aix-en-Provence; the period is of an empire, but not that of the Roman Empire. In choosing the period of

C

Napoleon III Giraudoux enables this age-old theme to be identified in a more modern, but not contemporary setting.

From the rise of the curtain we know this is tragedy, an all but Racinian tragedy. The action is already far advanced in a state of crisis at our first introduction to Lucile Blanchard (his Lucretia); within twenty-four hours in the play she is the victim of her virtue; we sense that Destiny is against her life, but her reasons for taking it are her own. As she sips her ice in a café on the Cours Mirabeau, the wife of the newly appointed imperial attorney at Aix has already as great a reputation for fidelity and virtue as her husband has for severity; already she is surrounded by enemies. She came to a city of love, and found that in the first month no man in Aix loved anyone else but her. At the end of this month Aix had become, through her morality, a city of original sin. She could not hide her utter contempt for the easy living, for women like Paola, women who loved and lived for promiscuity.

Paola is the evil force of the play. She is as hot in temper as in sex; harmless until hurt, until her husband learns through Lucile that she is not an angel. Then her flood of revenge knows no mercy, nothing will stem it. She is the most dangerous and the most eloquent woman in Provence. She accuses Lucile of being quite another character from what she pretends to be, a person who loves men but not her husband. "Whether your virtue be the domino of holiness or lust, no matter. You're all right within, buttoned up to the neck. But the day will come when the buttons will burst . . ." It remains for Paola to slip a sleeping drug into Lucile's glass, and in her unconsciousness to arrange her body on a slightly disordered bed so that when she wakes up she will believe the buttons have been burst — and by none other than the Don Juan of Aix, Count Marcellus.

The second act develops the intrigue. Marcellus is killed in a duel fought with Paola's husband (he was a former lover of Paola) without denying that he raped Lucile. In the last act Paola is all but triumphant. Lucile's husband has returned and far from listening sympathetically to his wife's confession of the trick that has been played on her, orders her out of the house. And by now, even though Lucile knows that she has not been raped, she prefers to keep the truth to herself. She admits that she doesn't love her husband, and when Paola prepares to celebrate her victory, Lucile replies:

LUCILE    No last resort? What a mistake! There it is in my own hands, my last resort. When you said a moment ago that

> I was beaten, I could laugh at you, for it was there already. It came to me from a little girl, of my own name, my own age who, when she was ten years old, took an oath never to acknowledge evil, and vowed to herself to prove, at the cost of her life if need be, that the world is a noble place and human beings pure. This earth has become for her a vile place stripped of all, this life only degradation; that does not matter, it is not true; for she still honours her vow.[1]

The last words fall to Barbette, the sorceress of the play, who closes the play with a tribute and a lament:

BARBETTE   You have been violated all right. But not by Marcellus. That kind is curable. Half a hundred have been cured. You quite thought so yourself. You got over it. But what you can't get over is the stupidity of men, the grossness of men, the wickedness of men. That came to you all of a sudden. It was too much. A gentle being like you dies of it.[2]

The language of the play does much to conceal some of the obvious failings, in the last act in particular. Can we really imagine that the husband would be so utterly unsympathetic? — and it is even harder to believe that Paola's husband would not have told the truth outright and in no uncertain manner. We have a sense of deception unworthy of Giraudoux.

There are those who accuse Giraudoux of being a literary dilettante in the theatre, presumably either those who do not hold so highly the purpose of the drama, or the existentialists, who see their paradise threatened by the influence of Giraudoux's universe, and who have therefore taken the critique of Giraudoux by their lord and master Sartre to heart. But all important writers have had their critics — Pirandello was responsible for riots in the streets of Rome and duels in Milan — and Giraudoux has had fewer than most. His reputation to-day in France stands exceedingly high, his plays have won international acclaim, and the possibility of Jouvet's prophecy that "if the language of Racine is still spoken in France in 200 years, the plays

[1] See original on p. 406.
[2] See original on p. 406.

of Giraudoux will still be performed" should not be lightly dismissed. For Giraudoux believes in good theatre, the theatre of the great dramatists. And Giraudoux's success has been as remarkable as his plays were unorthodox and his ideas unlimited. He can have no imitators. Yet he does point a direction in which young writers can follow, he has led them to a point of departure from where they can advance. Just as Pirandello experimented gradually away from the naturalist camp, Giraudoux has succeeded in turning the semi-circle in theatrical fashions and has freed the theatre from the stifling atmosphere of naturalism. With his impressionistic interpretation of life Giraudoux has shown how the world we live in can respond to the poetic sweep of imagination. His way is always towards a less sophisticated universe, and his creation of this little world which is more than a world, inhabited by characters which are more than human, is the testament of faith which Giraudoux has bequeathed to a world in doubt.

# THE MUSE WHO IS GRACE—A NOTE ON PAUL CLAUDEL

PAUL CLAUDEL is first a poet and only secondly a dramatist. The reason is not because he lacks dramatic power — power is what attracts us most in Claudel's work — but because when he wrote his theatre between 1890 and 1924 the public was not ready for a return to religious drama, or indeed for plays which appeared to be 'difficult' at all. Not until the middle of the second world war, when Jean-Louis Barrault presented *Le Soulier de Satin* at the Comédie Française, did the public recognise the existence of a poet who was soon to be acknowledged as one of the great figures in French literature. Like Pirandello, Claudel sees everything connected with man threatened and transitory, nothing human can be saved from destruction and death. The development of Claudel's career was the development of his own faith from the time of his conversion to Catholicism, and we follow his progress from the violence of a Paradise lost in a transitional play like *Partage de Midi*, to Paradise regained, with the culmination of his thought in *Le Soulier de Satin*. Claudel invokes the mystical element in his plays; where reason ceases to throw light he uses a symbol to take its place. He reintegrates his characters into this symbolism, and through the powers of the mystical he can change a soul from darkness to light. Claudel's plays are not simple mystery plays, but plays to counter the Reformation, and to counter it in a style which demands attention. His plays offend many in their harsh, uncompromising Catholicism, for Claudel, never at any time a willing listener to the arguments of the other side, is a writer who insists; as Gide writes in his *Journal*: "When he talks, it is as if something were released within him; he proceeds by sudden affirmations and maintains a hostile tone even when you share his opinion." He requires an effort to be understood, but his work repays study both for the richness of his language and the sweep of his imagination. Here we have poetry as a means of divine communication.

# FOUR

# THE DISCOVERY OF PAUL CLAUDEL

"Le combat spirituel est aussi brutal que la bataille
d'hommes."

ARTHUR RIMBAUD

IN the contemporary theatre, especially the French theatre, religion
once again plays a vital rôle; believers and atheists, both sides
contribute to and passionately disturb our living drama. This preoccupation with religious themes is a development of great significance;
it certainly cannot be called a return to religious drama, since for the
first time plays of a religious nature are being presented by a secular
theatre. Instead of addressing our spiritual beliefs, an appeal is made to
our intelligence and our doubts. Though certain of the plays of
Claudel, *The Tidings Brought to Mary* for example, take us back to the
Middle Ages, they do not follow the pattern of the medieval mystery
play. The mystery plays were essentially ceremonials to be performed
before a mass-crowd sometimes as large as those seen to-day at major
sporting events; they were the work of several hands; they were not
concerned with originality. It was, moreover, an audience of believers,
sometimes resembling "a cathedral in motion". To-day, on the other
hand, Christian playwrights turn from divine problems to directly
human aspirations, viewing man from the vulnerable side of uncertainty, his hope and despair, light and darkness, the trial of strength
between saints and the devil, the conflict between the divine and the
diabolical.

Cláudel, then, is a great Catholic writer. But can he be great to those
who cannot accept the Catholic faith, and to those who feel that the
acceptance of its dogmas imposes too severe a restriction on the
freedom of thought of any author to allow for greatness? It might be
suggested that such a view, itself sincere, denies the possibility of a

Catholic writer to be himself sincere. For a writer such as Claudel, it is his spiritual faith which completes the unity of his existence. His work is a record of man's struggle through successive stages towards the peace which comes with the "délivrance aux âmes captives" — the end of the pilgrimage of life. Claudel sees his faith as a source of light and hope in a world where darkness prevails. In his Paradise rediscovered, "the human soul", he wrote at the end of his life, "is something which is able to catch fire, in fact that was what it was created for, and when that takes place, or as we say 'the spirit descends on her', she manifests such joy, gives forth such a cry . . . that there is no other word except enthusiasm to describe it."

The appreciation of this enthusiasm, whether in its final stage in the "communication with God through poetry", or in man's earlier conflict between the call of the flesh and the vocation of the soul, can be of the greatest interest to non-Catholics as well. Claudel's plays yield themselves to anyone provided they are approached with the necessary tolerance to submerge one's own beliefs. They should be understood as a Catholic draws inspiration from the great paintings of the Renaissance. Obviously, those who would never set foot in Saint Peter's, or the materialists of the Anglo-Saxon school who view 'Popery' in the same light as the 'Wee Frees' in the Highlands, are not the audience for Claudel. Even those with open minds will require to initiate themselves into the meaning of his symbols which act as a key to his expression if they wish to appreciate the real significance of the struggle his characters fight against sin and temptation. Claudel's is a difficult drama even for Catholics; his plays never allow departure from the terrible reality of punishment for those who break the rules, and there is the necessity to be superhuman not to yield to the forbidden. Claudel's plays are intensely rewarding for those who wish to explore them. More than anything, it is his power which sweeps us along with him. He is, as Jean Vilar says, writing in *La Revue Théâtrale* (October, 1946): "The only contemporary dramatic poet who is able to invigorate us is a Catholic poet, enclosed in a confessional world against which all other religions, philosophies and the modern beliefs of mankind combine to assail." Claudel's ambitions are vast, he describes the setting of *Le Soulier de Satin*, for example, as being the world. He wishes to explore the whole range of human experience, and the only difficulty is to find the means of communicating our perception. He demands that an audience should complete what it sees by imagination; in other words, he asks for the collaboration of the audience. But just as his plays are intolerant and exacting he can incite the tempers of others. For this reason naturalist critics with a strong anti-Catholic bias are not likely to accept the world which Claudel introduces into his plays.

There is also the language problem, where it is almost impossible to give an adequate rendering in translation of the strange force of Claudel's poetry. In his penetrating study, *Maria Cross*, of the imaginative patterns in a group of modern Catholic writers, Mr. Donat O'Donnell draws attention to the symbolism which acts as a 'currency' in the interpretation of the meaning of Claudel's work, and to two words, 'gold' and 'water', in particular. As Mr. O'Donnell explains in his essay, the French 'or' (gold) has a significance quite different for French ears to that which it has for English-speaking people. 'Or', in French, immediately suggests 'corps' and 'morts', which have clear associations with the idea of communion and death which are the signposts of Claudel's writing. Water can be found to have similar associations with 'la mer' and 'la mère', or the adjective 'amère' (bitter) and the similar sounds of 'l'amour' and 'la mort'. How can these be expressed in English? The result surely is that the power of Claudel's poetry is never so direct, so forceful, in another language, and this may be as great a difficulty in the appreciation of his work outside France as is the religious content, which is not nearly such an insuperable barrier.

Though Claudel wrote the majority of his plays without a view to stage production, he had an intensely dramatic aptitude for the theatre, and if only, like Giraudoux, he had found his Jouvet, he would have been as great a dramatist as a poet. Consider, for example, the insight he gives into the theatre in the following speech from *L'Echange* (1933):

> The theatre. You don't know what it is? Really?
> There's the stage and the auditorium — the house.
> It all being enclosed, people come there in the evening and sit down row behind row, watching.
> ... They are watching the curtain in front of the stage.
> And what there is behind once it rises.
> And then something happens on the stage as if it were the real thing.
> ... I watch them, and the house becomes nothing but live flesh clothed
> Packed like flies from floor to ceiling.
> And I see hundreds of white faces.

Man grows bored and the ignorance he was born with sticks to
  him
And not knowing a thing about how it begins or ends, that's what
  makes him go to the theatre.
And he is looking at himself, with his hands resting on his knees.
And he cries and he laughs, and he hasn't the least desire to go
  away.
And I have a look too and I know the box-office man is there
  Who knows that to-morrow
His books will be checked, and the unfaithful mother
  Whose child has just taken ill
And the man who has just committed a theft for the first time,
And the one who has done nothing all day.
And they are all watching and listening as though they were
  asleep.[1]

Had he had an opportunity of seeing the immediate effects of his plays
on an audience as he wrote them, Claudel would have been a greater
dramatist, but he could not have given us plays of greater dramatic
content or literary value. When he died in 1955, he was the last of a
generation which produced a number of outstanding figures in French
literature. To-day one fears this golden age is finished.

Paul Claudel was born in 1868 at Villeneuve-sur-Frère, in Aisne, a
countryside which was to teach him in his childhood the reality of
being ever close to the land, and give him a feeling of the freshness of
nature which is to be found everywhere in his poetry. Just as a painter
learns to contemplate a landscape, so Claudel drew inspiration from his
own meditations. He was fourteen when he came to live in Paris and
attend the Lycée Louis-le-Grand. At this time he had abandoned his
early religious instruction, and believed — "what most of the so-called
cultured people believed at that time" — in a materialistic goal.
Little by little he fell into a state of despair. He tells how over many
months he had watched his grandfather consumed by a cancer of the
stomach, and he was haunted by the fear of death.

The revelation came to him on Christmas Day, 1886, when, for
nothing better to do, he attended Christmas Mass at Notre Dame. He
found the service somewhat ordinary, but decided to stay on for
Vespers. He writes: "And it was then that the event took place which
was to dominate my whole life. In one instant my heart was touched and

[1]See original on p. 406.

I believed. I believed with such a strength of adherence, with such a profound conviction, that there was no room for any sort of doubt. And since then all books, all the hazards of a troubled life, have been incapable of shaking my faith, or in truth, of touching it."

But though Claudel had, as it were, made his 'divine' conversion, he had still to make his spiritual one, which was to be a hard struggle. For he was plunged into a new world, a world repugnant to all his previously held convictions. He disliked priests. He had not a single Catholic friend. He did not dare to announce his conversion even to his family. During this period he attended the Ecole du Droit and the Ecole des Sciences Politiques and entered the French diplomatic service.

Religion became his dominant interest. He found comfort in the works of Arthur Rimbaud. Pascal answered many of his doubts. He read anew the Bible. But it was *La Somme Théologique* of St. Thomas Aquinas that was to enable him to make his spiritual conversion. He found there a key which enabled him to construct almost a grammatical interpretation of the universe. It is not our purpose here to examine in more than a brief outline the religious thought and development of Claudel, such as is essential to any understanding of his drama. The Catholicism of Claudel is that divine truth is outside us. God exists whether we wish him to or not. Man is not the source of religion.

We must not accuse Claudel of diminishing the dramatic intensity of his plays as he becomes more at peace with his own mind. Though his earlier plays are different in mood from his later works (Jean-Louis Barrault has called *Tête d'Or* his 'sap'; *Partage de Midi* his 'ordeal' and *Le Soulier de Satin* his 'synthesis'), the world of Claudel remains a dark world, where everything related to the flesh is threatened and salvation can only be found by transcending earthly things and seeking the message of God. His characters are on trial. They struggle with their minds and their flesh and find that a human being cannot be the supreme end of another human being. The quintessence of Claudel has been explained in some notes published in *"Cahiers de la compagnie Madeleine Renaud — Jean-Louis Barrault"* (1953) where Claudel gives us quite a new key to himself and his writings:

The mind . . . yes . . . but egotism, avarice, being hard, dry vain — the things God most detests.
The flesh? True, the need of the other one, being a slave to the other and recognising that the other cannot be reached, something not unlike hell.

But above the flesh there is the super-, the trans-flesh — there is the heart which too is flesh, that heart which has made us and knows more about it than we do. If God placed it in our bosom it is so that it may find its echo in some other person's.

In 1893 Claudel left for his first post as vice-consul at Boston in the United States. From 1895–1909 he occupied different posts in central and southern China. In 1909 he was sent to Austria as consul in Prague, and in 1914 he found himself Consul-General at Hamburg on the outbreak of war. During the war he was in Italy, Brazil, and at the time of the armistice was Minister in Denmark. In 1921 he was appointed French ambassador in Tokyo, in 1927 he became ambassador to the United States, and in 1933 he was ambassador in Brussels. And yet he managed to combine this active career with a no less active career as a writer. Neither career seems to have imposed on the other; it might almost be said that he gained from being absent from France in that he never came under the influence of any school; Claudel was his own 'maître'. No wonder he infuriated those who believed that he was wasting his talent as a diplomat, no wonder Antonin Artaud one day announced after a performance of one of the acts of *Partage de Midi*, "The act we have just presented to you is by Paul Claudel, poet, ambassador and traitor."

★

Claudel was twenty when he wrote his first play, *Tête d'Or*. "At twenty one is afraid of nothing", he apologised to Jean-Louis Barrault when he refused to grant him permission to present the play. "It is not because the play lacks sincerity. Good heavens no! It has too much. But it is precisely this sincerity — crude, clumsy, horribly naïve — which makes me shudder." Nevertheless, *Tête d'Or* is a remarkable first play, and one of the important plays Claudel wrote. It was to be Baurrault's choice for the opening of the Odéon under his directorship in October 1959.

Tête d'Or is a young adventurer, so called because of the golden colour of his hair. He believes he is a law unto himself, and respects neither law nor religion. Having saved his country from defeat by taking command of the army and driving out the enemy, he now feels that he has the right, through his strength, to overthrow the government. This he does, and proclaims himself King. He presents himself as a leader who will lead the nation to conquest; he does not offer peace and security. The old King is killed, and he drives the beautiful Princess, who represents beauty and joy, into exile. Tête d'Or then leads his army over the whole of Europe and to the frontiers of Asia. Everywhere he is victorious. He has one last battle to fight, in which he is mortally wounded. Everything has been in vain. Before he dies he hears a cry of anguish, and sees crucified to a tree the Princess he had driven from her country. She pardons him, and they die side by side. The soldiers return, having won a futile victory.

Here Claudel introduces the first temptation of man, that of power and possession. But no matter what success a dictator may achieve, he is doomed to failure, for no man can seek to rule the earth. In his next play, *La Ville*, this barren victory is followed by redemption. Avare is a man like Tête d'Or, seeking power through violence and destruction. Coeuvre is a poet restlessly seeking for art, and refuses to join the side of Avare and Lala, Coeuvre's wife, who has deserted him. Instead he finds his answer in entering the Church and devoting his life to the service of God. In the last act Coeuvre has become a bishop. Avare, although he has achieved power, cannot rebuild the havoc he has caused. He hands over his power to the Prince Ivors, the son of Coeuvre and Lala. The young prince receives his conversion from Coeuvre — the new city will be built not by the negative forces of life but with the spiritual faith which gives continuity . . .

The construction of this early work leaves much to be desired and cannot be said to be theatrically effective, even when given such an excellent production as that of Jean Vilar and his Théâtre National Populaire. Instead of dramatic tension mounting act by act, the drama in *La Ville* subsides and gives way to sermon. The young Claudel has revealed for us in this play many of his important ideas — ideas that he was to develop in his subsequent work more effectively. Yet even here he has mastered the use of a poetic language which is always admirable. But the dramatic content is not in harmony, and the play lacks the power that is so marked in Claudel's better work. As it is, the play lends itself better to reading than to performance.

*L'Echange* (1893–1894) is a very different type of play, much smaller in dimensions, human and bourgeois in appeal, and yet with an absorbing dramatic conflict which raises the play to Claudelian tragedy. An American, Louis Lane, soon finds that he has no time for his French bride Marthe, and is willing to 'exchange' her for a pocketful of dollars with a rich American, Thomas Pollock Nageoire. She is, after all, his property. Marthe believes in the beauty and dignity of marriage; she will not leave Louis. An actress, Léchy Elbernon, reveals to Marthe that she is already Louis's mistress. But Léchy, who loves Louis, knows herself how slight her hold is over him, and threatens that she will kill him should he desert her. She begs Marthe to help her prevent this. Marthe refuses, for what is to be must be. Louis is murdered.

*L'Echange* presents character studies drawn more to types than of interest as individuals, but the play holds an audience. It might almost be regarded as an exercise in play-writing, a model for instruction before embarking on *Partage de Midi*, where Claudel reaches the summit of his art.

"You know that I never wanted to discuss *Partage de Midi* for the theatre," Claudel wrote to Jean-Louis Barrault, "and that I have long ago recalled from circulation all the copies of the first edition. It is an ordeal which I suffered so strongly from in my youth that its effects have accompanied me all my life. Even to-day the play lives . . . what prevents me to-day is a kind of shame 'there are cries that a man has not the right to utter'. *Partage de Midi* is such a cry. It embarrasses me as if I were naked."

The subject of *Partage de Midi* is the limitations of love. In this one play Claudel places all the chances and all the obstacles of life. The characters do not seek a conjugal love, but that of a satisfied passion. The argument is both banal and complicated, but that has little consequence. Claudel admits this in the preface to the 1949 edition of the play: "Nothing apparently could be more commonplace that the twofold theme this drama is built around; that of adultery — husband and wife and lover — and that of the conflict between religious vocation and the call of the flesh. Nothing more commonplace but at the same time nothing of so long standing and I would almost venture to say — nothing more sacred. For the idea of that conflict between the Law and Grace (in the most varied and unexpected forms), between God and man, between man and woman, runs right through the Old Testament stories richest in significance."

From the rise of the curtain we sense an atmosphere of conflict which is rare, we are gripped almost with an element of terror. We are on a vessel bound for China, it is midday and the ship is somewhere in the middle of the Indian Ocean. There are four characters. Ysé, a young and beautiful wife of a prosaic trader De Ciz, meets Mesa, an intensely unhappy man who has a noble and spiritual disposition. On board there is also Amalric, a forthright man and something of an adventurer.

He knew Ysé before she was married, and is trying to have an affair with her. Ysé, however, rejects his advances, for she is attracted to Mesa.

So the four of them meet in blazing solitude. It is "midday in the heavens, midday in the centre of our lives". For midday is the central hour, the moment in life when one attains what one seeks. It is an instantaneous moment of obligatory choice. It can be one of chosing between dream and action. It is the supreme moment of freedom. It is the most difficult moment in life, for it is the moment when man is the farthest removed from God. It is the moment when he has to bear the heaviest responsibility, the responsibility of the direction of his soul.

Ysé senses in Mesa something strange and beyond her comprehension. "You don't understand me", Mesa tells her. "I understand that you are unhappy." She has tempted him, and Mesa is willing to become her lover. But Ysé suddenly becomes frightened. There is something wrong in her loving a mind like Mesa's. She tells him:

YSÉ    No, no, you must not love me.
       No, Mesa, you must not love me.
       It would not be right at all.
       You know that I am a poor weak woman.
       Remain the Mesa I need.


                    .    .    .


Tell me you will not love me. Say: Ysé, I will not love you.[1]

The second act takes place in the European cemetery of Hong Kong. Mesa and Ysé are to meet again and be left alone together, for De Ciz has to go away for a month. Ysé knows that the temptation will be too powerful for her to resist, and implores her husband not to leave her, but in vain. Alone with Mesa, Ysé gives herself to him: "I am yours, I am not holding back, you may do as you wish." But their passion is joyless, because they know that their love is a theft; a sense of guilt is between their union.

YSÉ    And what are the others to us? Since you are unique and I
       am unique

[1] See original on p. 407.

And your voice stirs my very entrails like a cry that cannot
be borne

And I rise up towards you with difficulty, a thing enormous,
massive, blind, silent and filled with desire.

But what we desire is not at all to create, but to destroy and oh!

Nothing exists any more but you and me, or in you but me,
or in me but being possessed by you, madness and tenderness,
rage to destroy you, no longer hampered

Detestably by those garments of flesh, and those cruel teeth
in my heart,

Not cruel at all!

Ah it is not happiness I bring you, but your death and with it
mine.[1]


A year passes. This tragic love has brought happiness to neither
Mesa nor Ysé. She decides to escape from this passion which resembles
death. She escapes to Amalric's plantation on the mainland, and bearing
Mesa's child, becomes Amalric's mistress.

Mesa searches everywhere for her and eventually traces her. She is in
great danger, for there has been a rising of the Chinese, and the Europeans are being massacred. In order to prevent their being taken alive
Amalric has laid a charge under the house so that they will not fall into
Chinese hands. While Amalric and Ysé are preparing themselves for
death, Mesa arrives with the means to save Ysé. De Ciz is dead, he has
a pass through the Chinese lines, and they can marry. But, seeing Ysé,
he reproaches her, asks why she has betrayed him thus; she remains
silent. Mesa speaks:

MESA   Tell me, Ysé, it is no longer the midday sun's full blaze.
        You remember that Ocean of ours?
        But the lamp of the grave is shining on your cheek, and your
        ear, and the corner of your brow
        And reflected in your eyes, your eyes in the mirror . . .
                *He blows out the lamp*
        The lamp's little flame is out. And extinguished at the same time
        The last sunshine of our love, that great mid-August sun
        Where we said our last adieu in the light devouring, separating
        us, as we desperately
        Signalled to one another across the widening distance.

[1] See original on p. 407.

Adieu, Ysé, you did not know me at all! That great treasure
   I bear within me
You were not able to uproot
To transplant, I was not able to give it. It is not my fault.
Oh yes! It is our fault and our punishment.
   I ought to have given everything,
And that is what you have not forgiven.
                                *Silence.*[1]

Amalric enters. By her silence Mesa learns that Ysé prefers to stay with Amalric. The two men fight, and Mesa is injured. Amalric takes Mesa's two passes and Ysé has to make her choice. She choses Amalric and, preparing to leave with him, strangles her child by Mesa. She believes she has made her choice, but at the last minute she returns to the condemned house. She has decided on certain death with Mesa rather than life with Amalric. At the frontier between life and eternity they discover the realisation of love. It is not the midday union, but the midnight union which has made this possible. The title, *Partage de Midi*, is thus symbolic.

His next play, *L'Otage* (1908–1909), is the first part of a trilogy, of which *Le Pain dur* and *Le Père humilié* are the other two plays, covering the period between 1812 and 1871. *L'Otage* covers the post-revolutionary years 1812–1814, but it would be wrong to view the play purely as a historical drama condemning the French Revolution. The story introduces Sygne de Coûfontaine, a girl from a noble family who were executed during the Revolution, who has with difficulty managed to restore the family property. Her cousin Georges, the only other member of the family who escaped, is attracted to her through the mutual pride of the family and distress at what has happened. They pledge their engagement. Through Georges Sygne becomes the possessor of a vital secret, that the man he has asked her to protect in her house is none other than the Pope, whom Georges has rescued from imprisonment. Toussaint Turelure, the Republican prefect of the district, the executioner of the parents of both Georges and Sygne, guesses the identity of their guest and presents Sygne with a choice which is to her nothing less than martyrdom. Ambitious to possess what Sygne has so diligently restored, he demands that she should marry him. Should she refuse, the Pope will be sent back into captivity. Sygne, although at first unwilling to make this sacrifice, eventually

[1] See original on pp. 407-408.

submits and breaking off her engagement to Georges she agrees to marry Turelure. She prefers to be true to her religion at the cost of her own honour. From this stage on she ceases to care about life, her mind is unconscious, her spirit extinguished. She exists. The play ends on a stroke of irony, Georges has been forced to seek Turelure's support some years later for the restoration of the monarchy, and thus compromises his own honour. In attempting to kill Turelure the bullet hits Sygne, and Georges and Sygne both die. Claudel has provided two endings to this play, one in which Sygne dies at peace with the Church by pardoning Turelure, the other in which she dies defiant. If religion demands the first ending, the play demands the latter.

The marriage of Mesa and Ysé had taken place on the frontiers of eternity, but it was a barren marriage. The marriage between Sygne and Turelure had filled Sygne's life with disgust; it was inhuman and could only engender hatred. In *L'Annonce faite à Marie* (1912, being the final version of *La Jeune Fille Violaine,* which dates back to 1892 and 1898 in first and second versions respectively) Violaine has to sacrifice everything in this world through no fault of her own. The darkness which separates her from Jacques is only removed in their final meeting before her death; for the first time they understand each other in perfect accord.

*The Tidings Brought to Mary* is a mystery play which admirably conveys the atmosphere of the Middle Ages, an age of faith, but also of suffering and darkness, of fate and destruction. We find in this symbolic play an avalanche of human misery which descends on characters ill equipped to struggle against it without an appeal to God's mercy. The good suffer with the evil, Violaine is a victim for her holiness, and has to suffer a terrible ordeal and fate for her compassion. Mara, her sister, who knows only jealousy, hatred, revenge, suffers less but finds no happiness when she achieves her ambitions.

In the prologue Violaine forgives Pierre de Craon, an architect who once made an attempt on Violaine's honour, but who has since been smitten with leprosy. Moved by sympathy, Violaine gives him a kiss. Her father, Anne Vecors, master of Combernon, announces that he is going on a pilgrimage to the Holy Land, and hands over his estate during his absence to Jacques, to whom he also betrothes his daughter Violaine. No sooner has he gone than Mara, his younger daughter, who is secretly in love with Jacques, says that she will kill herself should the marriage ever take place. Moreover, she has seen Violaine kiss the leper. She does not need to carry out her threat, however, since Violaine has contracted the disease and is banished to die in the distant woods. Mara is able to marry Jacques and a daughter is born to them, Aubaine.

Some years later Aubaine dies, and Mara decides to seek Violaine, now a blind and holy recluse, and beg her to work a miracle. At first Violaine refuses, saying she is not a saint, but she yields and Aubaine is reborn. The child has now been given Violaine's eyes, which causes Mara a fresh wave of jealousy. Realising that Jacques still remembers his love for Violaine, Mara kills her sister.

Such a brief outline is quite inadequate to give an impression of the quality of the play, through the richness of Claudel's poetry, or indeed suggest the emotions it disturbs. With *Le Soulier de Satin* it becomes impossible, for this vastly complex play — indeed, not one play but several related — is beyond the limits of a satisfactory synopsis. We shall therefore discuss some of the situations and the ideas rather than deal with this, Claudel's testament of life, which contains all that is essential in the evolution of his poetry and vision. Before we consider *Le Soulier de Satin,* let us mention in passing the remaining plays of Claudel, which include *Le Pain dur* and *Le Père humilié* of the *L'Otage* trilogy; *Le Livre de Christophe Colomb* (1927); and two short comedies, *L'Ours et la Lune* (1917) and *Protée* (second version, 1926. One writer has compared this satire as being close in *esprit* to Giraudoux's writing). These plays, however, add little to the body of Claudel's works, though that is not to say they should be dismissed. *Le Pain dur,* in particular, is among the most effective of Claudel's plays from the dramatic point of view. It is a natural sequel to *L'Otage* with Turelure remaining as avid as before both for money and love. We see how he hates his son because he reminds him of Sygne, and we watch the development of this hatred until the son is driven to make an attempt on his father's life.

In *Le Père humilié* we meet the next generation, Pensée, a beautiful girl who has been born blind as if she were paying for her parents' sins. Pensée is not specially religious, but she falls in love with Orian, who feels the spiritual 'call'. We see the familiar Claudelian theme unfold, this time against a definite historical setting which plays a leading rôle in the plot. Orian is willing to renounce everything for Pensée, but the Franco-Prussian war breaks out. He has a duty to do, and Pensée persuades him to go to the front. He never returns.

*Le Livre de Christophe Colomb* is interesting for the possibilities it offers for an imaginative *mise en scène*. The book is published with an introductory essay on "Drama and Music", delivered at Yale in 1930, where Claudel explained some of his basic ideas for making the theatre more than a theatre. He believes that instead of a static set we should allow pictures, suggested by poetry and music, to appear on a screen, which would open a road to dreams, remembrances and imagination. "Why," he asks, "when a flood of music, action, and poetry entrances the minds of an audience, reply with a false heaven as crude and trivial as a café mural? Why not utilise the screen as a magic mirror where all sorts of shades and suggestions more or less vague and designs may pass, follow, and eliminate each other. Why not open the door of this troubled world where the idea gives birth to sensation and where the ghost of the future unites with the shadow of the past?"

If Paul Claudel had been born a generation later, he would doubtless have set himself the task of "discovering the formula", as he puts it, to unite the new arts with the old, and embody them within the framework of the living theatre. For his greatest work, *Le Soulier de Satin*, offers the severest test for any producer; it is total theatre and requires all the resources of the modern theatre — and more. The play is not divided into acts, but into 'Days' of uncertain duration. The full text, which took Claudel over five years to write, is published in two volumes, but an abbreviated version was used for the Comédie Française production in 1943.

"The scene of this play is the world," Claudel writes, "and more especially Spain at the close of the sixteenth, unless it be the opening of the seventeenth century." The play roams far and wide, its mood changes from that of medieval mystery to classical tragedy, and at times it has an element of the ducking-stool of farce; each scene is a marked contrast ("it is essential", notes Claudel, in a word to producers, "that the scenes follow each other without the least interruption"). But we must not suppose that *Le Soulier de Satin* is an abstract work, on the contrary, nothing is obscure and the purpose and direction are never hidden. We are, it is true, very far from the real world, and it would be foolish to consider the events that take place as if they were true. That is not the significance of the work. It is concerned with the invisible, what takes place inside the mind, and Claudel uses symbolism in a concrete sense to enter there.

The subject of *Le Soulier de Satin* has been described as a resumé of *Tête d'Or* and the conclusion of *Partage de Midi;* whereas *Partage de Midi* is a transitional play in Claudel's career, *Le Soulier de Satin* affirms vigorously and clearly. Human love and divine passion; the fusion of two beings into a single whole. Carnal love is weaker than the unio n of souls; the love of the body may be strong, but that of the mind is always more powerful. Just as Tristan loved Yseult, Mesa Ysé, so Rodrigue in *Le Soulier de Satin* loves Prouhèze, because they were made for one another. We are concerned, however, not only with the desire to love, but desires under many forms, power, possession, envy. To all these there is only the Christian solution.

Rodrigue and Dona Prouhèze in *Le Soulier de Satin* replace Mesa and Ysé in *Partage de Midi*. Rodrigue is like Tête d'Or, full of ambition. Dona Prouhèze has already met Rodrigue, and although she has only seen him for a short time she knows that she loves him. But since she is married, it is a love without hope. Rodrigue, for his part, knows that nothing can extinguish his love for her. As he explains:

> And can you imagine the body capable alone of kindling in mine such deep desire?
> What I love is not what in her can melt away, flee me, be absent and cease one day to love me, it is the very cause of her, what brings forth beneath my kisses life, it is not death!
> If she learned from me that she is not born for death, if of her I ask her immortality, that star which, unknowing, at her core she is,
> . . . Ah, how then could she refuse me?
> It is not what in her is cloudy, mixed, unsure, that I would ask, what is perishable, neutral, inert,
> It is the stark naked being, the pure life,
> It is that love, strong as I am when filled with desire like a great raw flame, like laughter in my face
> Ah, might she give it to me (I droop and night is closing over my eyes)
> Might she give it to me, yet she must not give it to me,
> Never will her body, dear though it be, give me contentment enough,
> Never except through one another shall we succeed in overcoming death.
> Out of orange mingled with violet comes the purest red.[1]

Rodrigue is wounded, and other difficulties are placed in their way. Prouhèze's husband decides that the best way to enable his wife to resist temptation is to place in her way a greater temptation. He

See original on p. 408.

arranges for her to assume command of a North African garrison, with as her lieutenant a Don Camille, who makes no secret of his fierce love for Prouhèze.

After some years Prouhèze's husband dies, and she immediately sends a letter to Rodrigue. This gets mislaid, and only reaches him after ten years. Meanwhile for reasons other than love Prouhèze marries Don Camille, so that when Rodrigue eventually arrives it is too late. Prouhèze meets him on board his ship in what is one of the most moving scenes of the play. She refuses to escape with him from Don Camille, for she has given her word that she will return — although she knows that certain death awaits her at the fort, which is to be blown up in order to forestall an attack by the Moors. For Prouhèze realises that she can never love Rodrigue on earth:

PROUHÈZE    Would you have had me then, noble Rodrigue, let you
            hold an adulteress in your arms?
            And later, after Don Pélage's death, launch that appeal
            to you
            Who, it were better perhaps, should not hear it.
            I should only have been a woman soon to die on your
            heart and not that undying star for whom you thirst.[1]

Rodrigue is about to prevent her leaving, but she challenges him to say one word and she will stay. He cannot prevent her going.

The love of Rodrigue and Prouhèze, it must be remembered, is only a part of *Le Soulier de Satin*, although it is of integral importance to the dramatic conflict. In a work of the magnitude of *Le Soulier* we cannot help noticing Claudel's faults (especially in the Fourth Day), but we feel that compared with the conception of the play and the clarity of its expression, the occasional momentary lapses unworthy of such a subject do not destroy it, but are themselves destroyed. Whatever may be the task of a critic to analyse a play, *Le Soulier de Satin* inspires enthusiasm or nothing.

Critics are inevitably divided about Claudel, but then, like everybody, critics like to ride their Dada's and hobby-horses, and it would be a dull world if everybody was infinitely and insincerely polite. But it is not the critics who have discovered Claudel, it is Claudel who has discovered his public. André Gide once wrote that though the public thinks that it chooses its authors, it is in fact the artist who chooses his public. This is certainly the case of Claudel, who had already written the majority of his plays before he had secured one performance in the theatre. Even after Copeau had presented *L'Annonce faite à Marie* in 1912, and *L'Echange* and *L'Otage* before the 1914 war, it was not until forty years later that the French public had come to treat its theatre seriously enough to admit religious and philosophical subject matter. As for production outside France, a Claudel play is fragile, however universal his theme may be. *L'Otage* is perhaps his best-known play in Britain, and recently has proved admirably suited for radio. But the language difficulty together with the idiosyncratic methods of Claudelian craftsmanship and spiritual expression prevent his plays ever being widely appreciated outside France, just as Shaw and even Ibsen have never quite fitted into the French *esprit*. Claudel will always be one of the major French poets, and in his creation of plays which restore the place of religion in the modern theatre he has introduced something which is entirely new in French dramatic literature.

# THE IMPACT OF BRECHT

BRECHT did not found Epic Theatre. The first explorer of the possibilities of revolutionary style and Brecht the true creator of Epic a century earlier than Brecht had been Georg Büchner, who died in 1837 at the tragic age of twenty-three. In the Germany of the Twenties Piscator may be said to have been more influential for experiments towards Epic; and yet the full impact of the Epic tradition in the contemporary theatre was not to come until the late Fifties, entirely due to the productions of Brecht. It was not indeed until Brecht had founded his own theatre, the Berliner Ensemble, in East Berlin in 1949, that he was able to achieve international acclaim. For although *Mother Courage* and other plays of his had been produced at Zurich in a neutral Switzerland during the war, even Brecht himself had not participated in their production; it was the memorable visit of the Berliner Ensemble to the Paris Festival at the *Théâtre des Nations* in 1954 which was decisive. Their visit to London two years later — alas, a fortnight after Brecht's death — was to influence profoundly the whole style of production; 1956 was to be an historic year for the British theatre. Here was a long-awaited answer to a naturalistic theatre which had degenerated into a drawing-room comedy set with martini-drinking cocktail cabinets. Epic Theatre was a challenge to the fundamental conception of theatre. As far back as 1930 Brecht had propounded a grammatical table for the aesthetics of Epic as opposed to dramatic theatre, and in doing so he became the supreme agitator of twentieth-century drama; only Pirandello can claim to have had a greater influence, and even that may be overtaken by Brecht in the years to come.

Few of the younger generation of dramatists, fewer still of directors, have not been influenced by aspects of Brechtian technique. One

Brechtian disciple has gone so far as to follow his master's footsteps to East Berlin; whether Peter Weiss has Brecht's cunning to make use of the Communist Commissars without becoming their puppet remains to be seen. Brecht may be said to have gained the theatre of his theories — he rejects the pretension of "dreams" — in the Berliner Ensemble, but already he had written during his years of exile all his major works.

FIVE

# FROM EXPRESSIONISM TO EPIC THEATRE

"If you want the audience to profit from the reality of the play, that is, to learn something from it, the theatre must evolve a style of performance which prevents the audience from identifying itself with the principal character (the heroine)."

BERTHOLT BRECHT

"The hero of this play is petrol."

LEO LANIA

CLAUDEL and Giraudoux both led the French reaction against naturalism towards impressionism, each in his own way, but both were reasonable ways, without compulsion, regimentation or the sacrifice of aesthetic values. The individual is respected, an appeal is made to his sensibilities, there is faith in man as there has been throughout the tradition of French civilisation. The extreme reaction against naturalism, as perhaps was to be expected, came from Germany, where from the time of the first world war until about 1927 the Expressionist movement held sway — an example of the blind leading the blind through the chaos of destruction and taking almost sadistic pleasure in doing so. Expressionism was an all-out onslaught against any sense of values which had survived the disaster, as topsy-turvy in its thought, as intolerant in its ultimate results, as the backcloth of the Germany it reflected.

Expressionism, it may be claimed, became an international movement, spreading as it did to Czechoslovakia, Poland, England and Ireland (it by-passed France), and America. This is true, but the ferocity and impact of its mood and influence were felt only in Germany, for expressionism belonged so much to the German spirit of the times that abroad its associations were missing. In the plays of Auden and Isherwood, for example, or Priestley's *Johnson Over Jordan*, Elmer Rice or O'Neill, we only heard a subdued echo of the expressionist howl. It was as if the German nation had kept its emotions repressed under rigid conformity and Prussian discipline for too long, and in the sudden explosion logic and reason had given way to primitive emotions and declamation. Expressionism has been described as an exigency of the mind, a mixture of ecstasy and obscurity, both facets being peculiar to the German temperament and language.

These plays are depersonalised. In Germany, it seems, it was not considered right that the individual should be allowed his own interpretation; indeed to the expressionists as to the Nazis the very word individual is suspect. Who, then, were these expressionist writers and what exactly were their theories? Here we run right into the confusion, for expressionism in Germany is not a coherent movement with a developed style, but a group of writers varying greatly in style and even politics, and often abandoning so-called expressionism after their first attempt, choosing instead their own *mélange* somewhere between crude realism and expressionism. Frank Wedekind (1864–1945), Karl Sternheim (1878–1943), and Georg Kaiser (1878–1945) are generally regarded as the initiators, but their successors, Ernst Toller, Fritz von Unruh, Bertholt Brecht, and Walter Hasenclever were at one time included in the list. It has also been suggested that the later dream plays of Strindberg were an earlier inspiration.

The consequences of expressionism were as devastating as confusing, and it is extremely difficult to trace any pattern between, say 1927, when Toller's *Hoppla! Wir leben!* ("Hurrah! We are Living!"), one of the last of the expressionist plays, was produced, and the burning of the Reichstag in 1933. After the expressionists with their contempt for reality came those who wanted to return to reality, though not necessarily the naturalism of Zola. Erwin Piscator, introducing what he described as a "knock-about style", attempted to replace both naturalism and expressionism by epic theatre (*episches Theater*), and his theories were closely followed by Brecht, who gradually saw the scene set for his "narrative realism". This was a period, however, when almost every known style was being tried out in the German theatre, and notably play after play appeared based on German history (the Napoleonic war period seemed the favourite choice) — strong patriotic dramas and generally exceedingly bad plays. But these were the writers who were later to respond so readily to official demand and guidance, once the political battle had been won.

In short, if any style characterised the German theatre in the inter-war years, it was a style suitable for political drama. The theatre was used as a battle-ground for political warfare, and there was no possi-bility of its seeking refuge in some ivory tower. Even in the golden age of German literature, Goethe may at times be said to be political, as can Schiller in his historical political dramas, and certainly as can Kleist and Büchner. Hauptmann was not political, but the expression-ists with their revolt against convention could not help entering the political arena, and with Kaiser they become more overtly social-political in their approach. With the Communists Piscator and Brecht, the forces of Bolshevism fighting Nazism, the theatre came to represent the political and spiritual faith of the nation. It must be regretted that in the extremes there was no room for moderation; liberalism was squeezed out in the struggle between revolutionary Marxism and national chauvinism. When Piscator wrote: "The drama is only im-portant in the degree to which it relies on the testament of document", little did he realise that in the German drama of that decade, and es-pecially his own theatre, we can see a clear reflection of the appalling mental state and depravity of a Germany ripe for Hitler's plucking, an all-too-true mirror of the decay of society and indeed a "testament of document".

Expressionism, then, ensured that the stage was set for political offspring, and until they had to flee before Nazi persecution, many of the expressionists became militant in politics. Piscator was the first to enter the political theatre, opening the "proletarisches Theater" in a working-class district of Berlin. "The style of our actors," he declared, "as well as that of the author and producer, should be of a complete and concrete nature (like the manifesto by Lenin . . .)". There was to be "no expressionism" any more. Piscator stressed the collective nature of production which had to be transmitted to the audience so that they too should be inspired by the spirit of their work.

After working for a time as producer to the Volksbühne he founded the Theater Piscator. His first play was Toller's *Hoppla! Wir leben!*, which is to-day regarded as a culmination of the expressionist tech-nique. Toller's social satire (hardly brilliant) and methods were not radical enough for Piscator, who introduced in his *mise-en-scène* extra material in film (which occupied about half the production time) to give the punch he felt the play lacked. Episodes in the film develop the idea of war, inflation, boxing, dancing girls, and other scissors-and-paste effects from newsreels, etc. We have already seen that Claudel experimented in *Christophe Colomb* with the idea of using the screen as a 'magic mirror' to complete, as it were, the atmosphere of the text. The idea can be used in moderation with great effect (Piscator's methods were a sensation), but beyond a certain point the method becomes a trick as precious as a toy-like Cinerama. It is no substitute for good drama, and the temptations it offers for crude sensationalism are only too apparent.

Any separation of politics and the art of the theatre was quite out of the question for Piscator, for "the destiny of the masses" was the "heroic factor in the new drama". The task of revolutionary theatre was "to take reality as a point of departure and underline the discord of society so as to introduce the elements of accusation, revolution, and the new order". And thanks to the film this lofty theory could be put into practice by showing sequences of the Russian Revolution, flashing statistics one minute and showing the horrors of war the next, drumming blatant propaganda the whole time into the thick heads of his audience.

★

Brecht has taken up these ideas and applied them as a challenge to the whole fabric of Western drama. It was during the period of the Weimar Republic that Brecht found roots, where in his experiments with mask and shadow plays his own cynicism corresponded to the mood of the times. It was in reaction to the unhealthy nihilism of so many of the expressionist works that made him of a sudden turn to Marxism as a way back to certainty, an established order, stability and a grammatical explanation of history and war. The time had come to make a clear sweep of what was still left, the dramatist's duty as Brecht saw it was to change nature, humanity and the world. There must be no more of the "let's pretend" aesthetic of naturalism, nor was there any question of trying to strive for the ecstasy and magical elements which were responsible for the *hara-kiri* of the expressionist movement. On the contrary, what was required was the theory of 'alienation'. It was wrong for the audience to participate when they should judge, for an actor to play when he should report, and for a stage to be a stage when it should be what it is, a platform. So Brecht devised the alienation of emotion to prevent the audience from identifying itself with an actor, or from losing itself in the supreme moments of theatre, only to be brought down to earth with a bump when it was over. There were to be no supreme moments and consequently no fall. Emotional strait-jackets were once again in fashion.

Of course some illusion had to remain, if the audience was itself to remain in the theatre. The question was one of selection. There was never an attempt at complete illusion but one of selected illusion; a room may be depicted showing only part of it, such as one wall, a table and some chairs. In *Mutter Courage* for example there is the fastidious detail of her provision wagon, aging throughout the play more markedly than Mother Courage herself. It is all a questiton of omission and inclusion and those items finally selected are given very special consideration. The idea is not without momentary excitement — what are we to make of it?

First Epic Theatre has borrowed very many of the oldest stock properties known in the theatre. There is nothing new in bringing the audience into the argument, improvisation (pretended), song, commentary, montage sequences. Brecht has merely experimented in these tricks further than other writers. Unfortunately Brecht's political insistence often defeats its own ends; the Communists were the first to realise that he would not win converts, however much intellectuals in the West might point to Brecht as representing truth, socialism and the promised land.

Brecht is undoubtedly gifted, "unfortunately gifted" as Thomas Mann once stated. His dogmatic certainties reflect the uncertainties of his own life. Even his Christian name changes from Berthold in his unorthodox period to Bert in his creative period and Bertolt at the end of his life. Born in 1898 in Ausburg in southern Germany, Brecht first studied medicine and science. During the first world war he worked in a hospital where he sang his first songs inspired by Rimbaud and Villon (in his plays song of course is introduced not to heighten conflict, but to alienate it). In 1923 he became assistant to Max Reinhardt, and it was Reinhardt who first presented a Brecht play to the public, *Trommeln in der Nacht*. This sharp satire on military heroism. mocking a soldier's return to his defeated fatherland and unfaithful bride — bearing the child of an armament's manufacturer — won the Kleist-Preis. Piscator produced Brecht's version of Hasek's *Brave Soldat Schweik*, but it was the adaptation of John Gay's eighteenth-century Beggar's Opera, *Die Dreigroschenoper*, that made Brecht famous overnight. This supposedly merry romp of beggars, vagabonds and thieves served as a pretext for an assault on "bourgeois bad taste". But as Mr. Herbert Luthy has observed in *Encounter*, the public misunderstood Brecht's intentions, taking them as a pretext for the enjoyment of the pathos, romance and sentimentality of the original. This was not the only occasion the public have applauded Brecht for the wrong reasons. When *Mother Courage* had its premiere at Zurich the bourgeois audience took the play to be a testament of the indestructibility of people like Mother Courage, and no doubt identified themselves with her small trader's attitude to war and profiteering.

When the Nazis came to power, Brecht began his life of exile. In 1933 he went to Denmark where he was to live until the Nazi maelstrom threatened to overtake him there, and he was forced to move on, to Sweden, Finland, and just ahead of the German invasion of Russia across Siberia to spend the war years in California. In spite of the anxiety of exile Brecht seemed to take to the idea of always being prepared to uproot himself; Max Frisch described his apartment in Zurich in 1948 as suggesting that everything in the room could be packed in 48 hours. The life of an exile did not upset Brecht's creativity, on the contrary it was in these years that he wrote his principal works, such as *Der Gute Mensch von Sezuan* (The Good Soul of Setzuan) between 1938–1940, *Leben des Galilei* (The Life of Galileo) during 1938–1939 and *Mutter Courage und Ihre Kinder* (Mother Courage and Her Children) in 1939. It is difficult to give a conventional outline of "plots" in Epic Theatre, for as Brecht himself emphasized, "plots" as such become "narrative" and he regards such German expressions as *Gesamtkunstwerk* ("integrated work of art") as something to be suspicious of, rendering "the various elements equally degraded" and extending this "process of fusion" to the spectator, who thus "becomes a passive (suffering) part of the total work of art." "Words," he insists, "music and setting must become more independent of one another."

*The Good Soul of Setzuan* (which was first produced at Zurich in 1943) is a highly controversial parable which suggests that the good in this world can survive only through ruthlessness and cheating, while even the gods are not immune from corruption if they stay long enough on earth. Three gods descend from heaven in search of one truly good human being to justify the continuation of the world. After an unsuccessful mission they arrive at the gates of Setzuan to meet their by now customary rebuffs from the selfishness of inhabitants who refuse them shelter for the night. Only the prostitute Shen Te offers them a room and they reward her with a sum of gold for her hospitality. She buys with this a tobacco shop, but is immediately invaded by relatives and parasites anxious to share and devour her good fortune; in order to protect herself Shen Te impersonates her brutal cousin Shui Ta. Shen Te also saves an unemployed airman Yang Sun, from suicide. She falls in love and they plan to get married, but on the wedding day the groom rejects the bride because she does not have sufficient capital. She then impersonates Shui Ta again, and employs Yang Sun as foreman in a tobacco factory, as he is the best person to mercilessly exploit the workers. Meanwhile the gods are worried about the disappearance of Shen Te and fear that Shui Ta has murdered her. They have him arrested, and at the trial, where they act as the judges, Shen Te confesses that she is only disguised in order to protect herself. The gods are so relieved that the one good human being is still alive that they ignore the implications of her methods, and return to heaven. In the epilogue Brecht stresses the need to change a world where good cannot survive by itself; songs also emphasize the irony.

*The Life of Galileo*, which was first performed in Zurich in 1943, and in an English version made in collaboration with Charles Laughton (who played the title role) in Hollywood in 1947. Here we have a theme which is very much in support of Brecht's own personal solutions to life. Galileo Galilei claims as his invention a copy he has made of a Dutch telescope. This enables him to make his cosmic discovery that the Earth is not the centre of the universe, but in fact goes round the sun. Though the Pope's own astronomer confirms this, it is thought inadvisable to have this published, and the Inquisition silences Galileo. A new enlightened Pope continues the interdiction and further orders Galileo to be shown the instruments of torture and to recant. Galileo's pupils desert him when they find he is a coward and has recanted. He is allowed to live under house arrest with his spinster daughter who does not understand him; his life seems to become that of a sensualist devoted to food and luxuries. In fact however he has used his cowardice to buy time to complete his life's work and have this smuggled out of Italy. Although Galileo is ashamed he had not the courage to refuse authority, Brecht clearly is on the side of the course of action he took.

In *Mother Courage and Her Children* (first produced Zurich 1941) the miseries of war are revealed through the chronicle of Mother Courage's seemingly endless trek across the waste lands of the battlefields of the Thirty Years' War. She is the bourgeois equivalent to the mercenary who sells his services; she will sell her provisions to either side, and is only concerned with preserving her own family and her means of livelihood. She has three children, two sons and a dumb daughter Katrin. The play opens with the silhouetted characters of Mother and Katrin sitting in the provision waggon while her two sons pull it (the stage revolves as they do so) in the wake of the Swedish army; they are singing the song of Mother Courage. The stage is bare, suggesting the desolation of war, the war from which Mother Courage derives her existence, which she will follow to the end, losing her two sons, seeing her daughter assaulted by drunken soldiers, and eventually shot. Mother Courage will continue to pull her waggon alone; she never sees further than the money the war brings her. She has sacrificed and lost all without understanding. In spite of Brecht's intentions and the theories of Epic Theatre she becomes a tragic heroine. Perhaps after all Epic is not so much diametricaly opposed to Dramatic Theatre as complementary, for the audience do not watch uninvolved, detached, without feeling for her plight. No amount of alienation can remove Mother Courage's searing heart-felt cry from the darkness of human suffering.

Of the plays Brecht wrote in the States, two stand out in importance, *Herr Puntila und sein Knecht Matti* (*Mr. Puntila and his Hired Man, Matti,* 1940–1941) and *Der Kaukasische Kreidekreis* (*The Caucasian Chalk Circle* 1944–1945). Mr. Puntila, like Mother Courage, is a character who dominates the play, and not a good example of Brecht's theories. For Puntila drunk and benevolent is contrasted with Puntila sober and mean and businesslike. *The Caucasian Chalk Circle* is based on an old Chinese play of the thirteenth or fourteenth century, where a judge places a child inside a chalk circle and only his true mother will be able to lead him out. The first wife twice tries to snatch the child, whereas the other sits patiently and the judge, recognising the sincerity of her love, declares her to be the child's mother. Brecht opens his play in Soviet Georgia at the end of the Second World War, where members of two collective farms are in dispute over a piece of land; after discussion it is decided to let the fruit farmers have the land, and a singer reminds them of the old Chinese legend. In Brecht's version the child of the governor is rescued by a housemaid during a revolution and carried to safety. After the revolution she is arrested, as the Governor's wife has taken the case to court. The judge turns out to be a drunken rascal, but the judgement given is the same as in the original Chinese parable. The maid is awarded the child because of her gentleness. The

D

singer concludes his interpretation of the meaning of the chalk circle and the land.

*The Caucasian Chalk Circle* was the last important play Brecht was to write: his *Die Tage der Kommune* (*The Days of the Commune,* written 1948–1949 in Zurich) was much less successful. In October 1947 Brecht was summoned to appear before the Committee on Un-American Activities in Washington, from which encounter he emerged with colours flying and even a word of thanks and praise from the baffled chairman. Brecht had delighted in misleading his inquisitors and throwing them off the scent; but already he felt the atmosphere of McCarthyism and witch-hunting closing in. There was no room for liberal intentions, let alone those of a Marxist. One month after the testimony Brecht was back in Europe, temporarily in Switzerland while he considered his next move. It is during his year in Zurich that Max Frisch in his *Tagebuch 1946–1947* gives us a fascinating picture of Brecht:

> It's now six months since I've known Brecht, and as with every important person whose superiority one admits, contact is difficult . . . For myself, it's when Brecht humbles me with his dialectic that I profit least from our conversation; one is beaten, but not convinced.

And Frisch continues:

> The fascination that Brecht exercises without cease I attribute especially to the fact that his life is truly lived through thought. Brecht does not look at all for approval, to the contrary, he looks for contradiction . . . And he listens in spite of everything . . . Then he passes to the attack, and the storm breaks.

In 1949 Brecht decided, not without hesitation, to settle in East Berlin and found the Berliner Ensemble which the Communist Commissars had offered him as bait. It was what Brecht had always hoped for, but never found in the capitalist West. However, as Martin Esslin has examined in his excellent biography *Brecht: a Choice of Evils* (London, Eyre and Spottiswoode, 1959) Brecht took the precaution of arranging an Austrian passport to enable him to keep his contacts with the West. He also kept his bank account in Switzerland. Brecht had to pay a price — he never wrote any significant work following his return to East Berlin — but although he was in decline as a creator, the practical application of his theories and the production of the plays he had already written enabled him to realise his greatness as a complete man of the theatre.

Whether before the Committee of Un-American Activities, or his Communist Commissars, Brecht was nothing if not cunning; in East Berlin, as Esslin has argued, they used each other, and it is difficult to know who won. We now know that the message of solidarity Brecht sent to Ulbricht after the workers revolted in East Berlin in June 1953 was merely a sentence taken out of context from a long letter, and used by the Party against him. In the memorial volume of the East German literary review *Sinn und Form* there are a group of significant poems, dated 1953, in one of which Brecht refers to his feeling of guilt, and another where we gather Brecht was merely sticking it out. He obviously remained convinced of the necessity to change radically the edifice of society; he wanted the ideal but realised that this would not be achieved in his lifetime. For Brecht only lived with a view of the future. Like Galileo there was no room for heroics. He believed that "to project a world where peace reigns and justice and to throw oneself before the canons to become their victim is to behave with a view of the beyond; it's the heroic attitude, contrary to the behaviour oriented towards down here; practical, and which will transform our misery."

In one of Brecht's last works *Flüchtlingspräche* ("Exiles' Dialogues," published posthumously in 1961) Brecht takes the case of two Germans who, chased from the Germany of the Third Reich, discuss the civic virtues of necessity. He finds that "the best school for dialectics is emigration" and "the most penetrating dialecticians are the exiles". Here we have the portrait of Brecht, like Joyce's requirements for exile, "and cunning ... "; we see him with his unshaven face, puffing continually at a cigar, wanting the audience to pull out their cigars and walk around the theatre so as to destroy any possible illusion. We hear his grunt, his ironical laughter, his approbation of an idea. But there is no room for the participation of nature. The future must be determined, there is no place for the artistic dream of which we don't know the ending. Finally, we must be aware of emotion. Brecht's exile was a continual reminder of the intense emotionalism of the German race, who had been swept by a *Herrenvolk* mystique beyond a paranoic point of no return. The Germans, Brecht was convinced, were too easily roused, too easily led; they had to be taught to think. And yet Brecht the man, like Mother Courage, rises above the turmoil of the parts, the episodes, the chapters, the fears of the cold war and the inhumanity of the Berlin wall; towards a more permanent and tragic sense of the whole. If life must be lived with cunning and compromise and impromptu, without comprehension or making others understand, it is surely because in the end the pattern does become a whole; the partial picture is complete.

# IN SEARCH OF EXPRESSION . . .

## LORCA — COCTEAU — O'NEILL — ELIOT

THE extreme reaction of the expressionists against naturalism was itself over before the more important modern dramatists had appeared, but its influence had shown them glimpses of a broader horizon and had disturbed their ambitions. The search for expression, the need for writers to experiment in new forms, was a serious challenge. Our next four dramatists, García Lorca, Jean Cocteau, Eugene O'Neill, and T. S. Eliot, each attempted to find in diverse artistic media their individual aims, but of the four, only Lorca may be said to have found his strength. Lorca, the only important dramatist to be killed in the war (and right at the beginning of the Spanish Civil War, an innocent victim of political vengeance) was as great a loss for world drama as for Spanish literature — the more so as he only finished his experiment in the pure folk tragedy of his last work; undoubtedly he would have given the theatre his full genius had he lived. With Jean Cocteau we have an artist who throughout his life strove to find new means of expression, but whenever he caused a mild stir he suddenly turned away in pursuit of a yet newer idea. Eugene O'Neill was perhaps the only really professional playwright among them, an early follower of expressionism who in his erratic trials and errors has covered the whole artistic field up to existentialism, displaying promising competence and talent. T. S. Eliot sought to bring back poetry to the theatre in gradual stages, where the poet was disciplined and poetry kept in abeyance to meet the needs of an audience accustomed to polite naturalistic drama. Eliot hoped that later on more liberal use could be made of poetry, but as his plays proceeded they in fact reversed the process. It is as if the poet was ashamed of the poetic participation and was prepared to compromise. The result was transitory box office success and eventual failure.

And meanwhile, the search for expression continues with a younger generation of writers, must continue, if the theatre is to remain alive . . .

# SIX

# A SPANISH TRAGEDY:
# FEDERICO GARCIA LORCA

*Le ganó con la verdad de la muerte a la razón de la vida.*
("He was won for the cause of life by the truth of death.")
MIGUEL DE UNAMUNO

THERE is a word in Spanish which defies translation: *duende* (literally it means 'elf' or 'hobgoblin'). It signifies that incantatory force which distinguishes the artist from all others; it is a quality of greatness which cannot be acquired. But it is more than that. It requires a living interpreter at an 'exact present'. All the arts are capable of it, but in Spain they are inspired by it. We witness it when a dancer, for example Antonio, holds an audience by his *zapateado*, so that they feel and shake to the very tempo of his movements; unless a bull-fight is alive with it the ceremony becomes meaningless. For *duende* is something which can make even a modern sophisticated audience aware of primitive emotion. "One only knows that it burns in the blood" is how Federico García Lorca once described it in a lecture on "The Theory and Art of the *Duende*".

Lorca's own plays depend absolutely on the creation of this strange power. Since his drama is merely a natural extension of his ballads in terms of the theatre, the most important element is always the audience and their ability to identify themselves with his leading characters. From his very first theatre piece, *The Witchery of the Butterfly*, written with the delicate fantasy of a boy poet, to the grim realism of his last completed work, *The House of Bernarda Alba*, everything depends on their ability to come across to the audience, who will be not so much entertained as animated and haunted by an apprehension unrelated to reason. An audience on Broadway or Shaftesbury Avenue which does not know that it is already in Granada, which does not fear the wild mountain-sides of the Sierra Nevada, which remains indifferent to the strange lyricism, unaware of the mystifying bond between romance and death, unafraid of the tyranny of Bernarda Alba, can never hope to enter the spirit of his plays by any intellectual process. They will only see in such a performance what Wolcott Gibbs described in an American production of *Bernarda Alba* as "apt to seem more comic than really dramatic".

In an interesting article on "Lorca's Audience" by Mary Otis (*Theatre Arts*, May, 1951), this failure of Lorca to establish himself with American audiences is discussed, and Miss Otis suggests that his inability to do so is not because the productions have been too Spanish for American understanding, but "not Spanish enough". "In Spanish dancing", as Miss Otis emphasises, "the genuine thing is always unconsciously recognised". On the other hand, we have the comment of Rafael Nadal, who, writing on the New York failure of *Blood Wedding* (produced under the ridiculous title, "Bitter Oleander"), believes that "whether we like it or not, Spain is from many points of view a world apart, and an attempt to transfer, in Lorca's most Spanish poetry, Spanish values of men and things met with an almost unsurmountable barrier." This barrier is not only confined to the English-speaking public, for *Blood Wedding* also failed in its Paris production in 1938, in spite of an excellent translation, praise from Left-wing critics and the politically favourable atmosphere of the time. Arturo Barea, writing of this production, explains that it had to fail "because foreign spectators only understood it through a laboured intellectual process, not through the swift, piercing associations and sensations it produced in a Spanish public. Indeed, in any Spanish public — for in Hispano America it was as great and lasting a success as in Spain itself". It would seem that there is danger of Lorca's plays losing their *duende* more or less completely without an audience which, if not Spanish-speaking, has a knowledge of, and sympathy for things Spanish.

To understand Lorca, then, we have to understand Spain, the hopes and sufferings of Spain, the rules of conduct and honour in Spain, the pride of the people, life and death in Spain. "I am a Spaniard and it would be impossible for me to live outside my geographical boundaries", Lorca once told a journalist. Throughout his entire work, Lorca is excessively a Spaniard, both in thought and action. Spain has always presented life in a sharper perspective than that of other European countries; it is at once exaggerated in its simplicity and passion.

The strident colours are brighter and darker; a merciless sun hides nothing. In this nation with such a tremendous zest for living the elongated shadow of death is everywhere present. If in other nations death is kept in the subconscious mind, in Spain it is for ever in the conscious. The capacity for living is made one with a capacity for dying; death should be triumphant, not an euphemism which is to be politely whispered. With this vision of death, it is understandable that religion in Spain should be so vastly important, rigid and extreme. In religion, as in politics, as in honour, the Spaniard imposes the severest discipline.

It is not without consequence that Spain has remained throughout history isolated, outside the European sphere of influence and culture. Spanish writers have written directly for the Spanish people, and an attempt during the eighteenth century to impose a pseudo-classicism on the Spanish stage as in France was to kill the Spanish drama until a return to its own tradition was made in the nineteenth century. Spanish art and music are equally distinguished in their perception of national temperament. Indeed, the arts in Spain have not and never have had the civilising pattern of European arts, for as Lope de Vega wrote in *The New Art of Writing Plays in this Age* (1609): "But since we are so far away from art and in Spain do it a thousand wrongs, let the learned this once close their lips." Spanish individualism can swim against the spirit of an age and bring its own rewards.

Lorca was less successful when he tried to expand his horizon; he was never the poet of burning intensity away from his Andalusia. His visit to America did not result in any broad understanding of the American scene or interest in their way of life. His *Poet in New York* is a testament of his failure there. His voyage, however, terminated a vitally important stage in his career, for he was able to realise that he was not to be the poetical opposite number of his artist friend Salvador Dali, who seemed in his painting to possess a universality that made him as much at home in America as elsewhere. It was a very different Lorca that was to return to Spain, for he had decided to abandon his gipsy romances and devote himself more and more to playwriting. But it was still Andalusia that attracted him for his themes.

Not only was he regional in writing about Andalusia, but he chose his own Granada, with its ancient towers nestling beside the bleak mountain-sides, or Cordoba, "remote and lonely", rather than Seville with its softer colours and more inviting calm. Lorca was an Andalusian minstrel who selected his themes from the diversity of life around him, from the people he met, to be recited preferably to the people he knew.

Lorca immediately reminds us of Burns in our own literature. Both are poets of international renown, yet both are essentially regional poets who, writing about their own locality, become the national poets of their respective countries. Lorca in New York was no more at home than Burns would have been in Oxford; the very thought of an Anglicised Burns, a Burns with a 'B.B.C. accent', is beyond the wildest probabilities of farce. But in spite of the distance between Scotland and Spain, the poet of Tam O'Shanter might well have chosen the subject matter of *Preciosa and the Wind*, though their interpretation of ideas would reveal the fundamental differences between Ayrshire and Andalusia. These differences are, of course, national differences, not a different vision of poetry and its uses. Both Burns and Lorca were master of the ballad, and the *duende* that comes from good storytelling.

Because Lorca was never so happy as in his Andalusia, he disregarded the advice of his friends not to go south to Granada in July, 1936. His tragic murder, which has been dramatically investigated by Mr. Gerald Brenan in his book *The Face of Spain*, was to turn Lorca for a time into a Republican martyr, thus unfortunately identifying him with a political cause. His politics had never been more pronounced than wishing to be friends with everyone in all countries, and not sacrificing the latter for narrow nationalism. If anything, at any rate on the surface, Lorca was more conservative than progressive, and plays such as *Mariana Pineda* (1929), as Arturo Barea has pointed out, might well at another time have been taken up by the Right, instead of being championed as an attack on the decaying dictatorship and monarchy of the era.

The truth is that Lorca could not help becoming identified as a poet of the democratic movement, for it was the progressives who were the intellectuals and who had supported and encouraged him. Moreover, the emotional onslaught against the conventional rigidity of the middle class such as his folk tragedies ventilated, ensured powerful enemies. His plays portrayed much that was wrong in the state of Spain, and while some believed his satires an occasion for a political demonstration (much to Lorca's disgust), others took exception to the 'realism' they saw in the mirror. These were the years when Spain seemed on the road to freedom of thought and social justice; a new renaissance had arrived for Spanish literature. It was the Republican government who appointed Lorca director of La Barraca, a national theatre company which toured Spain with a repertory of classical plays by such authors as Lope de Vega, Cervantes and Calderón. This work stimulated Lorca and encouraged him also to write and produce his own plays for his company.

For the last six years of his life Lorca was a professional playwright working within his company; his earlier failures were a closed chapter, for now he had made contact with his public and gathered confidence in each play he wrote. His poetical evolution led him, ironically enough in his last play *The House of Bernarda Alba*, to reducing the lyrical element so drastically that he could go no further in this direction; he had written a play which had been pruned bare, consisting only of bones and the impact of Spanish realism. But even though Lorca rejoiced that there was not 'one jot' of poetry in this play, its whole conception is that of a poetic vision, a drama, with the economy and precision of a well-made ballad.

Those who only know Lorca through this severely disciplined work can have little idea of the gradual evolution of Lorca's arrival there; those, on the other hand, who know him only by his other plays would find it difficult to believe that a mind so unusually sensitive to the qualities of lyricism should have deprived itself so completely of its opportunities.

It is true that the struggle between poetry and prose in his plays does not always lead to satisfaction, but it is a conflict which all poets have to solve for themselves in the theatre. Their fusion can only be arrived at by experiment. In these experiments Lorca was tempted by other methods, such as surrealism, which he finally discarded, and rightly so, in order to concentrate on his pure folk tragedies. For it is by these that Lorca is remembered. In them he endeavoured to introduce into the Spanish theatre the folk speech, lyricism and poetic imagination while at the same time to reduce life to an outline or skeleton of bare essentials. He wished to replace the bourgeois realism of the commercial theatre of his day, which was not specifically Spanish, with a return to the beauty of the Spanish language as spoken by peasants who retained its purity. Lorca wished to ally this with a return to the traditional Spanish theatre, the models set by Lope de Vega and Calderón, which had been discarded. For though Jacinto Benavente had for so many years been acknowledged as Spain's leading dramatist (he was a Nobel Prize winner in 1922) he had surprisingly neglected much of the tradition of the Golden Age (in fact he shares with Lope de Vega only the distinction of having had a long life in which to write a superabundance of plays). Lorca delighted in the lyrical and emotional elements in Lope de Vega's plays, specially in his own productions of them. But possibly he revered more the austerity and spiritual exploration found in the plays of Pedro Calderón de la Barca, and especially his concept of honour which figures in many of his works. We must, however, remember that Lorca was only in the tradition of these Spanish classical writers, they were only the forefathers of a common heritage.

★

The world of Federico García Lorca (1898–1936) was from his early childhood an imaginary world of the theatre, and the whole of life was to him a mysterious drama in which he was an actor. In a preface to *Three Tragedies* his brother Francisco tells us how the first toy that Federico ever bought was a model theatre. Since there were no plays provided he had to make them up for himself. We are also told that one of his favourite games was to play as priest and deliver a sermon to his sisters, the servants, and any others who would willingly participate; the only condition was that everyone had to weep. Life was to Lorca an occasion for tears and laughter, and that was what he wanted of his audience.

It is not perhaps surprising that Lorca failed to establish a *duende* with his Madrid audience in his early career. Its urbanity was far removed from the childhood simplicity needed to give way to a flood of tears. *El Maleficio de la Mariposa* ("The Witchery of the Butterfly"), presented during the 1919–1920 theatrical season by Martinez Sierra, ran for one performance and was vigorously booed. Written before he was twenty, the subject matter of this piece was related closely to Lorca's verse written about the same time. He tells us of the longing of a sordid cockroach to know the world of a wounded butterfly. Eventually the butterfly is able to use its wings again and flies away to the world the cockroach will never know. For the cockroach life becomes unbearable because of the witchery of the butterfly.

In 1927 Lorca, with the aid of Salvador Dali, who designed the sets, had his first full-length play, *Mariana Pineda,* produced. The play, an historical romance, takes for its heroine a woman from Granada who embroiders a Republican flag in preparation for a revolution in the 1830's. When the police discover the plot the cowardly revolutionaries flee abroad and she is arrested; unwilling to betray the names of the conspirators, although they have deserted her, she dies on the scaffold. Mariana, however, is not made to die for a political cause; like Lorca himself, she is not interested in politics, but is an innocent victim caught in their web. It must be remembered that the place of a Spanish woman is at home; she would evoke little sympathy in dying for a political cause. It is, on the other hand, very much in the Spanish tradition for a woman to sacrifice herself for love. Mariana Pineda is in love with a liberal conspirator. How can she show this more fittingly than to embroider a flag for him with his party's emblems on it? It is through her love that she must die, and die alone, for all the revolutionaries are shown up as pitiable funks.

Lorca calls this play a 'popular ballad'. To the obvious dramatic opportunities in the theme he has introduced many lyrical passages of distinction, but it is not altogether a satisfying play. His greatest difficulty is to make his characters appear to live instead of remaining merely figures in a plot. Perhaps this is an inevitable danger for a writer of ballads, where so much less importance is attached to characterisation than in a play.

After *Mariana Pineda* Lorca started writing a series of plays which experimented with the folk idiom on the stage, and which were to clear the ground for his more important folk tragedies. *Amor de Don Perlimplín con Belisa en su Jardín* ("The Love of Don Perlimplín for Belisa in his Garden"); *La Zapatera Prodigiosa* ("The Marvellous Shoemaker's Wife"); and *Retabillo de Don Cristobal* ("In the Frame of Don Cristobal") form the three plays of this group. Perlimplín is a dear old rich bachelor who, urged on by his housekeeper Marcolfa, rashly asks for the hand in marriage of Belisa, a voluptuous beauty who lives next door. She accepts readily, but it is not long after their wedding night that Perlimplín learns that she has a lover. He tells her he will be content to love her as a father does a daughter. In the last scene Perlimplín approaches Belisa while she is waiting for her lover. He tells her that if she really loves her lover, he does not want him ever to abandon her, and "so that he may be yours completely, it has occurred to me that the best thing is to stick this dagger into his gallant heart". Perlimplín runs after a figure and after a while returns, wrapped in a red cape. He is wounded, and before falling dead in Belisa's arms rejoices that Belisa is now able to have a soul as well as a body. Through his own suicide he has given Belisa a soul. It is indeed a play for tears and laughter.

*The Marvellous Shoemaker's Wife*, the most successful of this series, may be described as a poetic farce, with song and dance interwoven in its theatrical structure. The young sensual shoemaker's wife is, like Belisa, married to a nonentity of a husband, far older than herself, and no match for her insatiable desires. In fact, for the poor shoemaker life is made a hell, and he is eventually forced to flee from his home. The marvellous wife turns his workshop into an inn which all her lovers frequent. The shoemaker returns in disguise and finds that with all the temptations available to his wife, she has nevertheless remained faithful to him. Everything would seem ready for a happy ending, but no . . . when the disguise is discarded we are back where we were, and the merry-go-round begins again.

*In the Frame of Don Cristobal* is a puppet farce, a highly spirited piece which opens with the poet addressing the audience about the meaning of his play, and having an argument with the producer about what he is allowed to say (the producer of course wins). Again it is a story of a faithless wife, Rosita, who having been bought in marriage by Cristobal, offers herself to any man, and when she gives birth to quadruplets pleads that they are Cristobal's children. He beats her to death for it.

There are two plays belonging to Lorca's surrealist period *Así que Pasen Cinco Años* ("If Five Years Pass") and *El Público* ("The Audience"). *If Five Years Pass* is a highly complex play, which has as many incidents, characters appearing and disappearing, as one might expect to pass through the mind when contemplating a span of five years. It is certainly too meandering for any adequate synopsis of contents, and the title itself tells us all we need to know about the plot. On the stage its violently surrealist approach must either conquer the audience or dumbfound them. A list of the characters: Young Man, Old Man, Stenographer, Manikin, Valet, the Friends, the Betrothed, the Rugby Football Player, Cat and Boy, three Gamblers, a Harlequin, a Clown . . . requires a fertile imagination to envisage them all as complementary characters in the framework of a play. There is no doubt that Lorca was attempting to rid himself of all the restrictions of dramatic conventions and achieve in the theatre the complete freedom of a poet. His other surrealist experiment, *The Audience,* may be considered as an attack on the commercial theatre, in which the audience itself is on trial.

After these *ballons d'essai* Lorca finally turned to his folk tragedies, where his genius was best fitted to assert itself. *Bodas de Sangre* ("Blood Wedding"); *Yerma   Doña Rosita la Soltera* ("Doña Rosita the Spinster") and finally *La Casa de Bernarda Alba* ("The House of Bernarda Alba") complete Lorca's drama. The heroines of these plays compel our admiration, for their portraiture of Spanish womenfolk is Lorca's superb achievement. In his plays the women accept the stern code of honour which is more important to them and their families than life, and should they fail, should they be driven by sexual passion to forfeit their virginity or honour they are aware of their punishment. An honest woman commits suicide to protect her purity.

In *Blood Wedding* (1933) the emphasis is on the word blood; blood is associated with the blood of old family feuds which have never healed. The characters in this play are nameless, except the one who causes the bloodshed, for this is a study not of characters so much as of attitudes and ethics. The only living son of a mother who has seen her husband and other sons killed in a feud murder, is planning to marry a girl who was previously engaged to Leonardo, a member of the family who took part in the murder. Leonardo has since married the girl's cousin, but it is not a happy marriage and Leonardo still loves the girl he was to marry. The wedding takes place between the son and the girl, but after the ceremony the bride suddenly elopes with her old lover.

When her father hears the news, he pleads: "It can't be she. Perhaps she's thrown herself into the cistern."

To which the mother curtly replies: "The pure and honourable throw themselves into the water. Not that one, no! But now, she's the wife of my son! Two clans. Here there are two clans."

They all join in the hunt to avenge the crime, and the mother knows that in doing so her only son is going to his death. "The hour of blood has come again."

So the young lovers are pursued through the woods, and in the beginning of the third act, set in the dark, supernatural atmosphere of the weeping forest, Lorca brings a sombre lyrical imagination to bear on the mounting tension of the human hunt. Symbolism is also present; three woodcutters represent a mournful Greek chorus; then the moon, the messenger of death, rises, lighting the stage with "an intense blue radiance". The moon gives way to the beggar woman, who personifies Death. In the final scene the bride returns leaving behind the bodies of both husband and lover, and submits herself to her mother-in-law's fury; the mother strikes her and she falls to the ground:

BRIDE    Leave her: I came to let her kill me so that I would be taken away with them. (*To the Mother*) But not with your hands:

             with hooks of wire, with a sickle, and with a force that will
break my bones. Leave her. I want her to know that I am
clean, that I shall go mad, but that they will bury me without
a single man's ever having seen the whiteness of my breasts.

MOTHER    Be quiet: be quiet: What does that matter to me?

BRIDE      But I went away with the other, I went. (*In anguish*) You
would have gone. I was a burnt-up woman, full of wounds
within and without, and your son was a spring of water
from which I expected sons, land and health: but the other
was a dark river full of branches which rushed towards me
with the song of its reeds and its stifled song. I ran with your
son who was like a little boy made of cold water, but the
other sent me hundreds of birds which impeded my course,
and left frost in my wounds of a poor pining woman, a girl
caressed by the fire. Your son was my aim and I never
deceived him, but the arm of the other swept me away like
a great sea-wave, like the butting of a mule, and he would
have swept me away even had I been old and all the children
of your son had been clutching my hair . . . Revenge yourself on me. Here I am. See how soft my throat is. It would be
less trouble to cut a dahlia in your garden. But not that!
I am chaste, chaste as a newly born child. And strong enough
to prove it. Light the fire. We'll put our hands in it — you
for your son, I for my body. You'll pull yours out first.

MOTHER    But what does your honour matter to me? What does your
death matter to me? What does anything matter to me?
Blessed be the corn because my sons lie under it, and it wets
the faces of the dead. Blessed be God who lays us out together to rest.[1]

*Blood Wedding* was the first play of major importance which Lorca
wrote, the first play where his maturity had developed to a point where
he was as much a dramatist as a poet.

    The following year Lorca was determined to move along the road
towards dramatic realism, while still retaining important lyrical
scenes. *Yerma* is still described as a 'tragic poem'. Like *Blood Wedding*
it is a tragedy which underlines the Spanish acceptance of sex as borne
by women and the torment suffered by the soul of a woman who adheres to the conventions and must reject all compromise. The word

[1] Translation by Mr. Roy Campbell.

'Yerma' means 'unsown' or 'uncultivated' and in this particular play it refers to a woman who is sterile, through no fault of her own. She only married to have children, but she fears her husband is impotent. She becomes obsessed with the desire for a child, and she is attracted by Victor, a strong shepherd whom she knows would be able to consummate her love. Clearly they were made for each other. But Yerma is a Spanish woman first. Although she is driven to hate her husband for his frigidity she has her code of honour. Although her body feels the need for children, her soul thirsts for children, better to remain barren than give herself to a man who is not her husband. In vain she consults other women, but they cannot comfort her. The behaviour of her husband drives her near frustration. He tells her that "life is sweeter without children. I am happy not having them". Yerma must resign herself to this fact, but this she will not do. Instead, in an embrace, she siezes her husband by the throat and in a mad frenzy of passion strangles him. Her tortured being could no longer accept, there was no other outlet for her emotions; what she did was instinctive. Now she can find peace, knowing for certain she will be barren for the rest of her life.

> Withered! Withered, now I know it for certain, and alone. I am going to sleep without ever waking in a start to see if my blood feels another new blood. Barren forever . . . what are you all looking at? What do you want to know? Don't come near, for I've killed my son. I myself have killed my son!

*Doña Rosita the Spinster* (1935) restrains the passions and there is little action or drama in its study of spinsterhood and old age in nineteenth-century Granada. But whether intentionally or not, the play makes a more open attack on the narrowness of middle-class life which was to be interpreted politically. Rosita waits in vain for the return of her fiancé, who many years before went abroad and who has actually married somebody else. The deception, however, is kept up by Rosita, who remains always faithful to him.

*The House of Bernarda Alba* completes the journey to dramatic — or should one rather say Spanish — realism. Everything is subjected to realism, right down to the names of the characters. In an article by Claude Couffon in *Le Figaro Littéraire* (26 December, 1953) Lorca's cousin Doña María told M. Couffon that "Bernarda Alba and her daughters really existed. They lived in a little village in the open country, where the parents of Federico owned property: Valderrubio.

The two houses were adjoining. The actual well was mid-way. It was one summer, when he was staying at Valderrubio, that Federico discovered this strange family of girls over whom their mother, widowed for many years, exercised a tyrannical guard. Intrigued by this, he decided to overhear the intimate life of the Albas. Using the well as an observation-post, he spied, studied, took notes. Two months later the play had taken shape." And we learn from Doña María that even the mysterious character of Pepe el Romano, who is behind the action in the play but never actually appears, played the same rôle in real life and had the name Pepe el Romilla.

There are no male characters in *Bernarda Alba*. The female studies of his previous plays had been so important — whereas one soon forgets his male characters — that it seems as if Lorca was determined to consecrate a play entirely to them. So we have Bernarda Alba, the domineering head of five daughters (aged thirty-nine to twenty), only the youngest of them attractive and not yet resigned to being a spinster. The daughters know nothing about what goes on outside their windows; they are barred, and the stifling atmosphere of repression, suppressed desires, results in a clash of wills. A marriage has been arranged between Pepe de Romano and the eldest daughter Angustia, but Pepe has already seen the attractive youngest daughter Adela and meets her in the stables. Their meetings are betrayed one night by another jealous sister who is also in love with Pepe, and Bernarda rushes out of the room with intent to shoot Pepe. Adela is given the false news that he has been killed, whereas in fact Bernarda missed. Believing him dead, Adela goes and hangs herself in her room. Bernarda orders them to:

> Cut her down! My daughter died a virgin. Take her to another room and dress her as though she were a virgin. No one will say anything about this! She died a virgin. Tell them, so that at dawn, the bells will ring twice.

For the others the house remains a prison, of jealousy, bigotry, unhappiness, ruled by the rod of iron of Bernarda.

In *The House of Bernarda Alba* Lorca reached the end of an experiment in playwriting, and it resulted in his most successful play. Throughout his life Lorca had never been content with doing things the same way twice, and whether he had at last found where he really wanted to go, or would, had he lived, have started new experiments, we shall never know.

That Lorca died in his prime of life is one of the greatest tragedies that could have happened, not only for Spanish literature, but for world theatre. Of all the dramatists of his era, he was the one who was capable of achieving the calibre of greatness. Many atrocities were committed on both sides in the Civil War; what is done is done. Lorca was a victim of the forces of violent death he himself described so vividly, for it was by always living in face of death that he lived so fully, with every moment precious to him. Death continually lurked by his side, haunted his imagination, and he lived forever under the presentiment of its shadow. Lorca found no consolation in the Catholic conception of death, and nowhere in his writing does he show any reference to a belief in any life beyond. For him, death was an eternal sleep which deprived one of the senses. So be it. Lorca has survived death, and lives every time his work creates that *duende* of which he was master. His name lives on as do his plays. As an epitaph we can quote his *Cásida de la Huída:*

> I want to sleep for a while,
> For a while, a minute, a century,
> But all shall know that I have not died,
> That there is a stable of gold on my lips,
> That I am the little friend of the West wind,
> That I am the giant shadow of my tears . . .

# SEVEN

# THE COCTEAU LEGEND

"It is not the business of the dramatist to bring life into the theatre but to bring the theatre to life."

JEAN COCTEAU

COCTEAU is no longer a name — he has become a legend. A legend of the 'twenties, who (alone of his generation) has continued the race for new means of artistic expression through the twilight of the 'thirties, the havoc and despair of the 'forties, and right into the 'fifties. "You're a wicked playboy", the great Colette once told him, "because you don't know how to relax without doing anything." That is as true of Cocteau's career as it is of his life; he can never be accused of resting on his laurels. If in his life he has sampled everything from opium to religion (to his credit he has never attempted the Marxist equation of the two) so in art he has tried everything. From poetry to painting, criticism to novel writing, and, of course, as *homme de théâtre*, there is no literary peak or band-wagon of fashion that Cocteau has not attempted to climb. But he refused to admit victory as he refused to consider defeat, for no sooner was he half-way up one peak than he was immediately more interested in what the view from the next one would be like. He was never satisfied with his own achievement; he no more believed in trying the same thing twice than loving at second sight. "Respecter les mouvements, fuir les écoles" (Pay respect to literary movements, flee from literary schools) is his conviction, his strength, and his weakness. So we have his *poésie graphique*, his *poésie de roman*, his *poésie de théâtre*, and his subsequent *poésie cinématographique*. His definitions are exact. He is not a poet attempting to bring poetry into the theatre; he wishes instead to seek a poetry of the theatre, in whatever style it can be realised. It is a vastly more dangerous height to reach and one which only the greatest poets attempt —

unless, like Cocteau, they have the balance of a tight-rope walker with the precision of a magician's sleight-of-hand.

The precision of a magician — the very French word *prestidigitateur* suggests euphoniously the lightness of touch that is required — is Cocteau's secret. But it is not the old professional magician who produces rabbits from top hats as if from slot machines, it is rather like an earnest young magician who is producing the rabbit for the first time in his professional career: since Cocteau is only interested in performing the trick once he does it creatively. With the irresponsible ambition of youth he has ransacked the history of the theatre, and given his version to the major periods; the ancient Greek legends, the folklore of the Middle Ages, Elizabethan passion, classical tragedy and romantic drama are not forgotten in his own *théâtre*. And to complete the history he proves that he can take a boulevard success and make his model that will hold its own with the box-office. You may perhaps question the word 'creative' when Cocteau so follows the footsteps of others rather than creates a new style of his own; yet Cocteau's signature is clearly evident in all his works, however diverse. Whatever the form of expression we are sure that only Cocteau could have been the artist.

Cocteau replied to such critics that he was a poet, bound by no school. He did not want, like his Orpheus, to suffer at the hands of the Saint-Germain-des-Prés mob, but he knew, like Orpheus, that one was never forgiven for not being faithful to a school, if one has once 'flirted' with it. It is not easy to-day, as he complained in a talk given on the B.B.C. Third Programme, to refuse lifts on the autostrade, to remain simply 'the cat who walked by himself'. Cocteau's freedom is the absolute freedom of an artist; freedom to exploit the full resources of poetic vision in its immensity. His talent demanded that he should 'reflect further', and since he never tired of life, he never tired of his seeking after the beauty of life. And in all his experiments Cocteau preserved the inquisitiveness of youth; his characters epitomised the expression of a youthful mind.

Youth is never satisfied, it fears nothing, for though it can be haunted by death, death remains an abstraction or some theatrical character who has not yet become a present reality. The young man can reflect in the mirror, the same mirror as in the *teatro dello specchio* of Pirandello, where he will see "death working like bees in a beehive". But for Cocteau mirrors are the means of passing from one plane of existence to another, the real to the unknown. Cocteau surveys the possibilities of the unknown with the limitations of the known. "Man is a cripple", he writes in *Journal d'un Inconnu,* "I mean that he is limited by the dimensions which surround him and prevent him from understanding the infinite where dimensions do not exist." It is the meeting of the real and the imaginary, the natural and the supernatural, that inspires Cocteau's poetry. He can only conceive the latter in terms of the former, for "reality alone, even when well concealed, has power to arouse emotion". Or, as the surrealist André Breton expresses it, "what is admirable in the fantastic is that there is nothing fantastic; it is only the real". Cocteau, even in his most surrealistic adventures, always describes his poetry in terms of the world we know and understand.

Cocteau was insatiable for the secrets of the great mystery; we feel he was not afraid of death, but regarded her rather as an artistic partner. In *Orphée* he introduces her to us not as a weird and midnight hag, such as we assume her to be in popular mythology, but as a glamorous, dark-haired beauty dressed for a ball, apparently because no one would recognise her in such an attire. And the ever-youthful spirit of Cocteau waltzes with her in order that she should lead him behind the scenes, through the magic mirror, but with the promise of a return ticket from the underworld.

Such are the methods of Jean Cocteau, where the mystery of life remains a mystery under the magician's wand, where we are always fascinated to go further, to know more, where we believe that the impossible is always possible, but where we must keep silence and not ask questions, lest we disturb the actors, who are playing very high and without safety nets, and cause them to fall from their great heights. We all know what happened to humpty-dumpty.

*

Jean Cocteau has been called "the spoilt child of the century". Certainly everything about his childhood had a touch of the 'silver spoon in his mouth'; born in 1892 and brought up in bourgeois luxury in the Rue d'Anjou in the centre of Paris, he was already a genius at the age of ten. Cocteau has continued his precocity throughout his life, and those who refuse to accept his behaviour as becoming a poet, willingly forgive him for being a publicity agent for the latest *snobisme*. The infant prodigy grew into a somewhat precious young man, who would be sure to 'dear' you in the manner of theatrical people on first meeting, and offer you some opium. Nevertheless his friends and acquaintances have included nearly all the outstanding figures in the French literary scene during this century: Proust, Claudel, Gide, Apollinaire, Mauriac, Giraudoux, Picasso. . . . But no wonder Gide despaired of him, when writing in his *Journal* on 20 August, 1914, he noted: "I have not had the pleasure of seeing him again in spite of his extreme kindness. But he is incapable of seriousness and all his thoughts, expressions, sensations, all this extraordinary dash of his ordinary speech shocks you as an article of dazzling luxury does at a time of famine and mourning." But how was Gide to know then what sort of 'brave new world' the armistice was to bring, or that 'articles of dazzling luxury' were to be the fashion! And by no means all the fashions that Cocteau wedded were as vulgar as posterity has decreed. The fashions went out with the 'twenties, but Cocteau's work survives. Somehow we have the feeling that Cocteau would survive in any age through his charm, so long as a place can be found for a poet.

Although we sense he was a lonely man, his life had been surrounded by friends, who have so testified their friendship that there have been times when they held Cocteau's judgment sacred, his tastes impeccable, when one word from him on a controversial topic was final. His early friends who met him every Saturday included Radiguet (his personal discovery), Picasso, Cendrars, Tristan Bernard, Rubinstein, and many others. Then suddenly in 1923 Radiguet died of typhoid fever and Cocteau was struck down with grief. Neither Monte Carlo, nor opium nor religion was sufficient, alone work offered an escape, a possibility to explore the mysteries through artistic expression. In the years that have followed, Cocteau has lost many of his friends (the Gestapo assassinated several) but his search went on, giving him little time for reflection or memories.

And so we come to Cocteau's work, and in this respect we shall concentrate on his work for the theatre, which is fully as important as the rôle he has played in the other arts. Each of his plays has brought a new horizon to the modern theatre, whether it be a return to the purity of Greek legend in *La Machine infernale*, the legends of medieval Europe in *Les Chevaliers de la Table Ronde*, the classical tragedy *Renaud et Armide*, or the brilliant monologue *La Voix humaine* where a wife holds a last and unavailing telephone conversation with the man who has left her for good. His theatre has caused famous scandals, notably *Les Parents terribles* which the Paris municipality condemned for its 'incest', and *Bacchus*, said to be anti-religious, and by which a friendship of youth, with François Mauriac, was broken in an evening.

Yet in all these plays there is the common element of, shall we call it, poetry, and in spite of the pre-war Paris municipality, taste.

Since his first work in the theatre, *Parade*, written in 1917 for the Diaghilev dancers (music by Satie, décor by Picasso), Cocteau has given us some seventeen plays, from which we shall select for consideration his admirable *Les Parents terribles*, his controversial *Bacchus*, his romantic *L'Aigle à deux Têtes*, his treatment of classical legend in *La Machine infernale* and also in his *Orphée*. Though outside the province of this book, Cocteau's career in the cinema has been an extension of his theatrical activity, and in the film version of *Orphée* Cocteau is justified in his claim to have realised his supreme ambition.

★

All Cocteau's plays have a great sense of the dramatic. No one knows better than he how to treat an old and worn legend, or for that matter a conventional boulevard situation, in terms of the theatre of to-day. In his first major work *Orphée* (1925), for example, we see how he turns to a familiar old Greek plot and makes it acceptable for a modern audience, giving it not only dramatic unity but contemporary interpretation as well. The legend becomes a means of expressing Cocteau's own preoccupations with the dividing line between the conscious and the unconscious, the real and the fantasy, humdrum life and the adventure of death. Orpheus becomes a poet whose inspiration is death, and his poetry responds to mysterious force instead of the poet's self.

All sense of time in the play is indefinite; we are neither in the past, present nor future. Orpheus has married Eurydice. Orpheus is the national poet of his country; Eurydice has left her secret cult and the Bacchantes (commanded by Aglaonice) to get married, and has consequently kindled their hatred against her. One day Orpheus is intrigued by a horse in a street and takes it home. The horse communicates to him, through an alphabetical system, mysterious phrases such as "Madame Eurydice will come back from hell", and gradually Orpheus is bewitched by the invisible power of this horse, much to the distress of Eurydice. She confides in Heurtebise, a glazier, who passes each day. Heurtebise in fact turns out to be an angel who watches over the destinies of Orpheus and Eurydice. While Orpheus is absent entering for a poetry competition Aglaonice succeeds in poisoning Eurydice, and Death arrives to carry her away. Orpheus learns what has happened and decides, with the help of the angel to go and bring her back from the underworld. As in the legend, he is allowed to do this provided he does not look at her on the journey, and of course the inevitable happens. On his return Orpheus is warned that the Bacchantes are coming to kill him, since they believe that he is a mystifier, having read his poem "Madame Eurydice will return from hell". Instead of saving himself Orpheus gives himself to the fury of the Bacchantes and to Death.

Cocteau adds, as it were, an amusing postscript where the Bacchantes declare to the police that they found Orpheus dead. The police arrest the angel Heurtebise, who, when asked his name replies: Jean Cocteau. The angel disappears to join Orpheus and Eurydice now united forever.

The little episode is an excellent *jeu d'esprit* on the lack of imagination which humans possess, and what could be more human than the prosaic plodding of police methods? The play is described as a 'tragedy in one act and one interval'. The description emphasises the timeless element of the play; we witness a scene in the middle of the play twice, as if in rehearsal. There are numerous such tricks throughout the play, some less effective, as when a member of the audience is asked for the loan of his watch, but on the whole the comedy and tragedy are carefully interposed, and the play has coherence. The two themes, poetry and death, become one whole, just as Orpheus and Eurydice are united in death. The premium then is on death, but death, as we have seen in Cocteau, leads to the revelation of the artistic unknown. The fusion of poetry with death is an adventure story.

*Orphée* was the first love of Cocteau. His return to the theme for his film deserves mention, if only to understand his development a quarter of a century later, and to see how his ideas had had an opportunity of spreading their wings in the greater freedom of the cinema, in ways in which the proscenium arch could never compete with 'the magic box'. The film *Orphée* is set in the contemporary world (the period is defined) and the realism is intensified. Orpheus becomes a modern poet who wishes to avoid the Saint-Germain vogue and consequently makes himself unpopular among them. Death is a Princess who drives about in a Rolls Royce; Heurtebise is her chauffeur. Eurydice used to work at a club called The Bacchantes. The whole accent is thus different from that of the play. The film sweeps through the mirror to the shades and desolation of 'no-man's land', the journey through the underworld. We make the grand tour. Then there is a most important variation in the theme: the Princess Death kills Eurydice for jealousy because she is in love with Orpheus. This is why Eurydice is allowed to go back with Orpheus, but this time it is Eurydice who forces him to see her. Orpheus is shot in a riot on his return, but the Princess returns them both while she must go another way, to face trial for her crimes.

The film is an adventure story derived from the play. Although the play never drags, it does not succeed in carrying the audience with it as does the film. Both the film and the play deal with the same unknown, an exploration of death through dream, a mysterious journey into the hinterland of the imagination. There is no need to struggle against death, for acceptance is so very much more exciting.

Cocteau turned again to Greek mythology in *La Machine infernale* (1932, produced by Jouvet in 1934), this time the old (not to say worn) legend of Oedipus. Once again he transforms it into something vital, alive and coherent. The inevitability of events is shown from the start, again in a manner acceptable to a modern audience. The horror of a son who murders his father and marries his mother is made real and convincing. Oedipus is a young man, full of conceit and certainties. How easy it is to disprove the oracle's prophecy that he would commit such crimes; all he has to do is flee from the land where he was brought up, Corinth, and go to Thebes (not knowing that this was in fact the country of his birth). As for killing his father, he has only killed one man in his whole life, and that was a stranger by accident (not knowing it was his own father). In Thebes there is a monster ravaging the country, and he is determined to kill it and claim the hand of the Queen (his mother). The monster is called the Sphinx, but when the Sphinx sees Oedipus she falls in love with him (to tell the truth she had already grown tired of killing). She saves his life by whispering the answer to the riddle that all must be asked when they challenge her. Oedipus in his conceit thinks he has beaten her, and not looking at her goes off to claim the Queen. The Sphinx in fury decides to let him go, for his punishment is a crime worse than death.

*La Machine infernale* is full of theatrical situations, where the audience already knows what Oedipus does not know. He understands nothing until it is too late. Each act is a decisive step towards the inevitable, but the final tragedy clears the crime of incest, for Jocasta reappears from the dead no longer as his wife, but as his mother, leading away the blind Oedipus.

*Les Parents terribles* (1938) must be considered on its own, for it has no comparison with any of Cocteau's other works. It is a realistic tragedy, bare in outline, devoid of those flamboyant frills which

Cocteau so often delights in; it is pure melodrama and admirable in its intensity. Nowhere else does Cocteau succeed so clearly as a man of the theatre, nor does he display in his other work the depth of character study that he has here created. The play is a biting social comedy concerning a mother's neurotic infatuation for her son, who has fallen in love with a girl who turns out to be his father's mistress. However triangular and contrived the plot may seem in outline, there is nothing artificial when reading the play or seeing it in performance. Yvonne, the mother, an invalid, neglects her husband and saves all her passionate affection for her son, Michel. Then there is Léonie, Yvonne's sister, who has always been in love with Georges, the man her sister married. She lives in the same household and as she suffers her own unfulfilled love, she is the witness and the figure of destiny. Emotions explode when Michel announces he wants to marry Madeleine. Yvonne refuses to share her son with someone else, while Georges forbids the marriage for other reasons. It is Léonie who helps Michel marry Madeleine in the end, a sacrifice more than Yvonne can bear, choosing suicide rather than acceptance.

Few plays in the modern theatre have the economy, the telling efficiency of *Les Parents terribles;* we have here a social satire more biting than anything of Becque's, the lies, petty jealousies pile up for the earth to open. Then in a Pirandellian fashion the masks are torn away from the characters and they see the truth for the first time. Cocteau concentrates on writing what he calls parts for 'great actors'. With no distractions, bound within the confines of the French bourgeois stuffiness, the claustrophobic atmosphere of *Les Parents terribles* is the backcloth for a genuine tragedy.

We shall not consider the boulevard 'portrait' *Les Monstres sacrés* written in 1940 and produced with success, but we shall mention more briefly Cocteau's two most recent plays, *L'Aigle à deux Têtes* (1946) and *Bacchus* (1951), neither of which adds to his status as a dramatist, though they both have considerable interest.

In *L'Aigle à deux Têtes* ("The two-headed Eagle") Cocteau turns to romanticism. We are in Ruritania (more exactly, "an imaginary castle in Germany"); it is the tenth anniversary of the assassination of the King on the day of his marriage. For ten years the Queen has been living in solitude, with the memory of her lover. The anniversary comes round and, as usual, she will dine alone in her bridal chamber. We hear the thunder of a storm, and then the sharp clatter of revolver shots. A young man jumps through the window. The Queen's bodyguard knock at the door and the Queen hides her intruder (who closely resembles the portrait of the King). They have come to warn her that an assassin is at large with intentions of killing her. The Queen does not give him up, but left alone with him they find themselves mutually attracted. But in a Cocteau play (as in contemporary French drama) there is no easy solution. Death alone can unite the two, which is melodramatically realised at the end by the assassin taking poison and the Queen, frantic, lying to make him kill her.

Like all Cocteau's work it is delicate. In Paris Edwige Feuillère turned the play into a triumph, as did Eileen Herlie, although in a very inexact translation, in London. But what a premium one has to pay for happiness!

The scandal of *Bacchus* seems completely unjustified. Only in its period and setting does the play have any similarity to Sartre's *Le Diable et le bon Dieu,* and even if Cocteau was attempting to outshine Sartre he has at any rate written a very different type of play. There is no character in *Bacchus* who represents the Devil. Criticism of *Bacchus* is justified not on the Mauriac line, but for the far simpler reason that it is not a very good play. Mauriac, as M. Stanislas Fumet explains in a debate on "Atheism in the Contemporary Theatre" (organised by the Centre Catholique des Intellectuels and printed in *Le Théâtre contemporain*) sees the Church as a mother, while Cocteau sees it as a theatrical partner. It is the clothes of the Renaissance, the ring of the bishop, the purple of the cardinal, that catch Cocteau's eye. The theme deals with the election in a little German village of Bacchus, who for five days will speak as master. The period is that of the Reformation and the Peasants' Revolt. The villagers choose the village idiot Hans for this task, a man who wishes neither to become a new Luther nor to assume the powers of the Pope, but rather to free the people from the oppression of the nobles and the Church. He hates tyrants in any form, he wishes to preach only the love of God and the freedom of the individual. But his ideals only make him hated by all. The people are going to burn him, and to save him it is suggested that he enters Holy Orders. But Hans prefers to remain free. He shows himself to the mob and is hit by an arrow. The Cardinal, however, is determined to cheat him, and announces that before his death Hans had entered the priesthood.

It is easy to understand why the play suggested affinities with the atheistic *Le Diable et le bon Dieu,* but Cocteau has merely taken a Sartrian subject and treated it in his own way, as he had done with Greek legends and romantic dramas in the past. Cocteau protests his freedom from 'isms', but may we suggest that this freedom is also the failure of Cocteau to give his undoubted artistry any sense of direction. He has squandered in tremendous diffusion his poetical energy, but he has never held this energy in check to assure an overwhelming victory. Even poets, after all, cannot be jacks of all media, and while all poets must experiment by trial and error towards the realisation of their creative genius, the truth must be faced that throughout his career Cocteau has only experimented. His was a genius which has only shown itself here and there in unexpected places, and he was to end up in the most unexpected place of all, with a seat among the 'Immortals' of the Académie Française. Had he had talent only he would doubtless have gone farther and secured a more important, though perhaps less controversial place, in the arts. But it seems somewhat niggardly to complain that a genius never showed more than promise in his works; would we exchange him on this account for a hard-working apprentice who believes that poetry and any of the arts can be taught in 10,000 difficult lessons?

# EIGHT

# A DRAMATIST IN THE WILDERNESS: EUGENE O'NEILL

"IF our life were endless and painless it would probably occur to no one why the world exists", says Schopenhauer. "Do not take pain away from us! It is our truth. Without pain there is nothing . . ." comes the O'Neill echo. "I do not know what eternal life is, but this one here is merely a wicked joke", says Voltaire. "The lie of a pipe dream is what gives life to the whole misbegotten mad lot of us, drunk or sober", is the philosophy of O'Neill's last-produced play *The Iceman Cometh*. Out of thirty-seven of O'Neill's plays it has been observed[1] that there are only five free from murder, death, suicide or insanity. In the others the score is eight suicides and one unsuccessful attempt, twelve important murders (not counting incidental episodes); twenty-six deaths, nearly all due to violence, and eight cases of insanity. Since this count was taken the victims have increased, but these figures will suffice.

It was not the way of Eugene O'Neill (1888–1953) to show restraint. His theatrical career was as restless as his early life (from gold prospector, seaman, to down-and-out) had been reckless. He was forever blazing trails in his writing to explore 'beyond the horizon', but somehow his imagination fails him; on the edge of the unknown he reacts like a flat-earther about to fall into infinity. His undaunted courage forever leads him into labyrinths from which he cannot extricate himself. It was because O'Neill never knew what he wanted out of life that he never knew where he was going, or what were the things for which he felt instinctively he should be searching.

As a thinker O'Neill's aspirations were too roaming, adventurous, romantic, to allow for profundity. He let others do the thinking for him, as in the two examples already given. Yet his indebtedness to

[1] Barrett H. Clark in *Eugene O'Neill*.

German philosophers, from Nietzsche and Schopenhauer to Freud, did not replace his Catholic upbringing and discarded faith with something positive; in his later work pessimism becomes an obsession and we feel the absence of any set of values as much as O'Neill does himself.

It has often been remarked that O'Neill's greatest failing was one of language; in setting out to write a great epic he seldom took into account his own limitations. The subjects of his tragedies demand a language approaching poetry, whereas they are clothed (except for one or two isolated lines) with a facile dialogue conforming to the pedestrian standards of modern inadequacy. Even the most important scenes of *Mourning Becomes Electra* could have been written by any good Hollywood scriptwriter. The exigencies, not of prose but of conversational expression may be severe in the English-speaking theatre, but no dramatist can do himself justice until he has freed himself of its petty dictatorship and found a style. It is style rather than poetry that the contemporary drama so sadly lacks. Without being able to distinguish his plays with either style or poetry, O'Neill was never able to translate adequately his chosen canvas in terms of the drama. Nor was he blessed with a sense of humour; his satires such as *Marco Millions* require a pungent, fiery wit that is the blessing and the curse of so many Irish writers — O'Neill never inherited this gift from his Irish stock.

Yet when all this has been said and taken into consideration (and they are serious faults to find with any important dramatist) O'Neill's reputation does not collapse like playing-cards. His achievements should no more be underrated than they should, as in the past among certain American intellectuals, be worshipped with superlatives. In the first place, O'Neill undoubtedly occupies the seat of honour among American dramatists. He has, so far, no challengers. Sidney Howard, Robert Emmet Sherwood, Elmer Rice, Maxwell Anderson, Philip Barry, Lillian Hellman or Marc Connelly — such candidates from O'Neill's generation look small in comparison. For O'Neill is the grand old man of the American theatre, he was the first dramatist to endow his theatre with a critical status. He was the first American playwright to achieve an international reputation, with his works performed the whole world over, from Russia to France, Scandinavia to South America.

If the speed of O'Neill's rise to fame is true to the pattern of a typical American success story, he was also to suffer the fate of old soldiers, not dying, simply fading away. It is a strange paradox that O'Neill was always as ahead of his times in the American theatre as he was behind them in the European. He stormed the barricades of Broadway without getting hurt and without even a publicity agency, a task which one might imagine would be much more difficult to-day. After he had found a small experimental group, the Provincetown Players, who were willing to produce any play O'Neill wrote for them, word soon got round. A professional production followed, and with this came a Pulitzer Prize. Nothing was to stem the O'Neill tide. Critics such as George Jean Nathan and Barrett H. Clark pressed his claims. The censors did their best to silence the rebel by providing him with the wrong sort of audiences. But literary awards brought their merits, and O'Neill's prestige culminated in 1934 with the award of the Nobel Prize for Literature. At the height of his fame he retired, and for the next twelve years no new play from O'Neill was published or produced. There were a few revivals, without great success, and his books, tucked away on library shelves, continued to be read by the faithful few. But O'Neill's name was no longer bracketed with those of Shaw and Ibsen.

During the years between 1934 and 1943 O'Neill was hard at work. In 1939 he completed *The Iceman Cometh,* in 1940-41 his autobiographical *Long Day's Journey Into Night,* and in 1943 *A Moon for the Misbegotten* and *A Touch of the Poet.* It was during the same period that O'Neill had ambitiously envisaged two cycles of plays. He completed first drafts of three double-length plays, *The Greed of the Meek, And Give Me Death* and *More Stately Mansions,* which he grouped in a cycle called *A Tale of Possessors Self-Dispossessed.* The first two he destroyed, and he intended to do the same with *More Stately Mansions* of which a handwritten manuscript survived, because he was dissatisfied with them as they stood and, already ill with Parkinson's disease, he was unable to undertake revision. *More Stately Mansions* reached the Stockholm Royal Dramatic Theatre — to which O'Neill had left *Long Day's Journey Into Night* as a "deathbed legacy" to a nation whom he felt had been more loyal to him than his own. It was published in 1964. Of the second cycle of plays, to be called *By Way of Obit* O'Neill completed only one one-act play, *Hughie.*

According to O'Neill's will all copies of *Long Day's Journey Into Night* were to have been locked in his publishers' vault for twenty-five years and the play was never to be staged in the United States. Copies were stored in the vaults of Random House and it looked as though we would have to wait until 1978 in order to see the *magnum opus* which O'Neill had once described in outlines to Barrett H. Clark:

All the dramatic episodes of my life I have so far kept out of my plays, and the majority of the things I have seen happen to other people. I've hardly begun to work up all this material, but I'm saving it up for one thing in particular, a cycle of plays, to be acted on nine successive nights; together they will form a sort of dramatic autobiography, something in the style of *War and Peace* or *Jean Cristophe*.

Three years after O'Neill's death, in February 1956, *Long Day's Journey Into Night* was published with Mrs. Carlotta O'Neill's consent though Random House preferred to cancel the contract rather than break the terms of the will. Meanwhile in Stockholm the play was received with enthusiasm. Subsequent productions followed in New York (7 November 1956) and in London two years later. *A Moon for the Misbegotten* was produced in New York in 1957 and *A Touch of the Poet* opened the 1958-1959 Broadway season. Although the majority of the critics highly praised these plays they have made far less impact than one would have expected from the major works of the leading American dramatist. Perhaps it is that for a man who had striven throughout his life at experiment in new forms, this retreat to the traditional naturalism seemed almost a surrender of his imagination. In these plays O'Neill returns to many of his earlier themes, but the fog thickens, the pessimism deepens, the characters become ghosts, and the dramatic conflict and power is submerged. We can feel the disease gaining hold. Written "in tears and blood", O'Neill was too close to his old and his new sorrows and it is only human in the circumstances for him occasionally to put life before creative art.

It is almost impossible to forecast O'Neill's position in the future, for even his present reputation is insecure. There are so many items which cancel out on the balance sheet. O'Neill is an 'all but' dramatist; he moved from realism to expressionism, Greek tragedy with modern psychology to studies of miscegenation and philosphical symbolism; yet he never 'quite' found himself in any of these experiments. The characters in his plays are seldom remarkable, his female portraits tend to be devoid of sympathy and human only through sexual thirst. Yet his sense of the dramatic in life and its realisation in the theatre is ever present, and certainly nothing can cancel out his innate ability to tell a story.

There is no shortage of plays to write about; fortunately it is not our purpose here to give a history of O'Neill's theatrical career, or a list

ARMAND SALACROU

JEAN ANOUILH

Tennessee Williams

Arthur Miller

of his works in chronological order, the majority of which are already forgotten and are unlikely to be seen again. Some critics have suggested that O'Neill has never equalled, even in his most far-reaching experiments, the stark realism and humanity of his four early sea-plays, *Bound East for Cardiff* (1916), *In the Zone* (1917), *The Long Voyage Home* (1917) and *The Moon of the Caribbees* (1918) — plays which are generally linked together under the title *S.S. Glencairn* and which were filmed in 1940 as *The Long Voyage Home*. This is perhaps true, for not only did O'Neill know the characters he was writing about, but he had also the ability to visualise certain dramatic situations which give shape, form and purpose to his playlets. But while with the realistic sea-plays he proved himself a promising young dramatist, he could never have achieved distinction and fame as America's leading playwright without his ambitious experiments and many-sided assaults on the conventional drama of the day. He brought to the stage a breadth of vision, showing the means whereby the theatre could reveal for its audience life, with its infinite possibilities, at once real and fantastic. No matter if O'Neill failed in his own plays, he influenced the American dramatists to think big, and to continue the attack. And even in his own plays, the surprise is not so much what O'Neill failed to do, but how much he did in fact achieve.

Which are the plays that have lasted? Undoubtedly his expressionistic *The Emperor Jones* (1920), a psychological study of how fear seizes a Negro's soul and sends him terror-stricken into the jungle, has lost none of its power. Here is a play which O'Neill might have written for broadcasting, for the effect on the nerves of the rhythmical beating of the drums is oppressively exciting and outstanding radio material. *The Hairy Ape* (1922) is half expressionist, half realist, and had not only novelty but dramatic intensity. In *Desire under the Elms* (1924) O'Neill gives us his first important work with a tragic vision where he reaches near the heights of his theatrical achievements. Set in a New England farm in the 1850's, *Desire under the Elms* explores the 'desire' to possess, in its different forms. Abbie, the young wife of the old puritanical farmer Ephraim Cabot, desires security; Ephraim, the love of his wife and sons which is denied him; Ephraim's thirty-two-year-old son Eben desires to possess what he believes is his birthright, the farm. Abbie gives herself to Eben, and the passions of desire unfold a misfortune which races towards a tragic disaster; life is presented naked and without hope, reciprocated love or comfort, indeed without meaning.

E

*The Great God Brown* is not likely to survive, in spite of — or perhaps because of — the use of symbolism and masks, but in one speech in it, O'Neill projects what may well be his own character and unhappy philosophy. It is also one of the passages where his language displays latent power.

Why am I afraid to dance, I who love music and rhythm and grace and song and laughter? Why am I afraid to live, I who love life and the beauty of flesh and the living colours of earth and sky and sea? Why am I afraid to love? Why am I afraid, I who am not afraid? Why must I pretend to scorn in order to pity? Why must I hide myself in self-contempt in order to understand? Why must I be ashamed of my strength, so proud of my weakness? Why must I live in a cage like a criminal, defying and hating, I who love peace and friendship? *(clasping his hands above in supplication)* Why was I born without a skin, O God, that I must wear armour in order to touch or to be touched? ... Or rather, Old Graybeard, why the devil was I born at all?

Neither *Lazarus Laughed* (1926), nor *Marco Millions* (1928) nor *Strange Interlude* (1928) has weathered the years. There remain for examination O'Neill's most famous play *Mourning Becomes Electra* (1931) his much discussed *The Iceman Cometh* (1946) about which critics have divided into the 'Ayes' and the 'Noes' camps, with an apparently unbridgeable gap between them and *Long Day's Journey Into Night*. Neither *A Touch of the Poet* nor *A Moon for the Misbegotten* have the same scope or staying power. There is good reason for selecting these plays for discussion; *Mourning Becomes Electra* is not only the best known and most widely acclaimed of O'Neill's works, but in it he set out to achieve definite aims, which he explains in an article contributed to *European Theories of the Drama*.[1] In *The Iceman Cometh* we have a vastly different type of play, which harks back to his early career for its characters and setting, although all resemblances to the sea-plays end there. It is a play of allegorical content, of waterfront types who are caught up in their own 'pipe dreams' and suddenly made aware that they must face up to their responsibilities and seek redemption. It has a signification which makes it one of O'Neill's most profound studies; one need hardly add that it is an intensely depressing play. *Long Day's Journey Into Night* reveals

[1] Edited by Barrett H. Clark, revised 1947, New York.

the secrets of O'Neill's own family — secrets which had already been
hinted at or guessed from his earlier work. He has attempted to write
his own tragedy "with deep pity and understanding and forgiveness
for *all* the four haunted Tyrones".

*

In the spring of 1926 O'Neill made the following note in his diary:
"Modern psychological drama using one of the old legend plots of
Greek tragedy for its basic theme — the Electra story — the Medea?
Is it possible to get modern psychological approximation of Greek
sense of fate into such a play, which an intelligent audience of to-day,
possessed of no belief in gods or supernatural retribution, could accept
and be moved by?" Two and a half years later when *en route* for China
the idea persisted. By April, 1929, he had visualised the period and some
of the departures from the story, coming to the conclusion "no matter
in what period of American history play is laid, must remain a modern
psychological drama — nothing to do with period except to use it as
a mask — what war? . . . Civil War is only possibility — fits into
picture — Civil War as background for drama of murderous family
love and hate".

O'Neill tells how he decided to follow the Greek practice and make
a trilogy of the Electra plot, the first play introducing Agamemnon's
homing and murder, the second following Electra's revenge on mother
and lover, using Orestes to help her, and the third play: "retribution
Orestes and Electra". By August, 1929, O'Neill had completed his
scenario of the three plays. The task of writing them occupied two
years, and in August, 1931, he was able to write: "has power and drive
and the strange quality of unreal reality I wanted — main purpose
seems to be soundly achieved — there is a feeling of fate in it, or I am
a fool — a psychological approximation of the fate in the Greek
tragedies on this theme attained without benefit of the supernatural".

So we have the trilogy realised. In *The Homecoming* we witness the
return of Ezra Mannon and his son Orin from the war, and the murder
of Ezra Mannon by his wife Christine, because of her affair with
Captain Brant. In *The Hunted* Lavinia, who loved her father and
despises her mother Christine, is aware of her mother's crime. She urges
her brother Orin, who despised his father and loves his mother, to
avenge the murder. Orin surprises Captain Brant and shoots him;
Christine as a result commits suicide. Orin believes that he is growing

like his father and is driven to suicide. Lavinia, left alone, tormented in her soul, accepts her punishment worse than death by living in the ill-fated Mannon house. The modern approximation of being haunted by the Eumenides is as devastating as any torment known in Greek drama.

The trilogy moves with melodramatic suspense, the Freudian undercurrents are subtly conceived, the mask-like face of Lavinia dominates the stage, a symbolic portrait to match the portraits of her Mannon ancestors on the wall. The tragedy remains strangely cold; we are in an ice-box of repressed emotions. In the end we realise that in spite of the tension, admirably built up, the mask-like figures are merely instrumental to the theme; they are not characters of flesh and blood nor are masks a substitute for language. Whatever our admiration, the trilogy lacks the essential substance to turn it into human tragedy.

*

Whereas *Mourning Becomes Electra* keeps emotion subdued and sheltered from the harsh winds of conviction, *The Iceman Cometh* smothers our emotions with a stifling atmosphere of booze, smoke, and 'pipe dream' credulity. *Mourning Becomes Electra* is a tragedy without tears; in *The Iceman Cometh* the time for tears is past. The curtain rises on a group of drunks who spend their days in Harry Hope's saloon, a cheap ginmill of the five cent whisky variety; the year is 1912. One of the drunks aptly describes the dive as:

> No chance saloon. It's Bedrock Bar, the End of the Line Café, the Bottom of the Sea Rathskeller! Don't you notice the beautiful calm in the atmosphere? That's because it's the last harbour. No one here has to worry about where they're going next, because there is no further they can go. It's a great comfort to them. Although even here they can keep up appearances of life with a few harmless pipe dreams about their yesterdays and to-morrows, as you'll see for yourself if you're here long.

Each of the drunks has his life behind him, either dodging the 'dicks' or merely as a down-and-out; each finds consolation in an alcoholic stupor. There is Larry Slade, a sixty-year-old Irish ex-anarchist turned philosopher who declares that all his pipe dreams are dead and buried. "What's before me is the comforting fact that death is a fine long sleep, and I'm damned tired, and it can't come too soon for me." Then Hickey arrives. Hickey is "a hardware drummer. An old friend of Harry Hope's and all the gang. He's a grand guy. He comes here twice a year regularly on a periodical drunk and blows in all his money." But this time when Hickey arrives he is a reformed and therefore unwelcome intruder. He is on the water wagon. He has finally had the guts to face life, throw overboard all the "damned lying pipe dreams" and find peace. Furthermore he means to save them all from their pipe dreams. "Just stop lying about yourself and kidding yourself about to-morrows" he tells them.

The results are the opposite of what he expected. The salvation cure just does not work with the others; instead the atmosphere becomes one of gloom and depression. Then Hickey confides in them that his wife, whom they used to joke about being left in bed "with the iceman" is dead. Later on he tells them the whole truth. He has murdered her because she loved him too much and he loved her too much. He has killed her to save her from the continual sufferings he caused her. He started hating himself for his weakness, and in hating himself he came to hating her. He knew that he could not control his cravings, and he had not the courage to rely on his wife's infinite forgiveness. It would eventually have broken her heart. He could not tell her he was leaving her, it seemed so much kinder not to allow her to wake up, to leave her in her dreams.

Suddenly in making this confession he sees that he must have been crazy to do such a thing, it had merely been a 'pipe dream' for himself. The others, who have listened in awe to his confession, breathe a sigh of relief and accept his solution as a return to the good old days before Hickey made them start thinking about redemption. Hickey gives himself up to the police, one of the drunks commits suicide and Larry, left alone, the philosophic commentator, remarks "Be God, I'm the only real convert to death Hickey made here. From the bottom of my coward's heart I mean that now." We are back where we were, the wheels have turned full circle.

Like all O'Neill's plays, *The Iceman Cometh* has its faults. Rich though the play is, one regrets that it was not abbreviated to a more economical length (the first night on Broadway started at 4.30 in the afternoon and continued until 10 p.m.) There is room for considerable pruning of dialogue among the secondary characters who add little to the body of the play, but O'Neill was never able to condense his thoughts. He has certainly managed to convey an atmosphere which is not easy to forget. It is a play of the day before yesterday, the days of O'Neill's youth which he spent on the waterfront, but it could not have been written in his youth. O'Neill is not here attempting any autobiographical situations such as, say, George Orwell did in *Down and Out in London and Paris*. He has attempted to show us his 'have beens' in a dramatic situation as he has done with his sea-play characters, only this time he is a wiser and a less contented man. For this is his most depressing play. But to deny its theatrical effectiveness, however distasteful its subject matter may be, we would ourselves have to indulge in some pipe dreaming hara-kiri . . .

\*

"Pipe dreams" were not only in Harry Hopes bar in 1912, but also in the living-room where the four "haunted Tyrones" set out for their solitary *Long Day's Journey Into Night*. James Tyrone, the father, is sixty-five, "but looks ten years younger"; he was once a popular actor and the stamp of his profession is still unmistakenly upon him. His wife Mary is a drug addict, though wishful thinking on the part of the family imagines she has been cured. The black sheep of the family is the elder son Jamie, a ne'er-do-well actor, with the signs of "premature disintegration" on his face. Edmund, the younger son is sensitive and has intellectual leanings. He is ill with "a bad summer cold" which like O'Neill in 1912, turns out to be consumption. He faces the possibility of death with a mixture of longing, fear — and anger. It is the anger which sparks off a series of recriminations on the part of each of the family. The father is a miser and thinks he can economise by sending Edmund to an inferior and cheap sanatorium. In the end he agrees to a better home — the one in fact which O'Neill went to and was cured. Gradually the fog seeps through your veins, the impersonal moaning of the fog horn resounding like the voice of fate on these tortured characters, veiling the truth of life and obscuring man's tragic ability to understand, either himself or others.

It has been remarked that it is the misfortune of the American drama that O'Neill should be its number one exhibit. In fairness it is an equal misfortune that O'Neill should have been elevated to the ranks of the exceptional when he was only the head of the youngest drama of the world. He had an outstanding sense of theatre and could write a good play; but he was not a genius and never wrote a masterpiece. He was the tallest figure among little men. He was a disciple of Strindberg and other European figures, but he remained a disciple, he never became a master. It was not in his generation that his nation was to reach artistic maturity. Through his work, however, the American theatre caught up with the European theatre. It started exporting as well as importing. The balance of cultural payments seems already at least equal, if America is not already repaying a cultural debt. The teacher can at last watch his pupils 'do'.

NINE

# T. S. ELIOT AS DRAMATIST

"To my mind, the drama took a wrong turning when the demand for realism led it to abandon the ornament of verse."

SOMERSET MAUGHAM, *The Summing Up* (1938)

"If the poetic drama is to reconquer its place, it must, in my opinion, enter into overt competition with prose drama."

T. S. ELIOT, *Poetry and Drama*

ALTHOUGH Eliot came from another generation than Claudel, and his environment and character were so completely different from that of the great French master, his point of departure as a dramatist traced a parallel course to that which Claudel was attempting in his plays thirty or forty years previously. There are the same liturgical echoes of ritual and the same search for a poetical language which would come to terms with the balanced rhythm of a sentence and be able to lead from ordinary conversational idiom to the rhetoric of chant and the intimacy of poetry. Religion also plays a major rôle in Eliot's drama, and he approached the theme of 'sin and expiation' with a religious zeal as urgent as in Claudel's own works. These similarities are often overlooked in the different direction Eliot subsequently turned since *Murder in the Cathedral* and *The Family Reunion* and in the concessions he made to the demands of naturalistic theatre. The work of Claudel and Eliot cannot be compared, the one in terms of the other. Both are among the greatest poets of their age, but whereas Claudel was primarily a poet and only viewed the theatre as a medium for his poetical expression whether audiences were there, ready to accept his work, or not, Eliot was a poet who turned dramatist, willing to "discipline his poetry" and put it "on a very thin diet in order to adapt it to the needs of the stage". He hoped "there may be a later stage, when (and if) the understanding of theatrical technique has become second nature, at which he can dare to make more liberal use of poetry and take greater liberties with ordinary colloquial speech".[1] Eliot went more than half-way to meet a public, accustomed to the conventions of polite naturalistic comedy, and became accepted as a popular dramatist. Claudel remained a poet and had to wait nearly half a century for recognition by playgoers; Eliot, on the strength of five plays was to be one of the most discussed dramatists of his time.

Here we have the major difference in temperament of the two poets. The one went his own way regardless, the other was determined to intervene directly and "bring poetry into the world in which the audience lives". Claudel did not restrict his inspiration; Eliot was a conservative, too consciously a critic to wander an inch from the theories of drama he so carefully propounds beforehand. The best criticism of Eliot's plays has been written by Eliot himself, and few theoreticians have proved their views so convincingly in practice. Eliot, a great poet, became both master and pupil of dramatic theory, yet however important his plays were, he was never to write a *chef-d'oeuvre*. His best play, *Murder in the Cathedral*, is noble in its theme and treatment, but lacks the natural abundance of creative genius. His cold, austere intellectuality is apparent in all his plays, and the more his plays have moved from spiritual to secular, the more onerous this has become in making his plays acceptable; if *The Cocktail Party* remains abstract, *The Confidential Clerk* aims to introduce human characters but not even *The Elder Statesman*, described as his "most human play", succeeds. Presented realistically, no wonder a play like *The Confidential Clerk* was roughly handled when it was performed at the first Festival International d'Art Dramatique in Paris in 1954. It is not surprising that *Le Monde* compared it to "a pyramid of happenings as unlikely as they are artificial", while *Le Figaro* said that "one has the impression of opening the door of a refrigerator". Naturalism has won and every vestige of poetry had, as planned, been removed. Lorca, it is true, did the same in *The House of Bernarda Alba*, where he claimed that there was not "a jot of poetry" to be found; but Lorca radiated his play with an intense and personal poetic vision, which Eliot was unable to achieve.

In diluting his poetry Eliot removed the power which, above all others, he possessed. Had *Murder in the Cathedral* been a beginning

[1] *Poetry and Drama.*

instead of an end of his full use of verse, Eliot might not have been box-office success, but his contribution to religious drama and dramatic literature might have resulted in works comparable to *The Waste Land* and *Four Quartets* in dramatic form. He might have given us a spiritual work in the tradition of Dante (on whom Eliot was an authority) and produced an English *Soulier de Satin*. We waited in vain for the time he would feel able to make "more liberal use of poetry".

*

Born in St. Louis, Missouri, U.S.A., in 1888, Thomas Stearns Eliot came to Europe in 1910, after his education at Harvard. He read literature and philosophy at the Sorbonne and subsequently studied at Merton College, Oxford, and in Germany. In 1915 he settled in England, worked first as a schoolmaster and then as a banker in Lloyd's Bank, London. After eight years there, he joined the firm of publishers which later became Faber and Faber. Already during the war years his work had started to appear in magazines, and then in small volumes, his first being *Prufrock and Other Observations* (1917). *The Waste Land*, his most famous poem, was published in 1922. During this time he began his editorship of *The Criterion*, a literary review which had great influence in the inter-war years.

In 1927 Eliot became a British subject. He defined himself as a Royalist, a Classicist and an Anglo-Catholic. In 1948 he was awarded the Nobel Prize for literature and he received the Order of Merit from King George VI. Up to his death in 1965, few writers have been more highly respected or more widely translated on the Continent, a return in itself for someone who believed whole-heartedly in the consolidation of Western literary traditions and movements.

For many years before his first experiment in dramatic form Eliot had shown interest in the drama, writing essays on "Rhetoric and Poetic Drama", "Four Elizabethan Dramatists" and "Dialogue on Dramatic Poetry". His first experiment in drama was *Sweeny Agonistes*, a fragment which could hardy have been made into a full-length play, though it is of considerable interest from the language viewpoint. A pageant play, *The Rock*, followed, written explicitly for the building fund of a London diocese. The invitation to write the words for the spectacle came, Eliot said, "at a moment when I seemed to myself to have exhausted my meagre poetic gifts, and to have nothing more to say". He learnt in *The Rock* to experiment with a choir or chorus, finding that the more voices there were, "the simpler and more direct the vocabulary, the syntax, and the content of your lines must be". But there is no need to linger over *The Rock*.

Preliminaries and tentatives over, Eliot was ready to give the theatre a major work, though it was only through the initiative of Dr. Bell, then Dean of Canterbury, that he was approached and commissioned to write a play for the Canterbury Festival. The result was the production of *Murder in the Cathedral* in the Chapter House of Canterbury Cathedral in 1935, an occasion which will be remembered in theatrical history. "He has reanimated a literary form which in England has been dead or dormant for nearly 300 years . . ." rejoiced *The Spectator*. Eliot had made full use of the opportunity, for he was in the unique position of being certain that his play would be attended by an audience sharing the same religious outlook and moral conventions. His religious play would be followed by a congregation, willing almost, as he puts it, "to be patiently bored". He therefore felt himself justified in the use of verse, and the only problem was the type to use. He wished to avoid any echo of Shakespearian blank verse and decided to keep in mind a variation on the *Everyman* type of verse. One cannot help remarking on Eliot's modesty, for the play has been widely performed and an outstanding success in the commercial theatre where there is no hint of the audience ever being "patiently bored", and only the 'sermon' has perhaps not been theatrically effective — but it, in any case, is not written in verse. It is the admirable concentration and the unity of the dramatic construction that interests the spectator, together with the ritual character of the setting. The introduction of the Chorus in the Greek fashion, but in the guise of the common women of Canterbury, adds both to the sense of foreboding and tension, and to the celebration of the Christian Faith as a link between Becket and congregation. For the subject of the death and martyrdom of Becket is not treated as a chronicle play, but as a kind of Mass in memory of an event which took place in the same cathedral 800 years earlier. Hear the urgency of the voices:

> O Thomas, return, Archbishop; return to France.
> Return. Quickly. Quietly. Leave us to perish in quiet.
> You come with applause, you come with rejoicing,
>     but you come bringing death into Canterbury:
> A doom on the house, a doom on yourself, a doom
>     on the world.
> We do not wish anything to happen.

> Seven years we have lived quietly
> Succeeded in avoiding notice,
> Living and partly living.

Or the Chorus can turn into a liturgical chant:

> We acknowledge our trespass, our weakness, our
>     fault; we acknowledge
> That the sin of the world is upon our heads; that the
>     blood of the martyrs and the agony of the saints
> Is upon our heads.
> Lord, have mercy upon us.
> Christ, have mercy upon us.
> Lord, have mercy upon us.
> Blessed Thomas, pray for us.

Thus does the Chorus provide the link as well as acting as narrator. But attention is centred on Becket himself in his isolation, his hour of crisis when he is tempted by the four tempters, who balance the later appearance of the four knights. We listen to the Christmas Day sermon, in which the implications of the ritual are elaborated. After the murder the four knights then come forward in a Shavian fashion to justify themselves, the intention being, as Eliot explains, "to shock the audience out of their complacency". It may have been a trick, but it is theatrically effective.

Great though the achievement was, *Murder in the Cathedral* did not satisfy Eliot, who in any case does not believe that success can ever be repeated, and "therefore one must always try to find something new". His aim in *The Family Reunion* was to explore the possibilities of a verse-play when applied to every-day life, and to find a "rhythm close to contemporary speech". He therefore decided to curtail his verse, to subordinate it to the exigencies of the ordinary business of life, a task which Eliot could not be expected to have accomplished in one experiment and which was, in fact, to lead him to *The Confidential Clerk*. *The Family Reunion* is a subtle and complex play, still ritualistic in spirit, though this aspect, like the poetry, is more hidden. It is a transition play, thought provoking, difficult, ambiguous, unresolved, and unsatisfactory — yet it occupies a central position in Eliot's dramatic development and cannot be lightly dismissed as a failure.

*The Family Reunion* is, one feels, a vehicle for personal experience, and perhaps it is because Eliot wanted to say too many things that the play is better read than seen performed. It makes too many demands on the audience. There are long scenes dangerously undramatic, and the experiment of using as Chorus four minor characters, whose sudden ritualistic chant seems quite out of harmony with their previous rôles, can only be described as embarrassing. For plot Eliot returned to the favourite Orestes pursued by the Furies theme, and transferred this to an upper-class country house called Wishwood in the wind- and rain-swept countryside of the north of England. The season is winter. Amy, the Dowager Lady Monchensey, is expecting her son Harry for her family reunion — the first time he will have attended for eight years. She has placed all her hopes on Harry's return so that he will take over the family seat and fortunes from her. Amy has, as it were, lived for the day when she can see Harry taking over his responsibilities, and she hopes that he will marry his cousin Mary, whom she has kept beside her these years with this ultimate intention. Even when Harry made an unfortunate marriage Amy never doubted but that he would return to the family, and now that he has lost his wife — she was drowned at sea in mysterious circumstances — Amy is prepared for the last family reunion and then to die in peace. This bourgeois plot gives way to quite another level at which the play asks to be judged; it is not only a conflict between the older and younger generations.

The arrival of Harry introduces the spiritual side of the play. He rushes to pull the curtains before he even speaks to his mother. We know he is a man sick in mind, pursued by the Furies, as in the Greek legend. They have followed him to Wishwood, yet no one else can see them. He is alone, apart, cut off from understanding:

> But how can I explain, how can I explain to *you?*
> And you will understand less after I have explained it.
> All that I could hope to make you understand
> Is only events: not what has happened.

The uncles and aunts who make up the reunion (but not Agatha) try to solve Harry's *angoisse* — he believes he pushed his wife overboard in mid-Atlantic — by the only practical methods known to them, questioning his butler and seeking the family doctor. But Mary, his cousin, and Agatha, his mother's sister, realise that it is only through spiritual discovery that Harry can be helped. Harry says himself that his illness is "deeper than what people call their conscience", it is neither his conscience nor his mind that is diseased, but "the world I have to live in".

Mary evokes for him the past, until he almost believes he could stay at Wishwood, but with the appearance again of the Furies he knows that that is impossible. Nevertheless, it is at Wishwood that he discovers where his redemption lies, the choice that he must make if he is to follow his salvation. By learning more of the past, he learns through Aunt Agatha that his father fell in love with her and wished to murder his mother while she was bearing him in her womb. Through this revelation Harry is able to be delivered from his conscience; the knowledge of transmission of the sin from father to son, his own desire to kill his wife, enables him to find redemption. For when he tells Agatha that it was possible that only in his imagination did he push his wife overboard, she replies:

> So I had supposed. What of it?
> What we have written is not a story of detection,
> Of crime and punishment, but of sin and expiation.
> It is possible that you have not known what sin
> You shall expiate, or whose, or why. It is certain
> That the knowledge of it must precede the expiation.
> It is possible that sin may strain and struggle
> In its dark instinctive birth, to come to consciousness
> And so find expurgation. It is possible
> You are the consciousness of your unhappy family,
> Its bird sent flying through the purgatorial flame.

Harry realises that the vengeance of the Furies is over and that instead of their pursuing him he must pursue them. The unknown way is the only way for his salvation and the realisation of his destiny. His choice must be between the tragedy of his mother or his own reconciliation with God and the rediscovery of his soul after eight years of despair and loneliness in the wilderness. His departure brings about the death of his mother, and with the symbolic "the clock has stopped in the night", what has been done or thought is over for ever. He has atoned, and will follow his calling wherever it may lie, leaving the others behind in a state of bewilderment (except Agatha) not understanding "a single thing that's happened".

This moment of choice is present in all of Eliot's plays, from *Murder in the Cathedral* to *The Elder Statesman*. The road to salvation is also the theme of *The Cocktail Party* (1949), written after a lapse of ten years after *The Family Reunion*. In the ten years we find a major change in Eliot's dramatic style; gone is the need for any Chorus, and the evocation of the supernatural has also been disposed of; rejected is any poetry "which could not stand the test of strict dramatic utility", and in *The Cocktail Party* there is only one runic chant which reminds one of *The Family Reunion*. Eliot himself believed "that it is perhaps an open question whether there is any poetry in the play at all". *The Cocktail Party* may be said to have broken almost completely with ritual and poetry, though not with Eliot's theology, which it attempts to interpret in the most secular and sophisticated circumstances possible. It is a spiritual investigation into the malaise of society and postwar futility, as depicted by the set who are to be seen at the right parties — the type Noël Coward has mirrored in his early comedies.

Described as 'a comedy', we must assume there is an ironic interpretation of the word for this most depressing play, concerned as it is with the breakdown of a sick society and an individual's inability to seek a way out of the super-civilised maze without calling on the assistance of the nearest psychiatrist. Our need for guidance "to work out your salvation with diligence" is examined by the divine investigator who indicates the cure and who gives his patients their moment of obligatory choice. The play opens with a cocktail party which is a failure from the start because Edward must do his best to carry on and hide the fact that Lavinia, his wife, has just left him. There is in the party an unidentified guest who in the second act turns out to be Sir Henry Harcourt Reilly, the doctor Edward has gone to consult about the nervous breakdown which is threatening him. Edward is suddenly confronted with his wife and they are examined together, for as Sir Henry explains:

> And now you begin to see, I hope,
> How much you have in common. The same isolation.
> A man who finds himself incapable of loving
> And a woman who finds that no man can love her.

After which advice it remains for Edward to say "Lavinia, we must make the best of a bad job".

No special treatment is prescribed apart from reconciliation, and their case is passed over in order to consider that of the next patient, Miss Celia Coplestone, whom we met at the party as Edward's mistress Hers is a very different case, and the most unexpected, in view of our introduction to her at Edward's party. She wishes to atone, to seek to be cured of the emptiness and failure for something outside of her. Sir Henry offers her the choice of living a normal life, marrying, the life of two people who do not understand each other, and breeding children they do not understand and "who will never understand them", or alternatively that of choosing faith, the faith which "issues from despair". This second choice has no destination, and the journey is blind and terrifying. Celia chooses this way of absolute sacrifice, which is her vocation.

In the third act we are introduced into an almost Pirandellian world where the masks are torn off. Edward and Lavinia now understand the loneliness of one another and are reconciled; their lot in life is to continue giving and going to cocktail parties. Celia, on the other hand, has reached the end of her terrible destiny, which was none other than crucifixion. Joining a religious order she was sent to a far land where there was a native rebellion and she was crucified and her body eaten by ants. Such was her martyrdom.

The idea of atonement as presented by Celia's sacrifice is in the tradition of certain Catholic conceptions, such as Claudel presented in his plays (i.e. the midnight reunion of *Partage de Midi*, or Violaine smitten with leprosy in *The Tidings Brought to Mary*), but its acceptance on aesthetic grounds is here open to grave doubts; it is not a question of what Sartre might contemptuously call "Dieu n'est pas artiste" (as he applied the phrase to Mauriac), for Claudel has shown that the most cruel atonement need not offend an audience but lead it to genuine compassion. Claudel's plays, however, are far nearer the ritualistic interpretation of Catholic dogmas (which are largely understood by his audience) than are Eliot's cocktail-drinking characters who, apart from the divine inquisitor, have nothing spiritual about them. Violaine, almost from the start of Claudel's play, is removed from this world and we can accept — as we cannot with Celia — her rôle as a holy recluse. Whatever the reason, Eliot's characters have too much the action of automatic robots responding to the strings of the high priest in a 1984 atmosphere; the play has an inhumanity which does little to recommend it to religious bodies. While there is no denying that it is a work of major importance, must a modern secular interpretation of a religious theme itself fall victim to the atmosphere of the disease it sets out to analyse and cure? *Partage de Midi* has made many converts; one wonders whether *The Cocktail Party* does not accentuate the inhumanity of despair.

In *The Confidential Clerk* (1953) one has the feeling that Eliot has attempted to make his characters of flesh and blood, and yet has failed to make us identify ourselves with these characters who remain strangely aloof. The last traces of poetry disappear, and Eliot has carried "the machine he set in motion" with *The Family Reunion* — when he wished to bring poetry to terms with a contemporary theme — to its logical conclusion. Eliot, it is true, preserves in his penta-metres a persuasive sense of rhythm, but can this "frothy, superficial humour", this narrowness of mental outlook and hollowness of philo-sophy, really for one minute make an audience believe that "they too could speak poetry"? The play can be judged, like *The Cocktail Party*, at different levels, but its most serious level seems to be a debate on the proposition: "If you haven't the strength to impose your own terms upon life, you must accept the terms it offers you." No longer are we dealing with matters relating to life and death, but merely to our choice of what we want to do in this world. Sir Claude Mulhammer wanted to be a potter, but rather than be a second-rate potter he chose to be-come a power in the city, where no one could deny his competence. Colby, whom he imagines to be his son and whom he has appointed his confidential clerk, decides in favour of being a church organist (and probably a second-rate musician) and (as an after-thought) the possi-bility of considering, later on, ordination. But his choice is a fairly safe, realistic, unadventurous one, and bears little resemblance to the suffering of Celia on her road to salvation.

The plot, again taken from Greek classics (the *Ion* of Euripides), is a far-fetched confusion of offspring and foundlings, where the need for self-knowledge seems to be the key to the solution of the cryptogram. The play does not gain significantly on second reading, and tends to close instead of open up mental horizons. For this reason it may be that this play, for all its supposed light-heartedness, is even more depressing than *The Cocktail Party*. The people are those with whom you would certainly not want to waste an evening, even those cocktail parties of Lavinia and Edward might be less dull. And the clash between the mundane and the wildly improbable situations makes the whole play seem out of focus. Something has gone wrong somewhere.

Nor is *The Elder Statesman* (1958) a very much happier play, though it is simpler in conception and more human in treatment. It again falls into the vein of ironic comedy, but the characters lack the delineation of light and shade to made them interesting as individuals. Lord Claverton — the statesman in question — might have suffered the anguish and torment of, for example, Ingmar Bergman's professor in the Swedish film *Wild Strawberries,* but in Eliot's study his rôle seems monotonous. The theme, however, is an ambitious one. Here we have a man, retired from the political scene in glory and with a peerage, who as he comes face to face with death sees for the first time the reflection of his true self, of a life spent avoiding reality and the sense of guilt which comes from moral cowardice.

The illusion of success must be kept for the sake of his loving daughter, Monica. At the rest-home he is confronted with two shadows from his past. There is Gomez, once a poor fellow student at Oxford, and who has served a sentence in England for corruption, whereas in South America corruption has enabled him to become a respected citizen. Then there is an ex-musical comedy actress Maisie Mountjoy, now Mrs Carghill, who had once tried to sue Claverton for a breach of promise. There is also his son Michael, in debt like Gomez had been, and wishing to break all ties with his family. It is Gomez who will give him a chance to succeed, under another name, in South America. For Claverton the only way out is confession to the one he loves, Monica. And Monica makes this easy by accepting at once her father as he is, with all his failings. Through her he achieves the serenity of perfect understanding.

The Edinburgh Festival Production, subsequently seen in London, was less satisfactory than the two previous Eliot premieres, although Martin Browne was again at the helm. For some reason miscasting made the characters appear at odds with the text, but it is doubtful if even perfect casting would have succeeding in making them cross the frontier from Eliot's own mythical world to appear as more than wishy-washy creations in our own world. Can it be that in bringing them down to humanity and the ordinary business of life Eliot has made them people without faces?

This culmination of Eliot's later dramatic vein must come as a great disappointment to those who had hoped that *The Cocktail Party* was the beginning of an experiment towards a new dramatic system. His real failing must be, as Mr. Lionel Abel has observed in *Partisan Review,* that he has not succeeded in this main task. Strindberg, Shaw, Pirandello or Giraudoux, yes, but "Eliot did not, though he did create a poetic system before turning to plays".

# THE APPROACHES OF DESPAIR

WITH *The Iceman Cometh* of O'Neill we have already reached the gates over which is written the grim warning "Lasciate ogni speranza voi ch'entrate." It is hardly surprising after the devastation of two world wars that our playwrights should have found a contemporary parallel on earth as it is in heaven. Sartre had in *Huis Clos* already discovered hell is other people; perhaps we could add that hell is just as often ourselves. "This century might have been a good one had not man been watched from time immemorial by the cruel enemy who had sworn to destroy him: that hairless, evil, flesh-eating beast — man himself." Such is the recorded message to posterity from Franz, the former S.S. officer in *Les Séquestrés d'Altona*. Man remains nothing other than the totality of his acts.

The characters of Salacrou are aware of their own uncertainty, of the mask of conventions; they have no grammatical interpretation of the universe to explain life — they simply do not understand. Lucie Blondel for example tells us that she is a woman like any other woman; she has the freedom Nora sought in Ibsen's day, but alas, this does not lead to happiness. If only, she is convinced, she knew what life was about then one day she could be happy. The characters of Salacrou speak and behave like children; they want to be happy. The heroines of Anouilh are obsessed with a nostalgic longing for a lost innocence, the memories of happiness, the recollection of days which are gone forever. The Americans, in contrast to Europeans, do not prize uncertainty, they fundamentally want to know, to probe relentlessly, through psychiatry, where the individual has failed and why. Arthur Miller in *Death of a Salesman* portrays the tragedy of the ordinary man who failed "to lick the system". In *The Crucible* the characters are victims of the witch hunts in Salem in 1692; Miller drew the parallel to the

McCarthy fanaticism in the States of 1953. To-day Miller endeavours to sort out his guilt complexes in *After the Fall*, making the audience his psychoanalyst. Tennessee Williams makes his characters suffer physically for the maladjustments of our age; the image of a "cat on a hot tin roof" may be applied to their own rendezvous with life, or as in the case of Mrs. Goforth in *The Milk Train Doesn't Stop Here Anymore* the arrival of the Angel of Death.

We are at the approaches of despair, but we have been saved the full shock treatment, as practised by the disciples of Arthaud and his Theatre of Cruelty, of abandonment to despair, which will lead us beyond the frontiers of the drama.

# TEN

# EXISTENCE IN THEORY: JEAN-PAUL SARTRE

"L'homme est condamné à être libre . . . l'homme est liberté."

SARTRE, *L'Existentialisme est un Humanisme*

"O liberté! Que de crimes on commet en ton nom."

MADAME ROLAND ON THE SCAFFOLD

AFTER the first world war came the heyday of the Dadas and the surrealists; after the second war it was the turn of the existentialists. No doubt there had to be something to correspond to the frustrated mood of a war-ravaged continent. In France the occupation had paralysed the community more completely than any plague could have done, while its stench lingered long after the liberation. Was man really responsible for this orgy of evil which had consumed nations? Were you, for example, to blame for the gas chambers of Buchenwald, the massacre of the innocents by bombing, the torture of patriots, the lynching of collaborators, the ravishing of women, the ignominy of starvation, the collapse of morals and morale? If many believed that man could only find hope in a return to religion and the realisation of human inadequacies when God is excluded, the pessimism of the age was to bring about an equally marked atheistic reaction: that man is nothing except his life and that consequently he is fully responsible for his actions. Man can save himself only through himself. He must choose for himself his course of action, and in doing so, he automatically chooses for everyone. He is not given the choice of inaction. In an existentialist world man is committed, whether he wants to be or not.

Just as the movement Dada had set itself the task of seeking a new order from anarchy, just as the surrealists had sought in Dali's words "the conquest of the irrational", so the existentialist writers condemn man to his liberty. It is, whatever Sartre may say to the contrary, a doctrine impregnated with pessimism and cannot in any way justify the claim to be a 'humanism'. It is not true that repeating a phrase like 'black is white' often enough makes people believe in the phrase — not at any rate where existentialism is concerned. In wishing to suppress God Sartre has so excelled himself that he has suppressed humanity. In sweeping away Christian ethics he has emptied out the baby with the bathwater. For Sartre's approach to man, living in a state of 'solitude in common', is not to bring him any message of hope to show his confidence in man; it is merely the introduction of a new vocabulary of Orwellian 'doublethink' to act as a key to his grammatical dialectics. Condemned to be free, our Sartrian superman finds freedom does not offer greater interpretation than would be the definition given by Radio Moscow, while descriptions such as 'lache' (coward) and 'salaud' (skunk) are applied indiscriminately to those situations and standards which are respected in any Christian — indeed in any self-respecting — society.

Though both the surrealists and existentialists have philosophic leanings, it is through their literary offspring that they have become known to the general public; recently existentialism might be said to have become almost entirely a literary movement — not without French philosophers breathing a sigh of relief. For existentialism as elaborated by Sartre from the theories of Martin Heidegger (who worked in defeated Germany after the 1918 war) is not of overwhelming interest to-day to a professional philosopher, and is in fact much less regarded in France than, for example, Emmanuel Mounier's *Le Personnalisme*. Nevertheless, the principles of existentialism are to be found in a massive volume of 724 pages, *L'Etre et le Néant*, which few people have attempted to read — and fewer still have been successful. But, like Karl Marx, realising that bulk counts more for prestige than popularity, Sartre has reduced his theories into a short existentialist manifesto, *L'Existentialisme est un Humanisme*, where the A–Z of his system is expounded in an ABC language.

His attempt, however, to bring philosophy into the theatre to reach a wide public is both his strength and weakness. From it all his limitations spring. It is responsible for his characters, who remain far too often merely abstract figures, never people of flesh and blood and human warmth. They are seldom complex beings but are created as theoretical types. It is true that in the better plays (not necessarily the most interesting) they do assume lives of their own; but the more Sartre's play is a *pièce à thèse* the less his characters reveal themselves to us. For propaganda is not the true purpose of theatre.

Yet this is precisely what Sartre holds to be the purpose of theatre. He is only interested in presenting a practical application of his philosophic theories, and one could write a complete exposition (and criticism) of existentialism from his plays alone. That he is not interested in character is admitted by him in an article on "Forgers of Myths" which appeared in *Theatre Arts* in June, 1946. "As a successor to the theatre of characters we want to have a theatre of situation", he writes. "The people in our plays will be distinct from one another — not as a coward is from a miser or a miser from a brave man, but rather as actions are divergent or clashing, as right may conflict with right." Situations are, it is true, vitally important (more important than most Broadway or West-End managements would care to admit) but the characters, whether they be mythical figures or not, are no less important. In the plays of Giraudoux or Claudel, even of Anouilh, the characters belong to life, not philosophy.

Though Sartre goes on to claim that the theatre he is writing about is not inspired by any preconceived idea, his own theatre most certainly is. It is the very essence of being committed. He writes his plays with the partiality of a system which must both be defended and rigorously applied at the expense of everything else, including, if need be, the artistic criterion (as in *Le Diable et le bon Dieu*). A critic who is old fashioned enough to judge a play first from artistic standards must decide whether he is to remain faithful to what he believes are permanent dramatic values, or whether he should, like ancient Romans watching Christians being thrown to the lions, 'get to know his times'. At all events we shall judge the plays of Sartre first as plays. But we cannot ignore the philosophy, since it is so much the *raison d'être* of the play. It is as if, in dialectical justice, Sartre forces a critic to criticise him (and nearly all critics have) whether they want to or not. At least he condemns a critic to condemn. But although condemned to suffer and criticise existentialism, there is an escape for the critic through the great literature of the past and even the present which is not *engagée*, even at the risk of becoming quite contentedly what Sartre contemptuously calls a "vieux critique". As Sartre would have it, the die has been cast.

There is nothing particularly revealing about the early life of Jean-Paul Sartre to suggest that he would one day become the celebrated demolisher of bourgeois morality — except that his own upbringing had all the middle-class respectability and conformity that any would-be revolutionary (theoretical or practical) could wish for. Born in Paris on 21 June, 1905, Sartre belonged to a half Protestant, half Catholic family; his father, a naval officer, died of fever in Indo-China when Sartre was still young; his mother remarried, but life under his stepfather seems to have been uneventful. He was, however, a delicate child, tormented with nightmares which made him seek reading and writing as an alternative to sleep at an early age. At six Sartre was writing alexandrines in the manner of the fables of La Fontaine, and he was soon absorbed by the scientific adventures of Jules Verne. At school he was a bright pupil in all subjects except mathematics. From a Baccalauréat in philosophy he proceeded to take his Licence in philosophy, and then, after his military service, to a post as teacher of philosophy at Le Havre. So far, a very ordinary career.

But during this time he had started his literary activities. At eighteen he had already founded a review with a Communist journalist, Nizan, called *Revue sans Titre,* in which he achieved print for the first time. Publishers, however, rejected his manuscripts, and his first success came in 1936 with an essay on "L'Imagination" contributed to *La Nouvelle Encyclopédie Philosophique.* In 1938 an essay called "La Nausée" was accepted, and the publishers, in order to promote its sales, described it as 'a novel'. This trick turned a philosophical essay into best-selling fiction, and had not its contents been so defamatory to traditional values, it would certainly have gained one of the literary prizes that are to French publishers what Oscars are to Hollywood.

Then came the war. During the winter 1940–1941 Sartre was a prisoner of war, but was repatriated for health reasons. During his captivity, however, he staged and acted a Christmas play, *Bariona,* which, "while pulling wool over the eyes of the German censor by means of simple symbols, was addressed to my fellow-prisoners. . . . As I addressed my comrades across the footlights, speaking to them of their state as prisoners, when I suddenly saw them so remarkably silent and attentive, I realised what the theatre ought to be — a great collective, religious phenomenon". Such was the premise of Sartre, a miracle play, perhaps too Christian in its existentionalism for him to allow performed out of its historical context.

Sartre was henceforth to combine playwriting and philosophy as his two dominant interests; in 1943 he wrote *Les Mouches* where, through symbolism and the use of classical legend, he was able to portray the sufferings of a France humiliated under the Vichy policy of repentance and collaboration. His classical parallel, which suggests on first sight (only) affinities with, say, Giraudoux, pulled the wool over the eyes of the German censors, and it was permitted to be staged by Charles Dullin at the Théâtre de la Cité (the Sarah Bernhardt Theatre renamed to appease Nazi racial policies). Along with Claudel's *Le Soulier de Satin* and Anouilh's *Antigone* it proved the outstanding success of the occupation years.

It was in 1943 also that Sartre's philosophical treatise *L'Etre et le Néant* was published. During the war years one can but wonder at Sartre's remarkable industry, writing secretly for *Les Lettres Françaises*, making valuable contacts with the Resistance and belonging to the Comité National des Ecrivains, an underground organisation for French writers. Officially he was lecturing on Greek drama. In May, 1944, Sartre's third play *Huis Clos* (produced in London under the title "Vicious Circle") was staged at the Vieux-Colombier, and continued triumphantly after the liberation.

Thus, whereas Sartre had before the war been little known to the public, he had by the end of the war established himself, if not as their leading writer, at any rate as their leading exponent of the school of 'Littérature engagée', which has been without doubt the most controversial and acclaimed development in post-war literature — an influence not confined to the frontiers of France. Truly in 1945 Sartre became the most talked about of men.

During that year we saw the rise to fame of Saint-Germain-des-Prés with its cafés where the *nouveaux-existentialistes* were soon replaced by the *nouveaux-riches*; more important, the year saw the birth of Sartre's review *Les Temps Modernes*, which still plays a leading rôle in French intellectual life. 1945 also saw the publication of the first two volumes of *Chemins de la Liberté*, and in addition to all this Sartre visited the United States as reporter for *Le Figaro* and *Combat*.

A generation later Sartre may be said to have survived the last existentialist. It is wrong, however, to accuse Sartre of ever having been a publicist — the wild and irresponsible youths who seized the existentialist banner were none of his doing. It was not publicity for himself that Sartre sought, but for his ideas. Not content with the theatre and novels, he turned to the cinema and to politics. A competent film has been made from his novel *Les Jeux sont faits*.

The politics of Sartre, like his philosophy, are negative and destructive. Having destroyed the *status quo* he leaves the ruins to take care of themselves. Sartre wishes to embrace and write for the masses without knowing how to arouse their interests. He is himself dazzled by the attractions which the Communist Party offers — not to himself personally, but to the "workers", and so the outcome of literature becomes inevitably "bound to that of the working-class". "To have the right to criticise a movement as important as the Communist movement", Sartre has written, "one has to work with it". Yet to his credit there were few more forthright criticisms of the way the Hungarian Rising of 1956 was crushed than that of Sartre. No one is more aware than Sartre that he would be one of the first victims of a Communist dictatorship, and yet he earnestly wishes and works for this end. In spite of himself he has not found a théatre *ouvrier*, and as Jean Vilar has remarked, Gauloises are a popular cigarette in France, and none the less popular because M. de Rothschild smokes them. It must have been with regret that Sartre has been unable to reach his public through the media of Television — although some of his plays have been presented successfully over the French networks — partly because he lacks a television personality and more important, because De Gaulle had immediately understood the potentiality of the new medium in politics. Thus denied the possibilities of political ambitions, Sartre seems condemned to the literary life. Having refused the Nobel Prize for Literature in 1964 on the grounds that it could restrict his freedom of action and speech, Sartre seems to have fallen victim to emotional impulses; in his hatred of the Monsieur Jourdain's of this world he seems prepared to reject with it the language of the people of the bourgeois gentilhomme; in its place there is the tendency to substitute a Marxist Jargon which Sartre has come to speak without his being aware of it.

Perhaps this is the place to explain briefly some early philosophical ideas of Sartre which are essential to any understanding of his plays. Here, then, are the golden rules of existentialism, which I summarise from *L'Existentialisme est un Humanisme:*

(1) Existence precedes essence. If God does not exist, there is at least a being with whom existence precedes essence, and this being is man, or, as Heidegger puts it, human reality.

(2) Man is nothing other than he makes himself, he is nothing except

his life. He exists only to the extent he projects himself towards the future, he is nothing except the totality of his acts.

(3) Man is thus responsible for what he does, and is also responsible for mankind. In choosing for himself, man chooses for mankind.

(4) When we choose, we of course choose the good, and not evil. Nothing can be good for us without being good for others. Thus our responsibility is much greater than we imagine, for upon our choice depends humanity.

(5) The only judgment which can be made of this choice is not one of value, but of authenticity. For if God does not exist, everything is permitted. Man is bound neither by laws nor orders, nor the necessity to receive them from others. Man is free, we are in fact:

(6) Condemned to freedom. Condemned because man has been thrown into this world — he had no say in the matter — and being free he is responsible for his acts.

Thus we find that in existentialism man is committed, and he commits in his actions the totality of mankind. Man, since God does not exist, is the legislator for himself. In short, Sartre claims that existentialism presents a coherent system of atheism. In this world which Sartre creates, a world without law or moral values, without help, without explanation, a world of violence which Sartre exploits to the full in his literary works, we must ask ourselves whether in condemning man to be free, M. Sartre does not at the same time condemn man without choice to a living hell. It is the logical conclusion of his dialectics.

\*

Unlike Claudel, Sartre did not have to wait for his audience. While in *la belle époque* no audience would have tolerated a play which set out not to entertain but to unfold philosophical situations, the post-war public has been willing to accept both Claudel and Sartre, and other playwrights treating religious and philosophical subjects within the framework of the drama. In the eighteenth century Voltaire had used the stage for his philosophic reflections, as had Diderot, but not in the way Sartre uses the theatre unsparingly to communicate his ideas, however abstract or complex. He sets out deliberately to attack the audience's mind collectively, to throw its prejudices into confusion, to leave it, if necessary, with a headache. His are plays which trouble our conscience, discover our anxieties, uproot our belief. Other writers have followed, such as Camus with *Le Malentendu*, and Simone de Beauvoir with *Les Bouches inutiles*, while there is the Christian existentialist Gabriel Marcel who has also had his very philosophical plays well received in Paris. But Sartre succeeds where others only partially do so because he has an unfailing dramatic sense, and whatever else he may be, he is never dull. Like the Ancient Mariner, his plays hold even a reluctant audience; there is no escape from his spell.

It is difficult to find a unity of inspiration in the works of Sartre; his plays may be divided into the symbolic, as represented by *Huis Clos* and *Les Mouches*, and the realistic, such as *Morts sans Sépulture* and *La Putain respectueuse*. His remaining plays could be grouped under a miscellaneous heading to include his melodramatic "potboiler" adaptation from Dumas, *Kean*, and his political farce *Nekrassov*, which has more in common with the work of a *chansonnier* than that of a serious playwright. From his first play *Bariona or The Son of Thunder* Sartre already masters the political potential of the drama as a means of making the public aware of its situation. What mattered in Christmas 1940 was the necessity to foster unity among the French prisoners, and in order to achieve this Sartre allowed himself to explore the Christian dimensions of Existentionalism. In ancient Palestine under Roman occupation he saw an immediate parallel with the German occupation of France.

Bariona is the name of a village chief, who believes the best way for them to resist the Romans is celibacy; no children would be born and eventually there would be no more Jews for the Romans to tax. His plan seems threatened when he learns from a Sorcerer that their Messiah is to be born. Alas, Christ is not a Bariona as the Jews had imagined, a soldier to follow and free them from the Romans. Instead they see "a mystical lamb, who preaches resignation". "Who", Bariona asks, "would have thought my own people would willingly lead themselves to the Cross?" Is this Christ not a collaborator when he says, "Render unto Caesar the things that are Caesar's?" Bariona decides to strangle the "King of the Jews" in his manger. An Angel implores him not to, but has to admit "we angels can't do anything against man's freedom of choice". Eventually it is Balthazar, as the Wise Man, who persuades Bariona to permit Christ to be born, for all the children in the world. Christ has come to teach man that he is responsible only to himself for his suffering, and that "if you accept your portion of suffering as you accept your daily bread, then you are beyond it". Left on his own to decide, Bariona discovers the meaning of freedom:

> Free ... O heart, stick firm to your denial ... you must accept,
> you must enter into this stable and kneel down. It will be the
> first time in your life ... You will be free—free. Free against
> God and for God. Against yourself and for yourself ...

In the end it is Bariona who organises the defence of Christ when the
soldiers are sent to kill him; his villagers will be the first soldiers of
Christ.

*Bariona* is essentially Christian in its existentionalism; through the
coming of Christ as a man, man is able to be free. In *Les Mouches*
written three years later, we are still in the midst of the war, and its
shortcomings are understandably those of an inability to treat the
enemy with sympathy or respect. Anouilh did not make this mistake
in *Antigone* where Creon presents his viewpoints so forcefully that
for a time rumours went round Paris that *Antigone* was in fact a Nazi
play. Certainly Sartre never spares his opponents, only when we come
to a play like *Le Diable et le bon Dieu* ("Lucifer and the Lord", 1951)
we are not sure we are any longer on the same side. By then Sartre had
made his "free" decision, and we are presented only with the aetheistic
side of the picture.

For *Les Mouches* Sartre has taken the Orestes-Electra legend, and
adapted it to suit his purpose. From the moment the curtain rises on
the square in Argos, with its walls stained with blood, with the stench
of carnage permeating the city, the swarms of flies infesting the air, the
wailing women dressed in mourning, we know that the city is being
punished and is repenting. Orestes returns unannounced to Argos with
his tutor. He meets Jupiter at the gates, but does not disclose his
identity. Jupiter (God of flies and death) tells him that the plague of
flies has been attracted to Argos since the death of Agamemnon
fifteen years ago. Jupiter goes on to describe the events that have
happened since the seizure of the throne by Aegisthus after the murder
of Agamemnon.

"Does Aegisthus repent?" Orestes asks Jupiter.

"Aegisthus? I should be very surprised if he did. But why worry?
A whole city is repenting for him", is the reply.

Piercing screams are heard coming from the direction of the palace.
Jupiter tells Orestes that these cries mark the beginning of the Ceremony of the Dead. Discussing the events of the murder, Jupiter raises

the name of Orestes, saying that he does not know whether he is really dead or alive, but hopes for his sake that he is dead. "Why?" demands Orestes.

JUPITER Imagine him turning up one day at the city gates ... I'd say to him: "Be off, young man! What do you expect to get here? You think to establish your rights, eh? You're strong and keen, you'd make a grand captain in a battle-thirsty army, you have better things to do than reign over a town half dead, a decaying, fly-infested carcase of a town. The folks here about are great fishermen as a rule, yet here they are now on the road to redemption. Let them, young man, leave them alone, do them credit for their painful endeavour, but tip-toe very far away ... Pleasant journey, young man, pleasant journey. Order in a city, like order in men's souls, is a fickle thing. Touch it, and you bring about catastrophe. (*Looking him straight in the eye*) A terrible catastrophe which will fall on your own head.[1]

But despite these dire warnings Orestes stays and meets Electra, who has just been banished from the city by Aegisthus for ridiculing the Ceremony of the Dead by discarding mourning and in fact being happy and dancing before the crowd. Electra tells him she will stay in Argos, and seek shelter in the temple of Apollo. She must stay, for she is waiting for her brother Orestes, who she knows is not dead and will one day return. Orestes then discloses his identity, but Electra refuses to believe him. She is suddenly afraid of him, for he is no longer the innocent Corinthian youth she had taken him to be. Aegisthus and Clytemnestra are killed by Orestes. Electra approaches Orestes with a candle after the crime:

ELECTRA I must light up your face, for night thickens and I can no longer see you very well. I need to see you. When I no longer see you, I am afraid of you. I must not take my eyes off you. I love you. I've got to think I love you. How strange you look.

ORESTES I am free, Electra; freedom has flashed upon me like a thunder-bolt.[2]

---

[1] See original on p. 409.

[2] See original on p. 409.

Together they seek refuge in the sanctuary of Apollo, the shelter of men — and flies.

In the last act Sartre expounds some of the essential ideas of the play when Orestes meets Jupiter and renounces him at the same time as he renounces repentance for his crime. Electra, however, is tormented by the thought of what has happened, and is willing to accept Jupiter's offer, paying the price of "a little repentance". With Orestes, however, compromise or obedience is no longer possible:

ORESTES  Yes, you are king Jupiter, king of the Gods themselves, king of the rocks and the stars, king of the waves of the sea. But — you are not the king of men.

JUPITER  Not your king, of course, cheeky grub. But who created you?

ORESTES  You did. But was there any need to create me free?

JUPITER  Your freedom I gave you to serve me.

ORESTES  I, Jupiter, am neither master nor slave. What I *am* is my freedom. You had hardly created me when I no longer belonged to you.

Learning from Orestes that the people of Argos are his own men whom he must enlighten and deliver from their feeling that they must repent, Jupiter has his own reactions:

JUPITER  Poor people! The present you are going to give them is loneliness and shame; the coverings I kept over them you are going to snatch away; and what they got for nothing, their mere existence, their drab obscene existence you will suddenly drag into the light of day.

ORESTES  And if the despair in me is their lot too, what right have I to conceal it from them?

JUPITER  What will they do with it?

ORESTES  Whatever they like. Aren't they free? And human life begins the other side of despair.

Jupiter takes his leave, warning that his reign — though drawing to an end — is not yet over, and that he is not abandoning the struggle. Electra chooses repentance. Orestes decides to leave Argos, and takes on his shoulders the responsibility for all its crimes. He compares himself to the piper of Hamelin, who with his flute attracts all the rats and leads them out of the city. So when he leaves Argos he takes with him the Furies and the flies; he rescues the city from repentance. Argos is free.

How in 1943 the very thought of freedom must have stirred the imagination! To-day we can be more dispassionate, and realise that the freedom offered by Sartre did not offer much scope to the imagination. Freedom to recognise one's despair, one's existence which had no significance anyway. In this play there are the seeds of an inhumanity which was to grow in each successive work of Sartre.

Let us now imagine a situation where three people, each guilty of a crime, are shut up in a monstrously ugly and uncomfortable room without escape, not for life, but for eternity. That is a fair approximation to the concept of hell given by Jean-Paul Sartre. "Hell is other people" ("L'enfer c'est les autres") is the theme of *Huis Clos*. The setting, with its barren walls, its bricked up windows excluding daylight so that night and day are alike, the space where a mirror once hung (for in eternity one must look at others, not oneself any more), is all part of a masochistic nightmare where continuity becomes an endless symphony of torture worse than any physical torture. There is no longer any hope, passion or human dignity. Love is as useless as hatred. There is no escape or intermission, neither sleep, silence, privacy nor death exists any more.

There are only four characters in the play, and the porter who shows the newly-dead to their room in the first place makes but a brief appearance. It is a drama of three, a sadist, a lesbian, and a child murderess. One man, two women. No love is possible in the presence of the third, no end is possible since the three must be together for eternity, "neither the knife, poison, rope" can enable them to escape this fact. The play presents an endless repetition, a study in monotony which, far from being monotonous, is in fact intensely dramatic and most seducing.

Sartre's next two plays do not sustain this level. *Morts sans Sépulture* ("Men Without Shadows" in London production) and *La Putain respectueuse* were presented in a double programme at the Theatre Antoine in Paris in 1946, and in London the following year. Of the two, *Morts sans Sépulture* is undoubtedly the better play, and should not be considered merely on the level of stimulating macabre sensationalism. It is a study of mental disintegration undergone in face of physical torture by a group of captured Resistance members in occupied France.

SEAN O'CASEY

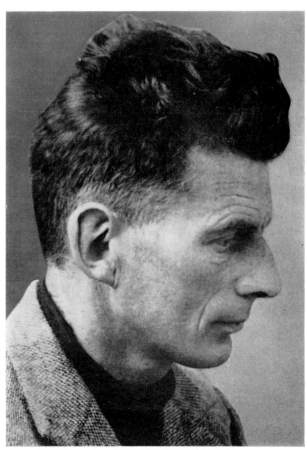

SAMUEL BECKETT

Eugène Ionesco

It is a dialogue between torturer and victim. The prisoners seek courage to enable them to keep their secret, one of them is raped, another leaps to death outside a window. But the secret they know becomes false. They can give it and save themselves. But one of the guards shoots them all the same. "They're just animals", is the justification for the torture.

*La Putain respectueuse* is an example of the supreme dangers of Sartrian theatre, the dangers of trying to over-simplify by crude melodrama and surface logic a problem which defies simplification. In dramatising the colour bar problem in the southern States, Sartre stumbles into all the pitfalls that a blatant propagandist in the name of Soviet realism might deliberately choose; the result is so outrageously false that this treatment is only one stage removed from mock-melo-drama.

The play introduces us to Lizzie, a prostitute newly arrived in a southern town from New York, where she is in trouble. On the train she witnessed an assault on two innocent Negroes by a group of drunken white youths. One of the Negroes is shot, the other one escapes. The youths, in order to defend their crime, have spread the rumour that the Negroes attempted to rape Lizzie. Everything depends on what Lizzie tells the court. The play opens with the Negro furtively knocking at Lizzie's door and asking her to tell the truth at the trial. Lizzie promises this, and slams the door in his face; for she is enter-taining her first client in the town, Fred, who turns out to be a cousin of the youth who shot the Negro. He tries to blackmail Lizzie to give evidence in his cousin's favour; Lizzie insists that should she be forced to go to court, she will tell the truth. The idea horrifies Fred, who warns her that she'll be testifying for a black man against a white:

LIZZIE    But it's the white man who's guilty.
FRED    He isn't guilty.
LIZZIE    Since he killed the guy, he's guilty.
FRED    Guilty of what?
LIZZIE    Of having killed.
FRED    But it's a nigger he's killed.
LIZZIE    Well . . .

And so it goes on, until the point is well rubbed home. Two inspectors start giving Lizzie the third degree when the Senator, Fred's father, enters and kills Lizzie's conception of kindness, not through violence

F

— but through kindness and an appeal to sentiment. Of course, he tells her, she must tell the truth since she knows the Negro is innocent, and he must go and tell his poor sister, the mother of the murderer, Lizzie's decision. Lizzie asks the Senator to help her. Then think, volunteers the Senator, how my sister might see the problem.

SENATOR    Just figure Uncle Sam stepping up to you suddenly . . . What would be his angle . . . He'd sure have a lot to say to you. Such as "Lizzie, you have to choose between two of my sons. One or the other must go. What do you figure you do in such a case? You keep the better one. Let's try? . . . Lizzie, this negro you are shielding, what good is he? Born by accident, heaven knows where. I've fed him and what does he do in return? Nothing . . . I wouldn't even notice his death . . . On the other hand, our Thomas has killed a black, which is very wicked. But I need him. He's a hundred per cent American, descended from one of our oldest families, studied at Harvard, an officer — we must have officers — and employs two thousand workers in his factory. Two thousand unemployed if he dies. He is a born leader, a solid bulwark against communists, the unions and Jews. He has a duty to live and it is your duty to save his life. That is the picture. Go ahead and choose.

Lizzie gives way under the stress of emotion, and signs the fatal document incriminating the Negro. The hunt is on.

The second scene of this short melodrama concerns the girl's efforts to hide the Negro. Already an innocent Negro has been torn to pieces through mob violence. The Senator and Fred pay Lizzie separate calls. Lizzie, too late, realises the Senator's trick, but she cannot bring herself to shoot Fred, for, as he tells her, "A wench like you cannot kill a gentleman". Lizzie accepts the compromise, with Fred's promise to install her in a large house. The Negro escapes until the next time; Lizzie prepares to give her body. As in *Huis Clos* there is no end to the cycle. The problem will end with the lynching of the last Negro.

It is surprising that French critics of repute have commended this play so highly, even to declaring it Sartre's *chef-d'oeuvre*, whereas outside France it has been attacked not only by critics but by any one who has a knowledge of the colour bar in the south, as well as by American Negroes. As a Negro from the south told this writer, "our problem is summed up in the words of the play by James Gow and Arnaud d'Usseau — *Deep are the Roots*". The problem is vast and complex. Lynching does not win much sympathy these days, and therefore Sartre is on safe ground for winning his case. He cannot lose it! For Sartre the whites are always black, and no doubt this mood suits the periodic outbreaks of Yankeephobia in France. Sartre understands the American colour bar about as clearly as Senator McCarthy did Communism — they both have made use of the same tactics in their attack.

*Les Mains sales* (1948) is a political melodrama of fierce excitement and intensity which steadily mounts until the final denouement; indeed the play might almost be a perfect model for its type, and writers such as Charles Morgan (who attempts the same hybrid form in *The Burning Glass*) might have taken lessons from Sartre the dramatist. True, Sartre does not make his characters human, but in this play abstract political figures are all the better for presenting mere silhouettes; the divine right of the Communist Party policies and the necessity to liquidate deviationists when new policies are enacted require an austerity both in language and characterisation. A little of this goes a long way, but it is justified here.

The action of the play passes in Hungary towards the end of the German occupation. The Communist leader Hoederer has been instructed to negotiate with the representatives of the government an agreement which will be hotly disputed and rejected by the mass of the party. Hugo, a young bourgeois intellectual who has made his choice and his revolt, wishes instead of editing the party's underground newspaper to prove his revolt in action, not words. He is therefore sent as secretary to Hoederer, with orders to kill him before he implements his policy. But Hugo is not a militant in spite of his ideals. The idea of to kill (or not to kill) torments him. Hoederer, on the other hand, is a born revolutionary, inflexible in his purpose and decisive in action. He senses that Hugo is going to kill him, but he believes that he can overcome Hugo through humanity, for Hugo cannot shoot him in cold blood. When Hugo does kill him, it is a 'crime passionnel' — the title of the play when produced in London.

In the epilogue, two years have elapsed. Hugo has been released from prison and returns to the yoke of his party cell, where Hoederer's views have now been accepted as official policy without a murmur, and consequently instead of being a hero he is a criminal. His ideals are challenged; he can only save his life by renouncing his idealism. He prefers the Communist firing squad, since he is "not fit for salvage"

"Although the action takes place 400 years earlier, *Le Diable et le bon Dieu* may be regarded as a complement to *Les Mains sales*", Sartre has written of his intentions in his most ambitious, philosophical and iconoclastic play.

> In Goetz, my hero, I have tried to create a character as far removed from the common run of his contemporaries as was Hugo in the other play, and equally torn by conflicting emotions. This time, it is a little less fine drawn. Goetz is torn because, as the bastard son of a noble and a peasant, he is rejected by both sides alike. The problem is how he is to break away from the anarchism of the right in order to throw in his lot with the Peasants' Revolt.
>
> I have tried to show that Goetz, a free-lance captain of mercenaries and an anarchist of evil, destroys nothing when he believes he is destroying the most. He destroys human lives, but cannot disturb society or social judgments; everything he does ends, to his fury, by benefiting the rulers. When, in time, he tries to perform an act of absolute good, and gives his lands to the peasants, this is equally without significance. Whether he tries to achieve the absolute through good or through evil, he succeeds only in destroying human lives. . . .

Such an outline indicates the essential fabric of theme and ideas. Sartre has taken for his existentialist hero a celebrated captain in the Germany of the Emperor Maximilian I called Iron Hand, who sold his services to the highest bidder and suddenly made a strange choice in heading the Peasants' Revolt in Germany in 1524. The play, as Sartre conceives it, falls into two parts. In the first half Goetz is the romantic anarchist who obeys only his evil passions. The citizens of Worms have defied their Archbishop who engages Goetz to besiege the town. But Goetz longs not only to capture it, but to set the city on fire, and wipe out both its treasures and inhabitants. The citizens, for their part, kill the bishop and threaten the 200 clergy they have imprisoned. Heinrich, an apostate priest who has the trust of the people, is given by the dying bishop a key which will enable the clergy to escape from the city by an underground vault. Heinrich realises that he also has the power with this key to hand over the city to Goetz. Heinrich chooses to do this.

Goetz is determined on evil, from his own personal actions, such as threatening to hand his mistress — who adores him — over to his soldiers, to his ambition to lay waste the city. When Heinrich meets him, he discovers almost too late the character of Goetz. He speaks up, and the voice of the priest returns to him. Evil, he tells Goetz, is such an easy thing. It is good that it is so difficult, if not impossible, to accomplish. Goetz falls for this argument. Throwing a die he decides to see whether fate meant him to destroy Worms or become a saint. He is to serve God. He has cheated from the start, for the dice was weighted. The idea of doing good for a year, of playing the holy man, amuses his imagination. Heinrich is then to judge him.

The metamorphosis in the character of Goetz is complete, but in intending to do good, he only succeeds in doing evil, of bringing in the train of his actions misery and destruction. He gives his lands to his peasants and thus leads to discontent throughout the country, and to a premature peasants' revolt. He is despised even by his own peasants, and in order to win their confidence he cheats again, by cutting his hands and pretending to be a stigmatist. Already in playing the saint he has lied. Goetz plans to build a city on earth as it is in heaven, but his scheme is doomed. His domain is invaded and the peasants are massacred. The Peasants' Revolt has broken out, but he refuses to lead them to victory, for man must not fight. So the year passes and Heinrich returns. Goetz must ask himself the question whether he has done good. He knows the answer and kills Heinrich. Neither God nor the devil exists; only man in his state of nothingness. It remains for Goetz to return to armour, lead the insurgents, in order to teach man that he is alone in the universe, or, as he says, "I shall remain alone with this empty sky above me, since I have no other way of being among men".

The play lacks unity (the unities which were so important to existentialist work in 1946) but a more serious objection is the confusion in the whole of Sartre's philosophic reasoning in this play. That we can believe Goetz is incapable of doing good nee 's no insistence, but it seems singularly false that Goetz cannot succeed in evil. As Phillip Toynbee remarked in his review of *Lucifer and the Lord* in the *Observer:* "As the most powerful military leader of his time and place there is no good reason for doubting his power to do evil, and Sartre, to elude this obvious difficulty, indulges in a typical piece of metaphysical sleight of hand."

For Goetz, even when trying to do good, is but a doleful masquerade of evil. Nowhere in the play does Sartre allow the voice of the Church to be heard; he sets out to prove that good is impossible by already assuming it is. The absence of the voice of God in reality is a sufficient excuse and indeed explanation for the absence of the case for Christianity in the play. How Sartre despises the Church! The abuses and corruption that have at times permeated the conduct of the clergy are unsparingly underlined; scandals such as the sale of indulgences to the poor in medieval times are very definitely equated with false hopes and deception which religion offers to-day. Since Sartre is an atheist he cannot be accused of sacrilege, but he can of insincerity. Sartre weights his dice before the house lights go down and he plunges man into darkness.

★

What are we to make of this existentialist progress in Sartrian theatre? We must not mistake it for a search for solutions, for Sartre does not believe that there are any. We must, if we insist, find our own solution. We must be sceptics. For it was through the scepticism taught him by his tutor before he reached Argos that Orestes discovered individual freedom (he allowed his sister Electra to get her own way). By the time we reach Goetz, however, Sartre is not only concerned with freedom for oneself, but also wishes to extend this to include the freedom of others; man must be liberated. From abstract situations we move more and more to reality. Yet whereas the notion of 'freedom' sounds exciting in the abstract light of *Les Mouches*, its glitter fades in daylight and does not even approach, let alone replace, 'faith' in the world of reality. *Les Séquestrés d'Altona* (1959) returns us to the depths of *Huis Clos*. It is a condemnation ostensibly of the Germans and their complicity in Nazism, but it is in fact as much an indictment of the French atrocities in the Algerian war — and it was produced at a time when no Paris theatre would have dared whisper a criticism of French conduct. Just as in *Les Mouches* Sartre had evaded the German censorship in his denunciation of tyranny, so in the midst of the Algerian war he was able to stir the consciences of the French; his play can be applied to both a situation and our times in general — we are all guilty in the name of humanity.

A German industrialist of the old school is dying of cancer; in order to assure the continuity of the family business he calls on his second son and daughter-in-law to sacrifice their own lives for the family interest. This is merely the point of departure of a four hour play which leads us to the darkness and stench of a cave, where we are subjected to the emotional tension and barrage of ideas in a work at once impressive and shattering. Why, for example, has Franz, the elder son, who is supposed to be "officially dead" chosen to sequester himself in the attic of his father's house? Sartre advances several explanations but each with an almost Pirandellian revelation proves false. We enter Franz's claustrophobic world and contrast the piles of rubbish which is all that remains of the furnishings with the stolid comfort downstairs. We listen to the plaintive justification of his actions as his conscience rages and the tape recorder turns; we watch him pelt the portrait of Hitler with empty oyster shells. Rather than face what he believes is a war-devastated Germany Franz lives out his hermit's existence, sharing secrets through an incestuous love with his sister Leni, who like one of the Furies mischievously hounds his conscience. In *Huis Clos* hell is others, here it is ourselves. Leni finds her domination threatened when Johanna, the wife of her younger brother, intrudes; she prevents a transference of affection by forcing Franz to tell Johanna that he deliberately tortured prisoners. When this truth is finally revealed neither sequestration nor love suffice, only a suicide pact with his dying father remains possible; only the voice of Franz remains as the tape recorder plays back his message to posterity:

> Centuries, here is my own one, solitary, deformed, accused . . . one and one make one, that's our mystery. The beast was hiding, we surprised his look suddenly in the eyes belonging to our near ones. Then we struck. Legitimate self-defence. I surprised the beast, I struck, a man fell, and in his dying eyes I saw the beast, still alive, in myself.

We are a long way here from any faith which requires man to fight for ideals and instead suicide appears as a possible solution for a conscience which is guilty. In this very Germanic play Sartre seems to combine a certain French *clarté* with German philosophic confusion, and the combination of these cross currents go far to explaining the inconsistency which he finds in his own "logically" held political convictions. It seems to me that a Sartrian hero is the product of confused thinking.

Their way of making men love is through hatred, or as Goetz declares, "we shall be sure of victory only when my men are more afraid of me than the enemy". It is as if having offered freedom through a revolt not unlike anarchy (free from giving or accepting orders, obeying laws, etc.) Sartre does not see beyond the blood bath any more than Marxists see beyond the withering away of the State. Condemned to be free, is this freedom really worth the having? There is and never can be absolute freedom, even for Sartre, since man is still bound to natural laws and this absurd life; the victim, whatever his existentialist will-power, to the unforeseen and unknown way.

# ELEVEN

# "THIS FEVER CALLED LIVING"—
# ARMAND SALACROU AND
# JEAN ANOUILH

> "When the World hath once begun to use us ill, it after-
> wards continues the same Treatment with less Scruple or
> Ceremony; as men do a Whore."
>
> JONATHAN SWIFT

IN an article in *Le Figaro Littéraire* Armand Salacrou has complained that the French classical authors ill prepare people for the
absurdity of life — because tragedies like *Le Cid* are disconcertingly optimistic. Perhaps the difference in religions, from monotheistic
to atheistic, does after all lie, as Schopenhauer contends, in whether
they are basically optimistic or pessimistic. In leaving the existential
pessimism of Sartre, the romantic pessimism of Salacrou and Anouilh
presents a world, if seen from a slightly different angle, in a no less
critical fever and radical despondency. Whereas Sartre strides forward
confidently, unfrightened by the void he has created, certain in a world
of uncertainty, neither Salacrou nor Anouilh can enter the existentialist paradise — for their profound regret comes from a paradise lost
which can never be recovered.

If Sartre is more concerned with philosophy and politics, Salacrou
and Anouilh look to morals. Salacrou knows instinctively that he will
never be happy until he finds God, Anouilh cannot forget that "there
is always a lost dog somewhere which will prevent me from being
happy". Salacrou is more directly concerned with religion, he understands "the necessity of God without being able to believe in God";
he is a man of faith who has lost his faith and yet cannot live without it.
Anouilh's violent fanaticism is for purity and unspoilt innocence; if

this has been stained, the stain can never be effaced; his plays are in fact *engagée*, not in the existential sense, but in the past, the lost purity of adolescence and childhood.

It is easy to link the name of Anouilh with that of Sartre and label him 'existentialist'; but even if, as M. Radine has observed, Anouilh used some of the main existentialist themes several years before Sartre, "as Monsieur Jourdain used prose without knowing it", his whole approach and reasoning are different. Indeed, the difference may be said to lie in the fact that Anouilh's characters do reason, while for Sartre it is the act of decision which matters; in other words, the choice, not the choosing. Anouilh refuses, Sartre revolts. Anouilh's refusal cannot in the true sense be called a revolt since it is negative, not positive. He seeks an escape from a world which has become vile and loathsome — he does not claim existentialist freedom. If Sartre depicts certain human beings as "not fit for salvage", Anouilh rejects the whole world. It is the refusal of an idealist, a perfectionist, a moralist; Anouilh delights in the romanticism of despair, where revolt comes to nothing, where the only escape and the sole absolution are to be found in death, where before the grotesqueness of life a fictional world is the safest refuge for human misery. If Anouilh was indirectly inspired by the Giraudoux universe for his shelter, he has made any parallel in life impossible, for happiness is out of bounds in a world where sin prevails, where love is banished and where man can never be redeemed. Unable to regain their lost paradise and innocence, Anouilh's characters are no longer masters of their destiny, as are those of Sartre. Nor does Anouilh, as Mr. Merlin Thomas has remarked, seek philosophical justifications, as Sartre does, to dramatic contexts. He is a moralist, not a philosopher. It is a very simple thing for which his characters search, yet vastly complex, much more so than the right to live their own lives — it is how to live in an absurd reality.

It is on the frontier of absurdity that we find the dividing line between Anouilh and Sartre; with Salacrou, more philosophic than Anouilh, less so than Sartre, standing between the two figures. Salacrou is absorbed by the practicability of how to make the most of absurdity. It is best to begin our journey to Anouilh by way of Salacrou, who is neither so bitter nor so aggressively nihilist as Anouilh, but who serves as an introduction to the mood of romantic despair. Salacrou does not believe in cruelty, he has infinite compassion, but he lingers in the shades of darkness and misery. Having rejected the possibility of an after-life he finds no comfort in Sartrian liberty. But, unlike Anouilh,

Salacrou is always ready to forgive, to have pity, and to make an attempt to understand our behaviour, since an understanding of life is beyond us. His picture of the world is both simplified and exaggerated, but he does not present the vehemence in his attack which we find in either Sartre or Anouilh. His characters are human with human frailties and failings, they do not respond to a system of philosophy, they want only to be happy without even being sure that they would know what to do with happiness should it ever arrive. Escape through death does not attract him. To Salacrou man is not God, nor is woman necessarily pure. Any man, as the title of one of his plays suggests, is merely "a man like others" and any woman, as his heroine Lucie Blondel puts it, is "a woman like others". His characters are like all the rest of us, trying to make the most of the ordinary business of life.

Salacrou, then, wishes to compromise himself with his time and period, to paraphrase a line in *L'Inconnue d'Arras.* He brings his audience as witnesses of the contemporary scene and daily problems. His characters are not exceptional beings, they are ordinary people. They know as little as anyone of how to lead a satisfactory and happy life. Salacrou does not believe in certainties; like Maugham the only thing he is certain of is that he is certain of nothing. This failure of man to find a faith becomes repetitive in all his plays, except perhaps in his tribute to the French Resistance, *Les Nuits de la Colère,* from which it is temporarily absent. His longing to know the mystery of life has the pain and the anguish of Anouilh's craving for purity; both are impossible.

Unknown and beyond understanding. But there is nothing hidden in the plays of Salacrou. Though his plays demand attention, they can be fully appreciated at one performance; they do not gradually reveal themselves like the works of Giraudoux or Claudel. They are immediately theatrical and effectively simple. Though we cannot quite apply the term 'well-made' to the experimental and often erratic technique of Salacrou, his theatre is nevertheless every minute dramatic.

Early in his career Salacrou fell under the surrealist influence, and though he found there an impasse he never rid himself of this influence. It is this which prevents his plays from becoming, to borrow from the title of John van Druten's play, "a camera", and himself a playwright of the boulevard. Salacrou looks not at the face, but the soul of the people he meets in the street. His characters are in every-day situations, he does not dare see more than the immediate present. The vision of Shaw or Claudel, Ibsen or Strindberg, Pirandello or Giraudoux is denied him.

If we must find him an opposite number, Salacrou takes his place somewhere above the plays of say Thornton Wilder.

Salacrou may not be a really important dramatist, but his plays do touch those problems which to-day's audience feels most acutely. He speaks to them in their language, ordinary commonplace idiom, often as ridiculous and banal as what crowds shout out at football matches. But this does not deny their serious intentions, and Salacrou does not intend his plays to be taken lightly. In his *Note sur le théâtre* (1943) he writes: "What I ask of authors, critics, the public, is, at the birth of a new work, to view it honestly, without trickery and not as means of passing the time, with the anguish of interpreting its soul. For me, it is in the theatre that at certain moments of great purity I feel nearest to approaching the inaccessible shore. And it is in the great theatrical works that I sometimes believe that I have found my salvation."

Again and again it is the religious enigma to which Salacrou returns. The concept of God in paradise and Satan in the flames of hell he finds as incomprehensible as the life of animals who 'officially' finish as they began: 'in the dark'. To answer his need, Salacrou confides, just as a Catholic finds refuge in heaven he from an early age found himself shrouded with a determinist philosophy; for him determinism became "a daily custom with as much incongruity as universal gravitation". It is not difficult to believe that this search for God can become the most terrible moral situation a man can know. In *La Terre est ronde* (the idea of a terrestial globe not suspended by any thread in the emptiness of infinity haunts the imagination of Salacrou) the futility of existence becomes a nightmare: "Do you realise that you are nothing, what was before you was nothing, and what will be after you will be nothing? All is nothing. And nothing exists, if it is not thou, the understanding of God." And how far are we from the hope that such an understanding exists. "You must not look for in my plays what I am looking for there myself", is Salacrou's reply. If Salacrou is less dogmatic than Sartre, less bitter than Anouilh, all three share a dominant pessimism. But of the three, Salacrou alone seems to feel human tears; the others have other preoccupations, liberty or escape.

★

Armand Salacrou was born at Rouen in 1899 and spent his childhood in Le Havre. His parents wished him to become a doctor and in 1917 he took his first year in medicine at Paris, and like Somerset

Maugham, came into contact with suffering humanity through his hospital experience. But student life in Paris also introduced him to an intellectual life, and in the summer vacation of 1919 he decided to abandon medicine. Instead he went to the Sorbonne, where he took his Licence in philosophy. A friend then found him a vacancy on *L'Humanité*, the Communist daily, where Salacrou was responsible for the entertainment column and the convocation of party rallies. A varied existence followed in the next few years, and in 1926 Charles Dullin offered Salacrou the secretaryship of the Atelier (it is interesting to note that Anouilh was secretary to Louis Jouvet), and to supplement his income he started a publicity agency in a small way which soon grew to mammoth proportions and made a fortune (Anouilh was also connected with a publicity agency for two years, though at the bottom of the ladder).

Meanwhile Salacrou had started his career as a dramatist. Under the strong influence of the surrealists he had written his early plays, *Le Casseur d'Assiettes*, *Tour à Terre*, and *Le Pont de l'Europe*, plays of little significance, but in which Salacrou was able to experiment and learn the craft. These attempts were ambitious, full of verbosity, wildly pessimistic, badly constructed, and made no attempt to come to terms with the theatre. But they had for at least one critic of the day the sign of better things to come — "Bear the name Salacrou in mind, I prophesy that this writer will one day speak about him again".

In 1927 Salacrou wrote his next play, *Patchouli ou les Désordres de l'Amour*, which was eventually staged, without success, by Charles Dullin at the Atelier in 1930. Indeed, the first night was a disaster, and whatever merit the play possessed certainly missed the public and critics. Dullin tried to save the play from their wrath by soliciting favourable judgments from important figures. Giraudoux found himself able to see promise in the young author, and wrote of *Patchouli*: "It is not an immature play, it is a play about youth. I listened to it with an emotion which, for the kind, was quite new." Immature or not, it was the last play written by the youthful Salacrou. With his next two plays, *Atlas Hôtel* and *Les Frénétiques*, there was a very marked development both in technique and ideas — his surrealist affair was finished and he came over in his next few plays to the side of naturalism with far happier results.

With *Atlas Hôtel* Salacrou for the first time knew success, and was even accused by the critics of "writing plays like everyone else", a reproach which was perhaps inevitable. The plays which were to follow, such as *Une Femme libre* and *L'Inconnue d'Arras*, were quickly to dispel these doubts. There is, it is true, in *Atlas Hôtel* the old triangular tale told under the burning passions and the blazing sun of Africa, and even the extraordinary erection of the hotel — half finished, with neither roof nor windows, and enmeshed with fig trees and cactus plants inside — is no more bizarre than that which audiences have been accustomed to from the days of *The Admirable Crichton* to *The Little Hut*. The hotel is a speculation of a certain Auguste, who has sacrifced everything for his enterprise. The wife of Auguste, Augustine, was formerly married to a poet who had deserted her — not for the sake of art but for pulp fiction and business rackets. Chance brings this ex-poet to Atlas Hotel where he once again tries to make love to Augustine and tries to persuade her to run away with him. In doing this he stoops to such low tricks that he loses her forever.

In both *Atlas Hôtel* and his next play *Les Frénétiques* Salacrou moves rapidly towards the naturalistic mood and his characters gradually assume more and more the reflection of ordinary people. In both these plays, however, something is missing, as if the realistic vein were alien to Salacrou's powers of imagination and thought. It was not until *Une Femme libre* that Salacrou was to emerge as one of France's rising dramatists; in this play the horizons at once expand, there is greater insight and depth to the psychology of his characters. The title "Une Femme libre" immediately suggests the theme of Ibsen's *A Doll's House*, and Salacrou's heroine Lucie Blondel has been contrasted with Nora. The comparison, while totally artificial, does at least enable us to say that Lucie Blondel is not a woman like Nora. Nora slams the door defiantly because she knows what she wants; Lucie knows nothing, except that she has her freedom like every other woman. Thus whereas Nora longs to enjoy her freedom with the sex consciousness of a suffragette, Lucie has never known anything else but freedom. When Jacques asks her where she has lived, where she belongs, she replies: "I belong to my twenty years. Don't you see? That's my country and family background I have left — my twenty years of life . . . We must just live from day to day with our age." Lucie belongs not only to her twenty years but also to the twentieth century; Nora steps bravely just a decade or so ahead of her times into the twentieth-century limelight; to-day her way is so much the way of the world that not even Ibsen, with the powers of greatness, can make *A Doll's House* anything more than a period piece, and a slightly boring one at that. If Lucie is, as M. Radine asserts, a wishy-washy Nora, she is not so far from what we might expect Nora's granddaughter to be; not an exceptional woman self-righteously leading a cause, but an ordinary woman who is frankly afraid of life and who does not know, can never know, the meaning of happiness and satisfaction. We can believe in the character of Lucie even though we cannot accept all the happenings of Salacrou's play, which is nearly shipwrecked as the result of his clumsy denouement; oh! for Ibsen, the master builder!

We meet Lucie when Paul, her fiancé, brings her to be introduced to his family, a caricature of bourgeois complacency, bigotry and prejudice. But as in so many bourgeois families there is one rebel, not her fiancé Paul (a business-man who fits well enough into the family circle and enables them to keep up their social standing with his income) but Paul's brother, Jacques, who has something of the artistic temperament. Lucie, already frightened by her frigid reception and afraid of what life has in store for her as a member of the family, meets Jacques, who warns her that one day she will take her place among the family portraits and in the family graveyard. "And we will one day be like them if we live like them", he continues, "that's what I call family life, the life amidst failures and corpses." But Jacques has made his decision; if Lucie is just beginning her life at the Miremonts, his is over there. Since there are "too many things in the world" to do and to see, he will leave the narrow little world of the Miremonts, and go out and face life. As he opens the door, Lucie decides to run away with him.

In the second act two friends of Jacques, Max and Cher Ami, wreck the happiness of Lucie with their theories of free love and freedom, in much the same way as Jacques in the first act destroyed Lucie's hopes of living with Paul. The idea of living with Jacques cannot be reconciled with the loss of freedom which that implies if she becomes his property.

JACQUES  Do you believe that you love me enough to love me for always?
LUCIE    Always? Let's leave the future alone.
JACQUES  Give me an answer.
LUCIE    Let's be content with to-day's happiness.

The third act finds Jacques and Paul reunited at their family house, both torturing one another with the memory of Lucie. In the six months that have elapsed, Lucie has become a much talked about lady about town, the type described in society paragraphs: "Mlle Lucie Blondel has just arrived Biarritz by air, a private plane piloted by Mlle Blondel herself, more sportive than ever". It is Aunt Adrienne, who has somewhat surprisingly taken a liking for Lucie, who recalls her to the house — she writes her that Jacques is dying, and calling for her. When Lucie arrives she meets Jacques, who is much taken aback, since he knows nothing about the letter. The questions pour out, why did you leave me? — what have you been doing? Lucie tells him that she feared that one day they would no longer love each other, but suddenly pleads with him to run away with her again. She is willing to renounce her career. But Jacques hesitates. He cannot forget the other men she has given herself to since she left him (are they as miserable as I, he wonders) and realises that it is through the many that she feels free. There is no hope for their love. Jacques cannot accept Lucie's assurance that they could be happy. Paul enters the room, but does not see Lucie. Jacques tells him that Lucie can no longer mean anything for them; that if she came to see them, they would have to tell her "You cannot stay here and we cannot follow"; that "she wanted freedom and must therefore pay for her freedom". At these words Lucie rushes from the room in tears, and the brothers once again resume their 'battle'. The three are condemned to solitude and suffering.

In his next play, *L'Inconnue d'Arras*, Salacrou was to turn away from naturalism towards a surrealist approach suggested by an original idea of a man, committing suicide because of his wife's infidelity, reliving his entire life in the fragment of a second between the pressing of the trigger and his death. So the play presents the characters who influenced the husband, Ulysse, in his life; the ghosts of his father, his young grandfather (killed at the age of twenty), his mother, his old school-master, the women he has known in his life, appear in short episodes. Among the women is the unknown girl he met one winter's night near the battlefield at Arras during the 1914 war. She had been abandoned and he had taken her into an empty house, where he had put his coat over her. This episode, which forms a vital link in the play, reveals that the husband had secretly been in love with this unknown woman all the rest of his life. She had told him that three days previously she had come to Arras to look for her sister, but the town had been evacuated. She was frightened and hungry and called out to him, and when she kissed him after he had given her his overcoat, he had punched her face — because she smelt of alcohol. Later that night Ulysse had returned with the intention of raping her, but finding her asleep, had been filled with pity and had left her food and drink. Returning the next day she had gone, and he had been searching for her ever since. He will never know her mystery or her name.

Salacrou uses the episodes to express some of his essential ideas; but it is a play of promise rather than fulfilment. From a technical viewpoint the episodes are expertly handled, but there is an unfortunate tendency to baffle the audience, so that even for some time after the rise of the curtain they are not quite sure whether the intention is farce, mock melodrama or grim humour.

Shortly afterwards Salacrou wrote *Un Homme comme les Autres*, where he becomes decidedly more interested in moral problems. His original idea, he tells us, was to write a play about a husband who is worshipped by his wife, a husband who in the eyes of his wife can do no wrong, but who in fact is like any other husband. In order to reciprocate the love of his wife, the husband longs to be loved for what he is. But when he tells her his wish, she cannot forgive him for not being what he is not! To this idea Salacrou has introduced a sub-plot of a young man who attempts to strangle an old lady for robbery, since he needs money to satisfy the expensive tastes of his girl friend. The man is sentenced to two years' imprisonment and when it is served he realises that he never loved the girl and cannot understand how he ever acted as he did. Forgiveness follows violence!

In *La Terre est ronde* Salacrou gives us his most important, as well as his most ambitious play to date; it is a passionate debate between reason and religion (since Salacrou is an agnostic it is a choice of 'either/or'), an intellectual and spiritual exercise which results in a futile victory of reason, reassuring us that the earth is but a round ball spinning in infinity as purposeless as are the lives of its inhabitants. Though written in 1938, the play has the full-fledged post-world-war pessimism of the nihilist school. Both *Le Diable et le bon Dieu* and *La Terre est ronde* lead us to the same *angoisse*, the 'all is for nothing' labyrinth; in the shades of such futility Charon is no more to be expected than Samuel Beckett's Monsieur Godot.

*La Terre est ronde* is a contemporary play merely dressed up in historical guise; like Goetz in Sartre's play, Savonarola cannot succeed in doing good, however much he tries. Goetz could not build his city in the sun because he was a man of evil; no more can Savonarola offer Florence, the pure and unspoilt 'flower', to God, because he hates man, the creation of God. In Savonarola's character there are more recent echoes, as M. José van den Esch stresses in his study of Salacrou, the realisation by the audiences who saw the play in 1938 that the 'Christ is King' greeting of Savonarola's was no more sincere that the 'Heil Hitler' that the Nazi mobs were then chanting.

The central character, however, is not Savonarola but Silvio, an intelligent young Florentine who is in love with Lucciana, but who cannot bring himself to marry her because he is worried about the mystery of life, and feels he must discover unknown lands to expand man's knowledge. Alas, Lucciana only loves Silvio without understanding his thirst for 'the reason why'; she can offer him her love, but she cannot satisfy more than his flesh. Because of this she must lose him. Silvio tells her one day: "I'm twenty-three and I know that people no longer marry, at any rate since this morning. I've learnt about an extraordinary happening. You see, Lucciana, it seems that the earth is round." Silvio does not leave on his voyage of discovery; instead he liberates himself by joining the cause of Savonarola, who is able to answer all his uncertainties. Silvio and Lucciana are still in love, but Silvio wishes their love to be something spiritual, and tries to persuade her to enter a convent. Meanwhile the public is already stirring against Savonarola, and demands that he should give them proof of his powers by a miracle: that he survive being burnt at the stake. Silvio cannot escape either, for he loves God as much as Lucciana. The final scene of the play is Salacrou's supreme achievement as a dramatist, and one of the best-written scenes in contemporary drama.

Salacrou's subsequent career has not maintained this standard, and the only other play of importance he has given us — a work which stands in isolation from the rest of his writing — is the tribute to the French Resistance *Les Nuits de la Colère*. The play, produced in 1946, admirably reflects the anger, heroism, revolt, degradation, felt by the members of the Resistance against the treachery, cowardice and decadence of those who either actively collaborated with the Germans, or those who accepted, who believed it possible to stay neutral, who in fact compromised with the Germans of the "Milice" while pretending they did not understand what was happening, what they were doing. But the anger of the Resistance tolerated no compromise. The play is a brilliant documentary, as realist in its selection of episodes (Salacrou uses the surrealist technique he had already tried out in *L'Inconnue d'Arras*) as any of the great Italian neo-realist films of the period. The play has but one purpose, as had the members of the Resistance. There is no place for religious or political controversy, the characters are either for or against; they are agreed to accept or revolt. The 'how to live?' which Salacrou continuously asks in his other plays, is here given a meaning. The purpose of their lives is realised in their death, so that the men who fell in the Resistance did so in order that their children would be happy, happy because free, and would never have cause to despair of life since in the darkest days of the occupation they in the Resistance had given their lives and had been able to live 'honourably'.

The action of the play passes in Chartres in 1944. A chemist, Bernard Bazine, married to a highly practical but extremely unimaginative Frenchwoman Pierrette, has chosen to live in Chartres with his three children in order that their lives may be as placid, imperturbable and have the same serene sense of permanency as that of the cathedral itself. One day, however, Bernard's oldest friend Jean, who is a member of the Resistance, seeks refuge in his house. He has just blown up a train carrying petrol supplies, and is wounded. Bernard and Pierrette panic. They hear the German patrols searching for Jean. He will bring an end to their happiness, he threatens their own lives and that of their children; they are giving shelter to a dangerous criminal, a man who blows up trains and destroys life, a man who breaks the armistice. Pierrette informs a collaborator and they naïvely believe that in handing over Jean he will be given a fair trial according to French law. When the curtain rises the Resistance have come to avenge the betrayal, and they kill Bernard. They also kill Pisançon, a collaborator, who as he dies shoots Rivoire, leader of the Resistance. The play then takes on the form of a dialogue between the traitors, the acceptors, and the resisters. There is also the parallel between the living and the dead. Rivoire is dead, as is Pisançon, the traitor, but whereas Pisançon believes that he has died for nothing, Rivoire has the certainty that his life has been a perfect success.

*Les Nuits de la Colère* is a mirror of the times through which France suffered. It is a record, just as *Journey's End* is a testament of the first world war for British audiences. Both plays have made a tremendous impact on their public, who relived the horror of those years in the auditorium. For Rivoire, the anger of *Les Nuits de la Colère* will never die; but will subsequent generations understand the reality of his anger? As a document, the play is witness that these things did happen; but it is more difficult to class it in theatrical literature.

Neither *L'Archipel Lenoir* nor *Dieu le savait* merits serious consideration. The former is a savage satire on how a rich family is driven nearly frantic at the thought of scandal, the latter is a highly improbable story dating from the Resistance, but in which courage gives way to sordid despair and fatalism. More recently *Le Miroir* and *Une femme trop honnête* and *Comme les chardons* have shown that Salacrou is out of touch with to-day's public, though his place among France's leading contemporary dramatists is assured. His work has a distinctive originality, and his virtuosity in describing the uncertainty of our times in terms of the theatre is never absent from his work. But one fears he is anchored to fatalism without hope.

However much the plays of Salacrou may disturb us, the pattern of life they present is depressingly clear; it is never far removed from the doldrums from which even the most optimistic of us occasionally suffer. The world of Jean Anouilh is at once more extreme, more mysterious and harder to understand than that of Salacrou. In the beginning were purity and happiness; they remain the axis of Anouilh's theatre, and our misfortune, suffering and *malaise* are a result of falling outside the orbit of their power. We have rejected the natural order by growing up to worship false values, to compromise, to lie, sin, be sophisticated. . . . The same themes are to be found again and again in Anouilh's plays, his obsessions grow work by work, varying in shade only in their relation to 'pièces noires', 'pièces roses', or 'pièces brillantes' in which, Shavian fashion, he groups them. Those who say an author is a man who repeats the same things throughout his life under twenty or so different forms may point to Anouilh, but this would be unfair. Anouilh is less concerned with themes than working in a tradition, and the links between him and the French classical tradition, as Mr. Merlin Thomas has stressed in a talk on the B.B.C. Third Programme, are very close. Again and again with mounting bitterness he returns to the same moral problems, which at the age of fifty have produced some of the most virulent attacks ever made on bourgeois hypocrisy and the corruption of society. Yet though this acrimony goes at times as far as the human mind can stand, it is those characters he brings in from outside like ventilation in a stuffy salon that gain our sympathy and enable us to share the romanticism for purity and the struggle for moral values. But alas, there is no escape for the heroes and heroines of Anouilh, for in a world which has become so debased that no salvation is worth the taking, a brutal refusal is the only way. And even in the artificial fantasies of his *pièces roses,* escape and happiness always in the end bring us to an impasse.

And Anouilh the man? About his private life he has always been shy in giving details, though we do know that he has never forgiven society for his having known the meaning of poverty in his youth. But his adult life appears to have been happy—a successful dramatist at an early age, a marriage to the woman of his dreams, and fortune at the same time as world critical renown. In Hubert Gignoux's study of Anouilh we learn the following bare outline: Anouilh was born at Bordeaux in 1910, and when young came to Paris. After a year and a half in the Law Faculty at Paris, Anouilh passed two years in an advertising firm, "where I learned to be ingenious and exact, lessons that took for me the place of literary studies". After the production of *L'Hermine* (1932) he decided to live only by writing plays, with a few odd film-scripts. He has never regretted that choice, and throughout his career he has rejected anything in the way of journalism, whether writing or the granting of interviews. "I shall keep the details of my life to myself." That is a more difficult ambition for a French literary figure than for an Anglo-Saxon.

In Anouilh's first play, *L'Hermine*, produced when he was only twenty-one, we have already all the features and tones to which we have grown accustomed in his subsequent work, indeed, in all his plays up to the present. The world is divided into rich and poor; for those who have money everything is possible, even happiness; for the rest everything is denied. *L'Hermine* tells of a poor young man, Franz, who falls in love with Monime (the first of Anouilh's heroines, a picture of perfection which only a lover is likely to accept and it is indeed the explanation for the idealisation of his love), a rich heiress whose family, ruled by the old Duchess of Granat, would never permit the marriage. Franz seeks money from an industrialist, Bentz, but when he is refused help he resorts to what seems to him the only solution, the murder of the Duchess. In spite of Monime's horror at the suggestion, he kills the old lady, although some moments previously he has learnt that Bentz has agreed to help him. He has killed her all the same. Now they have all the money they need, but it is too late. Monime tells him she can no longer be his wife, and Franz, with nothing left to live for, gives himself up to the police.

The next play Anouilh wrote was *Le Bal des Voleurs*, an exuberant high-spirited 'comedy-ballet' belonging to the most wild of his 'let's pretend' humours he calls *rose*. As this play was not performed until six years later, it is his next produced play — the second of his *pièces noires* — *La Sauvage*, that we shall consider. For *La Sauvage* is a work of considerable importance, less mature perhaps than subsequent works, but of great dramatic vision and power. The thirst for purity is already a driving passion, from which there is no escape. This purity is personified in Thérèse, a poor girl who plays the violin (and badly) in her father's second-rate café band. Her mother, a monstrous creature who is the pianist's mistress and schemes when she has the chance to sell her daughter's honour to the highest bidder, plays the 'cello; such is the world into which Thérèse has been born, and from which she can never escape. A world of disgust and shame. One day she meets a true artist, Florent, a musician of talent. He is rich, and could lead her into another world, the best of possible worlds. But Thérèse knows that she must refuse this happiness, because those who have known shame and misery can never escape from its punishment. What is done is done, and to-morrow will be too late. Only when Thérèse manages to make Florent miserable by telling him in sordid details and lies about previous lovers, does she momentarily believe she could be happy. Florent, however, settles back to his work and happiness, and on the eve of the wedding day as Thérèse listens to the music he plays at the piano she realises that she is listening to the sounds of a distant world which is barred to people like her. It is not for her to embark on the pilgrimage to the Isle of Cytherea. She instinctively knows that the secret of happiness is denied her by destiny.

For his next *pièce noire*, *Le Voyageur sans Bagage* (1936), Anouilh took the subject of a soldier who loses his memory in the war (theme dear to Giraudoux) and little by little discovers the horror of his 'forgotten' past. His nature revolts, and in running away from his family he is running away from himself.

*Eurydice* (1941), like Thérèse, is another of Anouilh's heroines. The Greek legend of Orpheus and Eurydice becomes the tale where true love is doomed, where the lovers flee from the impossibility of this world to find happiness and purity in death. Life is the tragedy, death the happy ending. The play opens in the buffet of a French provincial railway station. Orpheus, son of a down-and-out musician (like Thérèse's father, a common and vulgar man, but not a bad soul), meets Eurydice, daughter of a withering actress in a seedy theatrical touring company, and falling in love at first sight, they run away to a cheap hotel in Marseilles. Eurydice, however, cannot escape her past, and when she receives a note from the manager of the touring company, whose mistress she had been, she runs away from Orpheus. The bus she takes crashes and she is killed. A mysterious messenger of Death, Monsieur Henri, offers to lead Orpheus back to Eurydice, according to the legend, provided he promises not to look at her until dawn. When, however, Orpheus meets Eurydice, he must know the truth about why she ran away, and looks into her eyes. Eurydice disappears, and

Orpheus tells M. Henri that he cannot live without her. M. Henri advises Orpheus to meet her in death, forever. The father of Orpheus wakes up and asks where Orpheus is. M. Henri merely whispers "He is with Eurydice — at last."

*Eurydice* is a very typical example of Anouilh's style; it is a symbolic theatre, where the classical parallels are simplified and modified to moral purposes. The language is direct, the sentences short, the words bitter. The characters talk, not like reasonable adults, but like squabbling children. And of course Anouilh's theatre is a nostalgic longing for the lost innocence of childhood — those who have never grown up to lie and cheat. But these children are not masters of their own destiny; they live in a world where the power to find love is impossible. Not knowing who they are or what they are to do, the characters of Anouilh are intended as an approximation to the complete powerlessness of modern man; they stand naked before life, knowing nothing and unable to alter destiny. There only remains for them solitude, violence and refusal.

The *pièces roses* which Anouilh was writing at the same time present a juggling with reality and illusion, a topsy-turvy mélange of fact and fable, plays acted within a play, mistaken identities and what have you, situations in which one is never sure whether or not the whole delicate façade is going to crumble and the masquerade is to be disowned. The *pièces roses* are more than a divertissement, for behind the transparent veil of make-believe, reality is never absent; it is for Anouilh the supreme tragedy and the ironical joke. The influence of Pirandello is very marked in these plays, and via Pirandello, the blend of the serious and fantastic that we find in Jean Giraudoux. In *Léocadia* (1939) the theme is how a poor milliner Amanda tries to take the place of Léocadia, a sophisticated enchantress with whom Prince Albert believes he was desperately in love. She shatters for him the sentimentalised memory of the past by being Amanda living, and not Léocadia, dead.

None of his *pièces roses*, however, comes anywhere near the standard reached in *Antigone* (1942) which is Anouilh's best play to date. Once again Anouilh has been able through Greek drama to discover a heroine who could answer his summons for purity, who would reject compromise, who was born to say 'no'. The Antigone of Anouilh cannot accept any life other than the life she would have chosen to live.

The play, written during the war and produced while Paris was still under the German occupation, was immediately topical, and being overtly political, was capable of interpretation by either side as a justification for acceptance or rebellion. Anouilh, of course, was very much on the side of Antigone, but he stated the other case persuasively enough for the play to cause a controversy and even to be branded as a Nazi play.

The problems which Anouilh had raised in his previous works are concentrated here in two characters: Creon, who stands for order, tradition, observance of the law; and Antigone, who believes in opposition and in doing what she thinks right. For Antigone the only happiness that is possible is total happiness; for Creon happiness is purely relative. Both are in exactly the same *angoisse*, only they do not see their way out in the same fashion. Antigone, with her passion for purity, cannot accept reality. You cannot both accept the world such as it is and retain your ideal. She belongs to her solitude, and must die for herself. She does not even know why she must die. That vague word 'freedom'.

The Greek values of the play are cast aside and the doubts of the contemporary world substituted. Antigone sees in the modern compromise of Creon only false values. Nevertheless the arguments Creon uses are so convincing that he almost persuades Antigone to save herself. He uses the common-sense approach, so reasonable that the obstinacy of Antigone would seem ridiculous to most modern men. Yet we know that Antigone is right even if few of us would have the courage to reject such a reasonable argument. Moreover, Creon also knows that she is right, for she has belief, whereas he believes in nothing. And to live for nothing is the modern tragedy.

Somehow the plays since *Antigone* have not retained the same urgency and purity. As they have become more professionally 'slick' they have tended to create a picture which no longer rings true. It is easy to wallow in the sordid, to say life is very ugly, but how tired we get of hearing these endless repetitions of exaggerated ugliness. There is always, it is true, escape, but the highly successful *L'Invitation au Château* proves little except that Anouilh is a clever entertainer who can at any time turn his gloomier thoughts rose coloured and write a play which merely marks time.

In *Ardèle* (1948) we find the anger of youthful idealism and revolt has given way to middle-age frustration, collapse and hatred. Nathalie has accepted life, she has accepted Maxime, although she really loved his younger brother Nicolas. *Ardèle* is not a tragedy of lost innocence, it is a bitter, ironical tirade against lust, in which even the youngster Toto, aged ten, and his cousin Marie-Christine, the Countess's daughter of the same age, have been corrupted and imitate the behaviour of the adults. As for perfect love, we are invited to believe in its realisation in two hunchbacks who end by committing suicide. The whole play is ferocious to the point of explosion, a strange concoction of farce and pathos, the former intended to shock you into the latter. Along that road Anouilh can go no further. Already he is middle-aged in thought, and his romanticism of youth has been finally forgotten.

How different is *Colombe* (1950) from Thérèse! Colombe the flower girl only wants to be happy and make others happy. Julien, the 'pure' character in the play, brings Colombe to see his mother, a famous actress with whom he is not on speaking terms, because he wishes his wife to be looked after while he does his military service. His mother takes Colombe into her company and gives her a small part. Soon Colombe is surrounded by admirers, and after preserving her honour for a while, is eventually seduced by Paul, Julien's brother. Julien returns and after learning the truth asks for an explanation. Colombe replies:

> Oh, how difficult everything is with you! I have to think six times before I dare open my mouth, and to me it all seems so simple. Everyone's kind and doing their best; and all I ask of life is . . . a little happiness . . . just happiness.

Thus purity has capitulated; no longer do the characters revolt, nor do they any longer hold our sympathy enabling us to share their thoughts and actions. Julien is as caricatured in his simple honesty, Colombe in her innocence (which leads her to compromise) as are the intentional caricatures, the cynical Paul or the hysterical Madame Alexandra. It may be every character was intentionally made repulsive; at any rate we have here the savage cynicism of middle age replacing the youthful refusal of *La Sauvage*.

*La Valse des Toréadors* (1951) explores further the history of General Saint-Pé, who was a character in *Ardèle*. As well as the general's wife, whom the general does not love, we meet an aging lady, Ghislaine de Sainte-Euverte. The general has been in love with Ghislaine since the time in his youth when they waltzed together at the Saumur Cavalry School ball. That was the only time the general had ever known the meaning of love and discovered he had a soul; yet the relationship was purely platonic. The play becomes a tragic study of this true love, but the style is of course in the bitter farce according to the later

Anouilh style. We have the spectacle of both Ghislaine and the general's
wife trying to commit suicide at the same time. Then there are the
general's two impossibly ugly daughters trying to flirt with the
general's secretary. In the end Ghislaine goes off with the secretary,
who turns out to be the general's son (he was a foundling) and the
general resigns himself to stay with his mad wife and make love as
opportunity presents itself to the new maid in order that he may be a
"little less lonely in the darkness of the world". There is a strong suggestion in the play that man can preserve his soul in spite of everything,
and the play ends on a note of resignation. This acceptance through
remorse is a far cry from the *pièces noires*.

Anouilh's portrait of Joan of Arc, *L'Alouette* ("The Lark" in the
translation by Christopher Fry, seen in London), has been both
enthusiastically praised (M. Jacques Lemarchand in *Le Figaro Littéraire* compared it to the *Cyrano de Bergerac* of the half century) while
other French critics have dismissed it as a pot boiler. It might be
suggested that the play is effective theatre, but falls a good way short
of being a masterpiece, or even "better than Shaw".

The opening of the play recalls the mood of *Antigone*, a bare stage,
with neutral décor, benches, a footstool for Joan, a throne, bundles of
sticks . . . one by one the characters saunter on to the stage, then Joan.
Finally Warwick, a debonair young Englishman, enters with Cauchon,
the judge. The whole introduction is reminiscent of *Antigone* while
the opening words of Warwick have the startling directness of
Anouilh's style:

> Are we all here? Good. Then let's start the trial without delay.
> The quicker she's tried and burnt, the better it will be for
> everyone.

Cauchon restrains his exuberance; there is a whole story to enact, the
whole of Joan's short life. And so we are introduced to the various
episodes in the history of Joan of Arc; her father who does not believe
in voices, but believes it's the soldiers his healthy teen-age daughter
wishes to go with, and he corrects her with a good healthy beating.
Then there are the stages when Joan flatters and outwits captains and
persuades them to let her ride to see the Dauphin. The famous scene
follows when Joan recognises the Dauphin in his disguise. Perhaps
even more remarkable is the way she addresses the Dauphin, 'dearing'
him with the French 'tu' and convincing him both of his duty to rule

and to appoint her head of the army. Thus we reach the end of the first half of the play, which in book form goes directly into the second part without a break.

Anouilh's conception of Joan is the most French of all the studies made of her — that of a French peasant girl. He is not interested in the 'miracle'. For him, the mystery of Joan is largely explained because the social, political and military situations were ripe. If it had not been Joan, it would have been someone else. To use his own words in the programme introduction of the Paris production, there were candidates before and after her. Anouilh is careful, however, not to offend the Catholic canonisation of Joan. He stresses that "Joan is a saint who died in a political episode; God did not necessarily take sides against Henry VI of Lancaster". No other play about Joan has been so concerned with national characters. Joan is the epitome of the simple, honest, French country girl. Her mother and father are to be found all over France to-day; practical, hard-working, thrifty people. Warwick is the caricature of an English 'gentleman', not given to logical thinking but insisting on the practical necessity of his actions. The policy of His Majesty's Government demands that Joan should be burnt. Later on in the play he tells Joan that it is stupid for her to be burnt (the argument of Creon in *Antigone*). For the policy of His Majesty's Government, solemn renunciation is exactly the same thing. Joan refuses. Warwick continues:

> A useless suffering. Something ugly. No really, it wouldn't have done. It would even have been, as I said, a little vulgar and belonging to the mob, stupid to suffer a lingering death in order to be seen by everyone and cry defiance on the pyre.

Joan protests mildly that she is of the mob and foolish. Warwick then shrugs his shoulders and complains: "How sordid this all is. And vulgar. Of course you never can have dealing with these French."

Apart from this scene, the second half of the play is a long-winded and bitter disappointment after a more than promising beginning. Only in the very end does Anouilh again stir the audience by at the last minute saving Joan from the stake, since the story of Joan of Arc is a joyous occasion. And as far as His Majesty's Government are concerned, Warwick declares that Joan is already burnt and its political objective achieved.

The play is more than competent, but considerably below the standard that Anouilh might have reached had he written another

*Antigone.* There are delightful episodes in it, but somehow it lacks a driving force. This is expecially noticeable in reading, since the play was so beautifully acted by Madame Suzanne Flon in its original Paris production, and Dorothy Tutin also succeeded in the rôle in London.

*L'Alouette,* together with *Becket, ou l'Honneur de Dieu* (1958) and *La Foire d'Empoigne* (1960) may be considered in the category of *Pièces Costumes,* under which title they have been published. *Becket* is Anouilh's version of the confrontation between Henry and the archbishop. There is an ambiguity in his study of the archbishop, for Becket is clearly not spiritually apart; he is no saint until his murder made him one. As a result in this study of the love-hate relationship between the two men the king, straightforward and jovial in character, but quick in temper, is the more sympathetically drawn. The play opens with Henry kneeling naked in penitence in front of Becket's tomb; as he speaks Becket appears from behind a pillar as on the day of his murder, and reminds Henry to pray instead of chattering. The king replies he doesn't feel like praying, but circumstances require him to make this peace. "You have to pay the price — and you taught me that, Thomas Becket, when you still advised me . . . You taught me everything . . ." The king starts to dream of the past, and there is a flash-back to the time when Becket was the king's loyal friend and adviser. No one was more dedicated to the service of the king; when at Henry's request Becket becomes archbishop the loyalty is transferred to the Church, and Henry feels his friend has deserted him. Thus in a fit of rage the historical martyrdom takes place and in Henry's penitence the honour of God is saved, and the Saxon subjects acclaim in front of the cathedral the king at the same time as Saint Thomas à Becket.

*La Foire d'Empoigne,* the third historical play, concerns Napoleon's Hundred Days. Though there are interesting studies of a vain Napoleon and a kindly understanding Louis XVIII, the work may be passed over as a failure. Simultaneously with writing these *Pièces Costumes* Anouilh was continuing his *pièces roses.* In *Cécile, ou l'Ecole des Pères* (1954) everything is as false as false can be, especially the ending, when Aramithe, Cécile's young and attractive governess, accepts the proposal of Cécile's father. Gone for the moment are Anouilh's obsessions (a passing reminder of poverty is quickly dismissed); they return however in *Ornifle* (1955), his "comedy-portrait" of a present-day Don Juan. After various episodes have emphasised Ornifle's debauchery a young man arrives on the scene clothed in black. This figure of death is Ornifle's son who has come to take vengeance on his father for abandoning his mother — he pulls out his revolver and fires. Although the revolver has been emptied by Marguerite, his fiancée, Ornifle, collapses with a heart attack. The play was badly received by the French critics; M. Gabriel Marcel remarked that it meandered beyond the borders of vaudeville into a kind of no-man's land where plays which lack credulity and style belong.

The revolver with a blank cartridge also plays an important role in *Pauvre Bitos* (*Poor Bitos*, 1956) when Bitos, dressed up to play the part of Robespierre at a dinner party given by a group of society people, is fired at as a joke; in the dream sequences which follow Bitos becomes Robespierre. Bitos was the boring little scholarship boy who won all the prizes; his old school fellows are determined to have their revenge on "beastly Bitos" because as deputy public prosecutor he sentenced to death for war-time collaboration a school friend. What is more he afterwards bought a very expensive doll for the daughter of the man he had executed. So Bitos has been invited to a wig party to play the part of Robespierre — because he acts as if he were Robespierre. When Bitos turns up he has mistaken the wig party for a fancy dress one; alone he is wearing the full costume and from the start lays himself open to merciless ridicule. The parallel between Bitos and Robespierre is made clear when Bitos faints after the mock shooting and dreams he is Robespierre, linked with the injustices of his own life. When he comes round they decide to make him drunk but before they can complete their ultimate ridicule, Bitos is forced by Victoire, the girl who refused to marry him, to stop playing their game. "The only thing I could have loved about you," she tells him, "was your poverty. But like all precious things, poverty is very fragile. Keep yours intact, Monsieur Bitos." Bitos thus becomes the Anouilh hero, replacing the heroine. Whether we have any more sympathy for Anouilh's public prosecutor rather than say that of Dürrenmatt is another question. In *Pauvre Bitos* all the main characters seem grotesque and despicable. The satire is too savage, but as we expect of Anouilh, the craftsmanship of a play within a play is admirable.

In *L'Hurluberlu* (1959) Anouilh mirrors the feelings of the last days of the Fourth Republic. Here we have another engaging portrait of an inimitable Anouilh general, prematurely and we gather unwittingly retired, who devotes his energies in helping overthrow the republic in a spirit of reforming zeal. There is no shortage of targets in either the Fourth or Fifth Republics and failing everything, there is always the army. The range also includes Ionesco and Beckett, as well as the aristocracy. As the play develops personal issues become more important. The general's young wife is bored, and his inability to understand her point of view drives his eldest daughter from the house. Gradually the family disintegrates, the revolutionaries also desert him until he is left with only his small son Toto. *L'Hurluberlu* is hardly one of Anouilh's best plays, but through it, as the critic of *L'Express* remarked, Anouilh was destined to be a kind of "Molière of President Coty".

"Excuse the mistakes of the author, ladies and gentlemen, but this is the play I was never able to write," Anouilh makes himself exclaim as the curtain line of *La Grotte* (The Cavern, 1961). We recognise the cavern of Pirandello's imagination; here the stock characters from the repertoire of Anouilh's theatre are assembled. Anouilh inspects them as on parade and finds them restless; soon they are out of control escaping into parodies of the boulevard theatre or the crime thriller, because he himself does not know what he wants of them. From the stylised naturalism of Henri Becque they seem ready to enact a melodrama like *l'Arlésienne*. Frantically Anouilh intercedes "I have a horror of that kind of theatre. They're trying to shame me in front of the whole of Paris. I don't care, I just won't sign the playbill."

Right at the outset of the play Anouilh acknowledges his debt to Pirandello: "I can hear a critic whispering to his neighbour that he has already seen this in Pirandello. Well, you'll notice it isn't exactly the same and besides that just goes to show that he also had trouble play-writing — I mean Pirandello." In *La Grotte* Anouilh's characters endeavour to elude him, rather than accept their author. It is the characters rather than the contrived plot we have to follow; as we have come to recognise in Anouilh's universe, people are divided into the haves and the have-nots. We have a plot of master and servants in a Paris 1900 atmosphere; there is the handsome count, the cook who is murdered, the old butler who wanders through many of Anouilh's plays. The author's own comment on the theme is that it is a story which "never should have happened. I can't believe that life is as ugly as that. There are all the same decent people everywhere. It's my duty to say it and write plays where people are decent and kind."

Like Pirandello, Anouilh finds himself increasingly placing reality and illusion in juxtaposition, he is drawn towards a kind of Green Room between the form of theatre and the absurdity of life. Instead of interviewing his characters, his characters in *Cher Antoine ou l'Amour Raté* (1969) and *Les Poissons Rouges ou mon Père, ce héros* (1970) seem to be interviewing him. These plays followed a period when Anouilh worked closely with a group of actors as a director; when he returns to playwrighting we feel a sadness that he has not been able to keep up himself with the experiments of the avant-garde theatre he admires (he was one of the first to defend Ionesco's *Les Chaises* in *Le Figaro*). In the character of the boulevard playwright Antoine de St. Flour, Anouilh seems to find his ventriloquist for his cynical assessment of a successful playwright. The idea of *Cher Antoine* is as Antoine himself explains it in the play:

> A man has just died, without having lived particularly well, or given or received much either; anyway, perhaps through his own fault, love and friendship seem to have passed him by. The day of his funeral, all those connected with his life gather after his burial for the traditional meal—these are country customs, so let's say he died in the country. They draw up the reckoning, of him and of them. That's all. But it will be fairly funny.

Between the play within the play and his own life, we feel somewhere Anouilh's own illusions pass him by, not quite autobiographically. Just as in *Les Poissons Rouges* we seem to hear through the voice of "Sourface" his childhood friend, that of his inner conscience, the "there but for the grace of God go I" self-criticism. Even in *Ne Reveillez-pas Madame* (1970) the "Prompter" reflects how we pass our lives filled with our ineptitudes, without sticking to the text, and ending up one day or another with "curtain".

Anouilh cannot accept that he is a success, and is well aware he continues to "distract and entertain" the boulevard public for whom he has such contempt. The debate is not whether his prolific output, together with brilliant craftsmanship and a magician's wizardry of touch will assure his position as France's foremost contemporary playwright, but whether, in his very success, the purity of his vision, like that of his heroines, will become permanently tarnished by the box office. We feel Anouilh knows this, forsees his own obituaries, and regrets the trends of modern drama have overtaken him. For them he has served as a vaulting horse, he was not able to run their race.

# TWELVE

# BROADWAY CORTEGE—TENNESSEE WILLIAMS AND ARTHUR MILLER

"People in America of course live in all sorts of fashions, because they are foreigners, or unlucky, or depraved, or without ambition; people live like that, but *Americans* live in white detached houses with green shutters. Rigidly, blindly, the dream takes precedence."

MARGARET MEAD, *Male and Female*

THERE are two United States — the legend and the reality (just as there are always two Presidents — the institution and the man). "America" is an idealisation symbolised by the Statue of Liberty; America is a blue print of a nation where many complex questions have still to be solved. The majority of Americans never doubt "the great adventure"; they are, to use M. André Siegfried's phrase, "congenital optimists"; "Never take 'no' for an answer". "The difficult we do at once, the impossible takes a little longer", this is the soul of 'American dynamism', the very spirit of the nation. Everyone is fully geared to 'lick' the system, the childhood hero becomes the man who "started with the clothes on his back and ended up with diamond mines". The American way of life is the acme of civilisation and supersedes all the cultural heritage of the immigrants she absorbs; children of immigrants can say "I am a one hundred per cent. American, born and raised in the greatest country on earth and proud as hell of it." Confidence spirals upwards in relation to the dizzy climb of the trade cycle, only in a major catastrophe such as when the bottom falls out of the market or when their sons do not return home from the war does a different mood take possession, the "what the hell does it all add up to?" despondency. "Do you feel yourself to be spiritually unprepared for the age of exploding atoms? Do you distrust the newspapers? Are you suspicious of governments? Does further progress appear impossible to you?" The voice of doubt momentarily replaces the Voice of "America", the very foundations of the ideal are shaken in the eruption. The transformation of society and individuals "when big wheels crack on this street" is "like the fall of a capital city, the destruction of Carthage, the sack of Rome by the white-eyed giants from the North". The question is whispered "Could it happen to me?" and the echo resounds on all sides "YES". The gap between the heaven of the ideal and the *terra incognita* of reality shatters the illusion of the pioneer's dream. The man who set out to 'lick' the system eventually realises "I'm a dime a dozen, and so are you"; "You were never anything but a hard-working drummer who landed in the ash-can like all the rest of them!"

The above paragraph is an attempt to suggest the American scene as presented in the plays of Tennessee Williams and Arthur Miller, and typical samples of their dialogue have been taken at random to paint the picture. If the mood is a parallel to the European school for pessi mism, it is very different from the philosophical equations we find in existentialist pessimism or the romantic courting of death. We have here a typically American pessimism, the result of a deliberate optimism *manqué*. O'Neill's gloomy pessimism was much more in the European tradition, with Williams and Miller the American playwright becomes 100 per cent. American. If Tennessee Williams looked to Pirandello and Arthur Miller to Ibsen for their masters, they have so absorbed and integrated their teachings into the American way of life that they can now claim an American school in its own right.

It is almost inevitable to link the names of Williams and Miller together, just as in the past one spoke of Ibsen and Björnsen; both have the strongest support from their admirers. Perhaps it is wisest to leave it to time to decide an order of importance as any present assessment is inevitably provisional; born in 1914 and 1916 respectively, they are both actively pursuing their careers. Though they are sensitive inter- preters of the American ethos, their work shows the difference of their own personalities and their artistic approach. Tennessee Williams is the poet who delights in language and symbolism and exotic imagery; Arthur Miller is the prose writer in the tradition of the social purpose plays of Ibsen, a psychological playwright with a strong moral com- mitment. Williams is a Southerner while Miller was born in New York City. While writing their early works, both tried various odd

G

jobs and Williams roamed extensively in America and Mexico. Shortly before the war the Group Theatre awarded Williams a cash prize for four of his one-act plays entitled *American Blues*, which were concerned with the American depression. Miller saved to go to college, and within four years of studying play-writing at the University of Michigan he had won three drama prizes. In 1936 he wrote *The Grass Still Grows*, which won the Theatre Guild National Award. In 1938 he joined the Federal Theatre Project. He was rejected by the army on medical grounds and for a year worked as a fitter in Brooklyn Navy Yard. He was then asked to do a film script on army training, which became *The Story of G.I. Joe.*

In 1940 Williams was awarded a Rockefeller Foundation Fellowship and a 1,000 dollar grant for work in drama by the American Academy and National Institute of Arts and Letters. One of Williams's early plays received professional production, *The Battle of Angels*, but was abandoned on the road in Boston and never reached Broadway (In 1957 Williams rewrote *The Battle of Angels* under the title *Orpheus Descending*, which this time proved a success in London, New York and Paris). Miller's first play to reach Broadway *The Man Who Had All the Luck* ran for a week in 1944. In 1945 Williams finally achieved success with the production of *The Glass Menagerie*, and nearly two years later, in January 1947, Miller established his reputation with *All My Sons*, which won the New York Drama Critics' Circle Award. At the end of 1947 Williams gained his second outstanding success with *A Streetcar named Desire*, and in 1949 Miller achieved an equal triumph with *Death of a Salesman*. The names of both were firmly established; a new era in the American theatre was opened.

The next few years saw Williams actively turning out *Summer and Smoke* (1948), *The Rose Tattoo* (1951) and *Camino Real* (1953), but it was not until *Cat on a Hot Tin Roof* (1955) that Williams repeated the success of *Streetcar* or *The Glass Menagerie*. The shadow of Senator McCarthy affected inevitably the social consciousness of Miller, and his next play *The Crucible* (1953) is an outspoken condemnation of all forms of witch-hunting and mass hysteria, the parallel between the trials at Salem in 1692 and what was taking place in the States of the early Fifties being made convincingly apparent. Only to-day can we recognise the play as being an important one relevant not only to the unhappy period when it was produced. Between Miller's two short plays *A View from the Bridge* and *A Memory of Two Mondays*, produced in a double bill in 1955, and *After the Fall* nine years' elapsed;

In 1956 Miller had been summoned to appear before the Committee of Un-American Activities, where he refused to turn informer and name people he had seen at Communist Writers' meetings ten years previously; during these years Miller had married and divorced Marilyn Monroe, and in 1962 came the news of Marilyn Monroe's suicide. During these years Miller claims to have been writing more than at any other period in his life, but that "I couldn't formulate what I wanted to say satisfactorily." With *After the Fall, Incident at Vichy* (1964) and *The Price* (1968) Miller may be said to advance his claims as a moral playwright.

The theatre of Williams since *Sweet Bird of Youth* (1959), including *Period of Adjustment* (1960), *Night of the Iguana* (1961) and *The Milk Train Doesn't Stop Here Any More* (1963) shows a speeding up of his own theatrical conflict between tenderness and brutality and the irreconcilibilities of the society in which we live and search for an understanding; does not the iguana, tied up and fattened for the killing, represent the grotesque symbol of humanity? We pull this way and that, will no one cut us free so that we can escape and submit to the laws of the jungle and the survival of the fittest?

These very laws seem to have ensnarled Williams's imagination into a dramatic cul-de-sac. His frenzied desperation becomes a prelude to his own breakdown. *Slapstick Tragedy* (1966), *The Seven Descents of Myrtle* (1968), and *In the Bar of a Tokyo Hotel* (1969) mark, play by play, his decline. Since he came out of hospital Williams has revised his *Two-Character Play*, which was produced in England in 1967. The two characters are a brother and sister, Felice and Claire, and the setting is an empty theatre in a place which could be the North Pole.

Perhaps it is Williams's turn not to be able to formulate what he wants to say. Be that as it may, Williams and Miller, in their contrasting styles, have given us the American folk tragedy of our times. It is as if the society in which they live whips them into indignation, and their plays have a primitive driving force which is concomitant to life where materialism is master. In the plays of Williams the spiritual is rejected and nothing remains but animal motivations, the instinctive blind groping to follow the system and to take what life offers before the realisation of futility. The price we pay for Williams, the Southerner born in Columbus, Mississippi, is "desperation"; for Miller, with his adolescent memories of the great depression pursuing him like the Furies, there is a moral price to pay. You can do what you like provided you succeed, and if you fail, your worst enemy is yourself. The very possibility of victory makes tragedy possible, but Miller is closer to Ibsen with a Brooklyn accent than say O'Neill's return to the sources.

The broken image of Pirandello's theatre, the illusion so carefully nursed and brutally destroyed, the unfortunate victim unable to face the consequences of truth, this is the dramatic situation which Tennessee Williams evokes throughout his work. Often the image is broken through the use of a symbol, which expresses directly the author's intent. "We all have in our conscious and unconscious minds a great vocabulary of images," Tennessee Williams has written, "and I think all human communication is based on these images as are our dreams; and a symbol in a play has only one legitimate purpose, which is to say a thing more directly and simply and beautifully than it could be said in words." So in his first success, *The Glass Menagerie*, Williams has shown how a cripple girl, Laura, nurses the illusion of her own fragile childhood through a collection of little glass animals, one of which is different from the others by having a horn. When this horn is broken, she sees the symbol as her chance to live an ordinary life.

The idea of a woman coming to terms with life, and shattering the image which is no longer possible in the disintegration of society and the death of the old aristocracy, is the theme of *A Streetcar named Desire* and is also developed in *Summer and Smoke*. In *Streetcar* Stella and Blanche du Bois are from an old Southern family which has fallen on hard times. Stella has secured her future by marrying a great beast of a man, passionate and uncouth, who eats "more like an animal" than a human, and acts with primitive possessiveness of her. Stella has reconciled herself to being his slave because she has found sexual satisfaction. Blanche, on the other hand, has seen the decay of her aristocratic upbringing and has had a disastrous tragedy in her first experience of sex; she has fallen to prostitution and drink, but clings desperately to her shaken respectability and the possibility of leading a normal life and finding a decent husband. At her sister's house she nearly finds her salvation, but her sister's husband, who recognises her for what she is, brings about her final mental collapse and madness. The character of Blanche is complex; although a fallen woman she has never lost traces of the gentility of her upbringing and her need for kindness and — to quote the final words in the play as she is carted off to a mental home — "the goodness of strangers". She seeks protection from the harsh and revealing light of reality (admirably symbolised by her desire to hang Chinese lampshades round naked bulbs), but not even her sister can protect her from the inhumanity of strangers.

The play asks to be considered as a tragedy, but it is a tragedy of a heroine who has fallen from the start. We are all responsible for Blanche and detest a society which has not given her a chance to save herself, and spiritual values are lacking for any other kind of redemption. It is a tragedy of society, not of an individual.

In *Summer and Smoke* Tennessee Williams seems to return to the theme of *The Glass Menagerie*, the longing of a young woman to lead a normal life, and this time, a normal sex life. The play reveals the failure of Alma to find satisfaction of both sex and spiritual values in the man she loves. Her lover is as frightened of her soul as she is of his body; he could not feel "decent enough" to touch her. Since she cannot find true love, she destroys her spiritual quest and gives herself to the first travelling salesman she meets.

His next play, *The Rose Tattoo*, is a disappointment and seems more to provide effective theatrical tricks than reveal genuine drama out of a very Pirandellian plot. Nor can *Camino Real*, Williams's most ambitious play be described as other than a worth-while failure. The play baffled its audiences during its short run and numerous people at each performance stamped out and demanded their money back at the box-office. Those in favour of the play claimed that the audience refused to go half-way to meet a highly original and different type of play. It seems in my view that *Camino Real* is an exciting idea, but that in the play Williams has given us no more than a bare scenario, which could be made into a cycle of plays. In its present form the play has a crudity of harsh and strident paints which may well be the intention, but it is achieved at a sacrifice of characterisation. *Camino Real* must be judged in its total effect; it is not immediately communicative and the symbols do confuse instead of illuminating and simplifying the author's signposts.

Camino Real is presented to us as a town square or *plaza* surrounded by an ancient wall beyond which lies a desert called Terra Incognita. This desert is the only way of escape, and it is a way which requires the courage which so few possess. In the square itself on the left lies the luxury side of the street, containing the fashionable Siete Mares Hotel; opposite the hotel is Skid Row, which contains the Gipsy's gaudy stall, the Loan Shark's establishment, and a 'flea-bag' hotel, "Ritz Men Only". To the right there are a pair of arches which give entrance to the Dead End streets. Camino Real is a port through which travellers pass. Our first travellers are none other than Don Quixote and Sancho Panza. Sancho reads in his chart that at Camino Real he should halt, and turn back, "for the spring of humanity has gone dry in this place". Sancho decides to turn back leaving Quixote to his dreams. We then meet all kinds of travellers from all nations; some stay at the luxury hotel and others in "Ritz Men Only" but the price they pay for both is that of frustration. They are robbed of their money and their papers; they seek an escape, but they have not the courage. The mysterious plane, the Fugitive, arrives, but we know it will crash. And meanwhile the Street-cleaners eliminate all those who are on their lists with the horrific Belsen extermination thoroughness:

> Now do you want to know what is done to a body from which the soul has departed on the Camino Real! — its disposition depends on what the Street-cleaners happen to find in its pockets. If its pockets are empty . . . the 'stiff' is wheeled straight off to the Laboratory. And there the individual becomes an undistinguished member of a collectivist stage. His chemical components are separated and poured into vats containing the corresponding elements of countless others. If any of his vital organs or parts are at all unique in size or structure, they're placed on exhibition in bottles containing a very foul-smelling solution called formaldehyde. There is a charge of admission to this museum The proceeds go to the maintenance of the military police.

Such is Camino Real. Man here has become a guinea-pig, and when he protests, he is reminded that "we are all of us guinea-pigs in the laboratory of God". "I don't make it out," exclaims our bewildered man. "Who does?" replies the Gipsy, "The Camino Real is a funny paper read backwards!"

As can be seen from the idea, this is more a synopsis for an imaginative *mise en scène* and it is a play of silhouettes and atmosphere. Pessimism of course predominates, but there is a way out across the desert which the young American traveller Kilroy decides to explore, accompanied by Don Quixote. *Camino Real* is the rendezvous of man's inhumanity to man, but courage to face the unknown way is what matters.

What are we to make of *Cat on a Hot Tin Roof* (1955)? It has been observed by critics that Williams uses the fourth wall as a mirror, and that this expressionistic treatment is often in bold contrast to the realism of the script so as to shock an audience into attention. The mirror in *Cat on a Hot Tin Roof* reflects the most bitter, cruel, sensual of Williams's interpretations: a play of emotions where again all repressions are swept aside, and what remains is the stark animal ferocity of an individual's loneliness, his inability to face responsibilities he owes not only to others, but to himself. Here is a tragedy which is denied a tragic ending; here are characters whose experiences we suffer but whose sympathies we can never share.

Maggie loves her husband Brick, but her relationship with him becomes increasingly like that of a cat on a hot tin roof. Brick seems to live in a dream world (through the bottle) in an attempt to recapture the memory of his college days when he was a success as a football player. It is only since the death of his college mate Skipper that Brick has taken to drink, and it is more than hinted that this may have been due to homosexual relations, which would also explain why he and Maggie cannot live as husband and wife. It is, however, important for them to have a child, for Brick's father is dying from cancer (a fact that the father does not know) and Brick's brother and wife, who have four children, are scheming to get control of the estate for themselves. When the accusations are let loose truths are revealed, and as a climax Maggie tries to save the situation by saying she is pregnant. The play ends with Brick accepting the challenge to make good her lie.

The plot, however, is not important; it is merely the skeleton which signposts Williams's universe. It is a world of harsh, strident colours, where normality is non-existent, and where abnormality is the essential means of the discovery of oneself. In *Orpheus Descending* (1957) Williams returned to a play he wrote in 1940, *The Battle of Angels*. In a preface to his new version he describes how he spent a summer with a clarinet player who eventually became moody and suddenly disappeared. That was in 1939, and over the years Williams has brooded on this theme. "A play is never an old one" he comments "until you quit working on it and I have never quit working on this one, not even now." It is interesting that *Orpheus Descending* should contain the quintessence of all Williams's other work, his merits and his failings. Set in the decadent South, in a small town where passions smoulder and corruption is rampant, Orpheus is a guitar player who was once corrupted and would free himself, like an Anouilh hero, from the stains. He believes that by refusing all commitments and entanglements he has shaken himself free, but he has forgotten that he is a man and underrated those forces of desire which will overpower him. He successfully keeps at bay the advances of a nymphomaniac, but surrenders to the lonely passionate storekeeper herself trapped into a marriage with an elderly sadist who with other members of the Ku-Klux-Klan burnt out her father. Her husband has not escaped his punishment, he is dying from cancer. So she watches him in his agony, dreaming of her revenge and all the things she will do. She clings desperately to the guitarist for the love she has been deprived of and for the children she wishes to bear. Meanwhile the guitarist has not avoided other human contacts. A kindly but unwise gesture to the sheriff's wife, a religious fanatic, alerts the lynch mob who warn him not to remain overnight in the town. But he stays for the sake of the "lady". The husband in his last breath shoots his wife and accuses the guitarist of murder. It is too late, the dogs are howling for his blood. As he is thrown to them all that he leaves behind is his serpent-skin jacket, which the nymphomaniac keeps as a souvenir. Nobody wants the guitar.

In spite of some powerful scenes the play is far too long for sustained melodrama, the characters too exaggerated for tragedy. We breath a claustrophobic atmosphere of romanticism, we are obsessed with a puritanical frenzy where there is no forgiveness for those transgressors more sinned against than sinning.

*Garden District* (1958) consists of two one act plays, a curtain raiser *Something Unspoken* where a wealthy Southern spinster sits beside the telephone concerned only with her small world of club politics, and *Suddenly Last Summer,* a nightmare of hypnotic power. Here again the theme is sexual maladjustment in a luxuriant mansion in New Orleans with

> . . . a fantastic garden more like a tropical jungle, or forest, in the prehistoric age of giant fern-forests when living creatures had flippers turning to limbs and scales to skin. The colours of this jungle-garden are violent, especially since it is steaming with heat after rain. There are massive tree-flowers that suggest organs of a body, torn out, still glistening with undried blood; there are harsh cries and sibilant hissings and thrashing sounds in the garden as if it were inhabited by beasts, serpents and birds, all of savage nature.

We are in for shock treatment. A mother with an obsession for her dead son, who was taken from her in his last summer by a girl who witnessed his death. She has described his terrifying death and will tell the story once again, face to face with the mother and a doctor, who has been ordered to operate and remove it from her mind. Under the influence of a drug she describes how they were dining in a restaurant on one of "those white blazing days in Cabeza de Lobo" surrounded by beggar boys banging on jagged tin cans, until in trying to escape he was pursued by them up a hill. When she arrived with waiters and the police at the spot where he had disappeared they found him lying naked and devoured. The featherless little black sparrows had

> . . . torn or cut parts of him away with their hands or knives or maybe those jagged tin cans they made music with, they had torn bits of him away and stuffed them into those gobbling fierce little empty black mouths of theirs.

The doctor is not so sure that this can be removed from her mind, for the play ends on his words "I think we ought at least to consider the possibility that the girl's story could be true."

The hero of *Sweet Bird of Youth* (1959) is a blond gigolo called Chance Wayne. He returns to a small town in the Deep South where as a youth he had had a sweetheart called Heavenly, daughter of the political boss Finley who had chased him out. He hopes he is returning in different circumstances, under the wing of an ageing beauty queen who is approaching middle age with the help of hashish and other drugs. Chance sees in her merely a hope of gaining a foothold in the movies—she has just made a film which proves to be the means of her come-back at the end of the play—and the possibility of pursuing the stage career of a Don Juan. His return is rather different from what he had imagined, for as a result of his infecting her with veneral disease Heavenly has had her sexual organs removed. Chance falls into the hands of Finley's henchmen and takes his punishment of castration.

*Period of Adjustment* (1960) comes almost as a respite to these themes of physical mutilation. Sub-titled "High Point over a Cavern" Williams describes this as "a serious Comedy"; it has in fact the ingredients of a Frederick Lonsdale farce of the twenties except that all the characters are neurotic. The time is Christmas Eve, the place a "cute" Spanish type suburban bungalow in Memphis, Tennessee. Ralph Bates is restless for adventure and has just chucked his job, a tailor-made one provided by his father-in-law. As a result his wife has left him, and her Christmas present, a fur coat, remains unclaimed under the tree, together with their son's toys. Ralph was once a hero of the Korean war. Almost to remind him of the days when he was his true self, a friend who served with him, George Haverstick, arrives with his bride Isabel. Or rather Isabel arrives, and for the first act we are not sure whether or not George has dumped her on Ralph, following a disastrous wedding night spent in some motel. George finally arrives, also without a job and in search of adventure; he suggests to Ralph that they should buy a ranch and breed Texas longhorns for T.V. Westerns. In the midst of their reunion Ralph's mother-in-law arrives to claim her daughter's possessions — nearly everything in the bungalow, it included, are hers. The daughter however makes a final attempt at reconciliation, especially when she sees the fur coat Ralph had intended to give her. In the end both couples are prepared to talk things over and recognise their parallel situation; as George says: "They're going through a period of adjustment, just like us." The play ends on a sentimental note, as if Williams were writing a Christmas charade.

*The Night of the Iguana* (1961) in contrast, is back again in a luxuriant exotic setting (this time Mexico), with the overpowering elemental forces of sea and sun beating down on the lust and outraged hypocrisy of the puritan conscience — the psychiatric no-mans'-land of Tennessee Williams. The Reverend Shannon, a defrocked minister reduced to conducting a Blake's Tour party of eleven spinster schoolteachers from a Baptist College, together with a teenaged Lolita in their charge, on a tour of Mexico, arrives at a very Bohemian hotel on the Costa Verde. He is at the end of his tether, having made a pass at the girl. Miss Fellowes, a member of the party, is determined to issue a charge the moment they return to the States. In desperation Shannon seeks refuge at this hotel owned by a friend, an "affable and rapaciously lusty" widow, Maxine Faulk. Unfortunately this is not the hotel laid on by Blake's Tours in their prospectus, and Shannon has forced the bus to a halt by taking possession of the distributor cap. Among the guests at the pension are a party of noisy beer-drinking Germans celebrating the Nazi victories — the year is 1940 — which contrasts with the mood of the Tour party, led by Miss Fellowes, who are unable to have any enjoyment at all. Another arrival at the hotel is a strange enigmatic girl, Hannah, together with her grandfather Nonno, who at 97 is the oldest working poet.   Nonno has had a stroke and is in a wheel-chair; for many years he has been struggling to complete his final poem. Hannah is unmarried, she has a romantic conception of love without ever having found it. She devotes her life to her grandfather, travelling from hotel to hotel while he recites his verse and she does sketches and watercolours of the guests. By the time they reach the Costa Verde they are destitute, and Nonno is still struggling to finish his poem before death overtakes him.

Here are characters each in their way trapped like the iguana which the Mexican boys have caught and tied up under the verandah. Like the iguana they are trying to scramble away, but having reached the end of the rope they cannot get any further. Does Hannah, Shannon asks her, have any life of her own? Shannon slashes the rope and the iguana runs free; Nonno immediately after completes his poem, recites it, and dies. Hannah is then free herself; only Shannon's future is bound by the dictates of Widow Faulk.

*The Night of the Iguana* is a play which has many of the obsessive symbolic echoes of his previous works where the characters are lost in a claustrophobic labyrinth of maladjustment; the hypnotic character of "Cissie" Goforth in *The Milk Train Doesn't Stop Here Anymore* (1963) is also lost in her superficial memories of social success and the four husbands she has escorted to the grave, to return alone "with the loot of three of them". Like Dürrenmatt's Clara Zachanassian of *The Visit,* Mrs. Goforth also believes in the absolute power of wealth to corrupt absolutely, and yet it is beyond her power to buy what she needs most in life, time. Her extravagant flashy costumes cannot conceal the fact that she is a living corpse, her deadline in writing her memoirs is not that of a publisher, but death. Chris, the Angel of Death, arrives, "the opposite appearance to what is ordinarily encountered in poets . . . his appearance is rough and weathered . . . he has the look of a powerful, battered but still undefeated, fighter." Mrs. Goforth can brag of her love affairs, but it is too late for a last infatuation. Ten years previously Mrs. Goforth had invited Chris to stay, but invitations, like passports, expire. "Now it's my turn to go forth," she tells him, "you counted on touching my heart because you'd heard I was dying, and old people are your speciality, your vocation. But you miscalculated with this one. This milk train doesn't stop here any more."

Tennessee Williams has introduced a pair of stage assistants as a prologue and epilogue, who "function in a way that's between the Kabuki theatre of Japan and the chorus of the Greek theatre." He explains that his reason is to remove the play from conventional form since the play should be regarded as an allegory and as a "sophisticated fairy-tale."

We notice that in each of these plays the symbols become more strident until his work achieves a direct secular crucifixion. The characters move in a world where symbolic identification lets loose his hysterical frenzied hari-kari which seems to cultivate sensationalism easier than the warmth of understanding, or as Williams has admitted, "I prefer tenderness, but brutality seems to make better copy."

*

The work of Arthur Miller is committed in the fullest sense to a twentieth century tragedy, the tragedy of the common man. His plays are best considered in two sections, the first include *All My Sons, Death of a Salesman, The Crucible,* together with his two short works, *A View from the Bridge* and *A Memory of Two Mondays;* the second group moves us to the soul-searching subjectivity of *After the Fall, Incident at Vichy* and *The Price.* A gap of nine years separates the two groups, and we seem to have turned from the tragedy of the common man themes to the nightmare of an intellectual guilt complex and a moralistic confrontation of responsibility.

It is as if Arthur Miller himself was unsatisfied with the sufficiency of an undeveloped and complex free mind. Starting from the belief that the common man was "as apt a subject for tragedy in its highest sense as kings were" Arthur Miller admitted that his character Willy Loman in *Death of a Salesman* "lacks sufficient insight into this situation, which would have made him a greater, more significant figure". The question is not whether we are writing about 'kings' or 'ordinary' men, but 'ordinary' and 'exceptional' men, or if you prefer 'ordinary exceptional men'. It is very doubtful whether pure tragedy does not require an extraordinary mind to enable us to realise the true perspective of tragedy. The tragic situation tends to elude those whose horizons are limited, bourgeois and narrow-minded.

*Death of a Salesman* is nevertheless a very remarkable play, and if we don't make the claim for it to be a tragedy, we can safely claim that it is a most interesting psychoanalytic study of an ordinary man. Though the whole impression of the play is of stark realism and the dialogue is purely colloquial, it is conceived as a dream play, and characters and sequences overlap in the style of a carefully thought-out cinema montage. Willy Loman, the salesman, is caught up in the system he tried to 'lick'; he is a failure as a salesman and as a father. The two are related, for his elder son had found Willy out while he was still at school — the God-like mask had fallen from Willy's face when his son discovered him being unfaithful to his mother. Willy's own failure is all the more bitter to him because of the memory of Ben, his elder brother, who at seventeen walked into the jungle, and came out at the age of twenty-one, and he was rich! Willy, on the other hand, never a successful salesman at the height of his career, has been burdened by debts, paying a twenty-five-year mortgage for his house, for his refrigerator, his car, all the 'necessities' of the system — at the cost of his own life. The day arrives when he can face the world no longer, when no one knows him and even his old firm refuse to employ him. He suddenly grasps the futility of his own life. Meanwhile his elder son has been a wanderer (like Ben) and his younger son is also a salesman who has probably the same fate in store for him at the end of his life as has Willy now. Eventually, nagged on by the vision of his elder brother Ben (who we are told is dead), he decides to join him in the adventure in the jungle "which is dark, but full of diamonds", and from which one never returns.

The searching pyschological study of a character was not attempted by Miller in his next play, *The Crucible,* which is a kind of modern parable. Arthur Miller has explained that in this play he was not attempting "to give people a sense of reality in depth" as in *Death of a Salesman,* but to write a play where "the characters were special people who could give voice to the things which were inside them". *The Crucible* is about organised terror, where theme not character is all-important, and where in fact his characters are more inclined to become spokesmen for his plot. Thus, whereas the characters do not come before us as individuals but as martyrs for the author's moral purpose and sense of justice, the play admirably succeeds in its intensely dramatic exposition of theme and the forcefulness of its writing. The message of the play, a timely reminder of the historical facts of the Salem witch trials, carried out with so much bigotry and zealous intolerance and blindness, comes across without turning the stage into a pulpit, for the historical facts themselves have dramatic unity. It is interesting to remember also that twenty years after the executions, the government recognised that a miscarriage of justice had been done and gave compensation to the victims still alive. Thus the defeat of an ideal was turned into a moral victory. What is to be admired most in the play is the sweep of Miller's convictions, the power of his faith and the urgency of the subject matter. The play has survived the era of the McCarthy witch hunts which presented a parallel, and written with passion and sincerity, takes its place as Miller's most important play to date.

In *A View from the Bridge* (1955) Arthur Miller returns to his theme of tragedy and the common man. *A View from the Bridge* is the second of two plays which he links with this general title, the first play, *A Memory of Two Mondays*, setting a sombre mood in anticipation of the second which, in its Broadway production, proved the main event of the evening. Set in Red Hook, on the bay seaward from Brooklyn Bridge, *A View from the Bridge* shows the reaction of longshoreman Eddie Carbone to the arrival of two Italian immigrants (and illegal immigrants) to his house. Eddie has unconsciously grown to adore his first wife's seventeen-year-old neice Catherine, and when she takes an interest in Rodolpho, one of the immigrants, he determines to stop this by fair means or foul. He tries to show Catherine that Rodolpho is effeminate, that he is only wanting to marry her so that he can become an American citizen and regularise his illegal entry. When Eddie finds he cannot shake her even by humiliating Rodolpho in front of her, he denounces Rodolpho and his companion Marco to the immigration authorities. Marco in turn denounces Eddie to his neighbours, and it is against Marco that Eddie draws a knife and is killed in the ensuing fight. Such a rough sketch of the action gives little justice to the subjective complexity of the theme. For here again Miller has attempted a tragic canvas in terms of the man in the street; it was to be his last in this vein. A long silence followed, which suggests that this no longer satisfied as material the need for self-expression which was increasingly tormenting Miller. He was also becoming aware of the difficulty in orienting himself in form; the structure he liked best was the Greek— "as condensed and short as it can get"— and yet he was drawn more to the exploration of Shakespearian technique, "the juxtapositions of people with no transitions."

This conflict is apparent in the shape of *After the Fall*, which followed after a nine year's interval. I think that had Miller resolved his technical dilemmas he would have been better able to come to terms with his theme, which is none other than a semi-autobiographical trial of his conscience. *After the Fall* is Miller's most personal play; he identifies himself with his character Quentin, a successful New York lawyer who having reached his forties, looks back in guilt on his failings as a human being. The play thus takes place "in the mind, thoughts, and memory of Quentin"; in studied outbursts the flashing images of objective reality come crowding into the conscience of subjective truth. A parallel is drawn to Miller's own life, for Quentin had also taken part in some of the activities of the Communist Party, while in Maggie and in her suicide, written as Miller stresses, "with respect for her agony but with love" we cannot help but link her with the name and memory of Marilyn Monroe. Charges of bad taste were hurled at Miller when the play was first presented, yet it is difficult to reason why a playwright should not write out of his own experiences of life, even to the extent of autobiography, as for example O'Neill has done without similar outbursts of ill humour. What matters is that the work itself should be judged as a work of art; in *After the Fall* Miller is perhaps less concerned with art than treating the audience as his psychoanalyst.

The tragedy of Maggie is developed in the second half of the play, after she has already entered Quentin's life as his previous marriage was dissolving. Maggie is a pop singer who does not know how to live with her success or even attach herself to life. Maggie exemplifies — as Miller wrote of her in *Life Magazine*, "the self destructiveness which finally comes when one views oneself as pure victim . . . of parents, of a Puritanical sexual code and of her exploitation as an entertainer." She has become shrewish because of the way of the world which treats her as a sex symbol. She is in fact an innocent seeking salvation and hoping to find her master on Quentin; Quentin cannot save her as he is not innocent. He remains detached from her, incapable at the end of a little love; in her suicide he has to accept the responsibility that he has failed her absolutely.

*After the Fall* is like a meandering nightmare where we are asked to share the guilt of Miller's conscience and to judge the play less as an artistic unity than as the sum total of his purifying experiences. The first half of the play, which, although it does not highlight the character of Maggie, is neverthless the more dramatic, introduces us to the prigishness of Quentin's behaviour. There is the clumsy way he breaks the news to his ailing father of his mother's death; the relief he felt at the suicide of his friend Lou, who was facing an investigation by the Committee of Un-American Activities, and which now will no longer be necessary. There is a play somewhere in these many *crises de conscience* but as it is written the dialogue, or rather the monologue of Quentin's mind, offers more the staccato outpouring of extra-dramatic identification and therapy. There is some hope that Quentin will discover himself with the maturity of the German woman who may become his third wife, and that through Holga, herself a survivor of the horrors of the camps, he will at last share the hounding of the Furies of guilt and responsibility. *After the Fall* may eventually be

seen as a necessary failure to rid Miller of his obsessions before continuing his further essays in the theatre. And just as Quentin in a
moment of guilt consciousness left for Germany and visited Belsen
although he "didn't get the connection" at the moment, so Miller,
following the production of *After the Fall* at Lincoln Center, went
himself to Germany and attended the Nazi trials in Frankfurt.

*Incident at Vichy* comes indirectly as a result of this journey.
Apparently based on fact, Miller has set his play in Vichy in 1942, at
a time when the Nazis were all over Europe rounding up people in
the streets who then mysteriously disappeared and were never heard of
again. On this particular day ten people are so arrested and wait their
turn for interrogation; one of them is Von Berg, an Austrian Prince
who we know will certainly be released. But he gives his pass to a Jew
and accept the fate in store. Miller has identified himself with that of a
Jewish psychoanalyst doctor, Le Duc, who eventually accepts the card
because he is certain of his right to live, and that he is better for the
world than any of the others. We are not told how the doctor will
justify his life, nor do we know what happens to the Austrian prince
who accepts the guilt of the German people in his act of self-sacrifice
— it could be that he still believes he has influential friends in high
commands who will save his life. Of the other people arrested, there is
a Communist electrician, an artist, an actor, a waiter, a gypsy and an
old Jew who never says anything and is already resigned to his fate. It
is the Communist electrician who first discloses the possible reason for
the arrests, in telling how the previous day a trainload of Jews from
Toulouse passed through the zone on its way to an extermination camp
in Poland. The actor cannot believe that the Germans could have such
little respect for art, and that as an actor who plays the lead in Cyrano
he will be given special treatment, until Von Berg warns him of the fate
of his own musicians in Vienna. The detainees sit on the benches
waiting for the interrogation and discuss almost academically their
fate; only Le Duc rebels against their passivity, their unwillingness to
face facts and act before it is too late. The main dialogue is between Le
Duc and the Prince, for between them there is common ground of
agreement. With the German Major such common ground does not
exist and therefore they are unable to share the feeling of guilt. The
moral of the play, however, is not concerned only with the guilt of the
Nazis, but extends to all of us (one of those arrested was a gypsy and
not a Jew); in the words of Le Duc: "I want not your guilt, but your
responsibility." There is no denying the theatrical effectiveness of the

situation nor the stark simplicity of the structure, and yet having said this the play makes a less important statement than *The Crucible*.

The stream of ethical consciousness is again evident in *The Price*. Two brothers, Vic and Walter, meet after 16 years. Walter has become an eminent surgeon who has just built a new hospital; Vic has remained a policeman as he had to forgo his studies, although he was academically the more brilliant, in order to keep his father left destitute after his bankruptcy in the depression. Vic can never forgive the ruthless way Walter completed his medical studies, and when a successful doctor, still only sent home five dollars a month. Vic is too honest to suck up to people to achieve promotion and yet resents his own failure; he is almost ready through his wife Esther's insistent pushing, to phone his brother and ask him for a better paid job; unfortunately his brother's refusal to speak to him on the phone is the final blow to his pride. He decides to go ahead and sell the family furniture; the entry of Gregory Salomon, a larger than life figure, is Miller's happiest creation. Salomon brings with him the restless dynamism of the immigrant which in spite of his 90 years, contrasts with the "play-safe" behaviour of Vic. Salomon will offer his "price", what would seem a low one, though an honest one, but he has something much more to offer: humanity. When Walter arrives unexpectedly he is convinced that his brother is being taken for a ride by this beguiling old man. Walter, who is highly intelligent, immediately suggests a tax dodge whereby the furniture, with an overpriced valuation, could be given by him to charity. Walter is not presented unsympathetically; just as we feel Vic's resentment, Walter does not hide his fear, the need he feels to have a brother and a family (his own marriage has failed). Walter claims that their father was never destitute and that he invested 4,000 dollars for him. Walter fails in bringing about their reconciliation and Vic refuses to work with him. The furniture is sold and Salomon philosophically remarks that you only realise your luck at the last moment.

In the character of Vic Miller represents the dilemma of the "common man", more tragic in his inability to come to terms with himself than assume the dimensions of tragedy. There is a strong Ibsenite influence in Miller's recent work, concerned with the moral problems of the human condition. But if the Vikings discovered America it was the Pilgrim Fathers who settled there.

# THE LIMITS OF DESPAIR

LIFE is full of decoys, exterior artifices, which hide the relentless forces of existence. Fame, fortune, success, fleeting moments of happiness, the zest for youth and love, they alter nothing in the moment of our sadness, of our realisation we are alone. We communicate with others, in words, deeds and actions, but that changes nothing; faced with the ultimate truth we have only our solitude. We are already separated from the world, we can abandon ourselves to pessimism, but is not this because we fear the unknown, the truth? God does not show himself, we can no longer wait for Him.

The plays of Samuel Beckett lead us directly into this no-man's-land, where despair becomes one long interminable sentence which leads from sanity to madness because no human mind can support the condition of the human fate. Language becomes a means to try and make sense, but it is no use. The characters are no longer human, they are like puppets. They have already shed their qualities as human beings and passed on. There is no conflict, passion, emotion; we are out of space and time. There is no freedom of movement, comings and goings, there is no return, and looking forward, there is the meaningless emptiness of nothingness. It is the last ritual without absolution, the last memories of a life which is over, the chuckle of irony and the howl of anguish at the sudden realisation of nihilism.

Is this theatre or beyond theatre? *En Attendant Godot* was first produced at the Theatre de Babylone, Paris, in 1952, and in the previous editions of this book will be found my original critcism after seeing the Roger Blin production. Time now requires a reassessment of Beckett's influence following his international acclaim, although I remain firmly in the opposition camp. My case remains that Beckett, with the dark Irish side of irony and negation, evoked a morbid one-sided monologue which is like the contemporary cult of neurosis and despair, and which ends up by taking us beyond the boundaries of theatre where a ritual orgy of jabbering is the sum total of life. If Nietzsche asserted that God is dead, Godot died at the creation of the world, and failed to give it meaning. We have no longer a life-size view of the world, but an incomplete world because it is inhabited by puppets rather than people with minds—and here is the difference. You cannot try puppets because they have no minds; you cannot try man because as an English judge once said, "the human mind is not triable". And that is why Beckett's plays do not rise to the level of tragedy; they may be anti-theatre tragedy, but that is a different thing.

# THIRTEEN

# THE CASE AGAINST BECKETT

"In the Kingdom of the Father there is no drama but only
dialogue, which is disguised monologue."

RUDOLPH KASSNER

THE true face of pessimism is as different from its cult as
tragedy is from *grand guignol*. The great pessimists in literature
are the great revealers, their vision is personal, creative, and for
all time; they are not victims to the contemporary and transient
influences of the *mal de siècle*, the stimulant of so much of our instant
despairers. In the tradition of tragedy there is a profound and classic
understanding of humanity from the minds of the Greeks to that of
Pirandello; the anguished appeal "call no man happy until he be dead"
comes from an involvement and experience with life. It is not symbolic,
abstract, specialised, coldly intellectual, unsolved like a moronic riddle
as seem the aims of anti-theatre — the very word seems to take us
beyond the possibilities of theatre into a form which is not dramatic.
The present century may have given us little enough to hope for with
two world wars, cruelty beyond imagination—even Kafka's nightmares
have frequently become normality. And yet this is "man's inhumanity to man", human nature will only abandon itself to an orgy of
despair because of an incomplete view of life. The purely negative
approach is one which like Gresham's law, tends to drive out the
genuine.

We have seen how contemporary dramatists have led us to the approaches of despair within the framework of the dramatic tradition. With
Beckett we go beyond into a land unmapped by Dante, for here is
neither Paradise nor hell, nor purgatory; it is a void, out of space and
time, beyond feeling, communication, explanation, even revelation,

where the characters seem withered like atomic dust, in the infinity of nihilism. Beckett can weep like Alexander, for here there is nothing to conquer except the forlorn melancholy of a demented Irish soul with its grotesque flash of an eternal present. We are beyond both theatre and art, everything is meaningless. This is the *ultima thule* of the space age.

★

Samuel Beckett was born in Dublin in 1906. After studying at Trinity College he taught English at the l'Ecole Normale Supérieure in Paris in 1928, and became the friend and disciple of Joyce. He started writing in French novels such as *Murphy* (1947) and *Molloy* and *Malone meurt* (1951) but it was incontestably the production of his play *En Attendant Godot* at the Theatre de Babylone in 1953 which proved him the most controversial figure in the modern theatre; you were for or against — no one could pretend indifference. *En Attendant Godot* unites the existentialist refusal, the search for and despair of religious salvation with the merciless accusation of farce. With this play and its sequel *Fin de Partie* ("Endgame", 1957) he gave expression to a flood of misery which is both inspired by and epitomises the logical conclusion of the search for pessimism. Beckett may be said to have incorporated all the features of the void which confronts man in his present compromise with the world. For just as man cannot live by bread alone, he now realises that he cannot live by mere thinking or hanging on in vain to a thread of salvation which does not seem to exist. We have had many plays where a mysterious Stranger, always spelt with a capital "S", arrives, leaving no doubt as to the implication of his rôle; *En attendant Godot* is about the Stranger, the mysterious "Monsieur Godot" who never arrives and who never will arrive because nothing happens in the play at all; no one comes or goes; all is just nothing.

It is a searing penetration of pessimism. George Steiner, in his *The Death of Tragedy* has noted that Beckett is attempting "with a kind of queer Irish logic" to "bar from the stage all forms of mobility and natural communication between characters and yet produce a play". Steiner finds the result "crippled and monotonous. At best, we get a metaphysical guignol; a puppet show made momentarily fascinating or monstrous by the fact that the puppets insist on behaving as if they were alive." We may describe *En attendant Godot* as a grand guignol of despair, where man is reduced to the reactions of a puppet, where the world is left behind.

*En attendant Godot* combines many styles into a single mood; it has elements of circus and pantomime, philosophical musings and attempts at existentialist suicides (which is doomed to failure). We meet on some strange no-man's land two down and outs, Vladimir and Estragon. Their conversation leads them nowhere, nothing happens, their minds and their bodies remain numb as they wait, every night, for the Stranger. Here is a typical excerpt from the dialogue:

ESTRAGON    Let's go.
VLADIMIR    We can't.
ESTRAGON    Why?
VLADIMIR    We're waiting for Godot.
ESTRAGON    Ah! (*a moment's reflection*). You're sure it was here?
VLADIMIR    What?
ESTRAGON    That we were to wait.
VLADIMIR    He said by the tree (*he looks at the tree*). Do you see any others?
ESTRAGON    What is it?
VLADIMIR    I don't know. A willow.
ESTRAGON    Where are the leaves?
VLADIMIR    It must be dead.

And so on, and so on, page after page, until we meet two further characters, two strangers as mysterious as the mythical M. Godot himself. The following stage directions explain their appearance:

Enter Pozzo and Lucky. The former directs the latter with the help of a cord fastened round his neck, so that we only see Lucky first trailing a cord long enough for him to reach the centre of the stage before Pozzo emerges from the wings. Lucky carries a heavy suitcase, a folding chair, a basket full of food and an overcoat (on his arm); Pozzo carries a whip.
Pozzo (in the wings): Quicker! (crack of his whip. Pozzo appears. They cross the stage. Lucky passes in front of Vladimir and Estragon and goes away. Pozzo, on seeing Vladimir and Estragon, stops. The cord tightens. Pozzo draws it in violently). Back! (noise of falling. It's Lucky who falls with all his load. Vladimir and Estragon look at him, torn between the desire to go to his rescue and the fear to get involved with something which doesn't concern them. Vladimir makes a step towards Lucky, but Estragon draws him back by the arm.)

We have here plenty of symbolistic food for thought, and more is to come. Clearly Pozzo is not Godot, and on learning their mistake Vladimir and Estragon deny even knowing Monsieur Godot.

The play cannot be described satisfactorily or even read; its impact can only be felt in the theatre. Lucky, with his long hair flowing over a ghostly white face, his elongated figure, his thin chop-sticks of legs, stands burdened under his load without ever placing his suitcase and other objects to rest. He merely stands dumb and shakes rhythmically while Pozzo cracks his whip or eats a chicken. He is completely the slave, responding to orders from Pozzo to dance and think. This is his chance, words flow out of his mouth in a non-stop jabber; three and a half pages are filled without a punctuation or even half a dozen words of continuous meaning; doubtless the unrelated words and phrases are meant to convey deep meaning, but it overwhelms an audience as it does eventually the characters, who throw themselves on Lucky to put an end to his thinking.

The only other character in the play is a young boy who arrives with a message from Godot saying that Godot will not come that evening, but to-morrow "for certain". There is, however, something strange about this boy, who makes two appearances and yet denies, on the second, that he had ever been to see Vladimir and Estragon before. The play ends as it began, with the two beggars waiting in vain for Godot. The dialogue continues on its doleful repetitive course, the 'nothingness' of everything becomes insistent. There is nothing left for them but to try and hang themselves — but alas, we know that they cannot even succeed in doing that:

ESTRAGON  You haven't got a bit of rope?
VLADIMIR  No.
ESTRAGON  Then we can't.
VLADIMIR  Let's go.
ESTRAGON  Wait, here's my belt.
VLADIMIR  It's too short.

They finally make one last attempt at hanging themselves with the cord from Estragon's trousers, but it breaks. Eventually Estragon says:

ESTRAGON  I can't go on like this.
VLADIMIR  That's what you think.
ESTRAGON  If we parted that might be better for us.
VLADIMIR  We'll hang ourselves to-morrow (*pause*). Unless Godot comes.

ESTRAGON    And if he comes?
VLADIMIR    We'll be saved.

VLADIMIR    Well? Shall we go?
ESTRAGON    Yes, let's go. (*They don't move*).

## CURTAIN

What more is required in the way of comment? One should add in fairness that *En attendant Godot* comes across to an audience in its full pessimism, and the very avidity of its subject matter offers remarkable scope for actors and an imaginative *mise en scène*.

*En attendant Godot* was written in 1947-48 and produced on the narrow stage of the Left-Bank Theatre Babylone, Paris, on January 5th, 1953. In 1956 by way of a post-script Beckett wrote *Fin de Partie*, first produced in French at the Royal Court Theatre, London on April 1st, 1957. In this one-act moan of uncompromising gloom we are again immersed in a pessimism beyond all limits of suffering, life and art. We are like flat-earthers falling into space. We cannot save ourselves, and no one else will. We share the Beat philosopher's credo that "the existentialist cat dug like that the positive answer of nothingness, in the face of nothingness, is positivism — we dig that the positive answer of nothingness, to nothingness, is nothingness — Man, isn't that farther out?" The four characters are like outcasts, untouchables, in a dying world. Already as if in a coma they are beyond hypnotizing us with their misery. They are all cripples, Hamm cannot rise from his chair, Clov cannot sit down, while the other two, Nag and Nell, cannot rise out of the dustbins that imprison them. Here is the cruel imagery of suffering humanity, as one French critic observed, like in the nightmare world of Bosch and Breughel. Listen to their dialogue:

HAMM:    Nature's forgotten us.
CLOV:    There is no more nature.
HAMM:    . . . But we breath, we age, we lose our hair, our teeth, our youth and ideals.
CLOV:    Then she's not forgotten us.

or, as Nell says from her dustbin, "Why this play-acting every day?" Time has lost all meaning, it is the time it usually is. Hamm takes a tranquilizer in the evening and a stimulant in the morning, other characters are living by tears. "What's Nagg doing?" — answer: "He's crying." "Then he's alive." No more words, no more pity.

We are far beyond the frontiers of theatre, of what can hold an audience by its dramatic intensity, as *Godot* did. Perhaps Beckett may indulge in his pessimistic orgies better in the novel where he can address a reader individually rather than in the theatre where all depends on collectivity. *Krapp's Last Tape,* a monologue written in English, proved the more bearable part of the English production of *Fin de Partie* ("Endgame"). Here Krapp, racked with disease, almost blind, grey tousled hair sweeping over a ghostlike face, his beard badly shaven, recalls on his tape recorder the moment of intimacy he had, or believes he had, over thirty years ago, with another individual. The idiosyncratic Beckettian moan has also a tape-like resonance in his Third Programme play *Embers* (1959), where an old man on a sea shore relives his tormented past.

Beckett's characters are isolated from life, terrified in their isolation. His language is also one of isolation, and in his choice of French Beckett finds the language of his own separation from his native Ireland. In a short radio play, *All that Fall,* one of Beckett's characters says: "I use none but the simplest words, I hope, and yet I sometimes find my way of speaking very — bizarre." The language of Beckett has a purity, a simplicity, a style which is a dimension away. The language we hear is like our own echoes, but echoes resounding from the abyss of the infinite.

*Happy Days* (1961) continues the monologue with death; this time Beckett introduces a virtuoso feminine rôle. Winnie is "about fifty, well preserved; blonde for preference, plump, arms and shoulders bare . . ." In the first act she is buried up to her bosom, in the second up to her neck, so that she can no longer turn her head, but only move her eyes. Behind her, hidden by a mound, is her husband, Willie, about sixty. He is capable of crawling on all fours, but his presence is more a wall for Winnie's monologue; Willie's contribution is mainly monosyllabic grunts — he is allowed a total of fifty words throughout the entire play. Winnie is concerned with living — "Another heavenly day" is her opening remark; "Oh, this *is* a happy day, this will have been another happy day! . . . after all . . . so far." her concluding ones. Her chatter is an endless flow; the loss of her limbs do not prevent her recalling the happy days of the past. At the end of the play Willie on all fours tries to make a superhuman effort to climb the mound, dressed in "top hat, mourning coat, striped trousers, with gloves in hand . . ."; even Winnie herself wants to know if he is really after her . . . but in any case he fails to make it.

*Happy Days* is literally a static play, and makes great demands on the audience forced to focus throughout on the head of Winnie; it is up to the imagination to fill in the background to the words, but this surely is more material for sound radio or the printed word. It does not come over effectively in the theatre, neither in the production I saw with Madeleine Renaud and Jean-Louis Barrault, nor that at the Royal Court Theatre, London.

Beckett's contribution to drama, even to those like myself who are not admirers of his work, has been to extend the frontiers of theatre; but anti-theatre itself cannot, like great plays of the past, come across at different levels. In an age where more and more people are going to the theatre, Beckett paradoxically is for the few. His plays have the ring of unfinished sentences and words; in this no-man's-land we are beyond the unities and disciplines of art. His plays are like his anti-novels, it is the vocabulary which matters, and, as V. S. Pritchett has asked in the *New Statesman* (2 April 1960), does language become "a gabble-gabble ritual to make tolerable the meaningless of life?"

In 1969 Beckett was awarded the Nobel Prize for Literature for his works in general. In so far as Beckett reflects the spirit of an age, Beckett was their inevitable laureat. Here is the anti-hero of our times, where man's destiny seems none other than the eternal present of labyrinthine monologues leading nowhere, as meaningless as an introspective hurdy-gurdy. In the two decades since Godot was first presented, an alienated society has identified with this defrocked romantic, believing, as the critic of *Time* magazine wrote about a recent revival off-Broadway, "that man's journey through life is a pointless shuttle from nowhere to nowhere. When that view of man alters," he adds "the vogue for Beckett will end." In the meantime we should remember the story of Father William of Lewis Carrol, who when his son asks if he thinks it is right at his age to stand incessantly on his head, replies that "in my youth I feared it might injure my brain; but now that I'm perfectly sure I have none, Why I do it again and again." Has man lost, not only God, but his power of reasoning?

# FOURTEEN

# ANTI-THEATRE: EUGÈNE IONESCO; JEAN GENET; ARTHUR ADAMOV

"And what a romp they had! The bath-room was drenched with their splashings. Of such is the kingdom of Heaven."
ALDOUS HUXLEY, *Point Counter Point.*

EUGÈNE IONESCO has created a theatre full of adventure, paradox, parables, burlesque, surrealism, monodrame and scenic naturalism. All things are possible, reality is ourselves home in the evening, alone in our room, with the same dreams and nightmares as others, the same fear of death. "Like a naked body on a beach" Ionesco has written, "astonished at being there, astonished at his astonishment, beside an infinite ocean, alone under the penetrating sun, inconceivably and irrefutably there." So Ionesco marvels at his own journey through life, from his birth in Roumania in 1912, a childhood in Paris, an adolescence in Bucharest and a return to France where he has lived since 1938. His greatest surprise in life must have been to find himself a playwright with, in 1959, three plays running simultaneously in Paris and an international success.

For many years Ionesco remained a convinced enemy of the theatre. He could not reconcile its so-called tricks, its exaggerated world and the one in which he lived. In 1949 he wrote his first anti-play, *La Cantatrice chauve* ("The Bald Prima Donna") a parody making fun of other plays. Originally entitled *English Without Tears* he found the material for the first scene out of a French-English phrase book. It was not until the production of *La Cantatrice chauve* that Ionesco saw the theatre in a new light and recognised his mistake: the weakness of exaggeration became the theatre's strength, it was in fact essential to "exaggerate still further, stress and accentuate as far as possible, to push the theatre beyond the intermediate zone which is neither theatre nor literature, to its natural limits". From his discovery he was able to turn to the problems of technique with a fresh mind, free from the usual worries whether he should write in a naturalistic or anti-naturalistic style. He would write for the theatre, pure theatre, he would try and communicate "an incommunicable reality", but nevertheless a reality which can now and again — and that's its paradox, be communicated. For him the theatre becomes a confession of his inner mind. He writes with no axe to grind. "I try to say how the world appears to me" Ionesco affirms "as sincerely as possible . . . I try to be the objective witness of my subjectivity. When writing for the theatre I am only concerned with personifying, in a tragic and at the same time comic sense, reality. That shouldn't prove a difficult problem . . . trying to be *avant-garde* before writing, not wanting to be, or refusing or choosing which kind of *avant-garde* it is to be, is, for someone creative, going about things the wrong way."

In the same way it is not the duty of a playwright to give any kind of message (like Sam Goldwyn he would remind us to try Western Union) or to offer to save the world in any form. A playwright must content himself with being a witness, reflecting from his own sufferings, and from those of others, or perhaps — which is rare — his or their happiness. This statement on the rôle of a dramatist was made by Ionesco in reply to the famous *Observer* controversy of 1958, when Kenneth Tynan, who had been one of the most ardent critics to introduce Ionesco into Britain, suddenly had his doubts. Tynan feared that Ionesco had wandered off "the main road", and while his theatre was interesting and exciting it remained a marginal *divertissement*. His world was one of "solitary robots", an escapism, whereas a playwright is inevitably committed to reality, in his view social reality. Social reality, Ionesco retorted, was the most superficial kind, which had made Sartre (for political melodramas), Osborne, Miller and Brecht merely the "new authors of the boulevard" conforming to prescribed left-wing doctrines as sorry as any of those on the right. This reply, like his remark that Brecht was merely a "theatre of boy scouts" created enemies among those who might have been his friends. But as a playwright Ionesco is determined not to encourage any cult or faction, but to be judged on his own merits.

How far do the plays come up to Ionesco's intentions? Much has been said about their hovering between the sublime and the ridiculous, and no doubt there are complaints that *The Bald Prima Donna* is not about an opera singer. In fact no prima donnas enter at all to share the long English evening with the Smiths, and their guests, the Martins, or to listen to the irregular and nervous chimes of the clock with its expression of unutterable boredom. Everything is a reality turned upside down, even the discovery of the Martins that they are after all husband and wife "comme c'est curieux et quelle coincidence!" It is true that many of the mannerisms are French rather than English, English people seldom complain about draughts in the way the French do, even if it is for something to say. The final summing up on Ionesco's first play is that it is an amusing enough joke at the expense of the theatre, but hardly to be taken seriously. And yet out of this *reductio ad absurdum* a style emerges which sets the framework for his future plays.

Tynan's *divertissement* certainly applies to *La Cantatrice chauve* as to his next play *The Lesson*, where a professor proceeds to the murder of his fortieth pupil, a young girl who loses her enthusiasm and falls back on such excuses (real or invented) as toothache, while the professor changes from a mood of false gentleness to intolerance.

In *The Chairs* Ionesco first attracted more serious attention. It was produced in 1952, a few months before Beckett's *En Attendant Godot* (produced January 5th, 1953), yet already Ionesco has surpassed Beckett in imagination, though close to him in the expression of "nihilism". An old couple in their nineties live in a tower surrounded by water. Before his death the old man wishes to leave his legacy to posterity, and he and his wife invite a large number of friends and important personalities to hear his lecture. The guests arrive, invisible to us, but made real by the conversation of the elderly couple, who pile up more and more chairs in the tower. Everybody has arrived, generals, the emperor himself, and finally the orator whom the old man, fearing emotion might overcome him, has asked to deliver his message for him. But as the old man and his wife disappear out of the window to their tragedy, the orator turns out to be deaf and dumb and can only speak gibberish. *The Chairs* will remain Ionesco's *chef d'oeuvre*, and a minor masterpiece in twentieth century drama.

Six years later in 1958 Ionesco wrote another theological nightmare, *Tueur sans gages*, his second full length play. Like Kafka's *The Castle* the play opens with the arrival of the hero, Béranger, at a strange place without knowing how he has arrived. Béranger is an ordinary citizen anxious to help others; he finds himself in a model *cité radieuse*, magnificently designed with fine buildings, broad avenues lined with trees and gardens full of flowers. It is the lost paradise, and the architect is obviously meant to represent the almighty architect of the world. The city, however, is almost deserted, because a mysterious killer is roaming the streets. Béranger cannot accept the fatal indifference of the authorities, the architect is taken up with the problems of creation, the police with regulating the traffic; so he takes it upon himself to rid the city of this menace. In the second act he discovers documentary proof as to the identity of the killer, but on the way to the authorities, the architect, the chief of police, he finds himself alone on the broad highway, he has lost the evidence and is face to face with the killer. His only hope is to argue the case of humanity, but neither flattery, promises, concessions, or threats are of any avail. The killer is unmoved by pity, vanity, words. To each he replies with a cynical chuckle. Giraudoux would have won his argument for life, Ionesco loses it. After a glimpse of a spoilt paradise we are again in despair.

*Rhinocéros* (1958) presents another leap in the imagination, to a world where the inhabitants change from being human to become rhinoceroses. Again Béranger, who is himself suffering from the symptoms which have turned others into rhinoceroses, pleads the case for humanity. From the logical beginning of "how can human beings change their form into that of rhinoceroses" we are shown how easy it is, once a thing has been proved possible, for others to follow the crowd. The leader of the faction who believes it is scientifically impossible, himself becomes one, and even the hero's girl friend joins the others. The individual is like a specimen in the zoo, gazed at by a world run and inhabited by rhinoceroses.

With *Rhinocéros* Ionesco at last achieved an international reputation; henceforth his life was to be spent travelling, attending theatre conferences. There was a queue of theatres wanting to be the first to produce his latest work; Düsseldorf generally achieves this. They produced *Rhinocéros* before Jean-Louis Barrault's production at the *Théatre de France*, and subsequently have been the first on the scene for *Le Piéton de l'Air* ("The Stroller in the Air", 1963) and *La Soif et la Faim* ("Hunger and Thirst", 1964) though they missed out on *Le Roi se Meurt* ("Exit the King"). In this last play King Béranger discovers he is to die and is dispossessed of his possessions like a Job or Everyman; yet the play is no match for the intermittent brilliance of *Rhinocéros*. It seems with these plays Ionesco has taken on a new seriousness in his approach to life; as his approach to theatre changed so now he is no longer playing a kind of hide and seek with life; like George Borrow he would say "Life is good, brother, who would want to die?"

*Le Piéton de l'Air* is a fantasy; once again a Béranger figure appears, this time in the guise of a pioneer astronaut, not exactly of historical authenticity. The setting is in the English countryside of Ionesco's imagination, not exactly the same setting as in his *La Cantratrice Chauve*. The secret of flight is one which reveals an apocalyptical vision of a humanity hovering on the edge of a precipice. In *Le Soif et la Faim* Jean is a pessimist while his wife is an optimist, but these are days when there's more to say if you're a pessimist. After a *rendez-vous manqué* in the second act, a Faust-like character appears in the third and Jean is presented with a Kafkasque solution for his needs.

*Jeux de Massacre* (1970) is concerned not, like *Le Roi se Meurt* with the individual act, but with collective. death. Suggested by Daniel Defoe's classic on the Great Plague of London, here Ionesco stresses not only the absurdity but the reality of living with death, the agonies of watching others die, the ever present menace of contamination, and finally, the certainty that even if you escape the plague you are doomed to another death. The city has no specific identity, and the period suggested is sometime between 1880 and 1920. The play is presented in a series of scenes; we follow the plague's ravages as if it penetrated like an invisible death ray, sparing neither rich nor poor, the healthy or the sick. Its victims increase in geometric progression; the authorities realise it is the plague which has not occurred for centuries. There is no known remedy, they merely bury the dead and forbid public gatherings. The city becomes a prison with no escape, the actual prisoners are themselves free to come out and die, or die in prison. Looting, political riots, famine which drives people to cannibalism are diversions to the frenzied panic caused by the plague. In the final scene the plague disappears as suddenly and mysteriously as it arrived; the survivors go wild with joy until they realise that they have merely escaped death from the plague to be burnt alive in the great fire which consumes the city.

As a full length play *Jeux de Massacre*, in spite of its tragic meditation of the absurdity of death, lacks perhaps the depth and sustaining power of say Dürrenmatt. The ferocity is there, and although the author prefers the play to be without intervals, the piling up of corpses scene after scene does not seem to me to have sufficient variations to give light, shade and ultimately life size tragedy. The characters are abstract puppets rather than individuals. There is again proof that Ionesco can write dialogue, yet this comes into its own in his shorter pieces, even his sketches and charades, which are always delightful. There is his satire on the Baccalauréat scandal in 1964, which made Ionesco reply with a portrait of a Nobel prize winning professor who discovers he never sat his bac and determines to do so. *La Lacune* shows the shame he brings on his wife and family for attempting something beyond his powers, without arranging either to see the papers beforehand or having someone sit the exam for him.

Some will admire Ionesco most for the abstract quality of *The Chairs* or *Jeux de Massacre*, others will regret that for all his brilliance in improvising dialogue he cannot penetrate the human self. If Cocteau is a cat who walks by himself along the "main road", there is more than an element of truth in Tynan's quip that Ionesco is a "solitary robot". However much our civilisation is taken over by Capek's *Rossums Universal Robots*, the challenge of Burns's "A man's a man for a' that" has never been more dramatic or true.

★

### JEAN GENET

Already we are more in the margins of theatre than theatre proper; Jean Genet uses the theatre as his anti-social protest; like the visitors to Madame Irma's bordello, you take your pick; queen, judge, bishop, general, and proceed to turn topsy-turvy the ethics of good and evil. The theatre becomes the great hall of mirrors and illusions, like an orgy of inversion and distortion. Genet's world becomes like that of a ritualistic nightmare, a metaphysical dialogue on the sanctuary of evil.

Jean Genet (born Paris, 1910) was a foundling who was brought up by foster-parents; at the age of ten he was accused of stealing (up till then he had been considered quiet and even "pious"). Whether he had stolen or not, Genet decided that if that was what society expected of him, then he would be a thief. In his *Journal d'un voleur* he repudiated a world which had already repudiated him. His three "trinities of virtue" became theft, treachery and homosexuality; he studied his criminal catechism in a reformatory. In his twenties he delved into the underworld, no crime was uninteresting, but male prostitution attracted him most. His prison life began; his world of pimps, crooks and murderers increased, taking on the dimensions of a new hierarchical society. In 1940, while in Fresnes prison, Genet wrote his first poem "Condamné à Mort" and started his first novel. Seven years later he decided to turn to the theatre. Tired of prose

John Osborne

Max Frisch

Friedrich
Dürrenmatt

narrative he looked for in what he calls in *Notre-Dame des Fleurs* "the logic of the stage". His first play *Haute Surveillance* ("Death Watch", 1947) was a kind of incantantory ritual where it was shown that criminals were mainly concerned with personal relationships. The heirarchy consists of the superman, Snowball, a Negro who has murdered, who "has the right to kill people and even eat them". Snowball is at the top. The three prisoners who share the same cell are not of his grade; Green Eyes has also murdered, but is altogether subservient to Snowball. Lefranc is an ordinary thief and Maurice, aged 17, a mere delinquent. In contrast to Snowball, when Lefranc murders Maurice, the crime is without value because it has been committed to prove that Lefranc can also commit a murder.

Jouvet encouraged Genet to write *Les Bonnes* ("The Maids", 1947) and its critical success came at a vital moment in Genet's ambivalent dual existence. In 1948 Genet had been faced with the prospect of life imprisonment — under French law habitual offenders are eventually firmly locked away — but through the intervention of many leading literary figures, from Mauriac to Sartre, Genet secured a pardon from the French President.

*The Maids* presents two sisters, Claire and Solange, who take it in turn to play the part of their Mistress (who is young and beautiful) when Madame is out. Whoever plays the rôle of Madame exerts her arrogance to the utmost humiliation of the other. When Madame in fact returns they plan to poison her, but she leaves again without drinking the tea in which they had put the poison. The game is continued, only this time Solange insists that Claire hands her the poisoned tea which she drinks, ending the illusion. Genet has explained that he "wanted to bring about a situation where the characters would no longer be anything but a metaphor for what they are supposed to represent". He pleaded with Jouvet for the maids to be male actors, but this would have further complicated the incestuous Lesbianism of the two maids as he had written the parts.

The bringing of "the theatre to the theatre" was continued in *Le Balcon* ("The Balcony", 1953). Madame Irma's brothel is one "of noble dimensions"; here we have the possibility of experiencing our illusions, of indulging in secret perversions. For example, customers can be a bishop forgiving sins, or a sado-masochist judge inflicting punishment on a girl thief. Like a theatrical hire service, all the props are available. While business is as usual, a revolution is taking place outside. The Queen has been assassinated and George, the Chief of Police (who

H

holds the real power) persuades Madame Irma to take on the role of the Queen, and from her palace of illusions find the judges and generals and other members of the Establishment. Thus from playing out their fantasies reality intrudes. The revolution fails, and the Chief of Police is dissatisfied with his image. Finally when a new revolution breaks out Madame Irma returns to her old task as brothel-keeper.

In his notes on *Les Nègres* ("The Blacks", written 1957, produced 1959) Genet remarks that "one evening an actor asked me to write a play for an all black cast. But what exactly is a black?" He wrote a play then for a white audience to be acted by a Negro cast, but he instructs that should the audience be all Negro, then either one white person must attend each performance, or alternatively, the audience should be given white masks. In *The Blacks* the Negroes enact the ritual murder of a white woman before a court of Queen, judge, bishop, general, and valet, all of whom are Negroes, but with white masks. After the ritual murder, the whole court set off to avenge the deed, but are themselves trapped and put to death by the Negroes. Towards the end of the play the audience learn that the ritual they had witnessed paralleled the trial and execution of a Negro off-stage.

There remains *Les Paravents* ("The Screens", 1961) which was a controversial choice for Jean-Louis Barrault's production at the Théâtre de France in 1966. A Chronicle belonging to the literature of the Algerian war, it shows a decline in his dramatic powers which makes but a poor contribution to the anti-colonialist literature on the Algerian war. Genet's theatre remains, as already remarked, outside the mainstream; a combination of ritual and metaphysics, a bizarre twist of the imagination and flashes of lyricism, the theatre is for Genet part of his dream. The problem is that dreams are not under control, their intensity can momentarily shatter our grasp of reality, but reality does intrude. It seems to me that Genet has greater power of abstraction than sustained logic; his world has the momentary horror of a nightmare exposed to daylight.

*

### ARTHUR ADAMOV

The name of Arthur Adamov (1908–1970) is a familiar one in avant-garde circles. He left Russia at the age of four and had lived in Paris since he was 16. His plays may be divided into two, those written before 1956 and those written since. After beginning in the metaphysical anti-theatre he finally rejected it and turned to Epic Theatre, taking up the mantle of Brecht in his search for a revolutionary drama for the people. His early theatre is scant and arid, a theatre of solitude where solitude is recognised *a priori* and not therefore pronounced. In his plays such as *La Parodie, L'Invasion, le Professeur Taranne, Tous contre Tous,* everything seems made bare, including the human soul. Understanding between individuals is from the start impossible. In *La Grande et la Petite Manoeuvre* physical mutilation proceeds scene by scene with moral mutilation. In *L'Invasion* the discord of the mind is reflected in the chaos of the room in which his characters live. *Le Ping-Pong,* by far Adamov's best play, finally has charadters whom we feel exist. It is the story of two men; when we first meet them one is a medical student and the other an art student, who play regularly at a pinball machine in a cafe. The machine fascinates them to the extent that their lives are finally determined by it. These two individuals utterly lose themselves in the machine; they cease to exist without it. They become old men; the one dies leaving the other on his own. There is an overwhelming sense of futility.

Adamov's next work was his transitional play. *Paolo Paoli* (written in 1956 and produced by Roger Planchon's company at Lyon in 1957) is Adamov's introduction to the Epic Theatre tradition of Brecht. *Paolo Paoli* embraces a cause, the same one as *Mother Courage.* Set in the period before the first world war, Paolo Paoli is a butterfly dealer who has a German-born wife. Paolo prospers by the manufacture of gadgets made from butterfly wings, and this trade, like the pinball machines of *Le Ping-Pong,* becomes the replacement of man; only business matters, the trade it involves, money; leading to the ultimate disaster of power politics and world war. The play does not impress as much as *Le Ping-Pong.* It is best to pass over and forget his epic *Le Printemps '71* (Spring '71), which deals with the Paris Commune; a rambling disaster, where the artistic — no longer metaphysical — becomes overtly committed and politically banal.
artistic—no longer metaphysical—becomes overtly committed and politically banal.

★

Various names are proposed as disciples of anti-theatre. Georges Schéhade was born in 1910 in Alexandria of a Lebanese family, and now lives in Beyrouth. His best-known play *Histoire de Vasco,* which Jean-Louis Barrault produced in 1957, provoked a lively controversy at the time; it has since been translated and published by the review *Gambit*. Vasco wanders across life, an innocent who doesn't understand the ways of the world, let alone the war where he shall die for glory. The play may be described as a poetical satire on war, but it seems ineffective in the theatre — I still remember Barrault's meandering production, which was nicknamed "Histoire de Fiasco". His other plays include *Monsieur Bob'le* (1951) and *Le Voyage*, produced at the Théâtre de France in 1961.

From Jean Tardieu (born 1903) and one of the earliest of the dramatists of the absurd, to Fernando Arrabal (born 1932 and who now lives in France and writes in French), one of the discoveries of Maurice Nadeau in his *Lettres Nouvelles*, there is no shortage of candidates. Martin Esslin's book on the Theatre of the Absurd should be consulted; here we are concerned with the mainstream of the theatre.

There is an urgent need always to experiment, and the agitated mind is the possession of man the artist; nevertheless two world wars and the reaction to the materialistic victory of nineteenth century capitalism have blunted the mind and thrown it into confusion. The power to survive also depends on the will to survive, the most powerful force in life. It is a will to survive against an omnipotent fate which must ultimately win; but with genuine pessimists it is never a self-willed defeat of their own choice. The so-called anti-theatre seems as much an incoherent exaggeration of life as a movie trailer, with its lack of continuity. If we are living between two ages, we have not yet entered the new while we reject the old. Anti-theatre, or theatre of the absurd, is indicative of an interregnum stage in culture; in the theatre, as in the other arts.

# THE IMAGE BREAKERS

IT is easier to knock down than to construct. Are playwrights seeking to change society, or hold a mirror up to society? Are they planning to alter the nature of society, or hold a court revolution? It was the late John Whiting who once said "the danger in revolutions is not losing, but winning; and it relinquishes the possibility of further revolt". In Britain John Osborne has stormed the polite theatre of the drawing-room; he has kicked over the whole clap-trap of conventional values; the long slumber is over. Since 1956 Osborne has not mellowed, but he has aged ahead of his generation. He is already the spokesman for a generation which tried and failed. As he observes, the younger generation are less sensitive but free of guilt, they did not have the initial task of participating in the revolution; for them the going has been made easy.

The conscience of the neutrals has often been complacent; Switzerland has preserved an almost insular distance from the rest of Europe, where the Alps have acted as the English Channel has for Britain. From their mountains the Swiss look down on the upheavals of their European neighbours without themselves becoming involved; yet they feel their isolation threatened, by atomic warfare and large trading blocks like the Common Market. Can they still maintain the illusion of neutrality in a world transformed by the new techniques? The plays of Dürrenmatt make the most savage assault on the hypocritical values of bourgeois society, and the worship of false gods, money, power and security. The threat comes from the arrival of the catalyst who reverses the logic of events, and delivers judgment according to a moral and didactic viewpoint. To those who thought Judgement Day was for the hereafter, Dürrenmatt reminds us of its present reality. Frisch is more the witness than the prosecutor, more the extravert with a love of travelling and participating; Dürrenmatt stays at home and judges.

Another neutral country, Sweden, offered a haven for the German writer Peter Weiss shortly before the war. The conscience of Weiss is that of an exile aware of having escaped punishment and death in a concentration camp. He is not drawn to the mild Scandinavian socialism, nor does he feel affinity for Sweden. In his play *Marat* Weiss has resolved his personal dilemma, torn between the pull of the freedom of the individual (as represented by De Sade) and the exigencies of revolution (his hero is Marat). Weiss has now decided that Marat was right, and has since become a Marxist.

The image breakers have made us face up to the truth; but only with Dürrenmatt have we the feeling of being shown the absolute truth "absolutely".

# FIFTEEN

# THE INVECTIVE OF JOHN OSBORNE

LOOKING back on Raffles after half a century George Orwell remarked: "all he has is a set of reflexes — the nervous system, as it were, of a gentleman. Give him a sharp tap on this reflex or that (they are called "sport", "pal", "woman", "king and country" and so forth), and you get a predictable reaction". Orwell went on in this essay to compare the morals of Raffles with those of Miss Blandish, observing (in 1944) that in Mr. Chase's book there are no gentlemen and no taboos. The English novel had achieved its emancipation and Freud and Machiavelli had reached the outer suburbs. But the theatre did not follow suit in the post-war years; the plays presented tended to be as polite as restrictions and rationing seemed drab. The most that the new social revolution of the Labour Government achieved was echoed in the verbal tinklings of Priestley's *Linden Tree*, and soon Priestley was to cast himself into the wilderness. Long runs by star-studded casts were the order of the day, they had the formality of an eighteenth-century conversation picture where one could marvel at the way a famous actress would delicately finger a cream cake without making her fingers sticky.

This was to be the case until 1956, and it is perhaps largely due to the spread of television that things are different to-day. The Television Playhouse, whether B.B.C. or I.T.V., with its several million viewers, constitutes, as Ted Willis puts it, "the most vital, the most alive, and probably the most useful section of the community . . . but they are often limited by social conventions which are narrow in the extreme." To which Dr. Tyrone Guthrie has added that the drama has been relieved, thanks to television, of the onus of popular entertainment. All these circumstances aided the entry of Jimmy Porter on to the stage of the Royal Court Theatre, London May 8th, 1956, a decisive date which marks a turning point in recent theatrical history. Until there was a change in the intellectual climate, the blowing away of the cobwebs, a creation of a new sort of atmosphere in the theatre, there was little hope for the blistering honesty of a Jimmy Porter to succeed in the English theatre. A return to a direct language without polite euphemisms would only be acceptable to English audiences and critics from characters in Shakespeare and the classics, but not, as Osborne commented, "from one who speaks out of the real despairs, frustrations, and sufferings of the age we are living in, now, at this moment". Times had changed. For the first time the audience is ready, so enter Jimmy Porter, or if you prefer, John Osborne, for we cannot help feeling that Osborne has become spokesman for his generation in his very articulate hero. This ending of a theatrical stalemate, the raising of the dust to disclose a different approach to theatre, a vocal movement in embryo, was an exciting moment. Even if *Look Back in Anger* was not the best play of the decade, it can be called the most important, for whatever may be the shortcomings of Osborne, a play which establishes a new intellectual climate, a return to a directness of language long absent, can have an important influence on the future.

How then, would Jimmy Porter fit the Raffles description? We must quickly eliminate the "gentleman", the "Christian gentleman" of public schools. Like Raffles Jimmy Porter has no moral code, no religion, but unlike Raffles, he has a strongly developed social conscience. Give him a sharp tap on the reflexes of his nervous system and you get the predictable obsessions, against society, the Church of England, the Press, women, and himself. "Damn you, damn both of you, damn them all . . ."; "when you see a woman in front of her bedroom mirror, you realise what a refined sort of butcher she is . . . thank God they don't have many woman surgeons! those primitive hands would have your guts out in no time. . . ."; "No, as far as Michelangelo Brigade's concerned, I must be a sort of right wing deviationist . . ."; "I've no public school scruples about hitting girls . . ." and so on.

Jimmy Porter is introduced as a young man about twenty-five, "a disconcerting mixture of sincerity and cheerful malice, of tenderness and freebooting cruelty; restless, importunate, full of pride, a combination which alienates the sensitive and insensitive alike. Blistering honesty, or apparent honesty, like his, makes few friends. To many he may seem sensitive to the point of vulgarity. To others, he is simply a loudmouth. To be as vehement as he, is to be almost non-committal". Here we have an egoistical battering-ram, an enigmatic character who however much he has to offer, is constantly misunderstood. He will deliberately set out to shock, he has the utmost contempt for all bourgeois values, his favourite words are "phoney" and "wet". A portrait of a character of contradictions, a complex mixed-up mind, full of fire and fury and not simply the louse he might appear — at least superficially. "I may write a book about us all" he exclaims "written in flames a mile high. And it won't be recollected in tranquillity either, picking daffodils with Auntie Wordsworth. It'll be recollected in fire, and blood. My blood."

Cliff, who shares the flat with Jimmy and his wife, Alison, is a different character altogether. One is largely indifferent to his existence. Alison is the most elusive personality. She is tuned in a different key. According to Osborne "she really is incapable of loyalty, even to herself. She is caught between two uncertain worlds and cannot bring herself to declare her allegiances". Alison is something of a pipe-dream, too good to be true in this environment. She does not seem to have a mind of her own, but is ready to be moulded, by her parents in their status of upper-middle class comfort and boredom from which she has fled, or moulded by the squalid and frustrating existence she shares with Jimmy. She is ready to renounce everything: "I don't want to be a saint, I want to be a lost cause. I want to be corrupt and futile! . . . Don't you see, I'm in the mud at last! I'm grovelling! I'm crawling!"

This is the only stage at which Jimmy is willing to be at one with her, it is the culmination of a blind rage of invective, ridiculing her parents, her snobberies, and everything she could cling to for an anchor. He drives her away and she returns home. She is pregnant and has a miscarriage. While they are separated Jimmy carries on an affair with Alison's actress friend, Helena. But Jimmy and Alison are made for one another, and there is no solution for either of them. Alison returns knowing that there will be more fights, that they will destroy one another, and that only in a lover's fantasy of playing bear and squirrel will they ever find happiness. Osborne asserts that this ending of the play should be ironic, not sentimental, that as "little furry creatures with little furry brains, full of dumb uncomplicated affection for each other," they are merely following "a common pattern of behaviour among sensitive, intelligent people." Be this as it may, coming as an anti-climax to what has gone before it is difficult to avoid the feeling that this is both whimsy and sentimentality.

*Look Back in Anger* is a play where the characters take over, and one character in particular. Osborne's dialogue, a non-stop outburst of frustrated verbiage delivered with the brutality of the blackboard-jungle school, has a magnetism about it which holds audiences who are far removed from the world of the angry young men, American and French audiences, for example. True there is little to admire in the character of Jimmy Porter, far less than that of Amis's *Lucky Jim* who was the prototype of the new provincialism. One would hardly wish to have Jimmy Porter as a friend or an acquaintance, with his odious loudmouth egoism, and would quickly consign his destiny to a place in the James Dean mythology.

Nevertheless *Look Back in Anger* swept the theatre like an electrical storm front and the weather changed from drizzle to gale. Osborne's next play was *The Entertainer*, performed at the Royal Court in 1957, but an interesting play *Epitaph for George Dillon*, which Osborne had written together with Anthony Creighton before *Look Back in Anger*, remained unproduced until 1958. If Jimmy Porter is not exactly a young man who endears you to him, there are moments in both *The Entertainer* and *Epitaph for George Dillon* when we have some sympathy. George Dillon may have compromised with a system, but he has not opted out of life. He is a down-and-out actor who has written a play, but success is only possible by rejecting ideals and accepting the seedy standards of Barney Edwards, a show-business impressario. Thus the title of George's play is changed to 'Telephone Tart'; as for George Dillon himself, he recovers from tuberculosis to be crushed by a much more insidious disease.

*Epitaph for George Dillon* is a most convincing piece of theatre, which has a harmony and rings true. The anger is controlled, not self-pity or sheer temper for the sake of hitting at any sitting target, but an indignation which is felt. Perhaps Creighton was the restraining influence.

In *The Entertainer* there is a marked Brechtian influence, borrowed and submerged until the result bears only Osborne's own signature. In turning to the music hall and the fortunes of a family steeped in its traditions, Osborne writes:

> The music hall is dying, and, with it, a significant part of England. Some of the heart of England has gone; something that once belonged to everyone, for this was truly folk art. In writing this play I have not used some of the techniques of the music hall in order to exploit an effective trick, but because I believe that these

can solve some of the eternal problems of time and space that face the dramatist, and, also, it has been relevant to the story and setting. Not only has this technique its own traditions, its own convention and symbol, its own mystique, it cuts right across the restrictions of the so-called naturalistic stage. Its contact is immediate, vital and direct.

Much of the success of the play in performance was undoubtedly due to the virtuoso performance of Sir Laurence Olivier, as the dud music-hall comic Archie Rice. The audience Archie has to play to are "dead behind the eyes. They pay their one and sixpence and defy you to entertain them". In vain he goes through the whole patter of brash vulgar jokes and jingoistic songs, and as he does so he enacts his own failure, his own unbelief. The turns are broken up by a series of scenes depicting a contemporary tragedy, a portrait of three generations of the Rice family. First there is Billy, the grandfather, a grand 'old-timer', lingering in the golden memories of the Edwardian era. Then there is Archie and his sozzled wife Phoebe, and their children Frank, who has just served six months in prison as a conscientious objector, in contrast to his brother, who dies out in Egypt, a hero without a cause, and a reminder of the crazy Suez adventure of 1956, which took place before Osborne finished the play.

"Nothing touches me, emotion is dead", Archie Rice claims. But Osborne's own emotions are very much alive, and the fault of the political satire is that too much is felt, too little thought. Out of characters of flesh and blood he nowhere offers hope of their rising from their misery. They believe honesty eliminates belief. The younger generation are as complete a failure as their parents. The lights grow dimmer, the repetition of the music-hall patter becomes more stale. The laughter turns hollow, sour, the tragedy is unrelieved even by Rock 'n' Roll and a Britannia in the nude.

It is interesting to compare the mood and theme of Osborne's pessimism with the way Chaplin treated *Limelight* — truly a film of our time. In *Limelight* it will be recalled that a once famous clown Calvero has lost his ability to make people laugh. And a gifted young dancer has become paralysed. Both have faith in each other. Chaplin's characters are pure, the clown is no vulgar down-and-out, he has known how to make the whole world laugh, he can still make us in the audience laugh. They are characters who transcend their environment and become universal. Osborne's characters, on the other hand, are shut in their own little world, from which they cannot, will not, escape. Canada is available, but Archie Rice refuses. For the young perhaps there is emigration.

The Rice family are thus outside society. Slaves of their own conventions they feel they have been badly done by, yet one wonders what exactly life should have offered them. Like Sartrian disciples, they were thrown into the world from nowhere, and with nowhere to go. They wander around No Hope Alley.

Of Osborne's musical *The World of Paul Slickey* (1959), we may recall George Dillon's words. "There's no such thing as failure, just waiting for success." If Osborne is to write a successful musical he will have to study rather more closely the technique, and not imagine that blind swiping at whatever tilt catches his eye is necessarily better than the tinkling musicals of the Ruritania kind. Being like the proverbial Irishman, and agin' everything, becomes merely dull, and the trouble with a bore is that he never knows or imagines that he himself ever could be one. To write a musical of our times Osborne will have to take rather more pains and trouble over the marshalling of his material.

Paul Slickey is one of Osborne's despised columnists on the "Daily Racket". Strangely enough he comes from one of England's stately mansions, he belongs to the despised class he writes about. If he started off being a decent fellow, society has cured him. As his newspaper boss goads him on to write more and more scurrilously, so Osborne himself launches out at the Crown, the Church, the Press, stately homes, pop singers, the Royal Academy of Dramatic Art, and women, among other topics. The climax drags on interminably as the cast change their sex. And at all this Osborne fires wildly without aim; unfortunately a hit here and there goes almost unnoticed in the general pandemonium. There are good lines in Slickey, and good characters. Even the much discussed rock 'n' roll funeral scene was not in bad taste, many a Highland funeral, at any rate, has been a merry social gathering with whisky galore. What Osborne failed to do was to find a workable technique, a plan of action for song, dance, and devastating satire.

Up to 1961 Osborne had remained in England, written plays about England and primarily for his immediate audience; John Whiting had justification when he once remarked that Osborne used "his considerable power of invective to wither things that are unimportant". With *Luther* (first produced in Nottingham 1961) Osborne is no longer bound by "this sceptred Isle", nor the little world of columnist

Slickey; his horizons immediately open up. Maybe the influence of Brecht made him look abroad for his subject (rather than influence his treatment) and it was Luther the man that Osborne was drawn to, his existential alienation, from his family, from his Church and from God. *Luther* is not an historical epic about the Reformation; Osborne brilliantly reconstructs from the historical material and documentary sources his Luther, where his arguing is always close to cursing, his praying close to despair; he is always afraid, always lonely and always tormented. He is driven on incessantly by his own daemon; the irony is that the man who tears Christendom apart is himself torn, though this is quite in accord with the psychology of self-hatred. Only twice during the play do we see him at rest with himself, at the very end and in the middle when he has his 'inspiration'. In a life which was a desperate search for faith, Luther's great argument is against authority; his parents could not provide it, the Church cannot because it is corrupt. No man is the father of himself, but Luther is nobody's son; the hard lesson he must learn is that he was created by God. He may learn it, but he never quite feels it.

The moral drift of *Luther* is puzzling; there is no simple saying who in this great upheaval of the Church stands for right and who stands for wrong, because right and wrong are mixed — just as both good and bad flow from Luther's action. If Luther destroys the corrupt unity of the Church he replaces it with endlessly subdivisive disunity. Osborne is concerned with his interpretation of the man removed from the wider historical context; what impresses is his strength of dialogue but in spite of this something is missing, the historical perspective. Although *Luther* is a long play, it stirs our excitement as an overture; for the language itself — images of blood, bone, flesh and the jakes weave themes and echoes, themes that look forward, which are there to be developed; we want to know more.

The play opens with Luther, the young Augustinian novice, taking his ceremonial vows. Nothing could set the stage more significantly than the contrasted confessions of Luther and his brother monks; while they confess to petty sins he confesses the self-loathing and the dreams of blood, lechery and suffocation that rive his soul. The scene ends with Luther having a fit, a foretaste of the almost epileptic interplay that exists between his mind and body.

By Act Two Luther has become a scholar of renown. His approaching act of heresy is put in perspective for the audience by Tetzel, the vicious and venal hawker of Indulgences. The Vicar-General urges caution, for Luther has already offended the State in the person of the local Duke and risks serious trouble if he offends the Church. But it is not in Luther's nature to be moderate, and in the next scene he delivers a haranguing apologia for what he is about to do to the crowd at Wittenburg, and nails his famous theses to the church door.

The Church is now roused and the Pope sends his legate Cajetan to dissuade Luther from the path of heresy. Failing to persuade Luther to recant he pleads with him on the ground that man must not be left to find God in the darkness, alone, but Luther stands firm. Two short scenes end the act; in the first a glimpse of the Pope, a sly politician and a dandy given to hunting. In the second we see Luther denouncing the Pope and his own following of monks making a bonfire of Papal literature.

Act Three opens at the Diet of Worms, where, in 1521, Luther was summoned to appear before the Emperor and the Papal Nuncio. Luther is required to recant, not reason; he refuses unless it is proved to him by argument that he is wrong. Four years pass, and we are at Wittenburg. It is the most powerful scene in the play. The war has begun, the peasants have risen and been massacred, while Luther has refused to be on their side because they were a "mob". The fury and futility of war is symbolised on stage by the bloody body of a peasant. A dispossessed knight, weary of battle and puzzled by Luther's desertion, sees wars as a sort of upper-class cheat and Christianity with its insistence that Christ was more than a prophet as another. Angrily he smears Luther with the peasant's blood, which he holds him to be guilty of. Luther defends himself: the peasants deserved to die because they rebelled against the Church and because they 'kicked against authority'. The knight breaks his banner in disgust as Luther's bride appears and together they kneel before the altar.

In the final scene the date is 1530. Luther has become prematurely old, domestic, slack in his devotions. Katherine, Luther's wife, brings to him their child who it would seem is also troubled by dreams. Luther croons over him the lesson that he himself has learnt, namely that a man's true father is God. "It's hard to accept you're anyone's son, and you're not the father of yourself. So don't have dreams so soon, my son. *They'll* be having *you* soon enough."

Osborne's concentration on Luther's personal conflicts becomes truly alive; the dialogue is arrestingly dramatic without ever veering towards the melodramatic; it compels our attention. It is only towards the end of the play that we are aware not of an anti-climax, but the feeling that a play which promised so much ought to have continued, indeed the echoes of what we have heard fit new meanings on former ones and this now seems to be yet another point of departure. *Luther* remains a personal interpretation, we are aware of Osborne's "temperamental affinity" with the man. It is Osborne's best play, but it is also "his" Luther.

Certainly *Luther* represents a tremendous advance. In *Plays for England* (1962), consisting of two short plays, *The Blood of the Bambergs* and *Under Plain Cover*, we are back beneath the low ceiling of the clouds and suburbia of contemporary England, with the second play a provincial English casserole of Genet.

*Inadmissible Evidence* (1964) is a mature Osborne which has echoes reminding us of his first play *Look Back in Anger*. Bill Maitland, the seedy, tortured, disillusioned middle-aged solicitor may be a far cry from the loudmouth Jimmy Porter of his youth, but whereas Porter has some sort of future to live for, with Bill Maitland everybody walks out of his life; he is ignored (except by the Law Society which is on his trail), he has no love, no strength, no future; he is the complete failure. The play opens amid the "bones and dead objects of a Solicitor's office"— it is a dream where Bill is in the dock, where he is being judged by his managing clerk. Bill confesses from the dock:

> I have always been quite certain that this is where I should end up, here, I've seen it too many times . . .

The time has come to recognise his failure:

> I am almost forty years old, and I know I have never made a decision which I didn't either regret, or suspect was just plain commonplace or shifty or scamped and indulgent or mildly stupid or undistinguished.

Maitland's failure is not only his personal one, it represents the failure of his generation, the failure of the Welfare State, the final collapse of his ideals not to accept, not to take over, the conventions of the previous generation. The world was to be a better place to live in once a clean reject had been made, and what has resulted? As a solicitor specialising in crime and divorce Maitland is no longer able to solve the affairs of others in trouble, for he has not even the ability to solve his own. His tirade is not so much the voice of Jimmy Porter hitting blindly at an

Establishment sitting pretty like Humpty Dumpty as the sudden realisation of his own inadequacies; he speaks less with anger than with guilt. "I used to be good at my job because I had what they called an instinct and a quick brain." It is the realisation that marriage, mistresses, his children, himself were meaningless. "I don't know what you have to do with me at all and soon you won't," he remarks to his teen-age daughter. He knows that they have nothing in common, she does what she likes, travelling across continents, dancing in a way beyond his ability; she is unselfconscious, without guilt. So what? She hasn't, he tells her outright, "the little worm of energy eating away in me", nor is there much loving in any of her kindnesses, nor for that matter cruelty. The younger generation she represents can no more understand Bill Maitland than did the parents of Jimmy Porter understand the anger of his hopes.

*Inadmissible Evidence* is a tragedy on a domestic theme; *A Patriot for Me* (1965) moves from the condition of England in the sixties to the vast canvas of the Austro-Hungarian Empire in the two decades preceding the First World War. Osborne has based his theme on the factual case of a homosexual Austrian colonel who was blackmailed into becoming a spy for Czarist Russia. With such subject matter Osborne was to run into the dangerous territory of the Lord Chamberlain's censorship in England. Permission for public performances was refused unless three complete scenes were deleted and radical changes were required elsewhere, the result of which would have been a hypocritical avoidance of an adult theme which Osborne has treated in a responsible way. Osborne rightly refused to agree to the Lord Chamberlain's edict and the Royal Court, where the play was presented, was turned into a private theatre club for the occasion.

We first meet Redl as a young and promising lieutenant in the 7th Galician Infantry Regiment at Lemberg in 1890. He acts as a second for a brother officer who fights a duel and is killed; his participation is however overlooked and he gains a place in the War College Examination, where his merit is recognised in spite of his rather humble origins. He has occasional relations with prostitutes but without success; later he falls in love with a countess but is impotent. Shortly after this he discovers he is a homosexual. The second act is mainly occupied with Redl's attendance at a "drag ball" in Vienna in 1902. As the guests dance Osborne stresses in his stage directions that it is essential that the audience should only realise gradually that all the dancers and guests are men. There are "the paid bums" whose annual occasion this is, the discreet drag queens with their clothes especially made for the occasion, the more self-conscious rich queens who tend to masculine drag and "end up looking like lesbians", those who dress up to make women appear odious and finally those like Redl who don't make any effort but wear full-dress uniform and decorations. It is shortly after the drag ball that Redl is successfully blackmailed by the Russian spies. Following this, the play does not maintain the remarkable atmosphere of the initial scenes, where we feel the authenticity of the period, or the tempo of the drag ball; instead it rather tends to disintegrate, while following the inevitable results of Redl's downfall. His own side discover his treachery and it is left to him to commit suicide.

As in *Luther*, even with *Inadmissible Evidence*, certainly with *A Patriot for Me* Osborne might be said to have lost interest in his theme at the moment when we want to know more. We have followed the facts, admired the way he conveyed the atmosphere of the times, but we have only viewed the exterior actions of Redl. We have listened to his dialogue, but only in one passage, when he tells the countess who has just married the man he loves that she will never know Stefan's body as he knows it, does he emerge as more than the stranger. To have succeeded so much with theme and setting, to have written a brilliant first act and remarkable second is an achievement; we know that Redl has all the qualities that are required of an officer in a military academy: what Redl lacks is his introspective side, the creation of Robert Musil's Ulrich for example in *Man Without Qualities*.

Osborne's theatre now rests on an extended front; from the anger of Jimmy Porter to the cynicism of Bill Maitland, from the ambitious study of Luther to that of the blackmail of a homosexual officer in pre-1914 Vienna. There remains Osborne's adaptation of Lope De Vega's *La Fianza Satisfecha*, under the title *A Bond Honoured* (1966). Here Osborne seeks to reinterpret the Spanish ego in Leonido who is the personification of evil, who rapes his mother and sister, blinds his father, who will stop at nothing, so that after his death they can say "he played a good tune on vituperation". Osborne claims to have concentrated on Lope de Vega's development, and to have discarded most of the rest of the play, reducing it from three acts to one. Judging from seeing the play in performance, one wonders whether it was not best ignored in the corner of some dusty library shelf.

Neither *Time Present* nor *The Hotel in Amsterdam*, both produced in 1968, add to Osborne's reputation, though they demonstrate once again his ability to catch the contemporary idiom of his stratum of

London society in the way Coward reflected his generation of the 'twenties in such plays as *The Vortex* and *Hay Fever*. These plays are essentially conversation pieces. *Time Present* introduces us to Pamela Orme, 29 year old daughter of a once famous actor, now dying. Even the death of her father changes nothing; she continues to sit around aimlessly, never going out, sleeping all day for weeks on end, living on champagne, refusing to marry or look for work as an actress. Osborne contrasts her with a young Labour M.P. Constance, whose apartment she shares temporarily. Constance believes in fulfilment, and no doubt commitment. Eventually Pamela decides to leave and "manage within my own, my own walls. I've no ambitions . . . I don't want to be judged or categorised or watched. I don't want to be pronounced upon or do it for anyone." Only her homosexual agent friend, who fetches her, seems to fit these requirements.

*The Hotel in Amsterdam* is a more slender piece. A group of film people, who are "around forty but none middle-aged" decide to visit Amsterdam in order "for a few blessed days" to have no "K.L." in their lives. K.L. is described by them as "the biggest, most poisonous, voracious, Machiavellian dinosaur in movies". They have gone away without even leaving him their telephone number, until near the end of the play they realise he will have it through a friend who may have passed it on. Almost immediately the phone rings, but it is not K.L. They learn that K.L. has committed suicide.

We seem a far cry from 1956, from looking back in anger to our present apathy; surely it is more, not less than a generation ago? Osborne, no longer the *enfant terrible* has become a middle aged grouser. In *West of Suez* (1971) we feel that nothing will stop the flow of words from his different characters, and that each of them is speaking a monologue with Osborne the ventriloquist. Such is his capacity for dialogue that nothing will stop his characters talking, all else becomes unimportant, even a plot can be dispensed with. Is this really life on a paradise island where life has turned sour through too much sun, too many sun-downers, and the departure of the British governor general to make way for independence and boredom. We only wake up at the final curtain when the old writer Wyatt Gillman, who is visiting his married daughter now living on the island, is shot dead by the natives. Another playwright might have started his play there, but Osborne can hold our attention without really trying, and when he succeeds, such as in the mouth of Bill Maitland, he remains the spokesman for his age group.

The very success of his Court Revolution toppled the establishment sitting there like ducks in 1956; his invective was too much for the Lord Chamberlain in St. James's Palace, it was only a matter of time before he went, indeed, he was the last of the anachronist figures to go. Yet at the end of it all, a recent revival in London of *Look Back in Anger* came across like a period piece written by a confirmed Tory. Even Osborne's mysogynism is mild compared to that of Albee's vitriolic *Who's Afraid of Virginia Woolf?* Already in the 'sixties Osborne was able to leave behind the Raffles reflexes of the past, his socialist cant (never overt anyway as say Wesker) and as a younger generation came forward they looked at each other with mutual incomprehension. Osborne continued to talk his monologue; the rest was silence. From an ex-revolutionary he finds himself the last of the Mohicans.

# SIXTEEN

# THE CONSCIENCE OF THE NEUTRALS

## MAX FRISCH AND FRIEDRICH DÜRRENMATT

> "If you had listened to the voice of conscience, and heeded
> the stings of remorse, before you had urged your diabolical
> vengeance to this extremity, Frankenstein would yet have
> lived."
>
> MARY SHELLEY, *Frankenstein*

CAN you be a good Swiss and not believe in God . . . a good
Swiss and lead a double life . . . or get up at nine o'clock in the
morning? These were questions which visitors to the 1964
Swiss National Exhibition at Lausanne were invited to answer, and
they were promised that a computer would analyse their replies. The
spirit of conformism dies as hard as that of neutralism, while at the
same time within the frontiers of security man is forever aware of his
vulnerability. If you live in countries where *coups d'etat* come naturally
you grow accustomed to the Latin American concept of "the noise of
governments falling"; it is in those nations which have not participated
in the major upheavals of the twentieth century, who having escaped
two world wars continue to live with the conviction that it is the
world and not them that has decided to run riot, that the conscience
of fear falls hardest. It is the price of sanity that you may be threatened
by the outrageous at any instant. In the bourgeois respectability of your
own fireside the public prosecutor or the executioner might step right
out of the grandfather clock which belonged in fact to your great-
grandmother. What would you do if an anarchist entered with a time
bomb, or a fire raiser asked you for a match to set your house on fire?
Or if the President of the confederation gave you the choice: "Are

you prepared, Herr Doktor, to be executed as a murderer, or would you prefer, in order to restore law and order, to form a government?" The story of Job is ever present, the degree to which an individual can be held responsible, and yet the realisation that we are not the judges, we are the accused. The frontiers of the human mind between order and chaos, rationality and madness are as artificial and prejudicial as the physical frontiers between neutralism and the barbarians. "Someone must have been telling lies about Joseph K., for without having done anything wrong he was arrested one fine morning" Kafka had written of his city of Prague. In a small country like Switzerland of law and order and justice the very unreality of the possibility is an affront, and yet the conscience of neutrals like Max Frisch and Friedrich Dürrenmatt is not to be neutralist; escape from responsibility is the deadliest of the sins and perhaps the only one relevant to our age.

Perhaps a word should be said of the very special position Zurich assumed in the life of German letters following the outbreak of the Second World War; as the lights went out over Europe Zurich remained uncompromising and unchallenged as the cultural capital of the German-speaking people. It was only in Zurich that those German authors who had taken refuge in Switzerland and elsewhere could find a publisher; moreover the German Swiss showed neither inclination nor sympathy for the Nazi *Geist* and *Kultur*. Throughout the war the position of Switzerland was inevitably perilous, and on two occasions invasion seemed imminent. One of the Swiss frontier guardsman at that time was Max Frisch, who was doing his military service; the incongruity of the situation must have haunted his imagination, and was later to find expression in his writing.

The names of Max Frisch and Friedrich Dürrenmatt have become linked as being the two most important dramatists to-day of the German-speaking world. They are clearly very different personalities. Frisch, ten years older than Dürrenmatt, has Austrian ancestors and appears, from his *Tagebuch 1946-49*, to be the more cosmopolitan, happier out of Switzerland, a lover of good food and more important, *conversazione*. Dürrenmatt, on the other hand, seems the more austere figure. The son of a Swiss German pastor, he studied theology, philosophy and literature at the Universities of Zurich and Berne, but like Frisch, he did not complete his studies. Both Frisch and Dürrenmatt were to become freelance journalists after they had abandoned their studies. Frisch however took the opportunity of travelling in Eastern Europe, and on his return to Switzerland through the generosity of a friend was able to resume his studies. He decided to become an architect. He continued writing, and in 1943 a novel *j'adore ce qui me brûle oder die Schwierigen* attracted the attention of the director of the Zürich Schauspielhause, who suggested that he might care to write a play at some time. The same year Frisch won an architectural prize for the design of a Municipal swimming bath in Zurich, and an anomaly of this success meant that Frisch was able to launch out on his own as an architect and have more time for writing. His first play, *Santa Cruz*, dates from 1944. Dürrenmatt was not to become known until his first play *Es Steht geschrieben*, was produced at the Zürich Schauspielhaus in 1947. We shall therefore consider first the works of Max Frisch.

Already in *Santa Cruz* we have the mirror to the ambitions of Frisch. We sense his frustration at being hemmed in by the towering Alps and his wish to seek out some tropical paradise. A cavalry captain and his wife Elvira are visited by a vagabond called Pelegrin, who seventeen years previous used to be Elvira's lover. Pelegrin is dying, but his visit rekindles the ambitions which both husband and wife have harboured for so long. Romantic illusions, but it is the husband who is still ready to start out on his voyage of discovery, and the woman who understands that you cannot escape any longer from yourself.

Frisch then turned to an experiment in what the dramatic medium could offer him. In *Nun singen sie wieder* (Now They Sing Again, 1945) sub-titled "An attempt at a Requiem", he presents a Breughelesque canvas of the horrors of modern war, where reality and the supernatural join up as the living do with the dead. The hostages who have been shot by the German troops chant a hymn of hope for peace. The experiment in style goes much further and more successfully in *Die Chinesische Mauer* (The Chinese Wall, 1946), where Frisch attempts in dramatic form to enclose a thousand years of history and human achievement. What, he asks, is man's chance of preventing the total destruction of the world? The contemporary, who is an intellectual, carries out the function of the Greek chorus as he introduces and relates the various sequences; characters appear from history such as Columbus, Napoleon, Pilate, together with fictional characters, Romeo and Juliet, Cleopatra, Don Juan and others. Writers are also referred to, Schiller, Shakespeare, even Brecht and himself. All the great figures of history and fictional figures of literature fail to understand the Contemporary, who is awarded by the Emperor of China a prize for fiction when he warns him of the terrors of the atomic bomb.

The conclusion is that the Contemporary, the intellectuals and poets among us, are aware of what is coming but can do nothing about it other than share the guilt of entire mankind.

In Frisch's diary the idea for his first important play *Biedermann und die Brandstifter* is noted in 1948, but it was not until ten years later that the play was produced. His next play was chronologically *Als der Krieg zu Ende War* (When the War Came to an End), which takes for its theme a German woman whose husband is concealed in a cellar while she has an affair with the Russian officer who is billeted with her (the setting is post-war Berlin). When the woman discovers that her husband was guilty of war crimes and in order to save his own skin connived at her affair with the Russian, she commits suicide.

The first draft of *Graf Öderland* (Count Oederland) had been written in 1946, and was performed at the Schauspielhaus in Zurich in 1951. A second stage version was produced at Frankfurt in 1956, but subsequently Frisch forbade performance of the play until a definitive version appeared in 1956. Count Oederland (the name Oederland means "barren land") is a mythological figure who seizes the imagination of the public prosecutor. According to the old rhyme:

Count Oederland goes about the world
Count Oederland goes with an axe in his hand,
Woe
to him who stands in our path . . .

We meet the public prosecutor, the representative of law and order, at the moment when he comes to identify himself with the meaningless crime of a murderer whose trial he is prosecuting. It is as if the prosecutor has a bond of understanding: "We all work too hard, till something snaps. And then all our good jurors are surprised when someone picks up an axe." Next the prosecutor disappears, and soon stories of strange murders are circulating; we listen to the news bulletin that three local policemen have been murdered by a man who has called himself a Count. "Anyone meeting him," the announcer warns, "is advised to exercise extreme caution. An examination of the three victims has shown that the murder was committed with an axe." A scene follows where the count arrives in a luxury hotel, and although the entire town including hotel porters as well as police are looking for him, such is human incredulity that they refuse to defend themselves against his presence, although they are aware of it. The Count even

jokes with the policeman and tells him about his axe — "It's no laughing matter" comes the gendarme's reply. The axe becomes "a symbol of
insurrection and revolt". The Count makes good his escape and
becomes leader of a terrorist movement. He emerges triumphant
from the sewers and almost as inexplicably he finds himself back in his
house where he was sitting at the beginning of the play. He is sure that
he has been having a nightmare, only the muddy boots he was wearing
in the sewer betray the truth. It is all too true, this horrible fantastic
nightmare. The President arrives to offer him power, the Residency
Guard "as in an opera" appear, but the prosecutor is unable to accept
the horror of the reality.

After an unimportant work *Don Juan oder Die Liebe zur Geometrie*
(Don Juan or the Love of Geometry, 1953) where Don Juan was not
at all what legend made of him, but actually a woman only interested
in geometry, we come to what is Frisch's most important play to date,
*Biedermann und die Brandstifter* (The Fire Raisers, 1958), which he
describes as "a Morality without a Moral". Just as at the turn of this
century we were told that we were "all socialists now", so after two
world wars it has become increasingly clear that we are in fact to-day
nothing more exciting that a civilisation of Biedermanns. Biedermann
is a good solid unimaginative citizen, the common denominator type
who continues to believe in good, and that if there is evil it would
never affect him. He is a do-gooder, and he believes that if you give no
reason for offence you yourself will escape — for the simple reason that
there is no justification in harming you. Your very innocence is invul-
nerable. Frisch noted the idea for the play immediately after the
Communist *coup d'etat* in Czechoslovakia when the Fire Raisers were
the Communist infiltrators whose aim was to overthrow the West.
Through credulity and appeasement we were all victims in spite of the
dire warnings of the chorus of firemen. The parable could likewise be
applied to the guilty men of Munich, and many see also an allusion to
the atomic bomb, and our own disbelief that it could be used against us.

*Biedermann* opens with the warning by the fire fighters that
mysterious fires are breaking out all over the city; even Herr Biedermann exclaims that it was time that the "harmless hawkers" were
"strung up". At that moment two hawkers call and Biedermann
permits them, in spite of common sense, to spend the night in his loft.
As the evening advances Biedermann becomes increasingly suspicious
and helpless; in the end he even hands them the box of matches with the
conviction that they couldn't possibly abuse his generosity by using

them against him. Wishful thinking and false values lead to his utter destruction.

Frisch has written an *Afterpiece* to the play, where we meet Herr and Frau Biedermann and the two fire raisers in hell. The attempt, however, to answer the questions of the morality is less effective and seems largely superfluous.

The idea for *Andorra* (1961) is first mentioned by Frisch in his *Tagebuch* for 1946, where we find a prose sketch "The Andorran Jew":

> There lived in Andorra a young man who was taken for a Jew. The task would be to tell the supposed story of his origin, his daily contacts with the Andorrans, who saw in him the Jew — the ready-made image that was waiting for him everywhere . . . Most Andorrans did nothing to him. Which means that they did nothing good to him either.

Frisch takes up the theme of anti-semitism and shames us with the disclosure that the boy Andri was not after all a Jew. Though his foster-father had claimed officially to have rescued Andri from Jewish persecution which was taking place in the country of the Blacks which borders Andorra, in fact Andri is an illegitimate son of a woman of that country. His foster-father is the real father. Andorra is not meant to be the small existing state but to stand for any small nation with frontiers on a totalitarian state.

The play has been given distinct Brechtian overtones — Frisch was a friend of Brecht's during his stay in Zurich from 1947-8. Each of the Andorrans between the episodes address the audience and explain their behaviour and deny their responsibility. Andri, for example, had been apprenticed to a carpenter, but because he is thought to be a Jew the carpenter cannot imagine that Andri could be in life anything else but a salesman. Finally Andorra is invaded by the Blacks and Andri is dragged off by the Jew detector and shot. No Andorran suffers, only as Frisch noted in his diary, when they learned the truth about Andri "they saw to their horror that they themselves bore the features of Judas, each one of them".

This in itself places *Andorra* at the highest level; there is little need to remind ourselves that Andri follows the path of the son of God, and that He was sacrificed through the silence of his Father. In spite of this, it seems in the context of the play that the Father should not have kept the secret of Andri until too late, that there was no particular reason for him to conceal the truth. There are also certain structural faults in the exposition, especially repetitive in the first part. There is something heavy-handed about this, and the very use of symbolism, such as the three crows of the cock, seems all too obvious.

"If only we could begin again," says Kürmann in *Biografie, Ein Spiel* (Biography, A Game, 1967), "we would know what errors not to commit twice." Frisch enables his hero to achieve this through the "registrator", perhaps closer to a stage director than a bureaucratic deity (in the Zurich production the rôle was played by Germany's Number One TV Quiz-master). If mere chance could have given him a different life, what importance, Kürmann asks "can any human biography have?"

The play is not his biography, but the game of his biography. The catch is that he cannot change either his intelligence, his meeting with Antoinette who became his wife, or his destiny. It is like being in a maze with only one exit; each variation is tried up to the point where it cannot be different; we even witness what would have happened if he had shot his wife, in any case he was doomed to die. Frisch warns us that it is important that "the play does not give the illusion that what is happening is reality, rather that it is reflected". Kürmann also must not appear as an actor, but be himself throughout. In the last scene we learn he is dying of cancer and that these events are passing through Kürmann's mind. The registrator gives him permission to be free once again, to continue the game from where he met Antoinette seven years ago.

The form bears a marked influence of Thornton Wilder's *Our Town* which was produced in Zurich during the last war and made a strong impression on Frisch as a young man. His experiment here, however, seems to lead him more to the frontiers of the novel, where in for example his *A Wilderness of Mirrors* he has already explored the introspective variables of the mind far more effectively; in the theatre this risks being static, however much the actors play for comedy at the author's request.

In a recent interview Frisch seems to feel he has reached a dead end in the theatre and has declared he does not intend to write any further plays. Whether he adheres to this or not, his substantial body of dramatic work will ensure him an important place among contemporary playwrights.

★

"The artist has no need of scholarship", Dürrenmatt writes in his essay *Theaterprobleme* (1955), "scholarship derives laws from what already exists . . . but the laws thus established have no value for the artist, even when they are true. The artist cannot accept a law he has not discovered for himself." Dürrenmatt goes on to explain how for a dramatist the theatre can never be something purely objective; the playwright "destroys the object he has created again and again, forgets it, rejects it, scorns it, overestimates it, all in order to make room for something new". Here we have an insight into Dürrenmatt's own search and relationship between the playwright and his art. The playwright never, Dürrenmatt continues, leaves the battle without wounds, and his enemy, "the material" does not believe in fair play. "This forces the playwright to fight back with every permissible and non-permissible means"; all rules may be broken, all conventions are suspect, reality itself is nothing short of absurdity. The grotesque and the macabre are the shadows of law and order; the public prosecutor is driven through the retribution of justice to commit murder; the female doctor supposed to be looking after dangerous lunatics is in fact the only mad person; a bank is run by gangsters who murder anyone withdrawing their funds. . . . And there is always money which corrupts the world; only by dispossessing yourself of possessions or titles can you find courage and the discovery of self.

Starting from tragedy Dürrenmatt soon realised that the ironic twists of comedy were the way to communicate his themes, just as he is convinced that the crime story is the one form which has validity for our age. The danger of a theatre of the grotesque, like that of the crime story, is for the characters to become puppets and ignore the human condition. "The actor is to discover humanity behind each of my characters", Dürrenmatt emphasises, "otherwise they cannot be played at all." The old lady of *The Visit* for example, is certainly a sinister character in a wicked play, but she should not be played in this way, "for nothing injures this comedy, which has a tragic ending, more than brutal earnestness". It is as if Dürrenmatt regards his heroes as absolved from the rules of conventional society, like the Nobel Prize novelist of his radio play *Abendstunde im Spätherbst* (One Evening in Late Autumn, 1957) whom a retired civil servant discovers merely writes the dossiers of the murders which he has committed. When the time comes for him to find material for another book he merely commits another murder. Certainly Dürrenmatt is the master image breaker; the contrasts of logic seem to disappear, chaos can also be orderly, the human situation which he considers as a calamity has nevertheless to be faced with courage; there is no turning your back on life. The voice of his conscience, the neutralists nightmare, asserts itself.

In his very first play *Es Steht Gescrieben* (It is Written, 1947) we have an introduction to the themes which are to become obsessions in Dürrenmatt's future works. "I have no faith, but gold," the rich merchant Knipperdollinck remarks, anticipating the character of the old lady of *The Visit*. Knipperdollinck is already struck by the very precise commands of the bible: "It is written, sell what you have and give it to the poor and you shall have the kingdom of heaven." Why should it be so absurd if you carry these instructions out implicitly? We are in sixteenth-century Münster, where the Anabaptists are seeking to establish His Kingdom at Münster, just as the Jesuits in Höchwalder's play *Das Heilige Experiment* look to South America. Knipperdollinck chooses to divest himself of his wealth, abandon his family and live as a beggar; Johann Bockelson, the poor tailor from Leyden newly arrived in Münster, acquires his wealth. When the Catholic troops besiege the town and both Bockelson and Knipperdollinck are certain of their impending death, they dance like clowns on the roof tops. Knipperdollinck acquires faith in his heroic rôle, Bockelson sinks further in his despair. In this play we also meet one of Dürrenmatt's favourite characters, the executioner.

In his second play *Der Blinde* (The Blind One, 1948) the setting is once again historical, that of the Thirty Years War, but this has in fact only minor importance for the theme, the story of Job. "The blind Duke", Dürrenmatt writes, "believes he is living in a well-preserved castle whereas he is living in a ruin . . . the dramatic place is one and the same, but by means of the pretence carried on before the blind man it plays a dual rôle, the place seen by the audience and the place in which the blind man fancies himself to be." The Duke is thus able, in spite of the loss of his possessions and security, to retain his faith in an ideal.

Following these two early works, Dürrenmatt's dramatic force makes an important advance in *Romulus der Grosse* (Romulus the Great, 1949, second version 1957). Described as "An Historical Comedy without historic basis" it is Dürrenmatt's only play where he may be said to appear happy and almost carefree. Romulus Augustus, the last of the Roman Emperors, is the first modern hero, the first one, we might say, without a cause. The Germanic barbarians are at the gates of Rome; like the blind Duke Romulus goes about his ordinary life as if nothing had happened. He is more concerned with the daily laying habits of his poultry, who have such illustrious names as Tiberius, Flavius and Marcus Aurelius. The Empress and his family continue to talk of the greatness of Rome, while planning to flee to Sicily, the politicians find themselves powerless to do anything but sit and receive news of one disaster after another. Romulus meanwhile is resigned to his martyrdom, having ruined Rome by his laziness. "The Emperor knows what he is doing," he insists, "when he throws his empire to the flames." His duty is to remain and feed the chickens. In the third act Romulus justifies his stand, saying that he did not betray Rome, but that Rome betrayed herself, by choosing tyranny. "Do we still have the right to defend ourselves? Do we still have the right to be more than victims?" The emperor replies in the negative and orders no resistance to the barbarians. The emperor's family all drown while escaping to Sicily; Romulus prepares for his martyrdom as the Teutonic chief enters; to his amazement he is not a "barbarian" as was supposed, but a chicken fancier like himself. The chief tells him he didn't come to kill the Emperor but to subject himself and his entire people to Romulus. "Madness," Romulus gasps. "All I have done has become absurd." He pleads with the chief to kill him; they eventually agree that instead of a sacrificial death Romulus should go into retirement, and that the Roman Empire should cease to exist. As Dürrenmatt observes, "for twenty years Romulus played the fool and the world around him did not realise that there was a method to his nonsense." Romulus was great because "he had the wisdom and insight to accept his fate".

The main plot of *Die Ehe des Herrn Mississippi* (The Marriage of Mr. Mississippi, 1951) is that of how the Public Prosecutor Florestan Mississippi proposes to a widow Anastasia who has just poisoned her husband who was in fact having an affair with Mrs. Mississippi — in her turn executed by Florestan. Anastasia clearly committed murder, whereas Florestan merely broke the existing law which should, he believes, be replaced by the Law of Moses. Their marriage would be a means of atonement and mutual torture. Anastasia has no alternative but to accept. Five years pass, Florestan has been working with particular zeal and no previous public prosecutor has ever been so hated or achieved such a record number of death sentences, 350 to the gallows. And each one of them is comforted on his way by Anastasia, who becomes known as the Angel of the Prisons.

There are also two sub-plots in the play, the first concerns Frédéric René Saint-Cloud, a childhood friend who has become a Communist revolutionary and who is shot in a mock-execution at the opening of the play, before turning round to address the audience "like a cross between the director of a rather second-rate theatre and a Mephistopheles." The comedy, he informs them, apart from the title it has, might have been called "Anastasia and Her Lovers". For apart from Florestan and himself, there is also a third lover, Count Bodo von Ubelohe-Zabernsee, the doctor who supplied Anastasia with the poison and who fled to the interior of Borneo to escape Florestan's prosecution; strangely enough he is the sole survivor. Florestan is himself taken into hospital for examination by the whole of a psychiatric congress, the male nurses ignoring his confessions of guilt. The play is also set on planes of reality, and the author instructs that the comedy is "a story of a room" which at the beginning of the play should be as real as possible and which gradually disintegrates; the decor should not be unreal or fantastic, even though one window does look onto a northern gothic Cathedral and the other window a southern Mediterranean ruin, the rest the author insists can be left to the text.

*Ein Engel kommt nach Babylon* (An Angel Comes to Babylon, 1953) is sub-titled "a fragmentary Comedy"; the Angel in question arrives on earth with the maiden Kurrubi, who has been created by God in outward human form for the lowliest of men, Akki the beggar. In Nebuchadnezzar's kingdom Akki is the only surviving beggar; having failed by all means of physical persuasion "to persuade Akki to enter the service of the state" the king decides to disguise himself as a beggar in order to make Akki see for himself the shame of poverty. It is through this confusion that the angel introduces Kurrubi to the king by mistake before Akki appears on the scene. When he does Akki tries to show off how good he is at begging, and it is soon clear that the lowliest of men is not Akki but Nebuchadnezzar, with whom Kurrubi has already fallen in love. Alas, there is no hope for the king unless he disposes himself of his title and wealth and becomes in fact a beggar, and so the king is forced to reject Kurrubi. For Kurrubi does not want a throne, nor does she want Akki the beggar, whom she does not love. When the angel appears she begs the angel to take her back to Heaven, for she doesn't want to die on the earth. The angel however does not listen to a word she says, having been bewitched by the beauty of the world while flying around. So Kurrubi is forced to suffer her unhappiness and go off into the desert with Akki, while dreaming of the beggar she first met who was none other than the king.

The play has a satirical relevance to the present, and Babylon is not meant to be presented as a city of any historical period. The play is flawed by Dürrenmatt's worst fault, the verbosity of his dialogue. It is as if the situations had raced out of control and not knowing how to end the play the author had allowed his characters to talk themselves out.

The same accusation cannot be levelled against *Der Besuch der alten Dame* (produced in London and New York under the title "The Visit", 1956) which raises Dürrenmatt to the level of the leading playwright of our times. Not only is it a good play in itself, it is one of the most forceful statements ever made on the corruption of the power of money, a radical indictment of the values of our society and the hypocrisy on which it is built. Clara Zachanassian is described as "sixty-three, red hair, pearl necklace, enormous gold bangles, unbelievably got up to kill and yet by the same token a society lady with a rare grace, in spite of all grotesquerie". She returns on her "visit" to Guellen, the small central European town where she had been born, as the richest woman in the world. She had many years previously been forced to leave Guellen—after her childhood sweetheart Ill had deserted her and their child—to take up a life as a prostitute; it was subsequently she met the oil magnate Zachanassian. The inhabitants of Guellen have remained poor and they await her return fully aware of how she has it in her power to change the lives of them all; they need so little and she has so much. At the station, in the welcoming party among the local dignitaries is Ill, Clara's old lover. The inhabitants are unaware of his position, as he is himself unaware of his guilt. "Young and hot-headed, I used to be a bit of a lad forty-five years ago." Clara and her entourage arrive, including her seventh husband, an 80-year-old butler who wears sinister dark glasses. There is also an empty coffin, which is to be the price of Clara's "generosity". Everybody in the course of the play changes except the millionairess; she wants to take Ill away in that coffin. At first the citizens are horrified; this is Europe, the very heart of Europe, where they would prefer "to have poverty than blood on our hands".

It is not long, however, before the inhabitants begin to have second thoughts about their refusal of Clara Zachanassian's offer, and the millionairess is prepared to wait and give the inhabitants a sample of what they could buy on "credit". Knowing they have not the means of paying, Ill watches them all taking advantage of Clara's credit facilities; he realises what is happening but does not know how to protect himself. He goes to the station to leave the town and is followed there by the entire population who have come "to see him off". Although no one prevents him boarding the train, he finds he is for some reason unable to do so. He is ready to accept death at the hands of his people if that is what they want. He will submit to their justice which is no justice, he will not even commit suicide, they must do the killing. As the mayor announces the acceptance of Clara's offer, Ill is murdered. Officially he died of a heart attack "through joy". The millionairess departs with Ill in the coffin; the villagers have for the time being some extra spending money.

The part of Clara is a very exacting one. Dürrenmatt describes her as a Medea with a sense of humour, a rare grace as well as a wicked charm. Finally she is detached and in a rigid mould; there is no possibility for her development. Ill, on the other hand, is an almost empty character during the early part of the play, and it is only as death closes in on him that he becomes a man of strength and courage. Somehow he does not attract our sympathies until too late in the play; as long as the people of Guellen are on his side we feel he has conveniently forgotten the past. In all the productions I have seen of this play, including that of the Lunts (and also the film version with Ingrid Bergman) the part of Ill fails to reach a tragic dimension and measure up to the figure of Clara in the final scene.

*Frank der Fünfte* (Frank the Fifth, 1959) continues his virulent onslaught against the power of money. This time his "opera of a private bank" ends in the killing of the old head by the son. It proved a failure, and his next success came with *Die Physiker* (The Physicists, 1962). This time Dürrenmatt turned his attention to the madness which seeks to destroy the world. Here the accused are not the mad physicists who are in an asylum, but against the madness of people whom society believes sane and in whom we trust our fate. Set in a private Swiss sanatorium, "Les Cerisiers", the three patients, each a physicist, would be model patients but for the fact that the physicist who thinks that he is Sir Isaac Newton has recently murdered his nurse, as has in similar circumstances the physicist who believes he is Albert Einstein. By the end of the first act the third physicist, who believes he is in direct communication with King Solomon, has strangled his nurse.

In the second act the madness is proved calculating; it is not the three physicists who are mad, but the head of the sanatorium, Fräulein Doktor Matholde von Zahnd. She is moreover aware of the true identity of her distinguished patients; Newton and Einstein are atomic physicists who are acting as secret agents for their respective countries (East and West). Möbius, the physicist who claims inspiration from

Peter Weiss

Bertholt Brecht

JOHN ARDEN

CHRISTOPHER FRY

Solomon, is the true genius. He has deliberately sought refuge in a madhouse to prevent the world from using his discoveries. He tries also to persuade Newton and Einstein to stay with him, since were they to declare their sanity they would be murderers. Möbius further announces that he has destroyed all his papers, but too late, for the Fräulein Doktor has taken photostats of all his discoveries and intends to use them and become the most powerful person in the world.

In 1963 Dürrenmatt expanded his radio play *Herkules und der Stall des Augias* (Hercules and the Augean Stables), which had been written ten years previously, but this is a minor satire compared with the pitch black of *The Meteor* (1966), where Dürrenmatt rises to new heights as a jester with death. Wolfgang Schwitter is once again a Nobel Prize winner, who has been pronounced dead, but is Resurrected by the Life Force against his will. The play exposes the awkward and unthinkable consequences of his return to life; it is not merely a farce about what those who fear his return stand to lose, for they are all doomed to die before Schwitter, who is to survive them all. Meanwhile Schwitter, in the artist's garret where half a century earlier he had destroyed all his canvases before becoming a writer, now destroys his manuscripts and fortune in bank-notes, and prays for release. In the final scene where the "miracle of his resurrection" is being celebrated, Schwitter prays for mercy as the Salvation Army surround him.

No blacker satire could be supported, Dürrenmatt has become the iconoclast *par excellence* like the prophet of doom before Armageddon. Not only does Dürrenmatt assert his vision of the world, even in the adaptation of Shakespeare's "King John" which he made for the Basle Theatre, he interpreted and substituted a comedy of politics for what had been a dramatized chronicle. Even Shakespeare's call for English Unity was omitted, for Dürrenmatt views both the English, French and the Holy See as people pursuing their own interests and not serving the people. The bastard Falconbridge becomes his clown, and we should never forget that the Swiss have produced the most famous clowns of all time. So in *König Johann* (1968) the clown stands for reason in politics which are running riot.

In comparison with his compatriot Frisch, Dürrenmatt is brutally provoking and undoubtedly sinister; Frisch is the more sensitive, the spectator and witness. Dürrenmatt, who claims that he protects himself "by smoking cigars and wearing glasses over other smoked lenses and I stuff my ears full of cotton wool" is the introspective inquisitor of our times.

I

# SEVENTEEN

# THE THEATRE OF DISTURBANCE — PETER WEISS

> "Vice and the devil put a fallacy on our reasons, and provoking us too hastily to run from it, entangle and profound us deeper in it."
>
> SIR THOMAS BROWNE

THEATRE of absurdity some call it, theatre of cruelty others, but if we must have a label then perhaps Peter Brook is closest in calling it "the theatre of disturbance". You are born a Jew in the Germany of the First World War; twenty years later a concentration camp with gas incinerators is being built. You were destined to die there, but you avoid this because in 1934 your parents leave Germany for England. Had you stayed you might have adopted the English language, but at the time of Munich you are in Prague, the city of Kafka and where one morning for no good reason Joseph K. was arrested. Life seems impossible. As the Nazi tide insidiously advances you make for Switzerland, but this haven of neutralism is no refuge for an unknown artist without a bank balance. You have tried to stand on your own feet, to *épater les bourgeoises*, but it is no good. Everybody has to belong somewhere, to have visible means of support, to have a cream front door. Your parents have settled in Stockholm, and you accept their protection in order to enter Sweden. Another twenty years pass and you return to what was your country only to find yourself a stranger there; you visit the camp at Auschwitz where you were destined to die, and you have no relation to it.

Such is the strangely deracinated world of Peter Weiss, who found himself living in Stockholm and who continues to live there, while writing in German. As he has explained: "the cities in which I lived, in whose houses I stayed, on whose streets I walked, with whose inhabitants I spoke, have no definite contours, they merge into one another. . . ." In his autobiographical novel *Fluchpunkt* he is aware of having grown up without a country, and to-day "I could live in Paris, or Stockholm, or London, or New York, for I carry my luggage in the lightest of suitcases." If he prefers to write in German it is because "as an instrument of work" he finds it best, although he has "no emotional feelings with the country the language belongs to." Having no country he describes himself as a citizen of the world.

From surrealist painting Weiss turned to documentary film making; he also made a full-length film *The Mirage* which he has described as "a poem of a day in a city, a complex film about finding a way to exist". A way to exist, but how? In the twentieth century ways seem to grow out of desperation. The situation in which Weiss found himself in neutral Sweden was that he felt guilty for not being punished as all the others have been punished.

In an interview on the B.B.C. Third Programme Weiss told A. Alvarez that he had to be involved, even if he felt the whole world and the world of politics were a sort of madhouse. "So I have to take a standpoint even if I think it's mad. And this is the very, very great difficulty, because this sort of ambivalence between those two different points of view — on the one side extreme individualism and on the other the change of society in which we live in this madhouse world — and we have to take part in it."

Weiss does not believe that a writer should be an onlooker, but that he should set out to change the world with his writing. The problem then becomes, to avoid being merely destructive and negative, what is to be the new shape of society, the new vision? In desperation Weiss could appeal to the politicians, if only be could trust them, to take over from the creative mind. And yet was not the figure of Diogenes the greater respected by the politicians in refusing participation and honours? "When I read the speeches of the politicians", Weiss told Alvarez, "they are very close to madness to me, and then I reach a point where I don't understand it any longer. And at the same time now I have to understand, I have to find out what they are meaning, because it's their world I'm living in." Or again: "It would be much better if I could say of myself: 'Well, I am a Communist' or 'I am an extreme Socialist; I believe it absolutely.' Then I could say something. Now I am only in between. I have this third standpoint which I don't like myself."

Finally Weiss declared that he wrote in order to find out where he stood himself. It was a kind of frenzied dialectical battle where he had to take in all the doubts which produced his major work *The Persecution and Assassination of Marat as Performed by the Inmates of the Asylum of Charenton under the Direction of the Marquis de Sade* (1964). Just as Claudel had been tormented with spiritual conflicts while writing his *Partage de Midi*, so in *Marat* Weiss has given us one of the most important plays in the contemporary theatre, both considered as a text (the English version was made by Geoffrey Skelton, with verse adaptation by Adrian Mitchell), and the exciting possibilities of *mise-en-scène* to which it lends itself. Before considering the play in detail mention must now be made of Weiss's own conversion to Marxism, which he announced in May 1965. *Marat* must therefore be regarded as possibly a solitary and certainly a transitional work where the author discovered himself; he now claims that it was a production in Rostock in East Germany which alone grasped Marat's true heroic rôle and revolutionary mould, on whose side Weiss asserts he was on all the time. There is nothing in the text to make us believe that de Sade did not equally represent the author's intention in his stand for the individual and his prophetic vision, not to say cynicism, of the possible results of Revolution. That Weiss felt indecision unbearable is one thing, but his indecision was expressed in dramatic terms and conflict; to discover the purpose of his play through a Marxist-Leninist slant of production is to admit that the director has made up his mind and answered his doubts for him. *Marat* remains a play of authentic power, a play which very much disturbs us and which by its very nature does not offer us ready answers. It now looks as though Weiss has at last been driven to East Germany in the belief that at last he can find a home, a dogma, and that only by writing for the Communist revolution will his work be valid. After being a citizen of the world he now looks as though he is surrendering that title to become a citizen of the Commissars. But has he taken into account his own restless disposition might make the de Sade "individualism" continue to haunt his actions just as *wanderlust* might his imagination?

★

We are at the Charenton asylum on the 13 July 1808 — we, the audience, those privileged Parisians who have been invited to attend one of the regular theatrical "entertainments" which the enlightened head of the asylum, M. Coulmier, has included as part of the therapeutic treatment for his patients. This evening the subject is the assassination of Jean-Paul Marat by Charlotte Corday (which happened fifteen years previously), written and directed by the Marquis de Sade, himself an inmate since 1801. The play is being performed in the bath house of the asylum, and male nurses are completing some of the routine bathing and massage of the patients. The "moral rejects of the civilised world" are here in front of us, crouched in strangely embryonic postures or gazing with their glassy stares in schizophrenic attitudes. Sade appears, a pathetic figure, puffy and debauched (but rather by the privations society had inflicted on him through twenty-two years detention without female company rather than his previous notoriety) occupied with last minute preparations. The play begins, with the entry of M. Coulmier and his family, while Sade summons the players. Marat enters wrapped in a white sheet and enters the bath (which he was in life continually immersed in through a skin disease caught in the sewers) like in the famous painting by David. Marat stands for revolution:

> I don't watch unmoved I intervene
> and say that this and this are wrong
> and I work to alter them and improve them
> The important thing
> is to pull yourself by your own hair
> to turn yourself inside out
> and see the whole world with fresh eyes

Coulmier has to intervene several times in order to prevent Marat's revolutionary outbursts from getting out of hand, after all, aren't we all now "citizens of a new enlightened age?"

Sade takes up Marat's challenge with his position, and to counteract Marat's revolutionary fervour invites Charlotte Corday to whip him with her hair while he reminds us to where revolutions have led:

> To the withering of the individual man
> and a slow merging into uniformity

Marat is disillusioned with the way the Revolution has turned out, while pointing to the audience he remarks bitterly that "they" think the revolution has been won. In vain the chorus appeal to Marat:

Marat we're poor and the poor stay poor
Marat don't make us wait any more
We want our rights and we don't care how
We want our Revolution NOW

In the second part of the play, however, the chorus come to the support of Sade:

And what's the point of a revolution
without general copulation

The force of the debate almost overshadows the play within the play; Charlotte Corday, a melancholic patient who occasionally is roused from her trance-like sleep to act her part, finally gains entry to Marat's room and bath tub and momentarily becomes Charlotte in her act of killing Marat. The deed is committed but the patients, now overstimulated, want the play to continue. "Marat, we're marching on", they shout hysterically as they begin to go berserk and advance on the audience, the male nurses no longer able to control them.

There are many influences in the play, notably those of Artaud and Brecht. The play within the play enables Brecht's alienation techniques to be effective, so that the audience in Weiss's play is left in control of its own judgement, without surrendering either to Marat's revolutionary ideals or de Sade's cynicism; moreover, the fact that the play is being acted by lunatics raises a further question; both Marat and de Sade appear to be the prophets of the world we live in; indeed if Marat proposes a thesis, Sade disposes with equal sanity. It is the world which is mad and hypocritical, not the lunatics who are the misfits of man's own irrationality. In the Schiller Theatre production at Berlin the madhouse atmosphere tended to be aesthetic and abstract, whereas the Peter Brook production of the Royal Shakespeare Company in London (and subsequently in New York) had real and threatening madness in the air. Before the London production opened Weiss had already issued the astonishing statement that *Marat* is "a Marxist play. Marat should be the victor; if de Sade wins the debate, that is bad." Weiss may believe personally in Marat because "the things he says are the right things to do", but the pessimism of de Sade, foreseeing as it does the corruption of power and the road to serfdom, whether under Hitler or Stalin, may indeed make an uncommitted audience pause to examine the price of revolution, and whether the means is a justification for the aftermath. As in Hesse's *Steppenwolf*, we are between two ages, but this is not necessarily the capitalist and the communist, rather the old nineteenth-century capitalism and the new technological revolution. Even Marx once complained he was not a Marxist, and he would certainly be inclined to complain to the management on the strength of *Marat*.

Weiss is still working on an immense trilogy in the form of Dante's *Divine Comedy*. The intention was to continue the questions raised in *Marat*; in Dante's *Inferno* the sinners are punished in hell — Weiss has them live out their sins in this world and never get punished. They are the ones in power who should be punished. The second play, "Purgatorio", is supposed to express the state of doubt and "something of my own situation just now"; "Paradiso" is for those who were punished in this world and who have to live with the punishment all the time. During the trial of the Auschwitz functionaries in Frankfurt Weiss apparently had intended to incorporate some of the material of the trial. Eventually he decided to make a separate play of this, and he describes *Die Ermittlung* (The Investigation, 1965) as "an Oratorium in 11 Cantos." On October 19, 1965 the play had its *première* in thirteen West German theatres (including a production by Piscator in the Freie Volksbühne, Berlin), and the East German Berliner Ensemble, and a midnight play-reading by the Royal Shakespeare Company in London. One is numbed into submission by the incontrovertible facts, which are recited without emotion by the witnesses and stubbornly, haughtily denied by the S.S. defendants, in so far as they claimed to be obeying orders as mere pawns of a Satanic state. The personal witnesses are anonymous, since they speak for the hundreds who were called; on the other hand the defendants bear the names taken over from the actual trial. The play-reading of the Royal Shakespeare Company was a moving experience, the text as Peter Brook described it, was "transmitted at once to whom it may concern". It seems to me doubtful whether a set and music would have added to the text; there was something more arresting in the stark simplicity of a reading. In an article in *Encounter* (January 1966) Joel Carmichael complains that he found the play "singularly ineffective" and that "the first night audience in Berlin, in any case, was quite untouched". He would be proved wrong by the audience at the London play-reading, and I think the very facts recited without comment are overwhelming — I recall how even in Hochhuth's *The Representative* the pictures projected of the concentration camps sent the audience away in silence as if they had been at a service to atone for their guilt and complicity. Carmichael believes that Weiss "is determined to show that it was capitalism 'in its ultimate results' that produced Auschwitz" and that "the present-day implication of this is that in West Germany 'the hatred for Bolshevism is the successor to the hatred of the Jews'", I think the truth is that this excessive confrontation of man's inhumanity to man is not itself dramatic.

It took twenty years for the first play of Weiss, *Die Versicherung* (The Insurance Policy) to be at last produced in Essen in 1971. The plot concerns a chief of police who wishes to insure himself against all catastrophes whatever they may be, only to be hit by them one after another as he is negotiating with the company. His wife leaves him, his children turn against him, and in the end he is the victim of his own police, after horror has been heaped on horror. Weiss's play, surrealist and highly stylised, is immature and tedious; in the end it is the audience who suffers most.

*Nacht mit Gästen* (Night with Guests) was produced at the Schiller Theatre, Berlin in 1963 and at the Traverse, Edinburgh in 1965. This is a minor curtain raiser, an experiment in variations between mime and grotesque violence when a robber with a huge knife terrifies a peasant family and kills husband and wife. The casketful of gold he was looking for contains no more than gold turnips.

Also dating from this period is *Wie dem Herrn Mockinpott das Leiden ausgetrieben wird* (How Mr. Mockinpott was freed from his Fears) where Mockinpott has to run the gambit of human misfortune, the eleven scenes including prison, his inability to find employment, at the doctors, before the government, and finally his rejection of God, for in growing up Mockinpott has learnt his "destiny is Mockinpott".

After *Marat*, at the age of fifty, Weiss turned Marxist. His more recent works have been exclusively directed towards political rather than artistic ends, his attack on colonialism in *Angola Gesang vom lusitanisc en Popanz* (The Song of the Lusitanian Bogey, 1967), performed by the Negro Ensemble Company in New York, a theatre *verité* attack on the Portuguese in Angola, and the native rebellion there on 15 March 1961. Maoist red herrings are everywhere evident in his diatribe against American colonialism and the Vietnam war in *Diskurs über die Vorgeschichte und den Verlauf des lang andauernden Befreiungskrieges in Viet Nam als Beispiel für die Notwendigkeit des bewaffneten Kampfes der Unterdrückten gegen ihre Unterdrücker sowie über die Versuche der Vereinigten Staaten von Amerika die Grunlagen der Revolution zu vernichten* (Discourse on the Historical Background and the Course of the Continuous Struggle for Liberation in Viet Nam as an Example of the Necessity of Armed Warfare by the Oppressed against their Oppressors and Furthermore on the Attempts of the United States of America to Annihilate the Basic Principles of the Revolution, 1968). It has been said that Marx was determined to write *Das Kapital* in several volumes in order to be taken seriously; in the age of Marshal McLuhan a title you cannot finish suffices.

The following year he wrote *Trotzki im Exil*, again in a documentary style. We are promised a play on Holderlyn, the German Hellenist who believed in building a new community based on ideals at the beginning of last century.

For all this frenzy of political preaching, Weiss will be remembered for the non-commitment of *Marat*; Now that his inner conflict, like Herr Mockinpott, are resolved, even Hegelian dialectics are over and the world of creation as everything comes to a stop. Unlike Casare Pavese, when he remarked that "to go into forced residence is nothing; to come back from it is the worst" with Weiss to make his decision was everything, for he has chosen the course of no return. He is a preacher now more than a playwright, and it is always easy to preach to the converted.

# EIGHTEEN

# THE STATE OF DRAMA: BRITAIN

Page 255——

> "The inhabitant of a country has at least nine characters: a
> professional one, a national one, a civic one, a class one, a geo-
> graphical one, a sex one, a conscious, an unconscious and
> perhaps even too a private one; he combines them all in
> himself, but they dissolve him, and he is really nothing but
> a little channel washed out by all these trickling streams,
> which flow into it and drain out of it again in order to join
> other little streams filling another channel."
>
> ROBERT MUSIL, *The Man Without Qualities*

A NEW DRAMA OR WE FAINT!—this "money or your
life!" call for help was the title of a theatre book published in
1853. A century later the British theatre-goer had grown used
to sleeping, even stage villains had become as genteel as the rest of the
theatre. Playgoing had become dull, it was a safety-first theatre where
passions were hinted at rather than experienced. Revivals were the
order of the day, the star system dictated the choice. It was a theatre
of stale naturalism; it was an apathetic theatre unaware that the world
it was supposed to reflect was there no longer—it had become a
drawing-room museum. They were hardly aware there had been a
revolution; the knocking at the door was dismissed as anger without
cause. But the revolution really had begun, with Osborne, with the
production at the Royal Court in 1956 of *Look Back in Anger*.

The English Stage Company at the Royal Court succeeded under
the direction of George Devine in finding the new dramatists, by
initiating Sunday evening productions without decor and by having
the courage of its convictions, even when writers it believed in, such
as John Arden, proved box-office failures. Gradually London's theatre
life split between the commercial managements, and the new subsidised
theatres, first the Royal Court, and then the National Theatre together
with Peter Hall's brilliant direction of the Royal Shakespeare Company

which took over the Aldwych Theatre, and made experimental seasons first at the Arts Theatre club, and at LAMDA. Before the idea of subsidy had been generally accepted, mention must be made of the valiant pioneering work of Joan Littlewood at Theatre Workshops' Theatre Royal in Stratford in the East End of London. Her discoveries of Shelagh Delaney, Brendan Behan and the production of *Oh What a Lovely War* all proved box-office hits when transferred to the West End. Another new theatre of promise was Bernard Miles' Mermaid Theatre in Puddle Dock, built on the site of a blitzed warehouse and one of the most delightful theatres that has been built.

There has also been a stir of theatrical activity in the provinces starting with the Belgrade Theatre at Coventry, which first discovered Arnold Wesker and brought him to the Royal Court. Gradually the old touring companies of the commercial managements have come to a halt, and provincial audiences have come to accept the idea of a Municipal Theatre, again generally subsidised, following the experiences of the continent. The Nottingham Playhouse, the Municipal Theatre at Edinburgh (which had taken over the old Lyceum), the Yvonne Arnaud theatre at Guildford are among the new ventures. The Chichester Festival is yet another exciting new development.

More and more the realisation that good theatre requires subsidy has been accepted in Britain, and in the case of London's three main subsidised theatres, without much evidence of outside pressures. (The same is not always true, as in the experience of the Glasgow Citizen's Theatre and Glasgow Corporation's disapproval of their policy). Works like *The Devils*, Whiting's ambitious dramatisation of Huxley's novel *The Devils of Loudun*, and Shaffer's spectacle *The Royal Hunt of the Sun* or Arden's *Armstrong's Last Goodnight* would almost certainly never have been considered by commercial managements. The era of Cochrane's great spectacles is over; rising costs have made a new *Cavalcade* impractical, and television seems to have dwarfed the plays of commercial managements. The hopes of the drama in the period of transition lie in the outstanding productions of the National Theatre and the Royal Shakespeare Company, and the more erratic but necessary experiments at the Royal Court. The British theatre has a better chance than ever before of raising standards and taste; the challenge of television has been met. It is encouraging to report that the standards of acting and production in London are among the best in the world; the dramatists often come a poor third, but at least they are emerging, if some are not yet very sure of themselves or of what they want to say.

★

Before considering the younger generation of British playwrights, this would seem the right place to pay tribute to two great names which have marked our theatre since the days of Ibsen and Shaw: Sean O'Casey, the last and the most rejected of the great Abbey Theatre school which included Yeats and Synge; and James Bridie, a Scottish gadfly who had all but Shaw's wit, and certainly a more tolerant smile for the frailties of human nature. An Englishman, John Whiting will be the subject of a third tribute, for though Whiting was not of their generation, his premature death at the age of 48 robbed the British theatre of more than a potential, but a very real talent.

## SEAN O'CASEY (1880–1964)

Sean O'Cathasaigh, who changed his name to O'Casey after the Abbey Theatre accepted *The Shadow of a Gunman* in 1923, had a turbulent and short career in Dublin. *Juno and the Paycock* (1924) was followed by the *Plough and the Stars* (1926) which provoked such scenes of rioting that O'Casey, when *The Silver Tassie* was rejected in 1928, turned his back on Ireland for good and exiled himself in Cornwall, England. On the strength of these three plays alone Casey's name was established as a playwright of outstanding importance in the inter-war years, and a voice which has probably had greater influence on contemporary British playwrights than any other name that comes to mind, with the exception of Brecht.

Unfortunately the tragedy of Ireland was to become the tragedy of O'Casey, for unlike his compatriot, Shaw, O'Casey was a foreigner exiled from everything he believed in, and in his new environment his "Genius" which he had rightly proclaimed to his fellow Irishmen during the rioting at the Abbey theatre, gradually turned to bitterness, his poetry to politics, his nationalistic hopes to the hopes for a Communist international, and his darlin' son was born a red Commissar. O'Casey was never again to write a heartfelt tragedy after leaving Dublin; nor did he fare much better with the sophisticated tastes of West-End London managers than he had to contend with in the political timidity of the Abbey Theatre when they rejected his early works.

### JOHN WHITING (1915-1963)

One of the ironies in life and literature is that recognition of an artist's merit is often withheld until after his death. Certainly under-estimated both by critics, the public, and the new school of dramatists (perhaps not surprisingly the latter, for he had said of them, "we face the prospect of having nothing in this kind of theatre but plays for peasants"). Whiting is now praised as "a progenitor of the new British drama" and considered by many critics as the most under-valued writer of his time. Was there, we cannot help wondering, in fact, "a glass wall dividing us from what was happening on the stage", and has this now been shattered by his death, making the loss of a potentially great writer at last realised? Potentially, for Whiting seemed a man of imaginative ideas and dramatic power who was unable to express himself clearly and directly. His plays became too obstuse, too worked upon until the very simplicity of the theme was hidden and disappeared in the verbiage. Not verbiage in the then fashionable Christopher Fry sense of the early fifties, but more, as Whiting was to admit himself, of "a Websterian accumulation of detail which has confused and angered many people". Although Whiting had been an actor, in his own plays he was much more an intellect seeking not so much dramatic situations as an exploration of the theme of self-destruction. His theatre consists of five plays — a small body of work on which to have built a significant reputation: *Conditions of Agree-ment* (written shortly after the war), *Saint's Day* (1949), *A Penny for a Song* (his first play to be staged, 1951), *Marching Song* (1954) and *The Gates of Summer* (1956). Whiting then seems to have been discouraged by his lack of any real success and to have momentarily abandoned playwriting when Peter Hall, on taking over direction of the Royal Shakespeare Company, commissioned him to adapt Aldous Huxley's book *The Devils of Loudun*; *The Devils*, produced in 1961, was immedi-ately recognised as a work of major importance. With a theme near to his own heart Whiting in this adaptation had succeeded where he had failed with his own plays, to conduct an investigation into the nature of good and evil, and in the relationship between the two he was able to communicate in a memorable way the self-destruction of Grandier, the libertine priest in search of salvation.

There is nothing much to remark on in *Conditions of Agreement*, Whiting's first play. A genteel widow, Emily Doon, lives with her crippled son and dreams of the day when one of her old lovers returns and gives her a future. He does so, a retired clown, and "moves" in, like a character out of a Pinter play. Whiting subsequently adapted this play for television under the title *A Walk in the Desert*. Whiting's next play, on the other hand, caused a furore, for *Saint's Day* was the winner of the Arts Theatre Play Competition in 1951, and was violently attacked by the critics (*The Times* reported that it was "of a badness that must be called indescribable") while the three judges of the competition, Christopher Fry, Alec Clunes and Peter Ustinov, vigorously defended their selection.

The theme is of an elderly writer, Southman, who for many years has refused to have anything to do with the community where he lives and who has been ostracised by them, until one day a young poet and critic attempts to end the feud. The old man is living with his daughter and her husband, an artist who has refused to show his paintings to a world he likewise despises. There is a sub-plot of three soldiers who are marauding and the vicar who asks the old man for his help only to be refused. So far so good, but already the theme has become confused, and as confusion enters the text fails to sustain whatever might have been Whiting's intentions; the theme started off as ambitious and interesting, but the play does not make it as a play.

*A Penny for a Song* is very different in mood, the only happy one Whiting ever wrote. It has the elements of both farce and fantasy, dealing with two English eccentrics at the time of the Napoleonic wars; one of them, Sir Timothy Bellboys, believed he would be able to defeat any invasion by digging a tunnel and coming up behind the enemy lines disguised as Napoleon and ordering them to lay down their arms.

The atmosphere of *Marching Song* is again different. It reminds one of a play by Ugo Betti — only with something missing — the theme of a man who is a prisoner both in fact and also inwardly of his own conscience is one which Betti could have developed with depth. *Marching Song*, though not an important play, is nevertheless an interesting one. A general of a defeated army is released from prison in order to face a trial where he will be a scapegoat for the humiliation of a nation. In order to preserve the unity of the nation, however, the Chancellor tries to persuade the general to commit suicide, and it is this choice which the play develops in its conflict — for the punishment requires the general's disgrace. The general's conscience forces him to relive the horror when he ordered his mechanised brigade to mow down a swarm of children who had blocked their way in an attack. The general had made his choice then, and in the horror of the deed immediately afterwards, he had been unable to continue the pre-arranged attack. His pride for war had overlooked humanity, and for victory was substituted his defeat. In the decision he has to take after release from the prison, he has to find his own way out. For neither the woman he no longer loves nor the young girl whom he has just met and who momentarily inspires him with confidence can answer for him.

*The Gates of Summer*, which was never produced in London although it has had productions in Germany, is set in Greece in 1913. Unlike the Byronic theme which sparked off Whiting's original idea, the sensualist turns from his Don Juan pursuits to identify himself with a revolutionary cause. The idea is initially a good one, like so many of Whiting's ones. With *The Devils* the idea comes from Aldous Huxley's book, which Whiting follows very closely, though the dialogue is his own. For the first time he appears to have mastered his craft; the power of darkness and evil and self-destruction are all there. Grandier prays for salvation, his thirty-five years "heavy with pride and ambition, love of women and love of self. Years scandalously marred by adornment and luxury, time taken up with being that nothing, a man". Grandier has loved for lust, but with the girl Philippe whom he is tutoring he loves for love, and secretly marries her. Meanwhile sister Jeanne-des-Anges, a hunchback, prays not only to have her humped back taken away, but also to be loved, and cannot get Grandier out of her mind. "My beloved sister in Jesus seems to have fixed her mind on me," as Grandier remarks. And with love comes hate; furious because Grandier refuses to be her convent's spiritual adviser Jeanne pretends to be possessed by devils and accuses Grandier of being responsible. In seventeenth-century France such charges are taken seriously; Grandier is arrested and found guilty at his trial of "commerce with the devil" and that he used "this unholy alliance to possess, seduce, and debauch certain sisters of the holy order of Saint Ursula." Grandier is brought to the torture but he refuses to confess. Whiting here writes a remarkable passage on the meaning of pain, as put to Grandier:

It is very difficult for us standing here, both healthy men, to imagine the shattering effect of agony. The sun's warm on your face at the moment, isn't it? And you can curl your toes if you want to in your slippers. You are alive and you know it. But when you are stretched out in that little room, with the pain screaming through you like a voice, let me tell you what you will think. First, how can man do this to man? Then: how can God allow it? Then: There can be no God. Then: there is no God. The voice of pain will grow stronger, and your resolution weaker. Despair, Grandier."

We are eyewitnesses of the torture of Grandier, we see him maimed before us and his crippled body being dragged through the streets to be burned at the stake. Before the convent Jeanne and Grandier face each other, and Grandier tells her: "Look at this thing which I am and learn the meaning of love." Grandier has found salvation through his own damnation. Whiting once said in a television interview: "Every sensible man doubts the existence of God from time to time . . . it would be a very unwise man who doubted the existence of the devil." It may be that *The Devils* will be remembered long after Whiting's own plays are forgotten.

★

O'Casey, Bridie, Whiting, but where do we begin with the regiments of British playwrights who, like all good soldier Schweiks, refuse classification?

First, one name we have missed out, that of Sir Noël Coward. It was never part of the original design of this book to include those writers who seemed to belong more to the twenties and the inter-war period rather than to have influenced the present. However prolific Coward has been in the last thirty years, nothing has matched the brilliance of his early work, from *The Vortex* onwards; the sparkle of his dialogue belonged to an age where there was still leisure to enjoy champagne, before the trend setters followed Sagan to St. Tropez. The *menages-à-trois* of Coward are prisoners of their own conversation, they are earth bound, living another existence from the "Jet Set" of the Jumbo age.

Before considering the important work and names of the contemporary British school, certain playwrights form a non-classification group. Sir Terence Rattigan, who can claim to have taken over from Coward, has found his position unchanged by any of the revolutions at the Royal Court, whether of Osborne or the Edward Bond decades. Only the versatility of Peter Ustinov matches his commercial acumen. Christopher Fry, who was once such a white hope for the poetic revival of the English drama, has faded into the background, though his recent play *A Yard of Sun* enables an assessment to be made of his seasonal quartet, now completed.

Another bystander, left behind by the contemporary scene, is J. B. Priestley; both his time plays of the thirties and his social purpose plays of the forties are too irrelevantly pretentious to interest this day and age. On the other hand his real talent lay in the comic, and the recent successful revival in London of his farce *When We Are Married* confirms this.

A very different lone wolf is Graham Greene, whose contribution to the theatre in the end may not prove to be more than the now forgotten Charles Morgan; it is as a novelist that Graham Greene is unsurpassed in England, and will remain one of the great figures of the 20th century novel.

If we are to consider order of importance and influence, it is rather playwrights such as Harold Pinter, John Arden, Peter Shaffer, Arnold Wesker who should have precedence.

JOHN ARDEN

Arden presents an enigma to critics and public alike; almost anything that may be said of him can be contradicted, generally by Arden himself. You can, for example, claim correctly that he is the most Brechtian of British playwrights, and yet he does not commit himself to any one side. Is *Serjeant Musgrave's Dance* a pacifist play? At first it appears to be so, but in the end other cross-currents intervene, the serjeant outwardly strong is a simple confused man who does not know how to communicate his message or set his plans in action. Arden believes that it is objectively in the theatre which counts, in both emotion and causes — but who is to decide? "If a character starts off" Arden has written in *Peace News*, "by being sympathetic and then turns off in a direction that people don't like, that is in fact what often happens with people that one knows in life. I never write a scene so that an audience can identify with any particular character . . . it's not up to me to make audience's judgements on the various characters in the play." So much for Arden's intentions, but has he the vision to reveal things of which an audience was not previously aware, can he lead them into a new dimension by thinking faster, seeing further than them? Or is his view the average one of confusion, the incomplete crossword puzzle mentality?

Perhaps we are asking too much of him, by reminding ourselves of the standards of great writers, whereas maybe Arden will never be more than a writer in the old "popular tradition", without finding the public he deserves. For here is another anomaly, Arden has set himself against the current towards the metropolis and capital cities, and his reputation was confirmed not by London but the support of the provinces. Arden is in the best sense a regional writer; with the exception of his adaptation of Goethe's *Goetz von Berlichingen* (a free adaptation indeed under the title *Ironhand*), Arden has never in his plays left the British Isles. A post-war Council Estate in a north-country industrial town is the setting for *Live Like Pigs*, an old folks home is that of *The Happy Haven*, a mining town in the North of England eighty years ago for *Serjeant Musgrave's Dance*, a Yorkshire industrial town in *The Workhouse Donkey*; historically Arden has depicted the times of King John in *Left Handed Liberty* and the border raids and ballads in *Armstrong's Last Goodnight*. Arden has in the latter most successfuly combined his separate use of poetry and prose, the subject lending itself admirably to this purpose. In the prose of *Armstrong* he has brilliantly captured the vernacular of the sixteenth-century lowland Scots, so that the ebb and flow of poetry in the ballads and the prose seem completely natural, as if, in fact, we were watching a production of a play from that period. It proves fairly conclusively how wrong Eliot was to put poetry on a meagre ration and introduce it gradually and mildly to the public used to the cadences of naturalistic prose. But in the other plays of Arden the transition from poetry to prose is more obviously Brechtian in technique, and unconvincing.

John Arden was born at Barnsley, Yorkshire, in 1930. He studied architecture at Cambridge and Edinburgh Universities; while at Edinburgh students performed a play of his, *All Fall Down*, and he also won a B.B.C. Northern Region prize for a radio play *The Life of Man*, which was about an ill-fated last voyage of a packet-boat with a mad captain. This brought him eventually to the attention of the English Stage Society, who produced *Waters of Babylon* as an experimental Sunday-night production without decor in 1957. The play was received with critical bewilderment, and Arden's career might well have ended there. The following year, however, the Royal Court produced *Live Like Pigs* which proved a failure, and in 1959 *Serjeant Musgrave's Dance*, which was a disaster both financially and at the hands of the London critics. The Royal Court on that production alone lost

£5,820, the equivalent of its annual subsidy. In the commercial theatre no playwright could normally hope to continue with such a series of financial failures behind him, but in 1960 Arden had been awarded a fellowship grant at Bristol University, and while there he wrote and had produced in an Open Stage production *The Happy Haven*.

*Serjeant Musgrave's Dance* is a strange, complex and unsatisfactory play, which inexplicably has become a favourite choice in the provinces. We are in a snow-bound Northern town sometime between the years 1860-1880; Arden thinks of the paintings of L. S. Lowry in his description of the place. The town is isolated when Musgrave and three soldiers arrive; furthermore the miners are on strike, and the mayor and mine owner fear trouble. Serjeant Musgrave, in his thirties, tall, commanding, a soldier who "could have served under Cromwell" with the other rough and seasoned soldiers are not regarded as the deserters, but ask the protection of the law. We learn however that Musgrave's message to the townspeople is to be a pacifist one, for concealed in one of their boxes they are carrying is a skeleton in uniform of one of the boys from that town, whose murder in the colonies resulted in Musgrave and his companions undertaking terrible reprisals. Horrified themselves by the mass murder, they are convinced that the townspeople will share their shame:

> This town is ours, it's ready for us: and its people when they've heard us, and the Word of God, crying the murders that we've done — I'll tell you they'll turn to us, and they'll turn against the war.

By the time Musgrave confronts the population and the strikers events have almost overtaken them. The most pacifist among the soldiers has been killed and Musgrave has condoned the murder because the man was deserting their cause. By doing so he ruins his own case. In the end it is with a sense of relief that the Dragoons arrive, for Musgrave by now merely looks ridiculous, a religious maniac who, with the confusion of a simpleton, is not a tragic character. The bargee with his cynical cheek who acts as a chorus throughout the action, seems to prove his point. Musgrave is the disintegration of a man, and we have never met the Serjeant, the fighter, we have only met the man possessed with a demonic madness. The parallel situation when the play was written (1959) with the action of British troops in Cyprus in fact adds nothing to the play (the parallel seems another confusing issue, not the clear-cut one of Sartre's relevance of Algeria in his play *Altona*). The play where no one cares in the end, where Arden makes statements, and leaves them at that for his audience to interpret, produces the result that Musgrave is rejected by us as well.

In *The Happy Haven* (subsequently produced at the Royal Court, 1960), Arden makes a break with stage conventions; by song, mask and an open stage he aims at an effect of formalisation such as we find in the oriental theatre. *The Happy Haven* is a sardonic farce in which lyricism and acute observation are tempered by irony. The "haven" is an old folk's home: the inmates lead an existence on the edge of death and like the ancients at the end of *Gulliver's Travels* all they now know is "plotting and planning, avarice and spite". Their law and their Lord; the custodian of their destinies, is the Doctor. He to the point of parody is a man of the science age: strictly clinical in his approach to his patients, his entire ambition is to produce from test tubes the elixir of life. Conflict develops when the patients, after discovering his purpose by cunning, realise they don't want to be the objects of his experiment, for playing the truth and lie game forces them to the painful recognition that their past lives have all been failures and that they daren't face inevitable repetition by having their youth again. When therefore the Doctor arranges for a group of public dignitaries to witness the triumphant application of his elixir the patients switch the tables on him: *he* is the one that gets the injection and becomes a child again, while the stuffed shirt dignitaries flee, and paradoxically the patients have established by their act that there is still some fiat in their senile souls. In the last lines of the play the patients in chorus warn the audience to be useful and cheerful in their old age and to remember that they must die. But what finally is Arden's meaning? He has not used masks to stir our souls and he has not taken the themes of youth and age to engage our deeper sympathies. Where the play should be strongest, namely, in the presenting to our minds a coherent intellectual or moral thesis, it fails. The wider significance of its themes is not established and it remains a play more interesting for its technical experiment than for its meaning.

In *The Workhouse Donkey* (produced at the Chichester Festival, 1963) Dionysus comes into his own. The Comic Theatre, Arden remarks in his preface, was expressly formed to celebrate "noise, disorder, drunkenness, lasciviousness, nudity, generosity, corruption, fertility and ease." *The Workhouse Donkey* is a melodrama with musical accompaniment; its manner is Brechtian, its material complicated and intractable. Minor themes — politics, vice, civic corruption, class feeling — are submerged, their resonance muffled by the tempest of living. Arden, who appears to see all sides on all questions takes no side on any.

Arden would have liked his play to last thirteen hours, with the audience coming and going as at a fairground; as it is he should be given credit for his feat of compressing the material. The setting is a provincial Yorkshire town; Arden fills the stage with people of high and low estate who though slightly larger than life and touched with caricature are basically conceived in realistic terms. They have in common a sense of homogeneity of background; we see them at the civic function, in the council chamber, the police station, the illicit night-club and the pub, we are not surprised to see the same person at each. Themes and people are woven together on a very slender thread of story. Colonel Feng is a new chief constable who comes to the town to clean it up. He tries to maintain a strictly impartial course but in doing so he falls foul of both political parties, some of whose members are put in an embarrassing position by his investigations, and he is forced to resign. By far the most vital characters are Alderman Boocock, the ex-Mayor, and Dr. Blomax, a wily and venal physician. Boocock (The Workhouse Donkey) is the strong man on the Labour side, a prodigiously unselfconscious lover of power; but when his corrupt practices are exposed he submits to his defeat with the impenitent *panache* of a renaissance villain. Blomax, who is hand in glove with Boocock, is more fortunate but no less unabashed: he ends up marrying his daughter to Alderman Sweetman, the leader of the local Conservatives.

*Left-Handed Liberty* (Mermaid Theatre, 1965) is a play of words rather than action. The rather cumbrous material does not lend itself easily to dramatic handling, though Arden has done something to lighten it and quicken it by means of doggerel, occasionally vivid, at significant points of the story and a peripheral love interest. Characterisation, except in the case of King John, is subordinate to the weighty issue of the Charter over which the contestants fight. On the one side is 'bluntsword' John, wily, intemperate and unpredictable, with his followers about him (of whom Langton and the Marshal are the most prominent), and on the other are the bone-headed unpredictable barons, while the Mayor of London falls somewhere in between them and a greedy French king waits for his chance to cross the Channel.

In the background acting the role of smug chorus is the sly Papal
Legate. Of the characters by far the most interesting is John. He is
cruel, untrustworthy, cunning, humorous, capable of kindness; above
all he is wilful. To pacify the barons John sets his Seal on the Charter,
but neither side trusts the other and while the barons outbid John in a
deal with the Mayor of London, John recruits mercenaries in Flanders.
A month after Runnymede John and the barons assemble in council at
Oxford to see that the provisions of the Charter are being implemented
(which they are not); John promises to cancel his drive for recruits
and the barons agree to leave London; but John secretly countermands
his cancellation order and the barons invite the French into London.
In the penultimate scene John steps out of history to deliver a speech on
the Charter and an eloquent but largely irrelevant speech on the
character of women. Finally, marching with his army upon London,
he is overtaken by the effects of a surfeit of cider and peaches and
dies scrabbling after his jewels in the rising tide of the Wash.

*Left-Handed Liberty* was commissioned by the Corporation of the
City of London to commemorate the 750th Anniversary of the sealing
of Magna Carta; unfortunately in spite of its historical honesty it
offers too little in excitement, allows the thread of dramatic action to
become too nearly lost in talk, and all-in-all expects in the audience too
much enthusiasm for political debate.

"An Exercise in Diplomacy" is Arden's description of *Armstrong's
Last Goodnight* (first produced at Glasgow Citizens Theatre, 1964);
here is the important play for which we had been waiting. Arden is
interested in historical parallels — in *Serjeant Musgrave's Dance*
nineteenth-century colonialism had been compared with the action
of British troops in Cyprus — and he dedicates *Armstrong's Last
Goodnight* to Conor Cruise O'Brien. The similarities between intellectual characters like Dr. O'Brien and Sir David Lindsay came to
Arden's attention while reading O'Brien's account of the Congo
crisis in his book *To Katanga and Back*. "I was immediately struck,"
Arden writes, "by a number of pertinent similarities between Scotland
in 1528 and the Congo in 1961." However, Lindsay is not meant to
represent O'Brien, nor is Armstrong Tshombe. Arden has moreover
not based his play on the historical fact that Lindsay was sent to deal with
the Armstrong problem, though it is a fact that Lindsay was sent on many
missions for the Scottish crown, and Arden does not believe that Lindsay
would have taken a different line had he been sent as in his play.

The two characters, John Armstrong of Gilnockie and Sir David

Lindsay are admirably contrasted. Lindsay might be said to be "too clever by half," a Machiavellian genius who can outmatch most moves; he knows when to flatter, when to tease, when to be ruthless. Armstrong is "a great bull, or lion" of a man; he has a speech defect which prevents him talking coherently; his "exaggerated stammer" is only overcome when he is either "extremely excited" or when he sings. He is in contrast to Lindsay a simple man, an innocent unable to grasp the manipulations of Lindsay's tactics. "The King has callit me brither" is sufficient for Armstrong to dress himself for the occasion and accept Lindsay's word. Armstrong's pride is his greatness, and as Macbeth is no tyrant, so Armstrong is no ordinary border bandit when his end comes in the betrayal. A sub plot introducing a Lutheran Evangelist who might have stepped out of Arthur Miller's play *The Crucible* seems irrelevant to the duel between Lindsay and the untamed force of Armstrong. Arden may not have taken sides, but his vision and feeling for the period is overwhelming. It is almost as if he were like the Dutch art forger Van Meegeren producing an undiscovered original, perhaps by Sir David Lindsay himself (he did after all write *The Three Estates*, which in Robert Kemp's adaptation has triumphed at the Edinburgh Festival in the open stage Assembly Hall). It is indeed difficult to remember that the play has been written by a young contemporary dramatist who has managed to capture the authentic rhythms of Lowland Scots as well as the zest and restless roamings of the marauders like the Armstrongs.

This is indeed a vindication to those who had such faith in Arden from the start, who argued his case in spite of repeated box office disasters, and even plays which did not come across without a kind of blur and confusion in spite of great intelligence and a fine mastery of language. Even with *Armstrong's Last Goodnight*, which has now entered the repertory of the National Theatre, Arden is far from being the popular playwright; he has made his mark, but even in Britain the larger public are only just beginning to know his work (though he is studied in schools and dramatic societies); will he remain a regional writer, or will his interest in historical parallels between past and present also lead him to one of comparative literatures and become an important writer of his age?

## HAROLD PINTER

Harold Pinter is a counter-type John Bull, born in Hackney, London, 1930. It is difficult to imagine anyone more typically English than the characters of a Pinter play — their way of talking and reacting, their cold reserve, their dry humour, the laconic monosyllabic exchanges which betray the undertones of emotion — seldom has understatement been so effectively conveyed. Yet it is more than a theatre of under-statement, it is also one of irrational impulses ever present, which create an atmosphere of nervous tension. Suddenly the monotony of the social ritual is shattered and the characters are set in motion to explain the outcome of a situation about which we are given the minimum, and that often contradictory, of information. The world of Pinter is one where people live their ordinary lives like driving a car in neutral, until they are forced to respond by something external, the intruder who enters and reverses a stable situation or renders it ludicrous. There is much in Pinter's imagination of a Peter Pan who flies in through the window, flutters round the drawing-room — only Pinter's walls are without wall-paper — and startles the occupants by joining their parlour-game. The poetic element should assert itself here, but is defeated by the too realistic framework, for Pinter's flight's of fancy are conducted with his feet firmly on the ground. Nor are there any planes of reality, or the delineation between illusion and the actual which renders the truth of the world for which Pinter seeks beyond the confines of his constraint. As Julien Green has reminded us, "the sin of the modern world is the refusal of the invisible." Pinter's world is an incomplete one, his characters are expressly without qualities, his plays without a philosophy or the levels of communication which are essential if his drama is to have universal validity.

This is to ask more of Pinter than he would claim himself; he believes that "a character on the stage who can present no convincing argument or information as to his past experience, his present behaviour or his aspirations, nor give a comprehensive analysis of his motives, is as legitimate and worthy of attention as one who, alarmingly, can do all these things."[1] The only facts we have are within, the time and the address; outside everything is vague, uncertain, it belongs to a past which has slipped our memory and to which we can never return. The future is an unrelated *mañana*, only the present matters, the improvisa-tion that is necessary, the sudden release from inhibitions and the frenzy of sexual motivation, and then the return to "as you were", more small talk followed by those dreaded silences. The claustrophobic power of the closed setting seeps through us, we are trapped by the intruder who has created a variable, the tramp who hopes to take over,

[1] "Time and Tide," interview with Peter Lewis, 21 June, 1962.

the match-seller who will supplant the husband, the sinister arrival of the two visitors with a "Mission", the son with his doctorate from the States and his well "qualified" wife. Pinter has admirably captured the ways and understood the subtleties of the English class structure, better than overtly social writers such as Wesker. At the same time he has no message, no axe to grind, no significance is to be attached to his themes, nor do they mask any abstract idea; as he himself has admitted: "I wouldn't know a symbol if I saw one." We must accept Pinter's assurance that there is nothing in his plays other than what we see.

Pinter writes very much from his practical training as an actor, first at R.A.D.A. and at the Central School, followed by nine years in repertory. We are told he likes cricket, that he was once a chucker-out at the Astoria Dance Hall in Charing Cross Road and worked as a waiter in the National Liberal Club. Between the ages of fourteen and twenty-four he wrote poetry; since writing plays he no longer does so. It seems to be his drama school training which bears directly on what has become known as Pinterism, the pure improvisation of situations, creating characters out of the minimum of information, reacting according to the milieu they belonged. Pinter would argue that this is the way we meet people, and that when his characters first appear on the stage he knows no more about them than we do; the danger is that they remain mere automatons responding to group reflexes and although they strive to escape and assume an individuality of their own they do not know how to achieve this. In the end they fail to move us because they have failed to communicate, to establish a relationship.

All this may be seen from Pinter's first full length play *The Birthday Party*, which was produced in 1957 and condemned by the London critics as a whole; it is not without comment that a revival in 1965 received critical acclaim in London. *The Birthday Party* is a good example of Pinter's work generally, since he cannot be said to have advanced since then, for he does not have any particular goal. As in all his work we have the feeling that he improvises the situations as he goes along, invents confusions and misunderstandings, the intruder arrives normally and makes the menace of his presence felt; somehow in the end the characters muddle through as in life. We are in the living-room of a house in a seaside town. Meg and Petey, a man and wife in their sixties, discuss over breakfast their lodger Stanley, who soon appears in his pyjamas, unshaven. Stanley is alarmed to hear that Meg has two gentlemen lodgers coming. On their arrival Stanley slips out the back way. The two men, Goldberg and McCann ask Meg about her lodger, and Meg tells them it is Stanley's birthday. She jumps at Goldberg's idea of a celebration party. Stanley returns when Meg is on her own and denies it is his birthday. Nevertheless he accepts Meg's present which is a boy's drum and marches round the room beating it, first gently, then savagely.

Goldberg and McCann confront Stanley; they catechise him mercilessly with staccato questions. They accuse him of sin, defilement, betrayal, murder, finally of being dead. McCann and Stanley seize chairs and they circle each other until Meg returns and they assume normality. The birthday party begins and at Meg's suggestion they play blind man's bluff. Goldberg and McCann converge on Stanley who backs giggling away.

In the third act we learn from Goldberg that Stanley has had a nervous breakdown and that they will look after him. Stanley comes down to breakfast dressed like a city gentleman and sits silent and blank as McCann and Goldberg enumerate all the things they are going to do for him to re-integrate his personality. Petey tries hard to enable Stanley to stay with them, but Stanley by now can only make gurgling noises. Stanley leaves with Goldberg and McCann; Petey does not tell Meg that Stanley is no longer still asleep upstairs.

The play does not lend itself to an easy summary, for nothing is positive, even the idea of whether the boarding-house is a boarding-house at all, whether Goldberg and McCann were expected, since Meg tells them in reply to their request for accommodation for the night that it would have been easier last week — although she has no other guests except Stanley, her permanent lodger. *The Birthday Party* may not be Pinter's best play, but in it we find the quintessence of his style, the people who are themselves confused and not to be trusted to give a true account of what is going on. We listen to the dialogue which seems so improvised, so mundane and trivial and the silences betray more than declamation. Moreover in spite of the invention of situations the play achieves a remarkable structural unity; we acknowledge the hidden control of the playwright. Perhaps this is the danger of Pinterism, those who imitate his style without maintaining the discipline of structure.

*The Caretaker* (1960) is Pinter's best-known play. Though he has followed in the footsteps of his prophet Samuel Beckett we are struck more by the differences than the similarities of his tramp with those in *En attendant Godot*. Unlike Beckett's tramps, who belong to nowhere in particular and thus assume universality, Pinter's Davies is a real tramp with a social background and a past. He was a cleaner in a cafe and was sacked for refusing to do some work he considered too menial. Instead of a philosopher he seems more a grumbler. His whole aim in life seems to be to go to Sidcup for his papers, and even if we know he will never go there Sidcup exists, you can go to any railway booking office if you have the money. There is no suggestion that it, like Birnam Wood or Godot, will ever come to us. Davies is brought in by Aston, a purposeless man in his early thirties, to whom the room belongs. Davies is poking around amongst Aston's belongings when Mick, Aston's younger brother, grabs hold of him. It turns out to be Mick's flat, but Aston has offered Davies the job of caretaker. Davies thinks he can criticise Aston to Mick, and believes these tactics will win him Mick's confidence. Davies disowns Aston as a friend, while Mick outlines to him lavish plans for improvements in the flat. Davies goes too far when he calls Aston "nutty" and Mick turns on him, accuses him of falsely pretending to be an interior decorator, turns him out and pays him off with half a crown. Mick leaves and Aston comes in; Davies is conciliatory, then grovelling, but Aston is unresponsive. The tramp has nowhere to go. He's lost. He babbles of shoes to go to Sidcup, of putting up with draughts, but his plea trails away, unfinished, unanswered. . . .

There is not much to be said of *A Slight Ache,* first performed on the B.B.C. Third Programme in 1959, and in 1961 at the Arts Theatre Club. In this play Edward remarks to his wife Flora that he is annoyed to see an old match-seller outside the back gate. Flora assures him that the match-seller is a harmless old man. Nevertheless why does he stand all day at the gate? Flora talks to the match-seller, she is sure she has seen him before. Is he the poacher who once raped her? She guesses his name is Barnabas, becomes sexually alive to him and says she'll keep him. She tells Edward the match-seller is dying, but as Edward's energy flags the match-seller becomes youthful, and in the end Flora gives Edward the tray of matches to hold as Barnabas enters.

*A Night Out* (1960) was specially written for television and it is here that Pinter's art seems to come into its own. His success on British television can be judged by the top TAM rating the production achieved. In television his silences lend themselves directly to the visual approach, the close up of the camera which catches the repressed emotion. The theme of *A Night Out* is that of a possessive mother who tries to prevent her son Albert from going to an office party. Albert tries to back out of going and his friends tease him about "mum". At the party there is an incident and Albert slips away. Back home his mother catches him as he tries to creep past and after a lengthy self-pitying tirade from her Albert seizes a clock and the mother gives a stifled scream. Albert does not return to the party but picks up a tart at a coffee stall and in the tart's room he suddenly turns fierce, equates her with his mother and all women, and threatens her with a clock. He leaves and returns home after telling her that he's just done his mother in. He freezes when he sees his mother — he had only threatened her. She becomes emotional, solicitous, they'll go away together, he's not a bad boy. . . .

Both *The Collection* (1961) and *The Lover* (1963) were first written and presented as television plays; *The Collection* was subsequently produced by the Royal Shakespeare Company at the Aldwych Theatre, London in 1962, *The Lover* at the Arts Theatre Club in 1963. These two plays made up a bill in Paris in 1965 when for the first time Pinter scored a major success on the other side of the Channel. Certainly these two works deserved their recognition, for they represent the best that Pinter has yet given us, while being written for the medium in which he is most at home. *The Collection* has the ingredients of a more traditional farce, had not Pinter approached the subject of a night in a hotel in Leeds in an almost Pirandellian manner. Did Stella sleep with Bill while she was at a fashion show in Leeds or did she only play with the idea? James is first given all the details by his wife Stella, and goes to confront Bill, whom he terrorises into agreeing that they are true. He returns to Stella and thanks her for having introduced him to such a fine intelligent and cultured man as Bill. Meanwhile Harry, Bill's rich protector, visits Stella and learns from her confession that she made the whole story up. Bill says he confirmed it only for amusement, and James remarks that his wife had been overworking recently. Alone at last James asks Stella if her denial was in fact true. Stella looks at him with a sympathetic expression and says nothing.

In *The Lover* a young couple succeed in reconciling matrimonial respectability with free love; or in other words, they have a lover and a mistress during the afternoons. Richard asks his wife Sarah whether her lover is coming in the afternoon and when he returns in the evening he asks her some matter-of-fact questions about her lover. He confesses to her that he has a whore, not a mistress; the following morning Richard goes to work, afternoon comes and Sarah wears a sexy dress, high heels, and takes up a sensual pose when Max (alias Richard) enters wearing a suede jacket and no tie. She acts the virtuous wife waiting for her husband, Max says he can't go on deceiving his wife who thinks he's going out with a whore. He tells Sarah he would like to meet her husband. In the evening Richard returns and orders Sarah to stop her life of debauchery. She claims to have many lovers, complete strangers. Suddenly he acts the lover and she talks to him as though he were Max; she asks him why he is wearing the suede jacket, whether she should change too. He says yes, and calls her a lovely whore.

The short play seems more suited to Pinter's material, his almost jig-saw puzzle charade, than a full length work like *The Homecoming* (1965). Here the characters consist of the father, Max, ill humoured and sarcastic who used to be a butcher, his smart and quick-witted Cockney son, Lenny, and another son Joey, oafish and training to be a boxer. Into this household arrives the third son, Teddy, a lecturer in philosophy at an American college, accompanied by his wife Ruth, whom the family have never met. Lenny meets Ruth and Ruth seems intent on seducing him. The following morning there is a scene when Teddy tries to introduce Ruth to his father, but Max is furious with him for bringing "whores" into his house and orders Joey to throw them out. He punches the reluctant Joey, hits his brother with a stick and collapses. Suddenly he makes it up with Teddy and Ruth. Teddy realises that he has no means of communication with his family and more and more wants to get back to the States. While he is upstairs packing Lenny kisses Ruth, and then Joey goes off with her. Two hours later Joey has still not been able to go "the whole hog" which makes Max indignant for his son. Lenny proposes she be set up as a prostitute, and Ruth agrees on fairly demanding terms. Teddy leaves alone, and Ruth sits in a chair stroking Joey, while Lenny watches and Max, suspicious that she will do the dirty on them crawls on his knees towards her, sobbing that he's not an old man and asking to be kissed.

All this is supposed to have happened over two days, which rather stretches the realms of probability, and yet this is Pinter. Situations arise and require to be talked out, each character giving his recitation to himself. You aren't interested in whether old Max is a bully, this may or may not be the case in other families. Pinter is a story teller with a gift for capturing the rhythm of ordinary speech; either you accept his stories as such or you don't. It is a drama of intuition, but you don't have to be on the same beam; either they live and you accept or they don't and you don't. It is even possible for audiences to find traits in character which the author neither suspected or intended; at least Pinter is honest and makes no claims or pretensions.

In the six years which elapse between *The Homecoming* and *Old Times* (1971) there is a marked change in the direction of Pinter's growth. He had already tentatively "flirted" with the theme of intrusion of the past in his short plays *Landscape* and *Silence*; in *Old Times* the pressures from time gone by assert our present contradictions, their relentless presence blurs reality. "There are some things one remembers even though they never took place." The fact that people remember the same thing differently might seem to be a Pinteresque variation on a Pirandellian theme. Yet it is Pinter's deliberate obscurities which give the audience the possibility of either accepting their own interpretation, or of completing the silences and unspoken thoughts.

Deeley and Kate are a middle aged couple living in a converted English farm house near the sea. They are waiting for the arrival of Kate's best friend, Anna, who has been absent the last twenty years living in Sicily. Keeley has never met her, or so it seems, and is curious about the life they led when young sharing a bed-sit in London. Anna arrives, and she begins to chatter about their old times to Keeley, with Kate gradually withdrawing into an evasive silence. Or when Anna and Kate are engaged in conversation, Anna the stronger and more protective towards Kate, we suspect there has been a Lesbian relationship. Deeley in his turn seeks to possess Anna in his memory of those days, he claims to have picked her up in a pub, taken her to see the movie "Odd Man Out", he remembers looking up her leg at a party, and Anna confesses she had been wearing Katie's underwear. The trio become almost erotically linked in the past; both Kate and Deeley strive to have once possessed Anna. In the end their involvement is broken, Deeley is crying, Kate symbolically dead on the settee, Anna unpossessable.

Pinter's ambiguity almost precludes a rough plot summary, for it is not only his dialogue that matters, but what is left unsaid; here in the reconciliation of "old times" and present paradox are the flashes of irrational truths following the silences; it is instant intuitive theatre. He has found the means of approaching a vast public and making them curious. Perhaps no serious modern playwright has had a larger television audience. Unfinished approximations are close to all our predicaments. Gertrude Stein might have said, he is a playwright, is a playwright. The rest of the sentence is silence and silence is Pinter's means of identification.

ARNOLD WESKER

Orwell once described England as "a family with the wrong members in control"; Arnold Wesker, who was born in the East End of London in 1932, the son of a Jewish-Hungarian father and a Russian mother, is an active polemical writer dedicated to the task of teaching, enlightening, enabling the masses to share his enthusiasm for culture. Although an idealist, an optimist, Wesker is the first to admit with shame the truth of Orwell's statement. "If you allow yourselves to be treated as unimportant cogs, you will be treated as such," he asserts through the mouthpiece of one of his characters. The problem is how to make the public aware, how to bring culture to them. He believes this can be achieved by organisations, such as his Centre 42, and by writing plays, plays of purpose for those people he was brought up with, the bus drivers, the housewives, the miners and the Teddy boys. Wesker realises that all this may not be as easy as it sounds on paper, that there may be some built-in resistance on the part of Mr. Smith to his being made interested in politics and culture. In an article in the now defunct magazine *Encore* Wesker has replied that the Mr. Smiths of Britain (presumably unlike those who go to Washington), have at each crisis of their lives found that they were not equipped to handle the situation that arose. "It was not simply that no one had given him tools for living, but no one had told him he needed any tools beyond a job that would earn him money to fulfil responsibilities." The key word for Wesker is "tools", tools becomes the means whereby through art we may understand and hence change social injustices and so enable us to come to terms with life. Here we have Wesker's message, his views on culture which he wishes to impart with passion and sincerity, courage and conviction. Through mass culture will come the wider horizons, an appreciation of better things instead of the lethargic 'what's good enough for me is good enough for my children'.

Wesker worked first as a plumber's mate and a kitchen porter; he then learnt the trade of pastry-cook at which he worked for four years in Norwich, and later in London and Paris. He gave this up to study at the London School of Film Technique, where he wrote his first play *Chicken Soup With Barley*. He also wrote a short two-act play *The Kitchen*, which is best considered first, leaving the *Chicken Soup* trilogy as a whole. Wesker's premise in *The Kitchen* is that all the world's a kitchen and all the men and women merely cooks, waiters, and scullions. The conclusion follows from the premise, but the premise is never tested against reality, only stated, and herein lies the most obvious weakness of the play; what we have is a typically Weskerian rigging of the case.

*The Kitchen* is an extended metaphor. A kitchen, alias an office, alias a factory, alias any other sweat-shop in which modern man spends his working hours — is a place where there are too many people, where there is too much to do and too little time to do it in; in consequence there is no time for friendship, nerves become frayed and the sensitive go berserk. The chief characters are twelve cooks, a motley international set comprising English, Germans, and Cypriots, an Irishman, a Jew and an Italian. The cooks scurry about at their work, chat, quarrel, grumble and flirt with the waitresses according to their various dispositions. The conditions under which they work bring out the worst in them most of the time. There are old hands, grown inured, and young hands who will go the same way if they stay on long enough. Kelvin, a young Irishman, is the new cook and in him we can see expectancy swiftly become disillusion. The most interesting character is Peter, a German, with a boisterous, sardonic humour which keeps him buoyant until, goaded by a frustrated romance, his underlying idealism breaks into berserk rebellion against the kitchen; with one blow of a chopper he severs the gas pipe that supplies the ovens. Mr. Marango, the proprietor, doesn't assume his true significance till the very end. His world is the restaurant, the money it makes him. He does not see what is wrong: "I give work, I pay well, Yes? They eat what they want, don't they? I don't know what more to give a man."

*Chicken Soup with Barley*, the first of three plays with interwoven themes about four interwoven families, the Kahns, the Simmonds's, the Beales's, and the Bryants, was produced at the Belgrade Theatre, Coventry, in 1958. The theme is of those who care, or try to care, in a world that is indifferent. They are plays about the struggle to implement vision and, after the struggle, the defeat of vision; caring for the whole world shrinks to caring for one's own family. Hero and heroine set out with youth and ideals and come home with weariness and bitter knowledge; only two idealists survive, Sarah and Ada, the mother and daughter and they survive because their vision is like instinct, because being emotional rather than intellectual it is less vulnerable to the world's scorn. Sarah and Ada are the real heroines; they can't change the world themselves, but they lessen the significance of the men's defeat because they carry the seed of hope. Wesker does not allow

HAROLD PINTER, AS ACTOR

ARNOLD WESKER

defeat to encompass his ultimate socialist hope.

The Trilogy, *Chicken Soup with Barley* (1958), *Roots* (1959), and *I'm Talking about Jerusalem* (1960) is slow-moving, rich in atmosphere, sociologically authentic. The characters are credible, their speech is consistent with their emotion, their emotion with the life within them and around them. There can be no doubt that this is a Jewish family of the East End or that this is a family of Norfolk agricultural labourers. The weakness of the play is that in identifying himself with the people the author shares their inconclusiveness of thinking and that there is a tendency to view in simple terms of black and white (socialist = good, capitalist = bad) somewhat to the detriment of the message. Wesker is at his best when depicting the family of mum and dad, not the family of man. In all the plays Wesker's conclusions follow very well from the premises but the premises don't quite square with reality.

*Chicken Soup with Barley* opens in 1936. We meet Sarah Kahn, vital, emotional and staunchly socialist, Harry her husband, less staunchly socialist, Cissie, Harry's sister and a trade union organiser, Hymie, Sarah's sister and Ronnie and Ada, the two Kahn children. Among the minor characters Dave Simmonds is regarded as something of a hero because he is going to fight in the Spanish Civil War. Act Two takes us to the post-war England of 1946; the Kahn's have moved to an L.C.C. flat in Hackney. Ronnie and Ada have grown up and come into their own; she is waiting for Dave to come home from the war so that they can get married and fulfil their dreams of rural socialism. Harry has a stroke which is to leave him half-paralysed. In the last Act he has a second stroke which leaves him unfit for any work. There's a falling off in the zeal for socialism, and disillusion has crept in, only Sarah keeps her simple faith. Ronnie comes home from Paris where he is a cook; his faith and ambition are broken. Mother and son harangue each other, and against Ronnie's nihilism Sarah pits all her emotional energy, and desperately cries: "You've got to care or you'll die." The play ends on this sombre note with Ronnie showing no indication that he is big enough to care.

In *Roots* socialism as such is only a subterranean rumble; it is not socialism, but education in the broadest sense, that is the theme. The stark simplicity of the structure reinforces the theme, it helps to suggest the die-hard conservatism of the country mind, its impassivity, its refusal to awake to new sights, new sounds, new ideas, new feelings, and its satisfaction with itself. It is as though everything that really

K

matters in the countryman's life is static, belief and love in particular. Beatie Bryant is in love with the distant Ronnie and just as he has tried to pass on the good word to her so she tries to pass it on to her narrow-minded self-satisfied family. She represents a stage between Ronnie, the self-awakened awakener and the torpid country folk. She is both eager to learn and annoyed at being taught. In the third Act while the assembled family have been waiting Ronnie's arrival, when the bell rings it is the postman with a letter from Ronnie — breaking off the relationship. Beatie is at first stunned but pulls herself together and having been for too long a mouthpiece for Ronnie's views suddenly bursts into a speech that comes from her own heart.

*I'm talking about Jerusalem* is the story of the defeat of Dave's rustic dream. Machines and the city brutalise and make men strangers to one another, so Dave has come to the country to find joy and brotherhood in creative work. The play spans the years 1946-1959, but the dream of a new heaven soon falls through; Dave's employer sacks him for pilfering. Dave and Ada battle on but misfortunes come, they are nagged by friends and relatives, cheated, until eventually Dave is forced back to London, where of course Sarah is glad to have her family back with her once more. The rustic dream is over.

In *Chips with Everything* (1962) Wesker seems to accept the division of a class-conscious society into officer material and the rest; try as he does to find one there doesn't seem to be an alternative. He takes us to an R.A.F. training camp where for eight weeks the recruits are put through square bashing before the final passing out parade; it is as though the spirit of T. E. Lawrence's *The Mint* has survived wars and generations. Yet Wesker's assault is not, say, Kenneth H. Brown's virulent one in the case of the American Marine traditions in *The Brig*; however unbending and old school the commanding officer is, or relentless the drill instructions may be, Wesker's thesis is not so much concerned with officer-recruit relations, it is far more fundamental. Wesker contends that even before the course opens the choice is already made; the recruits may be put through their paces, but the only person willing to rebel against authority and resist cringing conformity is Pip Thompson, the rich banker's son, and potential officer material. It is he who organises the raid on the coke dump when without his initiative all the men would have been shivering round an empty stove; it is Pip who at an all rank's New Year's Party, prevents the recruits from being made a fool of when the C.O. suggests they imitate their favourite pop singers. Instead the recruits follow Pip's lead and turn to folk songs and a Scots ballad. Is service life a parallel to civilian life? Does this mean that when Pip accepts his commission at the Passing Out Parade, we have the key to what happens in society, *plus ca change, plus c'est la meme chose?*

There is already a departure from the naturalism we had learned to expect from Wesker in *Chips with Everything*, almost surprising when in such a short space of time he had established himself as one of the best naturalistic playwrights since the war. Here the characters are no longer the complete human beings of the trilogy or *The Kitchen*. And yet the staging, the breaking in of the raw recruits in the best sergeant-major tradition concealed the gradual change in Wesker's development as a playwright. This was still a play with the largest possible appeal, very much a social purpose play although one which ultimately admitted defeat on the questions raised. It was as if naturalism was becoming a hindrance to the creative experiments he wanted as an artist; whereas Giraudoux's Siegfried had searched for a country without past or future wars without success, Wesker wanted to find a country without class wars, where as he confessed in an interview in the *Twentieth Century*, he could write a play beginning "Once upon a time. . . ." *The Four Seasons* (1965) marks the retreat of Wesker from naturalism into a world of make-believe and illusion. From plays of purpose Wesker has written an elegy on love. Adam and Beatrice arrive in mid-winter in a derelict house; their relationship follows through the four seasons, the growing love of spring, the height of their love in summer, the mellowing with the autumn already threatened with the chill of impending winter, when their love dies, and they part. An abstract classical poem on love is the most ambitious aim which any playwright can attempt, only rarely with a great poet like Claudel in for example, his *Partage de Midi* does he succeed. Wesker has in this play revealed a personality little suspected, and although he has failed to communicate the theme and the variations on love, there are moments when he has an insight, as if he were afraid to look too closely. There are some beautifully written poetic passages, but unfortunately the play lacks the dramatic action or conflict to draw them out. Wesker's study of Adam is good, he knows what a man's reactions would be; it is his portrait of Beatrice which is not that of "a queen without a country" which he intends to portray. Instead of understanding a woman of the world, Wesker misunderstands the responses such a woman would make (far removed from his experiences with ordinary women) nor was Diane Cilento suitably cast in the London production;

the majesty of the rôle demanded more an actress like Eileen Herlie (we remember how she interpreted Cocteau's queen in *L'aigle a deux Tetes*), who could at least have more evenly balanced Adam's sensitivity. Wesker has however given her one line which rings true, "a beautiful woman will always be sneered at". In the end the collapse is due not only to Wesker's incomplete portrait, but also because he has endeavoured to make reality out of abstraction instead of abstraction out of reality. There are too many practicalities, the gas supply, the idea of going from derelict house to derelict house redecorating, until, finally running out of action in the last act, he returns to the certainty of the kitchen and makes Adam prove his love, according to Napoleonic principles, by making an apfelstrudel, an episode completely out of keeping with the whole lyrical mood of the play — but perhaps the only one understood and appreciated by Wesker's old admirers who had not come prepared for an anti-naturalist experiment.

The play unfortunately was very badly received by the critics, and few were willing to realise that by its very nature it was the most ambitious work Wesker has attempted. They seemed to regret that he was no longer the prophet of socialism, that he was not the protagonist for class consciousness; here there were no nationalities, no jobs or wages, only the kitchen scene could be applauded. Ambitious failures are seldom understood or forgiven.

*Their Very Own and Golden City* (1966) was a return to the didactic type we have come to associate with Wesker. As for *The Friends* (1970) Wesker presents us with a humiliating *auto-critique* of his generation, the young idealists who came up from the provinces to make a new and Socialist England in the fifties, who could associate themselves with the angry young men and presumably the early plays of Wesker himself. In the death of Esther "the friends" reflect what went wrong. They seem to have proved the truth of Harold Macmillan's "you've never had it so good"; they have opened shops and have made out at the expense of becoming morally bankrupt. Their solution and penitance is to make sure the shops go in fact bankrupt and they dedicate themselves once more to brotherly love and papa Lenin. Wesker forgets Shaw's advise to revolutionaries: "do not do unto others as you would have them do unto you, all tastes are not the same." On the contrary, he is trying to impose not only his political and sociological hotchpotch on the audience, but worse, he is like Arlecchino serving two generations with the same tried failures. Wesker at any rate remains in his land of make believe, not that of imagination and emotion, but rather of sentimentalism and class security.

## PETER SHAFFER

With the production of *Five Finger Exercise* (1958) it was apparent that in Peter Shaffer a very professional English playwright had emerged, a writer who clearly had something to say and had acquired the craftsmanship to construct climaxes, create characters — in short, he was instinctively a man of the theatre. Shaffer was born in London in 1926, and after studying at Cambridge he decided to write plays, though before 1958 he had only had two television acceptances, and these were without particular note. It is interesting to observe that in 1958 it was still the traditional play set in a drawing-room with five or six characters which prevailed; high budgets had telescoped plays the wrong way round; the days of spectacle were as dead as we imagined the *avant-garde* or the one-act play. So' at first sight Shaffer appeared to fit into the conventional pattern; as it was his ambitious concept of "total" theatre in his play on the Incas *The Royal Hunt of the Sun* had to wait six years, passing from management to management, until the subsidised National Theatre could budget for it. Apart from two one-act plays *The Private Ear* and *The Public Eye*, presented as a double bill in the West End in 1962, two other one acters, *Black Comedy* and *White Lies* and a minor defeat at *The Battle of Shrivings*, Shaffer's reputation rests on these two widely different plays, the spectacle *The Royal Hunt* and *Five Finger Exercise*. Each succeeds in its way without either being a masterpiece; the less ambitious *Five Finger Exercise* is the more important as a play, while the production of *The Royal Hunt*, which cannot be separated from the text, is the more memorable.

*Five Finger Exercise* takes us to the Harrington's week-end cottage in Suffolk during two autumn week-ends, a conventional middle-class family with money such as Dodie Smith used to portray, in fact we might have had another *Autumn Crocus* but for the arrival of a young German, Walter Langer, who serves as a catalyst and disturbs in turn each member of the family, and emotionally unable to extricate themselves they turn against him. There is Stanley Harrington, a self-made hard-headed businessman who now runs a large furniture factory; his wife Louise, who is socially above him and never allows him to forget it, culturally pretentious, terribly possessive of her son, Clive, and forever talking about her French ancestry and that she is a Parisian at heart. Clive, aged nineteen, is nervous, taut, and disturbingly young for his age —"the nakedness of someone in whom intellectual development has outstripped the emotional". Pamela, their fourteen-year-old daughter, is volatile, alternating between seriousness and teenage frivolity.

Walter Langer joins the family as a tutor for Pamela, and this is the first week-end he has been at their country house, which Mr. Harrington has recently bought on the instigation of his wife. Walter has now been living five years in England, where he wants to settle and take British nationality; he refuses to talk about his home or his parents, except that he says he will never return. He has discovered that his father was an S.S. officer at one of the concentration camps; his picture of England is in contrast idealistic, "here in England most people *want* to do what's good"; that is why he is so anxious to be accepted by an English family like the Harrington's, and already he looks on Mrs. Harrington as a mother figure for him. Unfortunately his affection for Louise is misunderstood by her, who unhappily married is looking for love; it is also mistaken by Clive who, has hopeless, unspoken feelings for Walter, when he discovers them embracing each other and who, because of his own hopeless feelings for Walter, provokes an outburst from his father; he has to share the anguish of what he has seen. Finally even Pamela develops a schoolgirl crush on Walter, and Louise uses this as a pretext to protect her own hurt pride and ask her husband to sack Walter. This Harrington delights in doing in the most brutal way possible, by saying that he intends to inform the Home Office how Walter forced his attentions on a fourteen-year-old girl in order to have him deported. Harrington further discloses his real reason. Walter goes upstairs ostensibly to pack and starts playing a record; when a few minutes later we hear the record stick we know something is wrong, Walter has tried to commit suicide.

*The Royal Hunt of the Sun* was written shortly after *Five Finger Exercise,* but was not produced until Sir Laurence Olivier bought it for the National Theatre at Chichester in 1964. The production was subsequently restaged so as to enter the repertory of the National Theatre at the Old Vic; in 1965 there was a Broadway production, and a film is being made in Peru. Like its splendid title, the play's conception is big in every way, the army of the Conquistadors crosses the Andes to the land of the Incas, there is a massacre on the stage of the sun god Atahuallpa's unarmed followers; there is the ritual mourning following the betrayal and death of the sun god, with the mourners wearing the golden masks of the Incas. It is the meeting of civilisations, the Conquistadors who crush the older and superior one of the Incas, which achieved a kind of State socialism where "no man could be rich, no man could be poor . . . but all might enjoy, and did enjoy, a competence" as William Prescott observed in *The Conquest of Peru*. Where likewise ambition, the morbid spirit of discontent, found no place. Not so with the Spaniards' civilisation, and the story of Pizarro's betrayal of Atahuallpa's confidence is one of the most insidious chapters in the colonial history of all times. So Shaffer's play becomes "an encounter between European hope and Indian hopelessness; between Indian faith and European faithlessness. . . . The Spaniard suspected joy as being unworthy of Christ. The Peruvian . . . was forbidden despair." Out of this material Shaffer declares that his aim was to create "an experience that was entirely and only theatrical". For such an experience we have to return to perhaps a Reinhardt production in the Berlin of the twenties; not even the prestidigital showmanship of Cochran's *Cavalcade* had the same sweep of power, for here we have the metal and the masks, the jungle cries of primitive people, the clash of civilisations and religions where neither Western civilisation nor Christianity come out very favourably. As an example of theatre devised as a spectacle it is difficult to separate the text from the means of production, and Shaffer's insistence on a visual lift to the play was the right one. The text itself is much less impressive; strangely enough the play does not make for reading, and it is difficult to conceive the impact without seeing the extraordinary comprehension of John Dexter and Desmond O'Donovan's production.

The character of Atahuallpa, the sun god, the Inca of Peru, is forcefully drawn, but the combat between religions is not an even one, as he reminds Pizarro:

> Pizzaro, you will die soon and you do not believe in your God. That is why you tremble and keep no word. Believe in me. I will give you a word and fill you with joy. For you I will do a great thing. I will swallow death and spit it out of me.

Pizarro is convinced, he asks what he must do. Atahuallpa is murdered, and the executioners cast his dead body at Pizarro's feet. Slowly, Shaffer writes in his stage instructions, the stage fills with all the

Indians, robed in black and terracotta, wearing the great golden funeral masks. They intone a strange Chant of Resurrection, and after three cries the sun rises, with its rays falling on the body. But Atahuallpa does not move, and they depart in despair. Pizarro feals cheated, the only joy is in death. "I lived between two hates:" he rages, "I die between two darks: blind eyes and a blind sky."

*The Royal Hunt* must be judged as a whole in production, because it was in its "totality" that Shaffer was attracted to the theme. Robert Brustein has accused Shaffer of probably taking Artaud's first scenario for his Theatre of Cruelty, "a tableaux sequence called *The Conquest of Mexico*" where Artaud hoped to "contrast Christianity with much older religions" and to correct the false views about Paganism and much older religions than Christianity. In contrast to Artaud's method Brustein accuses Shaffer of sentimentalising these myths with "a set of liberal notions about the noble savage, the ignoble Catholic, and the way brotherly love can bridge the gulf that separates cultures". There seems no reason why Shaffer should not apply his liberal notions to replace the theatre of cruelty of Artaud, since he has never claimed to be a disciple, and whatever the merits of Artaud's theories might be, they are not the exclusive and only ones. We can however, criticise Shaffer for not having the necessary power of language at his command. *The Royal Hunt of the Sun* is more than a spectacle, more than an elaborate pageant play, but it falls short of succeeding on all levels. It is a theatrical event, but not a masterpiece.

Of Shaffer's two one-act plays produced in a double playbill in 1962, *The Public Eye* is a considerably more effective study than *The Private Ear*, a slight piece about a shy young clerk and his ineffectual relationship with a pretty, but rather dumb, typist whom he asks to his bed-sitter for dinner. *The Public Eye*, in contrast, is a fairy story on the subject of marriage with the moral "how many people would stay married ... if they just shut up and looked and listened, and heard each others heartbeats in the daytime'. Julian Cristoforou has chosen for his profession to be a detective, for he has discovered that he was a man without a private life who could only come alive against a background of other people's affairs. Charles Sedley, a prosperous accountant, hires Julian to report on the activities of his wife Belinda, whom he suspects of having a lover. Charles rescued Belinda, who is twenty-two years younger than himself, from her 'hot black burrow of feeling' to give her 'facts, ideas, reasons for things'. The result in the end is that she can no longer distinguish between what she really feels and what she pretended to feel, so that she has merely learnt from him to respect her own feelings. Charles has become like a schoolmaster before whom she feels guilty; her lover, on the other hand, makes her feel alive despite the curious fact that they have never exchanged a word. It is Julian who prescribes the remedy, that Charles and he should swap rôles: while Julian takes over in the office for a month Charles shall follow his wife wherever she goes.

Shaffer has also written a short play *Black Comedy* which was produced at Chichester in 1965. Here the "trick" is that the house-lights go down and the curtain rises on a darkened stage, until there is a "fuse" which plunges the stage into light — as it were a "negative" for the audience, who watch the different characters stumble around, trying to see with the aid of cigarette lighters, and so on. The result is that through mistaken identities confidences are betrayed, secrets told to the wrong ears, an irate father hears more than he should, and by the time the fuse is mended everybody sees each other with new eyes.

*Black Comedy* was written as a curtain raiser. In order to transfer it to Broadway Shaffer wrote a companion piece called *White Lies*, later presented in London as *The White Liars*. The idea of this play is to bribe a fortune-teller to give a wrong prediction in order to dissuade a pop-singer colleague from having an affair with a girl. Shaffer asks whether it was mere jealousy. The play may have a moral, but it lacks the brilliance of *Black Comedy*.

In *The Battle of Shrivings* (1970) Shaffer again ventures on new ground, with equal ambition if with less success. The character of Sir Gideon Petrie, an aged English eccentric living in a medieval abbey at Shrivings in the Cotswolds, is essentially Shavian. We could imagine how Shaw would have made him meditate like Captain Shotover in *Heartbreak House*, as he guides a Peace Movement, and believes in the perfectibility of human nature. The catalyst in this play is a dipsomaniac poet Mark Askelon, who had been one of Sir Gideon's converts, and returns this time either to be conquered once again by the old man — or to conquer. In other words, will Sir Gideon be able to tolerate him or be driven himself to violence? In the end Sir Gideon has to eject nearly everyone else in his verbal duel with the aspiring Mephistopheles.

*The Battle of Shrivings* does not add to Shaffer's reputation; it merely suggests that Shavian situations require Shavian wit. Shaffer at least continues his experiments, which in the course of seven plays have taken in the historical epic, problem plays and the intimate hilarity of a farcical curtain raiser: he is a peripatetic professional.

## CHRISTOPHER FRY

Already the name of Christopher Fry (born 1907) has slipped into the theatrical past; he belongs to the period immediately preceding the Royal Court Revolution of 1956. In the midst of an unimaginative, stuffy drawing-room three-dimensional theatre of tired mannerisms and outdated conventions, Fry may be said to have taken up the challenge of Eliot's attempt to make room for poetry. Whereas Eliot believed the only way for poetic drama to compete overtly with prose was a temporary compromise which in the end defeated his intentions, Fry introduced such a bacchanalia of words and such a thesaurus of fine phrases that in his case too the audience, like Monsieur Jourdain, was not at all sure of the difference between poetry and prose. At any rate his very box-office success as a verse dramatist suggested that there was a large public ready to support any serious attempt to rid the English theatre of its triangular naturalistic plots; believing with Max Reinhardt that we carried within ourselves "the potentialities of all passions, all fates, all forms of life . . ." audiences were eager to escape the naturalistic framework and the politeness of hypocritical understatement; they were prepared to share with Fry his belief that "reality is incredible, reality is a whirlwind", but alas, to no avail. Fry's contemplation through a galaxy of words on the marvel of creation was confined to the naturalistic framework; his new poetic drama ended up in another cul-de-sac, different but as constricted as the one where Eliot had led us. It was almost in reaction to all this that the public listened to the thumping of John Osborne on the door.

Until Osborne the most talked about English playwright was undoubtedly Christopher Fry, a verse dramatist whose very success has done much to make box-office managers share his belief that "reality is incredible, reality is a whirlwind". Indeed it is. No wonder at the enthusiasm of the rejoicing, the sincerity that made many compare his plays with the tradition of the Elizabethan masters; premature, yes, but at least it indicated that not everyone was complacent about the dreary monotone of the naturalistic drama. It proved there was a large public ready to support any worth-while attempt to find a way out towards poetry and imagination. Fry has now given us sufficient work (three religious plays, one tragedy and four comedies) to enable the pattern of his development to be viewed in perspective with the trend of the modern drama we have been considering, though obviously such a judgment will be an interim one; Fry is still with us.

What strikes one first in the plays of Fry is his completely idiosyncratic style and his felicity for words; his language has a dazzle which seems to be almost an end in itself and is nearly blinding when, striving to ignore it, an attempt is made to understand the essential Fry. In a lecture to the Critics' Circle Fry has defended his use of words by declaring that while sometimes in his comedies the words are "an ornament on the meaning and not the meaning itself", "almost as often I have meant the ornament to be, dramatically or comedically, an essential part of the meaning". Since writer and critic must "start with the same premise" we must bear his words in mind. Fry's plays are moods, perhaps even "the stuff that dreams are made of", they are climatic but not dramatic. In these gay flights of fancy there is no attempt to build up dramatic sequences or lead the audience to anticipate events; there seems to be no direction in the flight and no more than a hint occasionally as to meaning and intentions. Nothing is defined.

In a talk on the background of his plays given by the B.B.C. Third Programme Fry has explained that he is attempting to combine the reality of amazement which is the province of poetry with the reality that is prose. What is different between the two realities, he contends, is 'implication'. "What I am trying to say is that a spade is never so merely a spade as the word spade would imply. I am asking for the sudden dramatic appearance of a spade in time and space, but I am equally asking for a spade which I can dig with. I am asking — now I come to think of it — I am asking for both kinds of realism at once." Now, in attempting this, it seems to this critic that Fry has completely failed to realise his aim. There are no contrasts with Fry, no planes of reality (as with Pirandello, Claudel, Giraudoux). There is but one dominant mood, bewilderment, which remains constant, with neither emotion, drama nor character, whether the play be comedy or tragedy, spring or autumn. All Fry's plays have a unity of mood, and this mood, it might be suggested, is not a combination of the reality of poetry and prose, but merely an embellishment of ordinary prose.

For Fry "we are plunged into an existence fantastic to the point of nightmare, and however hard we rationalise, or however firm our religious faith, however closely we dog the heels of science or wheel among the stars of mysticism, we cannot really make head or tail of of it." But the exploration of amazement, the "how lost, how amazed, how miraculous we are", which may certainly be considered the province of poetry, should yield a poetic vision of life, illuminating ideas, contrasts and ambiguities rather than shrouding them with a mist against which our sensitivities and our mind eventually rebel. Giraudoux also attempts to see reality in terms of amazement, but he succeeds through his ability to contrast the irrationality of the real with the rationality of the illusory. Fry's reality, on the other hand, never shows much spirit in venturing beyond the frontiers of naturalistic comedy. And this mood, a lingering swan song, extends until death, whether at the stake or like the death of the Countess in *The Dark is Light Enough*. The business of the play is never to be dramatic, nor to present life-size characters with whom we can share a bond of sympathy. The business is in words, like in an Oscar Wilde play, and while hints may be dropped with the epigrams, these tend to exclude discussion of more serious subjects which the theme itself provokes. We have a flow of words with which we may luxuriate as if in a steam sauna; but it is given to other races to have the courage to roll in the snow afterwards.

All this seems to me a direct negation of theatre, because it eliminates the dramatic, and consequently cannot claim to belong to the tradition of dramatic poetry, as can Eliot, for example. And it has led in Fry's later work, *The Dark is Light Enough* for instance, to a kind of poetic monologue, devoid of action and not overflowing with imagination. But these same faults were to be found in Fry's best play *The Lady's Not for Burning*, though in this case the originality of the plot, the natural inspiration of its treatment and the sparkle of some of the phrases could not help to excite — and blind the realisation that we were moving towards a dramatic stalemate.

The plot of *The Lady's Not for Burning* is probably familiar to readers; a young girl, suspected of witchcraft, is condemned to be burned at the stake (the period is the fifteenth century) and a young man, tired of the hypocrisy of the world in general and human beings in particular, demands that the local mayor should have him hanged. The girl pleads with him the cause for life, and through her love she persuades him to go on living. The appearance of the rag-man whom the girl was supposed to have turned into a dog saves her from the stake, and unofficially they are pardoned. It is interesting to compare this play (Fry's best) with Giraudoux's *Intermezzo* which treats a similar theme. With Giraudoux we have a perfect blending of the planes of reality, a poetic vision allied to the intellect. With Fry, however pleasing the poetical phrases and certain passages may be to the ear, the need for character study, a clearer, surer vision, a willingness to call a spade a shovel, becomes increasingly embarrassing. No, Fry is not the English Giraudoux, as some have called him, for his is essentially the naturalistic theatre, not Giraudoux's anti-naturalist style where lightness of touch is its own revealer. No serious dramatist can, however, afford to marvel about the mystery of the creation throughout his career without asking the audience to share with him his interpretation.

If we turn to Fry's most serious work *A Sleep of Prisoners*, which might be described as a passion play as it was originally produced in the University Church at Oxford (and later at St. Thomas's Church, Regent Street), we realise how completely at sea Fry can be when forceful exposition of ideas and meaning is required. This was the play which was to cause such a furore when produced by Jean-Louis Barrault in Paris, where the audience failed to follow it although they listened to it for the first half hour without interruption, and only, to quote one French critic, "after they had been the most insufferably bored that can be imagined" did they show their dislike of the piece. Nor was it purely a failure of translation, for the play, in my experience at any rate, fails completely to come across in English. This is all the more surprising as Fry has had a long training in the theatre and is not like Eliot, for example, an academician. Be that as it may, Fry explains in an introductory dedication that in *A Sleep of Prisoners* he is concerned with "the growth of vision; the increased perception of what makes for life and what makes for death". He continues: "In *A Sleep of Prisoners* I have tried to make a more simple statement, though in a complicated design, where each of four men is seen through the sleeping thoughts of the others, and each, in his own dream, speaks as at heart he is, not as he believes himself to be." Alas, the complicated design, the verbosity (in spite of a more urgent sense in the poetry), results in complete confusion. No doubt the audience realises that these four English soldiers, locked in a bombed church and thrown in each other's company, have in the dreams they enact from biblical sources, such as Cain's murder of Abel, some sort of allegorical significance, but just what, would defeat any average audience of intelligent playgoers. A clear driving force, a simple pacific message instead of the contrived rhetoric at the end, might have made *A Sleep of Prisoners* into a memorable work. As it is it is too complex and obscure to be readily appreciated on the level at which it invites to be judged.

*The Dark is Light Enough* is much less complex than *A Sleep of Prisoners*. Again the play is an appeal for pacificism, and we have the

prospect of the end of the civilisation we know. The Countess Ros-
marin Ostenburg, living in a country in revolution (the Austro-Hungarian Empire during 1848–49) is a supremely Christian lady, endowed
with wisdom and charm and the firm conviction of divine non-inter-
ference. But the times are against her and her Thursday salon, for her
ex-son-in-law Gettner, having stirred up a revolution, has now
deserted from the Hungarian rebel army and seeks protection and
hiding. The Countess offers him sanctuary, and her daughter's second
husband is taken prisoner in his place. Gettner repays the hospitality
by making love to his former wife, and then shooting the Countess's
son in a duel and wounding him. But none of this, or the fact that
because of her action the Countess has been turned out of her home by
the rebels and is forced to live in the stables, influences the Countess's
belief in human charity. Gettner is eventually converted to her philosophy, and before the play ends the political fortunes have turned, the
rebel colonel is given shelter by the Countess, who, dying, summons
up her strength for her last Thursday salon.

The play may be regarded as a commissioned work for Dame Edith
Evans, who played the part most beautifully in the London production.
The play, consequently, has the appearance of being contrived rather
than natural, and it is difficult to believe that Fry wrote it because
he felt compelled to do so, or because he had left unsaid something he
felt essential. It is merely the repetition of a mood, more sombre, with
his language held in check and used more cautiously. It is a monologue
for Dame Edith, and the other characters are the merest puppets. If
Fry is to remain a poet in the theatre he will in the future have to find
more dramatic material than that of the theme of non-intervention; the
idea of shaking your head at the way of the world and philosophising
in long, unoriginal platitudes may be the stuff twentieth-century
idealist dreams are made of, but it is unlikely to prosper or be very
healthy for the theatre. His growth of vision seems to have remained
where it did when he wrote *A Phoenix Too Frequent,* and his inability
to make head or tail of this poor world of ours is no excuse
for dramatic paralysis.

With *Curtmantle,* first performed in Holland in 1961, and subsequently at the Edinburgh Festival, Fry has turned again to dramatic
conflict, this time the theme of Thomas à Becket and King Henry. If
in *Murder in the Cathedral* Eliot gave us a movingly religious and poetic
play, Fry's version may be said to be at once secular and poetical; less
theatrically mature than Anouilh's interpretation, Fry has like Anouilh

presented a sympathetic study in Henry; he describes him as "simple and royal, direct and paradoxical, compassionate and hard, a man of intellect, a man of action, God-fearing, superstitious, blasphemous . . ." Just as Henry says of Becket

> It looks as if this island
> Isn't large enough to contain both of us.

so in the play there is hardly room for both men. Eleanor of Aquitaine laments of their clash of personalities:

> Between us, by our three variants of human nature,
> You and Becket and me, we could be
> The complete reaching forward. Neither of you
> Will dare to understand it.

The portrait of Henry evolves, and the theme of Law becomes the interplay between those of State and God. Becket warns Henry early on:

> What you see as the freedom of the State
> Within the law, I fear, as the enslavement
> Of that other state of man, in which, and in
> which only, he can know his perfect freedom.

and again, in reply to Leicester's assertion that all he possesses comes from the king:

> Nothing. Nothing from the King. Whatever the Church
> Holds is held in perpetual liberty.

The action of the play rises to the inevitable murder of Becket, and in the third and last act Henry lives out his life trying to shake free the shadow of Becket.

Fry is perhaps more modest in his presentation of Henry, claiming that "it adds up to no more than a sketch", and that "no single play could contain more than a splash from the brew"; yet a chronicle play is to be judged by the impact it makes, the revelation of character and the interpretation of the canvas of history.

With *A Yard of Sun* Fry completed what he has named his seasonal quartet: *The Lady's Not For Burning* represents Spring, *A Yard of Sun*, summer, *Venus Observed*, autumn, and *The Dark is Light Enough*, winter. It is not easy to understand why exactly *A Yard of Sun* should be associated with summer, except for the idea of the Palio of Sienna, which is taking place in the background of the play. The Palio is an annual Renaissance spectacle on horses:

> The old
> Stimulant: bells, trumpets, drums, flag-juggling,
> It's a heady mixture. It comes very near
> Even to seducing me, and I'm used to it!

complains Roberto, a doctor who has fought with the partisans, and has now returned to his father's Palazzo for a family reunion: the year is 1946. Of the two other brothers, Luigi allowed himself to be carried along with Fascism, while the real black sheep of the family is Edmundo, who spent the war years in Portugal, where he amassed a vast fortune. Their father Angelino has lived in the Palazzo resignedly until the return of his sons. Yet the inevitable tempers are not those of say Malaparte's Italy year zero; Angelino is determined that his family should have a reconciliation and think of the future. The arrival of a former prisoner in a concentration camp, Cesare, helps to remind them that "transformation" is much more important than revolution:

> "I haven't the simple faith that a man can be doctored
> Out of his tragedy into the millennium.

In the end nothing has changed, and a quarter of a century later Italy still seems a vast palazzo where brother enemies continue to live under the same roof in a *modus vivendi*.

Nothing has changed, either, in Fry's attempt at poetic naturalism; unfortunately the restrained sculptured phrases seem to me to make it impossible to think of his characters as Italians; somehow movement, and at least gesticulation, is as necessary for the Italian tempo as speed is for the Palio race. Fry has still to convince us that his poetry is more effective than prose.

### GRAHAM GREENE

Sooner or later a successful novelist will turn his eyes to the theatre. Graham Greene has written four plays, *The Living Room* (1954), *The Potting Shed* (1958), *The Complaisant Lover* (1959) and *Carving a Statue* (1964); an adaptation of his novel *The Power and the Glory* has also been successfully produced. As a novelist Greene is one of the outstanding contemporary figures, in the cinema he is a master of suspense in such films as *The Third Man*, but in the theatre the technique seems to stifle his broader vision — and the ability to carry us with him.

In *The Living Room* Graham Greene makes his own variations with stock characters — the two elderly sisters, the one terrorised by the other; the innocent (but soon not-so-innocent) Rose, who is unable to find happiness because she is the mistress of a married man (who is also a psychiatrist for the sake of the play) and cannot find absolution for her affair from a priest (because, for the sake of the play, he is her uncle). Now all these characters and the strange house which they inhabit bear no relation to life in general nor human beings in particular. Apparently neither psychiatry nor religion can save Rose from suicide, and we are left with the impression that it was no one person's fault, but a general despair and failure of the world. For those who like to put a premium on failure in life, Graham Greene's play suits the prevalent mood of despair; this is not because a suicide is in itself unlikely — of course not — but because the situations are so painstakingly contrived and never ring true.

The same weakness is apparent in *The Potting Shed*, where the plot takes on the character of a religious who-dunnit, with a detective played by a thirteen-year-old girl, a defence lawyer, and clues lying in the potting shed waiting to be unravelled in time for the final denouement. Instead of a murder we have a suicide, instead of a doctor to examine the body we have a priest, who as he leans over his young nephew, James, who has just hung himself in the potting shed, begs God to let him live, adding "Take away my faith, but let him live." All this happened many years before the play opens. Henry Callifer, a well-known Rationalist, is dying, and all his family, except James — who is asked to stay downstairs, for fear that the miracle of his life might upset his father in his last hours. It was in fact his miracle which destroyed his father's faith in atheism as much as his uncle priest's faith in God. The development of the play is an exercise in psychological suspense as the truth and reality of the miracle is argued and explained. But although Greene attempts to bring his characters to life they remain the stock protagonists of his own invention. Maybe a Claudel or some other great poet could convince us that you can bargain for a miracle, but the naturalism of Greene's theatre is all against our belief. Like Alice's pudding, or after reading an ingenious murder-story, we feel that it was merely a clever thing to invent.

*The Complaisant Lover* is a very different type of play, or one might even say two plays in one, for there is an abrupt change of tempo from the first half, which has all the ingredients of a French bedroom farce, to the second, where the hilarity ends and we are reminded that there is a serious problem of human relations to be solved. Victor Rhodes is not the tiresome practical-joker or the unromantic and insensitive dentist husband he appears to be in act one; this facade is shattered, the reality revealed, when he discovers his wife's infidelity at the beginning of act two. His emotional breakdown comes as the climax and transitional turning point to what went before and the subsequent *denouement*. Had we really been so unkind as to laugh at the situation in the Amsterdam hotel bedroom where unsuspectingly he confronts his wife with her lover (instead of old school friend Jane Crane who should have been there) without realizing that anything is amiss? Even his Dutch dental colleague who couldn't speak English probably understands more than the wronged husband.

Nevertheless a way out must be found, and it is here that Rhodes, the practical joker now turned moralist, suggests an English compromise. He will allow what he cannot prevent on condition that his wife keeps the home together. Moreover the husband knows that eventually the lover will tire of his wife and leave her, so that this unconventional design for living turns out to be a feasible and practical solution. The husband is at the end of the play, a wiser, if a sadder, man.

This leap from farce to the serious is not necessarily as easy as Greene believes. "I have always believed," he writes as an 'Epitaph' on *Carving a Statue*, "that farce and tragedy are far more closely allied than comedy and tragedy. This play was to me a game played with the same extremes of mood as *The Complaisant Lover*." Yet in an interview with J. W. Lambert, published in *The Sunday Times*, commenting on the failure of *Carving a Statue*, Greene says he would like to see it played as a farce, adding: "I still think that's what I meant it to be." The problem is that Greene, far from writing the play to appear like a farce, or a first act which should be "almost completely farce", has in fact given us a small play on an enormously ambitious theme; we have not a farce about "human inadequacies", so such as a tragedy of a bad sculptor who attempts the perfection of God. Can we laugh at this pretentious amateur who wastes his life in seeking to carve an image of God, sacrificing the world, indifferent to his son, and even finding the death of his wife merely "a shocking inconvenience"? Is there any denouement possible other than the one which Greene presents us, that instead of creating God the Father he has ruined "a fine piece of stone". The statue was a means of escape from his "indifference and the world's pain".

*Carving a Statue* is indeed a small play; such action as there is comes from the introduction by the son of two girls, one an obvious vamp whom the father seduces, the other a deaf and dumb girl whom a lecherous doctor tries to rape and who is killed in a road accident while running away from him. It is through these scenes that the alienation in tempo between farce and tragedy is attempted, but the alternance of farce and Soho sordidness seems to obscure the simplicity which Greene was attempting. The failure of *Carving a Statue* is a complete one, altogether as Greene admits, "a painful business". It seems that in the theatre Greene remains an outsider unable to explore the dimensions with that same life-size moral vision which encompasses his serious novels; although a skilful writer of dialogue he is a prisoner of his own limitations. Greene appears to have found in the theatre a kind of cul-de-sac; his reputation as a playwright is almost without importance, an unfortunate conclusion for the most important English novelist of our times.

### JAMES BRIDIE (1888–1951)

The plays of James Bridie present an optimist's window on the world. Bridie (Dr. Osborne Henry Mavor) was a tolerant moralist, little concerned — unlike his Yorkshire contemporary J. B. Priestley — with social propaganda. The experience gained as a medical practitioner made him an acute observer of man, and at the same time he delighted in poking fun at our foibles without preaching. His characters are without exception interesting people, the good are never too good and the bad are always human. "I find a few facetiae light this wilderness of a world like glow-worms", exclaims Dr. Angelus after he has finished poisoning his wife and mother-in-law, and goes on to confide with the audience that he is a rare combination, a man of science and a philosopher. In his characters Bridie has a bond of understanding and sympathy, and transfers this to the audience even for characters they would not normally feel affection for at all (i.e. John Knox, or the Wee Free minister in *Mr. Bolfry*).

Throughout his work — some thirty plays — Bridie shows an innate sense of theatre, and even in his poorest plays he never bores and even offers just a wee dose of idiosyncrasy which is the signature of Bridie's own civilised intellect. They are always interesting but often slap-dash. It was as if he had so many ideas in his fertile imagination that he rushed on to the next one without doing justice to his last one. As so many critics have complained, a play by Bridie has the appearance of being unfinished. It is more like a first draft, often in urgent need of revision and structural alteration. His refusal to take pains is regrettable, but fortunately a born playwright does not depend on that.

One can do him more justice by attempting a general picture of his work than by presenting a classification of his plays starred according to an A.A. handbook. Bridie never gave us a masterpiece by which he may be remembered by succeeding generations, but there is no reason why his themes should date. For he delighted in using the fantasies of a biblical story to give flight to his own wit and flow of language, and he thus finds himself perfectly at home in such plays as *Tobias and the Angel* and *Jonah and the Whale*. And surely the body-snatching of Burke and Hare which is described in *The Anatomist* will never fail to hold an audience.

Among Bridie's other works perhaps the best known is *The Sleeping Clergyman* (1933), where heredity and the way in which it is affected by environment is traced over three generations. In the third generation Bridie maintains his belief that however true it may be that the worst features of heredity are passed on, at the same time no man is wholly evil and the genius that is the better self may also grow stronger and defeat evil. A word perhaps also on the theme of *Mr. Bolfry*, where Bridie asks us to imagine the possibility of a group of young people who, in the severe atmosphere of a Free Kirk manse in the Western Highlands, decide one night for want of entertainment to experiment in witchcraft with the aid of an old book on the subject. To the accompaniment of thunder and lightning the Devil arrives, dressed as a minister of the Church of Scotland. On the morning after the visitor has departed, all think it was an ugly nightmare, until they discover the proof, Mr. Bolfry's umbrella, which walks out of the house on its own, to their amazement.

The typical approach of Bridie can best be described by examining his treatment of a theme like *John Knox*, one of his lesser known plays, which was written for production at the Edinburgh Festival by the Old Vic, but which had to be abandoned owing to casting difficulties and was produced instead in 1947 at Bridie's own Glasgow Citizens' Theatre. Bridie presents the career of Knox episodically, linking the sequences together through a commentary provided by a present-day divinity student and his girl, who see Knox and other historical characters of the period as ghosts on Hogmanay. In the final episode Bridie reconciles the two. Mary sympathises with Knox, because to this day he is regarded as a villain, but when she suggests that they're really lucky to be dead, Knox explodes in anger and starts preaching at her once more — even in heaven!

Bridie came to the rescue of the English theatre when there was no one left after Shaw who could write the polished and witty conversation pieces which English audiences had grown to admire and demand instead of tragedy. It is ridiculous to call Bridie the Scottish Shaw (just as it is to call Edinburgh the Athens of the North or Amsterdam a northern Venice); his plays have an atmosphere of their own. His imagination, the sharpness of his intellect and the flow of language (he often makes his characters slightly tipsy in order to encourage the whirlwind of words to come more naturally!) have assured Bridie his own place of honour in the theatre since Shaw.

## SEAN O'CASEY

At one time in his career, after the productions of *Juno and the Paycock* (1924) and *The Plough and the Stars* (1926), Sean O'Casey would have been described as the most exciting dramatist in the contemporary theatre, and certainly these two plays are among the few outstanding works in the theatre of the inter-war years. Unfortunately the tragedy of Ireland was to become the tragedy of Sean O'Casey himself when he turned his back on Ireland and settled in England, for unlike his fellow Irishman Shaw, O'Casey was a foreigner exiled from his own land, and in his new home his genius turned to bitterness, his poetry to politics, his nationalistic hopes became hopes for a Communist international and his "darlin' son" was born a Red commissar. There can be no better example of how art dries up when even in absolute sincerity a writer endeavours to help the Communist cause. O'Casey has never been able to write a heartfelt tragedy since leaving Dublin, even *Red Roses for Me* falls considerably short of his tragedies such as "Juno".

Born in a tenement house in the back streets of Dublin, O'Casey had a harsh upbringing. His father died when he was three and his mother (who undoubtedly inspired the character of Juno) had to provide for the family as best she could. At fourteen O'Casey became a manual labourer, and in his spare time taught himself to read and spent his earnings on books (though he had been nearly blind since childhood). After a strenuous day's work and though he had never known good health, O'Casey took to helping the causes of Irish nationalism and the Irish Labour struggle.

We shall not attempt to deal with any of O'Casey's plays in particular; his two masterpieces are too well known to invite approval at this late date, and in the others the failings do not require to be analysed at any length. In his early (and best) work, *The Shadow of a Gunman* (1923), and in *Juno* and *The Plough and the Stars* O'Casey was a realist, but in *The Silver Tassie* he turns to expressionism. There is a different and more bitter mood in this study of the football hero who returns from the war maimed to live in a society itself a cripple. The method of expressionism and symbolism (which had been used as a contrast to realism in *The Silver Tassie*) is carried to greater extremes in *Within the Gates*, where his poetry deserts him and becomes as insipid as the characters are cardboard. Poetry returned, if we bypass and quickly forget the naive Communism of *The Star Turns Red*, written for Unity Theatre in 1940, in a rich fantasy of life in *Red Roses for Me* (1943) reminiscent of his earlier writing. O'Casey was inspired here by the Irish railway strike of 1913, and by his own memories of the period. The central character is Ayadmonn Breydon, a young railway worker who loves life and art and who dies under fire from the police at the head of a worker's rally. O'Casey has recreated in this play not only the past but also his present hopes. Yet in spite of the sweep of its action and tragic understanding, which suggested that O'Casey had at last succeeded in re-establishing his contact with his own countrymen, the play was only a moderate success.

*Oak Leaves and Lavender* (1946) was a salute to our Soviet ally when already the cold war tide was encroaching, but *Cock-a-Doodle Dandy* (1949, produced at the Edinburgh Festival ten years later) is a satire full of gusto for Irish rural life, with its rival team of killjoys, including the village priest and policeman, and the young of heart who flout them. But somehow this type of play is limited in its appeal to those who can appreciate the significance of what to those unfamiliar with Irish temper and idiom might seem a rambling and parochial allegory.

O'Casey was never able to find roots or understanding in England. Even the best and most human of his plays written in exile, *The Bishop's Bonfire* (1955), would be largely meaningless before an audience unfamiliar with the religious framework and practice in Ireland. The problem is a peculiarly nationalistic one, for it is the Irish interpretation of the Roman faith which 'has led to criticism, such as the burning of books, which is the symbolism of O'Casey's bonfire. Religious fanaticism is the theme of the play, but it is more the study of character types that makes the play come to life from time to time. A village awaits the coming of its bishop (he never appears in the play) and to this plot are allied a number of sub-plots — the frustrated love affair because of class, the frustrated love affair because of faith and the vow to virginity, the priest whose interpretation of Christianity differs from that of his immediate superiors. Frustration, drunkenness, cynicism; and yet *The Bishop's Bonfire* rises above the level of defeat because its characters reveal O'Casey's ability to depict in passages the richness of Irish humour which is sufficient to banish despair. Arguments become less tedious when Irish eyes are smiling.

O'Casey was both discovered and rejected by Dublin. He understood and had the genius to give expression to the feelings of the Irish people. No Irishman, not even Joyce, has been more alienated from his homeland, and no Irishman, we feel, has so regretted his exile. Joyce could play with language and its academic concomitant, form, in *Ulysses*. For O'Casey there was no substitution for the ordinary sounds of spoken Irish, the poetry even of an Irish "paddy", the romantic and exaggerated gesture, finally the comic that is the microcosm of a man's heart. In his need to share memories of the Irish jig, not to mention the irreverences of a "wake", O'Casey comes alive again. He was neither a moral or didactic preacher, his politics, like his pacifism, were idealistic. However out of his depths he may have found himself in his search for a new way of life and new forms of dramatic expression, the two great Irish plays, *Juno and the Paycock* and the *Plough and the Stars* belong to the classics of world theatre.

## J. B. PRIESTLEY

John Boynton Priestley (born 1894) seems to have moved through three distinct periods as a playwright; first there is the pre-war Priestley of the Time plays. The second period belongs to his adherence to the Labour Party and the ardent faith he once had for Socialist utopias and ideals. Finally there is the "in the wilderness" period of disillusionment, when he realised that the City he wrote about was no longer to be reached through party politics, and viewed from the wilderness his common sense told him it was no longer practical. After being for so long a man who knew all the answers he has become a man of doubts;

he still has his pipe in his mouth but it has gone out. After various misadventures, including *The White Countess* (written in collaboration with Jacquetta Hawkes), and *Mr. Kettle and Mrs. Moon*, Priestley's adaptation with Iris Murdoch of her novel *A Severed Head* (1963), proved at least a box-office success.

We should not forget that humour is Priestley's forte. How robust is the humour of *The Good Companions*; has Priestley ever bettered his North Country farce *When We Are Married* with its Yorkshire fun and games? Even his more sophisticated comedies such as *Ever Since Paradise* are extremely competent and entertaining. But these are not the plays which Priestley would consider important. His first period includes plays like *Time on the Conways* and *I Have Been Here Before*, both written in 1937, where he explores in dramatic form the time theories of Dunne and P. D. Ouspensky's *A New Model of the Universe*. In his second group, that of the social and propaganda plays, we have *They Came to a City* (1942), *The Linden Tree* and *An Inspector Calls* (both 1947).

*They Came to a City* was a topical play which embodied the hopes of a nation at war and for a peace which would resolve the social injustices of the pre-war world; it reflected the political idealism of a brave new world and was argued with down-to-earth common sense. A group of people divided into two caricatures, the privileged conservative classes of yesterday and the ordinary man and woman of the street who shall have their lives to live to-morrow — these people find themselves unaccountably outside the walls of an unknown city. The capitalists of yesterday are afraid to enter the city and horrified with what they see when they do venture inside; but the younger generation and members of the working class have no fears — and find the city answers their dreams. After a quick look round at the show places (like a conducted party in the Kremlin or Peking to-day) they return and must decide individually whether they wish such a city or not. Two of the younger generation decide to leave the city behind, like the horrified capitalists, in order that they may teach others the truth of this city:

Not every man, not every woman, wants to cry out for it, to work for it, to live for it and if necessary to die for it — but there's one here, one there, a few down this street, some more down that street — until you begin to see there are millions of us — yes, armies and armies of us — enough to build ten thousand new cities.

But in spite of this impassioned rhetoric — and also perhaps because of its electioneering spirit — the play is no more than well-intentioned. Priestley has failed because his characters are no more than types and his city is only a political city. It is doubtful whether Priestley would be so easily thrilled with the idea of such a community city to-day — would he not wish to remain in the wilderness there also? But the real failure of the play is not character or language, but the lack of any spiritual power and mystery which alone would make a theme of this magnitude a work of art. Materialism seems an unpromising end in itself, however much the commissars may insist.

In *The Linden Tree* Priestley is still overtly political, but he is writing here not about another utopia, but about how the silent revolution during the years of the Labour Government from 1945–1950 has affected the lives of a middle-class family in a drab north of England town. Mrs. Linden, who is worn out after the war years and discontented with the continuation of rationing and restrictions, longs to get away from the environment, while her husband Professor Linden feels it his duty to stay on at the university, although he has now reached retiring age. The professor's son, who has made a fortune during the war, wishes them to settle in a large country estate he has just bought in the south of England, and the Linden's second daughter feels that her parents should come and share her privileged aristocratic life in the south of France, where she has married a Frenchman and is in the process of accepting a way of life which is out of touch with the world. The eldest daughter is equally uncompromising on the other side, as a Communist materialist, and only the youngest daughter believes in her father and urges him to stay on. The theme is therefore a reflection of the dilemma felt by many middle-class families, but again — though less marked than in *They Came to a City* — Priestley has selected characters almost too black and white, and in their clash of political and ideological beliefs he makes a plea for a better understanding of post-war England and all that it stood for.

Only in *An Inspector Calls* does Priestley really come to grips with his theme; here all his characters are responsible for the death of a poor girl. They have not murdered her according to the law, but they have killed her nevertheless through the inhumanity they have shown her. The father has sacked her from his works, the daughter had her dismissed from a shop (merely because she was feeling grumpy and was jealous of the poor girl's smile), her fiancé had had the poor girl as a mistress and then deserted her, while the son had given her a child and had then disowned her, and the mother had refused her application for charity. The year is 1912. The inspector who calls and makes the enquiry is not a real police inspector, but as one of the characters describes him, "he was our police inspector all right". And there remains the description of him by the father, a rich industrialist: "probably a Socialist or some sort of crank — he talked like one".

Priestley is a playwright who has attempted to break out of the conventions of the naturalistic drama, tending sometimes towards a modified form of expressionism, at other times breaking up the illusion of the box-realism deliberately, as in *Ever Since Paradise*. He would fly if he could, but he has not the power of poetry to sweep him over and beyond the immediate present. His blunt Yorkshire idiom and common-sense outlook make this alien to his character. Although an idealist, he is most successful when he realises his limitations; an intelligent thinker, he has not a serious mind. But he has a flare for the theatre, is masterly in his technique, generally topical, and a writer to whom good humour comes naturally. It is one thing to prefer the wilderness, another to discover the wilderness, and suburbia are one and the same.

Robert Bolt (born 1924) first revealed his ability to convey dramatic situation together with character insight in *Flowering Cherry* (1957), an English variant of Arthur Miller's tragedy of the common man theme. Here Jim Cherry, an insurance agent, dreams of ideals and escape from the world of reality through the bottle. His children are no happier than their parents. The Somerset orchard which is the ideal becomes at last a practical possibility, but Jim is no longer able to grasp it and accept his wife's offer. Right up to the final moment of decision and truth the wife clings to her illusions of hope and pride; Jim prefers the rustic dream; his failure is complete.

*A Man for all Seasons* (1960) is a skilfully constructed play with a genuinely tragic tone; its language is eloquent and its characterisation sure. For all that it fails to achieve full dramatic power. The reasons may partly be that as a play it is altogether too smooth; the central figure of Sir Thomas More, subtly and compellingly drawn though he is, is not full-bodied enough to carry the burden of the tragic theme. Bolt's More is a complex, interesting and credible man: he is a canny and reluctant saint who chooses to hide from the eyes of God and kings in the 'thickets of the law' where he knows his agile mind can serve him best. He is a lover of the good things of the world without being worldly; he is a man of inflexible conscience who would go to almost any lengths to prevent his conscience being called to the test. The real excitement of the play derives not from the conflict between More and the king or More and Cromwell, but from the noble manner in which More takes his stand upon conscience. His words in the last scenes have a ringing authority that seem to echo far beyond the confines of the play. Bolt however makes a mistake here: by borrowing the words of the historical More he undoubtedly elevates the later part of his text but by so doing he both betrays a certain lack of confidence in himself and admits inconsistency into his language — for the speech cadences of Bolt's More are separated from the speech cadences of More himself by several hundred years (Arden is a dramatist who would have caught the speech patterns of the period so that the actual words could have been included and passed unnoticed).

Little needs to be said of his other two plays; *The Tiger and the Horse* (1960) is too blatantly a *pièce à thèse*, a kind of *Linden Tree* dealing with the theme of Nuclear Disarmament, individual conscience, with Charles Morgan characters having wandered into the wrong play. Following the failure of *Gentle Jack* (1963) Bolt made a successful box-office come-back with *Vivat! Vivat Regina!* (1970) where Mary Queen of Scots and Elizabeth of England are placed, as it were, mirror to mirror, and their creativity as women compared with the force of circumstances. While almost all playwrights have had their say on either Mary or Elizabeth; the Tudor pageantry with the two magnificent feminine rôles cannot fail to carry an audience.

## N. F. SIMPSON

"It takes a trained mind to relish a non-sequitor" says the 'author' at the end of *A Resounding Tinkle* and it is evident that a respectable degree of mental training lies behind the calculated "retreat from reason" of Norman Frederick Simpson (born 1919). Simpson, who before the war worked in a bank and is now an adult-education lecturer in London, loves logic and like Lewis Carroll he tries to stand it on its head; inverted logic is the key to his dramatic method. His feeling for inversion extends to making the ordinary appear extraordinary and the extraordinary appear ordinary; the world he gives us is one of carefully worked out topsy-turvydom. His name first came to the public's notice when he won one of the third prizes of the *Observer*'s play competition in 1956 with *A Resounding Tinkle*, which was first performed in a one-act version at the Royal Court in 1957. The setting is a suburban drawing-room inhabited by two perfectly ordinary-seeming people, the Paradocks; they have some weird friends (two comedians) and say and do the most extravagant things in the most matter-of-fact spirit possible. The play comes to life through the language rather than the characters, indeed words seem to have an existence of their own. As it's a world in which nothing surprises, Mr. Paradock doesn't so much as raise an eyebrow when at the beginning his wife tells him there's a man at the door wanting him to form a government; nor of course is the audience surprised when the Paradocks complain that the elephant they have been sent this year is far too large and exchange it for their neighbour's anaconda.

*A Resounding Tinkle* is a little uncertain in its touch and it is undoubtedly too long, but its chief fault is an irritating archness that Simpson introduces by putting on stage at intervals an 'author', a technician and a group of critics all of whom discuss the play with the audience. These interlopers on stage are presumably intended to give the audience a sense of Brechtian rapport with the actors, but artistically they are a mistake. The main characters, the Paradocks and the comedians, are indefatigable talkers and talk is what the play mainly consists in. Sometimes the Paradocks hold the stage, sometimes the comedians, and then they hold it all together. One never learns quite why the Paradocks have invited the comedians round, but that doesn't seem to matter. They discuss a host of things, calmly and flatly; at one point Mr. Paradock pretends he's a Bergsonian comptometer (whatever that might be), and lets forth all kinds of statistical nonsense when he is 'plugged in'.

Simpson's second play *The Hole*, a one-acter which completed a double bill at the Royal Court with the shortened version of *A Resounding Tinkle*, is a slight piece with even less plot about a hole in a road and the various interpretations given by different people about what is happening and what it might be for. Simpson did not however achieve any real success until his third play *One Way Pendulum*, which he describes as "a farce in a new dimension". It was first produced at the Theatre Royal, Brighton in 1959.

*One Way Pendulum* is more tightly constructed than *A Resounding Tinkle*, though it has the same logic, the same deadpan fantasy, and the set is the same kind of suburban living-room. The play is concerned with Kirby Groomkirby's obsession with black, which he has worn ever since he was born. In order to satisfy his logical mind that thus dressing himself in the colour of mourning is not unreasonable, he has had to have recourse to murder (total number 43 before the play begins); but now since murder conflicts with the law he takes his mind off it by occupying his entire time with trying to get a massed choir effect from some 500 speak-your-weight machines. Kirby's ineffectual self-important father is obsessed with the law and is not satisfied until he has erected a do-it-yourself Old Bailey in the living-room. Aunt Mabel, Mrs. Groomkirby's sister, is somewhat potty and confined to a wheelchair. She is obsessed with travel. All the characters live in their little world of obsession and are almost entirely oblivious to anything that goes on outside them.

In the First Act we see Kirby working away with his machines (one refuses to emit any other noise than 'fifteen stone ten pounds' despite the fact that the others are singing the Hallelujah Chorus), his father is struggling to erect his court, which by Act Two dominates the living-room and the father appears as witness for the prosecution. He is smugly cocksure at first but then has his confidence gradually broken down by the withering line of questioning of the prosecuting counsel and the judge who treats him rather as the accused than a witness. He confesses to having lived in a world of his own prior to coming to court and to having practised masochism for three or four years. The judge remands him in custody. Kirby who has not yet appeared is judged in his absence, Sergeant Barnes, who had arrested him before he could commit his 44th murder appearing for the defence. (Kirby disposed of his victims in a kindly manner telling each a joke before striking him with an iron bar, so that he could die laughing.) Questions reveal that Kirby's hidden motive with the weight machines was to lure so many people to the North Pole where he would instal them that the sheer weight of the earth's axis might be tilted a little to one side, thus provoking a new ice age so that many people would die. Though the judge is not prepared to take a lenient view of the case, he discharges Kirby on the ground that if he sentenced him he would be putting himself beyond the reach of the law in respect of the crimes he had not yet committed.

Kirby is jubilant and conducts his mass choir with the recalcitrant machine joining in. His father tries unsuccessfully to assume the mantle of the judge, but it is the machine that has the last word. When the father tells the imaginary jury what weight they must give to the evidence he has put before them, the machine chimes in 'Fifteen stone ten pounds.'

Simpson, in an interview with Simon Trussler in *Plays and Players* says that he wrote *One Way Pendulum* "intuitively". In the six years since then he claims to have written "a lot of abortive stuff, pieces written more or less as technical exercises, or pilot plays". His new play *The Cresta Run* produced at the Royal Court in 1965 proved a disappointment. Here Simpson is dealing with the world of the Secret Service, which lends itself to extravagance and hocus pocus all the way from the Whitehall corridors of secrecy to the suburban drawing-room. Simpson has confessed that "I've lost my faith in the power of reason, but it still exerts a powerful hold." Less, however, than in *One Way Pendulum*, and that is perhaps why *The Cresta Run*, though still clearly written with the Simpson signature, is not the play for which we had hoped. It is certainly almost as difficult to place Simpson's future as it is hard to place him at all, except as Martin Esslin might claim, in the company of the theatre of the absurd.

Brendan Behan (1923-1964), on the strength of *The Quare Fellow* (1956) and *The Hostage* (1958) looked at one time as though he might have filled the mantle left vacant by O'Casey. *The Quare Fellow* ("quare fellow" is prison slang for the "condemned man") takes us inside prison walls to meet the inmates, wardens, governor, each drawn with a human authenticity that could only come from someone who had lived, worked and suffered with them. Behan spent eight of his forty-one years in prison for "terrorist" activities on behalf of the Irish Republican Army. While the play lacks form, the brute force of the dialogue sustains the action, which passes on the eve of a hanging. Here we are, listening almost to a tape recorder which had been left running, much in the same way as in his autobiography *Borstal Boy* Behan left nothing to be added by way of a commentary. And this same impartiality is present in *The Hostage*.

The theme of *The Hostage* concerns a young Cockney national serviceman whose life is in danger when he is held hostage for an I.R.A. man in Belfast who is to be hanged. Nobody in the play wants this to happen, but all things are possible, tragedy can lead to tears, fate may decide as easily as you can dance an Irish jig.

Behan arrived too late for the great days of the Abbey Theatre, too late for nationalism. Gone are the figures from Yeats and Synge to O'Casey. It was fitting that Behan should have found his way to London through Theatre Workshop. Here he was at home as he could never have been in respectable Dublin. It is the dusty counter, the riff-raff, the honest swear word that Behan delights in; not for him polite drawing-room fare. He would like the audience to spend an "Irish" evening with him, not merely to watch a play. The actors must improvise ("The author should have sung that one — that is if the bleeding thing has an author") or, after a devastating satire

"But praise God that we are white
And better still are English."

he adds "Well, that's brought the show to a standstill". All this seems much nearer the *Commedia dell'arte* tradition, with actors talking to one another, addressing the audience, enjoying the bawdy song and Irish jig, than to the Brechtian influence which many London critics have recognised. In fact the Brechtian overtones in Joan Littlewood's Theatre Workshop production are used to suit Behan's, and not Brecht's, purpose. It is the irresponsibility with flashes of acute perception which made Behan approach ordinary people in extraordinary circumstances, and out of such material had he lived Behan might have developed his sense of the dramatic to have been more than a passing figure; he will remain more legend than either poet or playwright.

### PETER USTINOV

Peter Ustinov is the Orson Welles of Shaftesbury Avenue. In his career to date there has always been something of the boy wonder about him, and in his unflagging energy he seems to dissipate his talent in a round of acting, films, producing, television and, last but not least, playwriting. He is a little too much the jack of all trades. He is an uneven writer who either succeeds or fails; his successes have included *Love of Four Colonels* (1951), *Romanoff and Juliet* (1957) and *Photo Finish* (1962); when on the other hand Ustinov is down he is down, as in *No Sign of the Dove* (1953), which *The Times* critic described as being not merely one bad play, but three — "a bad play in each act." Ustinov had his first play produced when he was twenty-one, and in *House of Regrets* (1942) he was able to portray a group of Russian émigrés in a London boarding house (a set Ustinov knew so well), living on the memories of their past, and where only the younger generation realised that their place was to live the present as members of their adopted country. *Blow Your Own Trumpet*, produced by the Old Vic the following year, was a complete failure, but with *The Banbury Nose* (1944) Ustinov gained his first long run. This play is a biography spread over three generations of life in an army family, the military tradition defeating each generation. The technique of the play follows the quotation "Life must be lived forwards, but it can only be understood backwards." Ustinov, in telling the story backwards, uses this trick successfully.

Among the plays which followed in quick succession are *The Tragedy of Good Intentions*, *The Man behind the Statue*, *The Indifferent Shepherd*, and *The Love of Four Colonels*. In this last play Ustinov takes us to the four-power occupation of Austria and in doing so offers a lively satire on the national characteristics of each nation as depicted by their four respective colonels. The colonels are led by two immortal spirits, representing good and evil, to a deserted castle which turns out to be the traditional home of the Sleeping Beauty. Each colonel sees in the figure of the sleeping princess his own ideal, and the transposition of the castle into a stage enables each colonel to enact his chosen scene and period with the princess of his heart. Each man thus reveals in his conception of love his hidden self. The Frenchman chooses to play a scene in the tradition of Marivaux, the Englishman naturally chooses the Elizabethan drama. It is left to the American to turn missionary and rescue the fallen princess from the hands of a gangster on the run, while the Russian prefers of all times the Czarist days and Tchekhovian chatter. Each little play within the play provides Ustinov with a magnificent opportunity to parody literary styles, which he does in the best tradition of the *New Statesman* competitions. It is entertaining and as a light and frivolous satire on national behaviour should not be judged too critically.

The Romeo and Juliet theme is transferred to the rival Russian and American embassies which face each other in the main square of the smallest state in Europe; as such *Romanoff and Juliet* cannot fail but make fun of both Communist lack of humour and American foibles. Romance, this time with a happier ending, is common to both East and West, and Russian Romeo with his American Juliet are not to be defeated by the Cold War. *Photo Finish* is a highly original play; we meet Sam Kinsale at the different stages of his life in the Einsteinien sense of the immediate present. Sam aged eighty is confronted by Sam aged sixty. "There is something about you I recognise. A quality of mind" Sam remarks to Sam aged sixty. Soon Sam aged forty enters, having just had a row with his wife Stella and in fact in love with Miriam, who will always remain an illusion because she is inaccessible. In the second act the three Sams meet Sam aged twenty, on the day he became engaged to Stella and was forced to break the news to his father, Reginald; Sam aged eighty and Sam aged twenty are different people "with the same name." "You don't yet know what it's like to

Edward Albee

Thornton Wilder

Federico
Garcia Lorca

Ugo Betti

be me, and I can't really remember what it was like to be you" and yet they are both nearer to understanding each other than Sam aged forty and Sam aged sixty — "They're both full of complications . . . when a man struggles with all the problems of maturity, and has no time and too much strength to care about simplicity." Following his father's refusal to allow the marriage, Sam aged eighty addresses his father and accuses him of driving him into Stella's arms and marriage because he forbade it. When the father forbids Sam aged eighty to talk to him like that "if you are, as you say, my son" there comes the magnificent reply: "You have no right to forbid me anything. You may be my father but I'm older than you are! In fact, I'm older than you ever will be . . . you don't live to be my age. You die!"

The final arrival is Sam the newborn, and Sam aged eighty is given the baby to hold in his arm. The baby cries, the "starter" has fired his gun. Now the race is almost over, and at the end of the race all the Sams' will cross the line in "one glorious photo finish".

Unfortunately the dialogue is not sustained throughout the play on the level of the originality of the idea; the play is supposed to take in the period of the First World War, for example, yet this does not seem to affect Sam aged forty other than a passing Zeppelin makes his wife afraid. This disregard of the outside world is like pulling down the shutters and concentrating on a family portrait with the small talk of the English upper middle class ("I have already written to the head-master of your old school, and made an application to have him entered", Stella informs Sam when she learns she is pregnant.)

We have then in *Photo Finish* an example of Ustinov's flashes of brilliance and at the same time his inability to give substance to his imagination as if it was the very fertility of his inventiveness which is his own worst enemy. Throughout his playwriting career covering nearly a quarter of a century Ustinov has remained the entertainer, but there is no advance in depth or maturing of philosophy which are required of a playwright who will last. However unfair it may be to complain that such versatility makes for the partial rather than the complete, we have always the feeling with Ustinov that he is play-acting situations rather than writing.

### SIR TERENCE RATTIGAN

As a highly successful playwright whose plays offer entertainment to large numbers of people, Terence Rattigan may be said to have found the recipe for producing box-office hits, and it is perhaps ungrateful to sound carping here because he only uses the theatre to entertain. Rattigan does not believe in the so-called play of ideas, but that "the character makes the play". And he contends that this is true not only of his serious plays, but also of farce. He believes in "the farce of character". "Plot", he continues, "in a farce is necessarily so extravagant that it is usually believed impossible for the author to introduce even the elements of characterisation without destroying the illusion and killing laughter. But if the plot, however extreme, is at the very beginning rooted in character, it is possible with a little forcing, to mould the plot into the most extravagant and farcical shape without exciting the audience's disbelief."

There is no reason to doubt that this is the reason for the success of his farces such as *French Without Tears* and *While the Sun Shines*. Rattigan's failure is not when he writes a farce of character, but a serious play of character. In his farces we do not ask that his characters should be complete individuals, whereas in a serious play the character must be a creation. The main criticism of Rattigan's work, then, is a fundamental criticism, namely, that his characters are wishy-washy creatures with neither nobility in their thoughts nor individuality in their actions. They are types we know exist, and though we might recognise them, they are certainly not people we would want as our friends. Nor is it true that it was the characters who made *The Winslow Boy* a worth-while play, but the concept of freedom which the Archer-Shee case presented. That Rattigan altered the historical facts to suit his characters makes no difference to the contention that it was the topical idea which was responsible for the great success.

It is a *coup de théâtre* that makes for the success of *The Deep Blue Sea,* a play which compels admiration in performance but which does not bear examination in reading, for we can have no admiration for his characters. The story of a lonely, sex-starved woman who tries to commit suicide and is eventually reassured that life is worth living (though we have our doubts as far as she is concerned) is a tragedy only of twentieth-century drabness; if the character makes the play here, we have a drama of the sickly minded. In *Separate Tables* Rattigan takes us to a Bournemouth boarding-house for two one-act studies of loneliness which hardly rise above the level of a plot-formulated "magazine story". The usual jokes are made at the expense of the intellectuals and Left-wing journalists and politicians, and the dialogue throughout is insipid. If this is Rattigan attempting to be serious, let us long for an early return to the happy-go-lucky *French Without Tears*. For his limitations as a dramatist were surely proved in *Adventure Story,* where Rattigan chose his most ambitious character, Alexander the Great. When critics complained that the subject matter was beyond his powers, Rattigan replied in a short article in the *Radio Times* that the fact remained "that neither Shakespeare nor Shaw has written a play about Alexander the Great and I have; and as this is, they say, a free country it is hard to see why a subject should be banned to a playwright, however humble, merely because two great dramatists might have chosen that subject themselves, but did not". From such a statement Rattigan would have us believe that a critic should praise him when he tackles a gigantic theme and fails, just as when he tackles a light-weight comedy and succeeds. No critic is banning Rattigan from writing about Alexander the Great, but Rattigan in his turn must not ban criticism, and the more ambitious the play the higher always are the critical standards. A play beyond an author's power may be well meant, but it is never good theatre.

An example of this is *Ross* (1960) which might have been an important work, for clearly there is material for a play on the life of Lawrence of Arabia. Rattigan has approached *Ross* as a chronical play, opening and ending the play at the R.A.F. Depot near London in 1922, with flash-backs to Lawrence's life in the desert. Whether it is that Rattigan has not the same control of craftsmanship here as in his closely knit comedies, the play fails to reveal the man and the mystic.

From the epic to the small screen, *Heart to Heart* (1962) was specially commissioned by the B.B.C. Television is very much a craft, and Rattigan proves his complete understanding of the medium. Where Pinter uses dialogue, together with those silences and unspoken menaces which enable the camera to make the point, Rattigan's approach is more an exploration of the medium, taking us through a gruelling television interview to the other side of the screen. *Heart to Heart* opens with a famous T.V. "grand inquisitor" interrogating his victim, a "time-serving" Q.C. with the obvious purpose of catching him out and ridiculing him in front of the viewers; to our surprise the interviewer slips up and asks the same question twice which the legal mind throws back at him. We are no longer watching a T.V. interview but a play where the camera invades the private world of television personalities. David Mann, the "inquisitor" of the programme, is drinking too much. The Controller of Programmes is worried about him and feels that his questions are sometimes too "near the bone"; he is particularly anxious that the next "victim" of the programme, Sir Stanley Johnson, the new Minister of Labour, should be spared the relentless assault which has become Mann's customary treatment. Mann refuses to ease up, and is even more resolute when some information from Sir Stanley's former secretary throws fresh light on Sir Stanley's involvement in a Riviera scandal from which his name had been cleared. Sir Stanley had allowed a man called Lopez to pay his Cannes hotel bill, thus avoiding currency regulations. Not a major offence, but sufficient to force his resignation and probably end for good his political career. "Heart to Heart" comes on the air, and Sir Stanley, thinking he is cornered, and unaware that the Controller has arranged to have the sound cut should Mann go ahead with the question, makes his own confession. The twist is that the vast majority of the viewers prove to be on Sir Stanley's side, and only three favour Mann's self-righteous indictment. I rather suspect that in reality it would be the inquisitors of this world who would have public support, no matter what the cause.

Rattigan's next play *Man to Man* (1963) is loosely based on the life of Kreuger, who would indeed have been the ideal "victim" in a "Heart to Heart" T.V. interview. Here we have a financial wizard who "by 1929, had achieved every ambition that any great financier could hope for, a man who was already acclaimed as the Saviour of Europe, whose advice was sought by Presidents, Ministers, and Kings, who, in a financial sense, ruled the whole world", whose personal fortune in 1929 was over fifty millions, built up and acquired through swindling and forgery. Gregor Antonescu (the Kreuger of the play) listens to a radio announcer recite the above description of himself as he is in hiding. The play however does not resolve the question why he did this. We have to be content to follow Genet's "Thief's Journal" and accept that his talents are criminal, and the best scene in the play is when Antonescu offers a homosexual company president his own son as a male prostitute.

After an absence of seven years, during which time he wrote mainly for the cinema, including *The VIP's, The Yellow Rolls Royce* and the script for the remake of *Goodbye Mr. Chips*, Rattigan returned to the theatre with *A Bequest to the Nation* (1970). The bequest in question (one which went unhonoured) was that made by Lord Nelson to his King and country on his mistress, Lady Hamilton's behalf, that after his death "they give her an ample provision to maintain her rank in life". The play concentrates on the period just before he set out for Trafalgar, and ends three weeks after the famous victory when news of his death is brought back. The portrait of Nelson is a complex one, the contrasts between the commander of genius and the petulant side not necessarily at odds with this. Emma Hamilton, an exhibitionist who had embarrassed half the society of Europe, is outwardly depicted as a drunken, middle aged woman; yet his portrait is sympathetic. Nelson's wife, who everybody pitied as the crippled "poor Tom-Tit" is the estranged wife. The inclusion of a number of letters and memories from the archives blend into Rattigan's own dialogue without difficulty, and give the play an authenticity that comes with "theatre verité".

Since then Rattigan has completed the first play of a double bill, a "spoof" of Sardou's *Tosca* entitled *My Proud Beauty*. It would be sardonic if history should ascribe a place in the history of the English theatre for Rattigan not unlike that of Sardou's in the French theatre of the last century. For both were masters of the well-made play, both were entertainers rather than thinkers, both were prolific, with subjects ranging from historical epics to farce; neither cared about the social problems of their time. Finally, both won accolades, with Sardou elected to the Académie Française in 1878 and Rattigan awarded a knighthood in the Queen's Honour's List in 1971.

Ann Jellicoe (born Middlesborough 1928) aims from her first play to bypass intellect and via rhythm, music, noise and irrational gesture to create basic stimuli that will reach down to the deepest fears and conflicts of the psyche. In her method words are emptied of their rational connotations and assume significance as subconcious gesture. The obvious danger in this method is that an audience while very ready to submit to musical jazz may be quite unprepared to submit to verbal jazz. *The Sport of My Mad Mother*, won third prize in the *Observer* drama competition of 1956. The play is intended to give an impression in performance of improvisation, and this it does. While she was writing it bits gradually fell into shape to form a whole; Miss Jellicoe even goes so far as to tell us that she didn't know herself what the play was really about until some time after she had written it. There is almost no subject matter, for emotion is made its substitute. She has chosen a group of confused and inarticulate East End youths, moulded into the semblance of a gang under the awesome dominance of a school-teacher-cum-mother figure called Greta. The gang are outcasts from the tribe and from the womb; they exhibit their feelings without the inflections of thought and submerge themselves whenever possible in group ecstasy. Through the din and dance, the demotic chantings and the occasional blows and flashings of a knife several dramatic opposi-tions emerge, such as between Greta and Dean, a young American, and between Greta and her boy-friend Cone. Dean is a run-of-the-mill liberal intellectual who opposes love, generosity and responsibility to Greta's destructiveness; Cone is a vociferous adulator and little besides. Both are defeated by Greta's strength of spirit: Cone commits suicide and Dean threatens to. Greta, the hard cold queen-bee, ends the play ecstacising about children and actually having one on the stage. The question remains whether the suppositions that underlie *The Sport of My Mad Mother* are deep down sentimental ones. *The Knack* (1961) is the best known of Miss Jellicoe's plays, largely due to the splendid film adaptation, where the camera takes over verbal situations and plays a visual ping-pong. The knack in question is the ability to seduce girls: Tolen has it, Colin desires it and Tom seems to be indifferent to it. The action takes place in Colin's house where Tolen and Tom rent rooms. Tom, whose main purpose is to act as the stumbling block to Tolen's desires, is redecorating his room; Colin, a frustrated schoolmaster, is shyly trying to get from Tolen instruction on how to acquire the knack. Tolen boasts of his prowess and speed. The stage is set 'for Nancy, whose arrival precipitates the action. Young and innocent, she appears at the window and asks the way to the Y.W.C.A. She never does get there: the three men and finally her own wishes intervene. She becomes caught up with the trio. Tolen deliberately rouses Nancy, who is both fascinated and repelled by him, and caught between conflicting desires faints into the arms of Colin. When she comes round she gets it into her head that she has been raped. While Nancy chants rape out of the window the three men discuss the best action to take. Should Tolen actually rape her? Tolen demurs. Should they use force to keep her quiet—or negotiation? Finally Nancy switches her attention from Tolen to Colin — to whom in fact she had been attracted to all the time. Tolen has to relinquish her.

After these two experiments in verbal virtuosity Miss Jellicoe surprised everyone when in *Shelley* (1965) she turned to a documentary-type biography of the poet's life. Her reconstruction is melodramatic but it lacks the spontaneity we had expected of her; it seems to be a turning in the wrong direction, for Miss Jellicoe has both insight and intuition into the words and thoughts of teen-agers.

Henry Livings, who was born in 1929 and has a working-class background is one of the more unpredictable of the new dramatists. As well as writing for television, two of his plays have been produced by the Royal Shakespeare Company, more recently a singularly unfunny farce *Eh?* (1965) and during their lease of the Arts, *Nil*

*Carborundum* (1962). Here we have a play which has whirling vitality, clever construction and simple aim. It seeks to illustrate the futility of conventional militarism in a nuclear age. The R.A.F. becomes a farce, and it makes fools of those who serve in the forces. The tragedy inherent in this futility is brought out in the persons of the Camp C.O. and in Sergeant Bull, both of whom realise the waste they are making of their lives and hate themselves for it. The C.O. had his hey-day as a bomber pilot during the war but now in peace-time his natural aggressiveness has become sour; Bull stays at his job because he knows he won't be able to make it in civvy street, and drowns his sorrow in drink. With the exception of the new cook, Neville Harrison, all the other characters illustrate the point that the military system encourages the bad qualities while stultifying the good ones. Livings is angry with the R.A.F. for what it is, not in the Wesker sense by using it as a universal metaphor for social consciousness.

Livings has one man who stands apart and refuses to accede to the demands made; he is the cook Neville. Having quickly realised that joining the R.A.F. was a mistake all he wants is to get back to civilian life: 'I want a job where it's a good thing if you *do* it, not one where you're more use idle'. His complete indifference to what is going on around him, his refusal to care, make us characterise him as a wise man. A less ambitious play than *Chips with Everything*, but in its way a more satisfactory one.

Peter Luke (born 1919) has found in the enigmatic personality of Frederick Rolfe, self-styled Baron Corvo, a dramatic figure which dazzles both an actor of ambition and the audience alike. Working freely from the biography by A. J. A. Symons "The Quest for Baron Corvo" as well as from Rolfe's own writings, in *The Play of Hadrian the Seventh* (1967) we follow his life both in his doldrums and in his imagination. A convert to Catholicism, Rolfe wanted to take holy orders but was expelled from the seminary at Rome because of his eccentric behaviour and his *folies de grandeur*. As a result his hatred turned against the ecclesiastical authorities. So he lived on in debt, scrounging on others, waiting for a pardon and written apology from the Church. Twenty years pass and when the play begins illusion seems to become reality. Two bishops arrive and he is reinstated; he leaves for Rome and before he even knows the Papal reply, he is elected Pope, Hadrian the Seventh.

Rolfe as Pope is never divorced from the past; he seems more concerned to remedy the abuses from which he had suffered than to save the world. He gives an audience to his old char-lady Mrs. Dixon, and mistakenly to his old landlord, a violent Orangeman from Ulster who shoots him. Thus dies Hadrian the Seventh. In the final scene of the play we are back in London where Rolfe is finishing his book. The bailiffs come to carry off his furniture, and when they enquire about his manuscript he replies that it is a novel of a man who had the error of being ahead of his epoch.

*Hadrian the Seventh* has all the makings of a theatrical *tour de force*. The transition which makes Rolfe Pope is never questioned. Yet in the end it is an unsatisfactory play: it lacks greatness, it lacks the Nietzchean quality of the Superman. One would have thought the ambition of a Pope would be more than petty revenge, rather to attack the impossible, the making of heaven on earth. Rolfe becomes a psychoanalytical study of arrogance and failure; he is closer to being the first Hippie, his excessive paranoia excluding the need for LSD for his "trip". Nevertheless, *The Play of Hadrian the Seventh* has, in a lean decade, proved an outstanding success because of the acting and ceremonial possibilities of the title.

Light and faith are quenched by dark forces as in a ritual purge of witchcraft in *Afore Night Come*, which the Royal Shakespeare Company produced in their Arts Theatre Season in 1962. David Rudkin (born 1936) lives in Birmingham and has written the play in Midland's dialect; the setting is a pear orchard in a countryside significantly termed Black. The characters are a strange brood, even more forbidding by what they are than what they do. From this refuse-tip of unremitting darkness, pessimism is enforced by bringing nature to act as a livid, rumbling chorus.

Larry, Jeff and Roche are new to the orchard; the others are not. The newcomers are immediately seen to be misfits, Jeff by his town ways, Larry by his education and Roche by almost everything about him. Roche is part tramp, part poet, mingling quack learning with genuine poetic observation, he is like the walking embodiment, in parody, of some bygone Gaelic civilisation. He is the focus of evil fears and desires and in the end their victim. Spens, the foreman, makes to throw him out but weakly relents: Roche, like some huge moth fatally attracted to its doom keeps coming back to the sinister group under the trees who are preparing first their minds, then their knives, for his slaughter. Roche at the end is deserted; stabbed, a bloody cross is scored on his chest and even his head is cut off; then his body and head, treated respectfully as befits a sacrifice, are hidden in the ground. After that he ceases to exist and all will go on in the orchard as before.

On the strength of this one play with its focus on fear and the forces of "the dark side of the moon" Rudkin has established himself as a regional member of the Theatre of Cruelty; but it is too early to assess his likely development.

James Saunders (born 1925) has described himself as an "introvert", a man standing "beyond the confines of conventional society and looking in, observing, criticising and maybe envying a little". In *Ark* (1959) he makes the character of Noah rather different from what we had assumed, uninterested in the rest of mankind. Saunder's other two important works, *Next Time I'll Sing to You* and *A Scent of Flowers*, are closely allied to death. The first takes its theme from Raleigh Trevelyan's book *A Hermit Disclosed*; in Saunder's version an actor interprets what the hermit might have been like. *A Scent of Flowers* concerns the suicide of a young girl, and her search for truth and grace during her life-time. The dead girl watches her own funeral, and in flashbacks we follow the moments of crisis in her own life. These plays seem to belong to a more genteel, old fashioned theatre which Osborne almost swept away. As if aware of this, Saunders turned in *The Borage Pigeon Affair* (1969) to a play which as he describes it: "deals with tattiness, shoddiness and squalor". The author goes on to instruct the director to "think of himself no better than Loathing, the actors no better than the characters they are playing . . . what is presented in the play is not people but the visual and verbal trappings they have put on. . . . If anyone wants to get beneath the surface, let them find another play."

Saunders, in my view, was to prove more successful with the contemporary idiom in *Games after Liverpool* (1971) where the first part of a double bill is an attempt to act out the failure of two men and two women to communicate, a theme which runs through all Saunder's work. The second play is a contrast between a Reuter's report on the trial of Lt. Calley and the way the actors decide to re-act the courtroom scene for themselves, until they become dissatisfied with what they think happened and search for what might have happened.

In previous editions I have remarked that Saunders is a playwright with ideas, but too ambitious in his subject-matter to have the dramatic power to give us an important play. With his recent experiments, Saunders is reaching out to involve his audience. In seeking meaning in a mad world Saunders knows he will fail; but as an *homme de théâtre* Saunders will, I hope, continue his search for dramatic forms.

Tom Stoppard (born Czechoslovakia 1937) does not deny his enormous debt to Beckett and *Waiting for Godot*. Writing in *The Sunday Times* (25 February 1968) Stoppard declares that Godot "redefined the minima of theatrical experience. Up to then you had to have X; suddenly you had X minus one." *Rosencratz and Guildenstern are Dead* (1966) is in fact an echo of Beckett minus one, Beckett's Irish saving grace. The vulagisation of the two non-entities of Shakespeare's *Hamlet*, "overheard as it were from the wings" here hold the centre of the play, with Hamlet and the other characters making ironic, stylised intrusions. Meanwhile we are asked to examine the relationship between conscious and subconscious levels, or "the wrekage of propositions which he had made only two minutes before". I found it an evening of complete banality and boredom.

*Enter a Free Man*, although produced after, was in fact written before *Rosencratz and Guildenstern are Dead*. It is much more a halfway-house between the conventional theatre and Beckett. The free man in question, George Riley, is an inventor; a bore at home he is nevertheless a good drinking pal. Riley has been working for years on completely useless inventions (such as fabricating indoor rain); though he still believes in himself his wife has long since given up trying to reason with him, although his trendy daughter has a try.

One wonders whether Stoppard is not too derivative to be a positive force in the new English theatre.

### OTHER PLAYWRIGHTS

Among other playwrights who have established themselves, the names of David Storey, (whose *Home* provided a brilliant vehicle for Guilguid and Richardson in 1970), David Mercer (*Belcher's Luck*) and Charles Wood (*Fill the Stage with empty Hours*, 1966, and *Cockade*, 1963) come to mind. They are, in their different ways, very much the voices of contemporary England.

Giles Cooper (1918-1966) first attracted attention when the London Club Theatre triumphed on the fringe of the Edinburgh Festival in 1950 with his play *Never Get Out*. The setting is a house doomed to be bombed; the characters an army deserter and a woman seeking suicide. His play *Everything in the Garden* (1962) opened the Royal Shakespeare Company's experimental season at the Arts Theatre Club. At first the play appears a conventional middle-class comedy about a husband and wife where everything in the garden is almost all right, until Cooper produces a Pirandellian twist by making the husband step out of the action to address the audience. Until then we had heard about the domestic problems, the wife always wanting more money, the husband, with taxation and a son at a public school, not knowing how he can provide. Suddenly the wife has a brilliant idea, she will take a job — but the job she finds offered at 25 guineas an afternoon is in a high-class brothel of a Polish Jewess. There is the question, should she? shouldn't she? until she discovers that many other suburban housewives do not have these qualms, in return for bank-notes to help the bank balance. This becomes a play with a decision, which is not the same thing as a play with an ending.

This becomes a play with a decision, which is not the same thing as a play with an ending. *Everything in the Garden* was "re-made", in the best "Ghost Goes West" tradition, by Edward Albee in 1967 for its New York production; something went astray in the crossing — Cooper's satire — while Albee was all too ready in the theme to see a moral justification for his mysogynism.

*Happy Family*, produced at the Hampstead Theatre Club, London, in 1966, reveals Cooper at his best. A brother and two sisters have managed to preserve their childhood world, until an outsider breaks the circle to reveal adult reality. To the very end they cling to their memories, Deborah has even chosen an apartment where there is no cupboard under the stairs where she can be sent for "Punishment B", though in her turn she can still threaten her brother "Punishment D for Dark" by pulling out the fuse. Childhood games and taboos are not always as idyllic as imagined; they can also bring about deception with life. One wonders whether Cooper's own death in 1966 was not the climax of one of his plays where accidental death is caused by stepping out of a suburban train.

Christopher Hampton (born 1946 at Fayal in the Azores) is resident dramatist at the Royal Court Theatre, London. It was there that his first play *When did you last see my mother?* was put on for a Sunday night production. *Total Eclipse* followed in 1968, and with *The Philanthropist* (1970) Hampton clearly established himself on both sides of the Atlantic.

The theme of *The Philanthropist* may be said to be that of the contrast between negative and positive forces in life; those who accept too readily must be responsible for the way the world is. Philip, an ageing bachelor about to get married, a philologist fascinated by words and yet unable to express himself, belongs to this type. He is indeterminate, ineffectual, kind and content; finding some good in everything he is completely uncritical. The play opens with his praising the efforts of a young playwright who has just finished reading his script to Philip and Philip's critical friend, Don. Suddenly the playwright blows his brains out. The subsequent scenes are unrelated to this episode. We meet Celia, Philip's fiancée, who can't bear cooking (although she cooks), working (she works) or Philip (who, in the end, she decides not to marry). The engagement is broken off following Philip's night with Araminta, one of those girls who merely wished to add Philip's name to the long list of men she had slept with. Philip was too timid to say "no" and too shy to succeed; nor was he strong enough to hold Celia after she had found out. In the end we realise that there is more to love than the Beatle's song "all you need is love"; loving everything like Philip leads directly to the inability of loving anyone. Hampton's play is a remarkable study of a present reality; it is not so much his characters we recognise as the ethos of a contemporary environment he depicts.

John Mortimer (born 1923) became a barrister in 1948, and while working at the bar wrote a number of novels and a play for radio, *The Dock Brief* (1957), which won for him the *Prix Italia* and brought him to the theatre. The brief in question has been assigned to a broken-down barrister, who is to defend a murderer in what seems a hopeless case. Though the barrister loses his case, the murderer is freed owing to the incompetent way he was defended, the barrister being unable to find anything to say in favour of the accused. The murderer believes that the barrister deliberately planned it that way.

Of Mortimer's full length plays, *The Wrong Side of the Park* is a fairly conventional play about a wife who is convinced that her second marriage is all wrong and that her first marriage was all right, whereas exactly the opposite was in fact the case. His second play *Two Stars for Comfort* (1962) concerns the owner of the Riverside Hotel, Sam Turner, and his last experiment with pleasure when young students come to stay (his wife is absent) and he has to crown the Regatta Queen. In his hotel he only speaks comforting phrases which customers want to hear; but in doing so he is no longer an individual. In the end Sam Turner is left to wonder, alone, what it is that everyone wants other than a word or two of comfort.

Joe Orton (1933-1967) would certainly have qualified for the prize in the Black comedy category; as it is Orton was the winner of the London Critics' "Variety" Award for the best play of 1964 for his *Entertaining Mr. Sloan*, while *Loot* won the *Evening Standard* award in 1966. There is something "Arsenic and Old Lace" in the necrophilic callousness of the situation contrasted with the extreme gentility of his dialogue. In *Loot* we watch Hal dragging his embalmed mother from the coffin to hide her upside down in the cupboard. He plans to fill the coffin with "loot" and with the money safely buried he will dispose of his mother's body. As a Catholic, however, he cannot undress her, nor can he tell a lie, not even though he knows Truscott, who forces his way in on the pretext he is from the sanitary department, is from "the yard". In playing hide and seek with the corpse from Truscott, the play becomes a savage attack on the police and police corruption. "The British police force used to be run by men of integrity", protests the not-so-innocent nurse Fay. "That's a mistake which has been rectified" comes the reply. In the end Truscott takes his percentage of the "loot", arrests an innocent who is guilty before he has invented a charge.

In 1967 a double bill, *Crimes of Passion*, consisting of *The Ruffian on the Stair*, and *The Erpingham Cup* was produced, but Orton's dramatic career was cut short by his own death, in a manner reminiscent of his own plays.

Bernard Kops (born 1928) is of a London working-class Jewish background, which he used in his first play *The Hamlet of Stepney Green* (1956). David Levy's dead father communicates to his son in a séance. The son, while working at a fish-stall, dreams of becoming a pop singer. Meanwhile David believes that his father has been poisoned, by his mother and her widower friend. David becomes a Teddy-boy Hamlet, although the father realises that his wife's remarriage is a good thing. In the end instead of poison we have a love potion administered, and all is set for a very different ending.

*The Dream of Peter Mann* (first produced Edinburgh Festival 1960) is a result of his being knocked unconscious while taking his mother's savings. In the dream Peter runs away with his childhood sweetheart Penny to look for uranium. Twelve years later he returns to a world run riot, with everybody prospecting for uranium, and Peter is nearly executed as no one recognises him. Five years later Peter is prosperous, having through his talk convinced people to work for him. His factory is manufacturing shrouds, as the bomb is about to fall. As the bomb falls Peter is in his shelter, everybody else is killed, and a voice tells him he is dying, and his mother sings a lullaby. As he dies, he is woken out of his dream, and returns to consciousness. Peter no longer wants to steal his mother's money, and he now knows he loves Penny and will take her away with him. As he exclaims: "What will you bid for life?" and asks us to make the most of it before it's gone. The play is not entirely successfully constructed, but at least Kops has, on the strength of these two works proved his imagination, his sense of understanding of theatre and his ability to portray the lives of ordinary people.

# NINETEEN

# U.S.A.

"If the theatre must bring us only what we can immediately apprehend or comfortably relate to, let us stop going to the theatre entirely. . . ."

EDWARD ALBEE

THE brightest prospect for the American theatre is that the stage is set, and, as showmanship would put it, the potentialities are tremendous. Eyes look not on the achievements of the past — for there are few worth looking at — but on the future, the period in which the new one hundred per cent. American drama will grow to maturity. Up to the present American playwrights have learnt the lessons of European masters, first O'Neill and more recently Tennessee Williams and Arthur Miller, though the plays of these last two writers are more than merely works of disciples, their steps are surer and the immigrant strain less conscious. The playwrights, then, are coming, the stars have had their names glittering in lights for some time, and there is money in the Broadway till. But when will Broadway (and Broadway "On or Off" *is* the American theatre) become a centre of good theatre and the cultural leader in world drama?

Whereas America has been forced to assume her rôle as leading power in the free world, there is no such urgent necessity for her to play such a missionary part in the theatre. That she will do so one day, if the theatre survives, is almost inevitable, but in the meantime American drama has hardly had time to have reached a golden age; it is sufficient that each decade since the 'twenties has been an advance on the previous one. Had the theatre been capable of organising itself like Hollywood as a centre of dream-producing products it would be very different, but there are no short cuts to success in the living traditions of theatre.

Can we really expect a drama to flourish when subjected to the exploitation of the 'box-office or bust' rule?

Since the 1914–1918 war, the American drama has been brought into existence from scratch. The Theatre Guild, for example, when it was founded in 1918, had only $19.50 for its second production (apart, of course, from the idea which had led to its formation), yet from importing foreign plays to begin with it soon encouraged American authors to write directly for their own theatre, and thus it found its playwrights. Yet even so, the Theatre Guild has not developed into an Old Vic or a Comédie Française, and unfortunately all attempts to set up a permanent American National Theatre (A.N.T.A.) have not proved too successful. Moreover, in the 'thirties the Left-wing Group theatre may claim to have done as much for American drama as did the Theatre Guild, which had modified its policy. We are not concerned here with elaborating the politics of the American theatre, nor to give more than a glimpse of the background of its organisation, without which it would be almost impossible to view a list of its better known playwrights in perspective.

The American dramatist is far from equalling the novelist in modern American literature. University schools of playwriting have not overcome the practical difficulties of an unknown playwright finding a backer, which seems to be more difficult in the States than in Europe (indeed Albee has had two of his plays produced in Berlin before American production). In the regional theatres, subsidies are provided by the Ford and Rockefeller Foundations, but few of these theatres make provision for new plays, apart from Dallas Theatre Centre (eighteen new plays in six years) and the Actors Workshop, San Francisco, who average four new plays. Scope is therefore limited, and as Richard Schechner, writing in Tulane Drama Review (Fall, 1965) observes:

> Significant new plays do not come. Off-Broadway, for all its ills, incompetence, and Broadway-mimicking, still provides more excitement.

The artist, as Mr. Schechner concludes, "is alienated within his institution rather than outside it".

What then, is the solution? The death of the theatre has often been predicted in general, and of Broadway in particular. The Broadway theatre has not in the past few years been at its healthiest; it seems to prefer the importation from London and Europe rather than rely on its own inspiration. Thus plays like Peter Weiss's *Marat*, John Whiting's *The Devils*, Peter Shaffer's *The Royal Hunt of the Sun*, John Osborne's *Luther* and *Inadmissible Evidence* set a standard which local products do not match. Even the promise of Jack Richardson's *The Prodigal* is quickly dashed by two successive failures. Broadway has become a luxury which backers can no longer afford — at any rate where risk is involved. There remains the off-Broadway movement, which developed in the twenties, and in the fifties had been responsible for such names as Jack Gelber, Kenneth H. Brown, Edward Albee, Murray Schisgal and Arthur Kopit. Eventually the spiral of costs hit the movement, and the one function that it could best serve — the discovery of native talent — was threatened by its policy of imitating Broadway itself with revivals, importations, and gimmicks.

Whatever future developments, New York and Broadway are the inevitable pulse of the state of the American drama; from time to time Broadway produces a faith which must surprise itself. A consideration of the drama of the last thirty years reveals its ups and downs, its achievements and its flops. The American drama is in transition as elsewhere; but it is young and still unsure of itself. It is in its uncertainty that lies its promise.

### EDWARD ALBEE

With both Tennessee Williams and Arthur Miller we are aware of the existence of the two Americas, the legend and the reality. Edward Albee (born New York, 1928) sets out to equate the two and call it the American dream; as he says in *Tiny Alice*, when memory exists is there any way of establishing the difference between the real and the imaginary? The younger generation of American playwrights, such as Kopit, Schisgal and Jack Richardson, seem mysogynists at heart; with Albee mysogynism is an obsession. He knows he cannot escape the claw marks of the all-American shrew. The American male can only play games, the "kidding" which turns both man and woman into mythomaniacs. The gorgeous young man is the replacement for the defective model originally supplied in *The American Dream*, he seems to need a flying trapeze and he would just sail through the air, for he is completely empty within. He is the image of the son George and Martha invent in *Who's Afraid of Virginia Woolf?* and whom George has to kill in order to reveal the truth, the whole truth, that the American dream doesn't exist. Here Albee stands on his own; Miller would have spoken out for truth in an overtly political context, but as an American would accept the basic American premise. Albee, no less one hundred per cent American (though of course we can't be certain as he was adopted when he was a month old) does not accept the American way of doing things, does not assume the American optimism, the sense of the virility and dynamism of their society. Although it is difficult to try and place him in any category (and no American one) Albee may be said to find more sympathetic inmates in the theatre of disturbance, or if you prefer, the theatre of the Absurd. As such it has now crossed the Atlantic.

Albee has to date established an impressive reputation on the strength of only two full-length plays, four one-act plays, and an adaptation of Carson McCullers' *The Ballad of the Sad Cafe*. His first play, *The Zoo Story*, a one-acter written in 1958 and produced at the Schiller Theater Werkstagg, Berlin in 1959, has a Pinteresque quality of menace about it. Peter, the good middle-class citizen is dressed in tweeds and smoking his pipe on a bench in Central Park on a Sunday afternoon, when Jerry, a downtrodden-looking man in his late thirties, falls into conversation with him. Peter wishes to be left alone, but not be unfriendly; Jerry is desperately anxious to communicate with someone: "everyone once in a while I like to talk to somebody, really *talk*; like to get to know somebody, know all about him". To which Peter replies uncomfortably "And I am the guinea pig for to-day?" Soon Jerry has found out that Peter is married, has two daughters and an executive job in publishing worth eighteen thousand a year. He on the other hand is a homosexual, an outcast. His only real contact was with a dog he once tried unsuccessfully to poison; afterwards he loved that dog and wanted the dog to love him, and for twenty seconds he believes he did make contact. Jerry gets intense. He tells Peter to move off the bench, which suddenly he wants and when Peter refuses, starts to tickle him and edges him off. Jerry tells Peter to fight, and to make things more equal flings Peter a knife. Peter, appalled, holds the knife to defend himself while Jerry impales himself on it, and dying, thanks Peter for having comforted him. To the theme of menace Albee has added that of homosexuality.

*The Death of Bessie Smith* (1959) follows the incidents following the death of a famous Negro Blues singer who was refused treatment by white hospitals following a road accident. Albee however is less interesting as a social writer than when he turns to stylisation. *The American Dream* (1959-60, produced New York 1961) is, to quote

Albee's preface to the play "an examination of the American scene, an attack on the substitution of artificial for real values in a society, a condemnation of complacency, cruelty, emasculation and vacuity; it is a stand against the fiction that everything in this slipping land of ours is peach-keen". There is little wonder that the defenders of the *status quo* took offence. The typical American family consists of Mommy, Daddy and Grandma; Mommy represents the American shrew, never allowing daddy a word except to repeat what she has just said — in order to prove that he was paying attention to her. Grandma they would like to have put away, but it's not so easy — after all, she's an older shrew. Still, she did warn Daddy about her daughter ("a tramp, and a trollop and a trull to boot, and she's no better now".). In fact, Mommy would have Daddy "carted off too, if she thought she could get away with it". A Mrs. Barker calls, not about granny, but about the complaint made of "the bumble" her adoption service provided. For it turned out the bumble didn't like its Mommy, but had eyes only for Daddy—so they were gouged out. Then they cut off its sex organs and wrists and when it called Mommy a dirty word they cut out its tongue; when it grew bigger it didn't have a head on its shoulders, it had no guts, it was spineless and its feet were made of clay, and then as a last straw, it died — after all had been paid for. To counter this a gorgeous young man enters "like a breath of fresh air"; they are all agreed he's exactly what they want. The young man, however, who was separated after birth from his identical brother, feels that he is incomplete, he doesn't know what has happened to something within him, but he has no touch, is unable to make love, to see anything with pity; in fact he has no feelings. Psychoanalysts might explain part of *The American Dream* through the fact that Albee was himself adopted at one week old and didn't get along with his parents. The obsession against Mommy is the dominant feature in Albee's work.

The Mommy and Daddy of *Who's Afraid of Virginia Woolf?* (1962) are this time given names, Martha and George, thus becoming individuals in place of abstract characters. Martha is 52, George six years younger; they have been unable to have children, so that their love is mixed up with sexual humiliation, a strong love-hate relationship which makes them want to hurt and claw and wound each other because they know each other and cannot do without one another. George has by now become resigned to Martha's verbal assaults ("He made the mistake of loving me, he must be punished for it"); he has also become resigned to much else besides; he owes his job to Martha's father, who is founder president of the New England college where he lectures in History; he has resigned himself to the fact that many years previously his father-in-law made him suppress a novel he had written full of his feelings and emotions on the grounds of the effects it might have on the college. So George now plods on without ambitions; on this particular night he and Martha have been at a party in the College given by his father-in-law, and Martha has invited a young biologist, Nick, and his silly young wife Honey, in for drinks. Unlike George, Nick believes that if you get to know the right people and say the right things you can make a short cut to the top; he has certainly come to the wrong household for that. Not only is he witness to the humiliation of George and Martha, Nick and Honey merely act like a couple of inexperienced tennis players on court with professionals. The personal relationship of Martha and George only shows up the hollowness of the young couple, for Honey is afraid of pregnancy.

The early hours of the morning pass, a prodigious amount of spirits is consumed, the partners become exhausted from the non-stop barrage, and when one falls momentarily out of the fight the other enters. Martha tries to seduce Nick; Honey is violently sick; the kidding game gets more involved until Martha announces that they have a son. False, true, where's the difference and who cares? George tells her that she has broken the rules, and reacts quickly. He breaks the "terrible" news that their son has been killed in a road accident. Martha refuses to accept this — "You didn't have to have him die, George" until Nick and Honey realise to their own embarrassment that they have made it all up. The party is over, this long night of Walpurgis on the campus. Out of the cross-fire of love and hate George and Martha need each other, like children afraid of the "big, bad wolf".

*Who's Afraid of Virginia Woolf?* has not only some of the best dialogue to be written in the American theatre, at least on a par with that of Osborne, it has also proved an immensely popular play at the box-office. And yet, having said that, has the play anything significant for us other than the wholesale destructive or at any rate disruptive insight into a hypocritical way of life and the sterility of the society it engenders? I think not, but at least Albee's views on the American shrew are clear and we are left with no doubts as to the content of the play, which is more than can be said for that of *Tiny Alice* (1965) where the theme and the ideas are so abstruse, the symbols so vague and elusive, that we feel we have here more the notebooks for a play

Albee has in mind to write one day rather than a completed work. As it is there is no doubt that this is the most ambitious play Albee has yet attempted, but for interpretations an audience has to guess, and there is a rather Pirandellian "right you are if you think you are" conviction in the various explanations. Who then is Alice? We have no answer other than to say that like Dürrenmatt's Clara she is the richest woman in the world. At the moment the play opens she has just announced that she is to give one hundred million a year to the Catholic Church for twenty years. She also lives as a recluse in a château, and when the Cardinal's secretary Julian, a lay brother meets her, she appears as a hag — but this is merely to disguise the fact that she is a highly desirable and sensual woman. The library of the château is inhabited not by ghosts, but by other tiny and tinier Alices, for there is an eighteen foot miniature model of the château, and in it we see a tiny Alice, the butler, Julian or whoever may be in the room; and inside the miniature model in the library is another model, in which is an even tinier Alice. . . . We may as well assume the inverse, that the stage reality may only be a replica of many gigantic châteaux outside the universe, and that Alice lives in a beyond, though whether she is controlled by the giant Alice, the tiny Alice, or herself independently we do not know. Which one are we supposed to be in is the unresolved problem?

The other character, Julian, is even more complex. It has been suggested that he is meant to be a symbol of Jesus who finds out he is not the Christ; or he may be Joseph. Once in an asylum he dreamt he raped a patient who thought herself to be the Virgin Mary, but doctors have assured him this never happened. Alice may be seen as either the temptress or the truth. In the chateâu she gives her body to him; later she marries him, although in the last act he is told he belongs only to the tiny Alice of the model. In the end Julian is doomed to die, and as the lights go out in the château we hear the magnified heart beats and heavy breathing of the dying Julian. Quite what the logic of this conclusion is again remains a mystery. Is this meant to represent an attack on the illusion of religion with the truth revealed, but if so, what does it reveal? There are all the shock tactics of the theatre of cruelty, the play is intriguing, but it leaves us unsatisfied and exhausted.

In a sense none of Albee's plays are ever over; his obsessions are continuous. There are moments when his misogynism becomes overbearing, notably in his adaptation of James Purdy's *Malcolm* (1966). If *Malcolm* merited its failure on Broadway, *A Delicate Balance*

(1966) deserved a longer run than the four months it survived. Friendship and fear are the inter-related themes of *A Delicate Balance* where the verbal massacre is reserved not only for the family of Tobias and Agnes, but for their best friends Edna and Harry who are almost identical to them. In their suburban home where they have been joined by Agnes's younger sister, Claire, who hits the bottle every now and then, and Julia, their daughter, who every three years leaves her latest husband, Edna and Harry one day for no particular reason decide to join them. As they move their belongings in they confess that they were suddenly scared of being alone, of the dark, and the fact that "there was nothing to be frightened of, but . . .". Agnes believes that they have brought their fears into the household like some plague for others to catch, but from the start of the play it is made clear that Agnes and Tobias are chronic sufferers. Agnes fears that one day she will lose her mind, just as she lost her small son Teddy, since whose death Tobias has stopped sleeping with her. Tobias also has never forgotten the way his cat one day, long before he met Agnes, for no particular reason, stopped loving *him*; how the cat seemed to be judging him and how he had had to take it to the vet to be destroyed.

As the "intruders" Henry and Edna, gradually take over the Tobias household both Julia and Claire feel they are unwanted; even Agnes suggests that Tobias would secretly like to be rid of her. Their fears continue when Harry and Edna do leave, Agnes seems to talk to herself to fill the silence.

The adaptation of Giles Cooper's play *Everything in the Garden* (1967) is rather like Albee seeing better than the butler what there was to see. In *Box* and *Quotations from Chairman Mao Tse-tung* (1968) Albee returns to the abstraction of his early one act plays. *Box* is a monologue about the fall of civilisation; the second play consists of this monologue and three others, that spoken by an old lady, that by a middle aged lady, and finally Chairman Mao reading maxims from his little red book. Here Albee finds a way of exploring, in essentially an a-political vision — the decline of a civilisation Splenger and many others have been aware of for over half a century.

The confusion left in the air after *Tiny Alice* seems to take more definite shape in *All Over* (1971). We have a larger than life character who is dying; the course of his death is explained to us by his doctor and nurse throughout the play; those who were close to him in his life, his wife, his mistress, his best friend, and so on, recall their moment of reality which his death will terminate; this is an elegy where memories and recriminations await the final curtain.

In his theatre Albee is by a long way the most audacious of the younger American playwrights; if he has yet to produce a masterpiece he is clearly not content to rest on the laurels of his success, for already he has ranged from box office to abstraction far removed, but perhaps closer to an universality which may one day ensure his reputation as that of a major playwright.

### THORNTON WILDER

No single dramatic work in the American theatre has had greater influence on both sides of the Atlantic than Thornton Wilder's highly ingenious *Our Town*, produced in New York in 1938. The reasons spring from Wilder's own dissatisfaction with the theatre of his time. In the Preface to his collected plays he explains why he lost pleasure in going to the theatre: "I felt that something had gone wrong. . . . I began to feel that the theatre was not only inadequate, it was evasive." The answer he felt was that the box-set proscenium arch tended to isolate the theatre from life and reality, while the more the stage was loaded with specific objects and props fixed and narrowed "the action to one moment in time and place". Wilder noted that there were no chairs in the golden age of the Elizabethans and Spanish drama. He began to write one-act plays such as *The Happy Journey to Trenton and Camden*, where four kitchen chairs represent an automobile and where a family could travel 70 miles in twenty minutes. After this and other similar experiments, Wilder was ready to turn to the theatre seriously and in *Our Town* he presents not a plot, but daily life, love, marriage and death in a New Hampshire village called Grovers Corners during the years 1900-1913. "Our claim, our hope, our despair are in the mind — not in things, not in 'scenery' " he reaffirms. It is a very ordinary town, "little better behaved than most. Probably a lot duller." Certainly "nobody very remarkable ever come out of it, s'far as we know."

As the audience arrive they see an empty stage in half light (there is no curtain.) The Stage Manager, who is also the narrator, sets a table and three chairs downstage left and the same downstage right, to represent the neighbouring homes of the two main families in the play, the Webbs and the Gibbs. The ordinary life begins. The lives and conversations in each house are so alike that while Mrs. Gibbs is telling her children to get ready for school the children in the Webbs' home in answering their mother are also replying to Mrs. Gibbs' lines. As day breaks on 7 May 1901, Dr. Gibbs is returning home after having delivered twins to a Polish family. He stops to say hello to the milkman and to the newsboy. The doctor's black bag is as imaginary as the newsboy's papers and the milkman's rack. We follow the lives of these people through an ordinary day.

Act Two takes place three years later. Life is the same but now George Gibbs and Emily Webb are going to be married. On the day of their wedding we witness their ordinary fears, comforting parents, tears and the pleasure of tears. Nothing is extraordinary. In Act Three it is now 1913, and twelve chairs placed in three rows to the right of centre represent graves in the cemetery. The narrator is telling a visitor of some of the changes in the past nine years. Emily died in childbirth of her second child. As the narrator and the visitor are walking around the cemetery, the dead people are talking. They don't like it when the "living" come to visit — it's just that they know more now and see life differently than when they were part of it. We see this when Emily joins them, a little nervously at first. She asks if she can visit, pick a day she'd like to relive again. The dead Mrs. Gibbs warns her to pick the least important day because any other might be too painful. She does and sees how beautiful and un-ordinary the day was. She asks whether human beings ever realise life while they live it, and the answer is "No, except for poets or saints, maybe." And the Stage Manager bids us good-night.

The year after *Our Town* Wilder wrote *The Merchant of Yonkers* which in 1954 he revised under the title *A Life in the Sun* for the Edinburgh Festival, subsequently produced in Broadway and London as *The Matchmaker*. This is a parody of nineteenth-century playgoing, based on an 1842 German farce by Johann Nestroy. There is little need to dwell at length on the farcical complications, the matchmaker in question is Dolly Levi who promises to introduce Horace Vandergelder, a wealthy but miserly widower to Mrs. Irene Molloy, a young widow and milliner. In fact Dolly intends to marry Vandergelder herself. Mr. Vandergelder's underpaid, overworked clerks also decide to go to New York that day for an adventure, and two of the clerks rush into Mrs. Molloy's shop to avoid meeting Vandergelder. Confusion follows confusion, mistaken identities, instructions, but everything is settled happily, Dolly gets Vandergelder, who promises in future to be a little gentler with his clerks. This is, it is true, an American parody, but it lacks the sparkle and gaiety of say, *the comedia dell arte* tradition.

*The Skin of Our Teeth* (1942), however, is a very different matter; Wilder has, as in *Our Town*, escaped the narrow confines of the box stage techniques, not so much in making fun of them, as rejecting them and escaping time and place. For the Antrobus family have been married five thousand years, and although living in modern times in New Jersey they have as pets a dinosaur and a mammoth. Mr. Antrobus has invented the wheel and is working on the alphabet and the multiplication tables; his wife has invented the apron. Their son Henry was once called Cain and killed his brother with a stone.

The play opens on the coldest day of the year — although it is August. Sabina, the maid, tells us that we are waiting for Mr. Antrobus to get home from the office, waiting and worrying day after day, year after year. As she is waiting she reverts back to herself as Miss Somerset, the actress with the rôle of Sabina and complains she is fed up with the part. Back to the play, a telegram arrives saying Mr. Antrobus will be an hour late. When he does arrive it's with hundreds and hundreds of refugees from the cold, which has been getting worse. It's been rumoured that an iceberg is moving closer and closer and that this may well be the end of the world. Among the refugees are the Muses, Homer and Judge Moses. Mrs. Antrobus only lets the refugees come into the house on condition that the animals go. Mr. Antrobus suggests that the children should be taught something in case the world does end but the children survive.

In the second act we are at Atlantic City, New Jersey, celebrating Mr. Antrobus's election as president of the Order of Mammals, Subdivision Humans, at its 600,000th Annual Convention. Sabina wins a beauty contest and tries to win Mr. Antrobus away from his wife. She almost succeeds when the storm signals and concern for his family change his mind. He takes his family onto a boat with all the animals, two of each kind; Sabina goes along too, although Mrs. Antrobus knows all about her and her husband.

For the final act Sabina is dressed as a Napoleonic camp follower, *la fille du régiment*, and the war is over. Henry returns not as a son but as evil. Mr. Antrobus is relieved that at least his books have been saved for he wants the chance to build new worlds and books are the voices that guide us. The play closes with Sabina looking again out of the window and waiting: "This is where you came in" she tells the audience, "we have to go on for ages and ages yet. You go home. The end of this play isn't written yet."

From the allegory of ordinary folk in *Our Town* we have moved to an allegory of man through the ages and the disasters he overcomes. Thornton Wilder has certainly helped the modern dramatist to find "new ways" in how to express the world in which we live. Himself influenced by the German expressionist techniques, he was to become their master when they literally disappeared in Nazi Germany. The production of *Our Town* in Zurich in the early part of the war made an enormous impression in the city which had become the intellectual capital of the German-speaking world. Moreover, young and as yet unknown names such as Max Frisch were immediately impressed by this breaking of the box set image and the opening up of the old conception of theatre. Frisch's early plays, such as *The Chinese Wall*, show the extent of the influence of Wilder. I think we can agree not only with Wilder's claim to have prepared the way for new dramatists, but also his satirical observation on the contemporary play, that in playing his part he is "exceptional in one thing — I give the impression of having enormously enjoyed it". Can it be that the younger generation take themselves too seriously, while lacking the humility and the sense of humour which goes to the understanding of man? As such Thornton Wilder, on the strength of his two main plays, will be remembered when most of our new playwrights are forgotten.

The shock treatment of reality was an "at home" discovery of Julian Beck and Judith Malina while their Living Theatre was still based in the States. The two American playwrights they may be said to have brought before the public were Jack Gelber and Kenneth H. Brown; indeed, the very success of their plays and their handling of certain "taboo" themes may well have incited U.S. tax inspectors and fire authorities to do their best to extinguish the Living Theatre's fire. Between 1964 and 1968 their Company chose voluntary exile in Europe, and it could be said that they have been continually en voyage since then (at the time of writing in August 1971 they have run into trouble with the Brazilian authorities). Since their emigration the Living Theatre has abandoned realism in preference for Artaud's theories in "The Theatre and its Double"; as such the Living Theatre has moved to different frontiers of the drama, leaving its two American playwrights as milestones in its quest for greater freedom of expression.

Jack Gelber's *The Connection* (1959) introduces us into the world of the "junkies", the heroin addicts who seem to hang around, like waiting for Godot, for the next connection or fix:

As you have gathered, we are, as they say in the tabloids, dope fiends. We are waiting. We have waited before. The connection is coming. . . . Suicide is not uncommon among us. The overdose of heroin is where that frail line of life and death swings in a silent breeze of ecstatic summer . . . but existence on another plane is sought, whether to alleviate the suffering from this one, or to wish for death, it doesn't matter.

There is no theme, there is no play. The playwright brings along some of his junkie friends and realising that they would rather loaf around in a morose stupor sets them to improvise — the old idea of a play within the play. What they say is less interesting than how they say it, with a complete vocabulary of beat *argot* to ring the changes with a jazz quartet. Eventually the junkies speak the situation out and we all go home, the only line which stays in the ear at all being:

> Every thing that's illegal is illegal because it makes more money for more people that way.

The other feature of the play is the author's notes that the parts are interchangeable between Negroes and Europeans, so that there is no colour consciousness.

In *The Apple* (1961) the characters are members of a bizarre drama group who perform scatty improvisations as the mood takes them. The atmosphere is surreal, anything can happen, no one listens to anyone else for long, the characters are bent on satisfying immediate needs, the performer is lost in the person and the person in the performer. This is consciousness as it were with the lid off, drug-released; speech and action are like primitive gestures of the psyche, they mingle and twist and split up and re-form like molecules. Irrationality holds sway but there is a strain of pseudo-mystical philosophising (e.g. "All goeth out. All returneth within. There shall be an end of ends."), and a desultory preoccupation with brotherhood and healing. The persistent symbol of the apple suggests that the characters are all seekers of the truth however weirdly they go about it. Clues to the author's dramatic intentions can be found in statements like "No design is a grand design."

Throughout the performance voices from the back of the theatre and occasional direct addresses combine with the wild informality of the proceedings on the state to make the audience feel "they cannot see the cast for people".

Gelber's assault on the brain, the attempt to make the audience "witness" and "take part in sole destructive scenes" takes a different form of disarranging the senses in *The Brig* (1963), by Kenneth H. Brown. Set in Japan in 1957, the Brig was a green wooden building at the foot of Mount Fujiyama which served as a penal institution for the American Third Marines. Brown writes that "Because it was a place of horrible disciplinary extremes, it was feared and ignored by those members of the unit not directly connected with it. It stood as an example of the consequences for those who would not, or wished not to conform to the rigid routine of the Third Marines." There were endless rules, such as "No prisoner may speak at any time except to his guards, when he must first ask permission to do so"; at any time the guards could "break down for a frisk" or "break down for a shakedown" prisoners returning to the brig from outside. In other words, the American Marines in their wish to create Spartan discipline have succeeded in recreating for civilised man in time of peace many of the horrors of the Nazi forced labour camps of the war. Gradually the prisoner accepts that his only existence is a number in the U.S. Marines, and the play inevitably shows the crack up of one of the prisoners who seeks to remain a human being. Yet for all its anger, as in the plays by Gelber, we are given a shock treatment of reality on a stage where in fact nothing happens, where there is no dramatic sequence other than the endless monotony, in this case, of discipline. This is the theatre where imagination belongs to another world; the right reflexes are those of being an unwilling witness. A strident shock to our sensibilities however, is not the drama which will make the theatre live. . . .

William Inge has been both unfairly dismissed by critics as "a lowbrow Ibsen" (as Bamber Gascoigne has called him) and a playwright who has somehow compromised between serious intent and box-office. This is to do him less than justice. "I have never sought to write plays that primarily tell a story", he writes in a Foreword to his *Collected Plays*, "nor have I sought deliberately to create new forms. I have been most concerned with dramatising something of the dynamism I myself find in human motivation and behaviour. I regard a play as a composition rather than a story, as a distillation of life rather than a narration of it." Inge has compared a play to a journey "in which every moment should be as interesting as the destination". He does not aim at the type of craftsmanship where plot construction culminates in the last act to "a big emotional pay-off'," and he seeks, dramatic values in a relative way, for instance, as he explains, "one character in a play of mine might seem quite pointless unless in comparison with another character".

His first play *Come Back Little Sheba* (1950) is the story of Doc Delaney, a benign man who three years previous went to Alcoholics Anonymous and hasn't had a drink since, and his wife Lola, who wears a dreamlike expression and speaks like a little girl to Doc. She talks of "little Sheba", a dog she loved and who has disappeared; she is lonely and spends her days doing nothing. Marie, their attractive 18-year-old lodger, is engaged to Bruce, a boy from back home, and in the meantime has a boy friend, Turk. A telegram comes for Marie saying that Bruce is to arrive next day. Turk spends the night with Marie, and Doc, deeply upset about this, takes the whisky from the cupboard. The following evening as Lola is preparing a dinner to welcome Bruce, she notices it has gone and becomes panic-stricken. Leaving Marie and Bruce she goes in search of Doc, who does not come home until the following morning, very drunk, and rants and raves at her. The men from A.A. arrive and take Doc away. Meanwhile Marie has decided to leave and marry Bruce. When Doc returns a few days later he is as we first met him and tells Lola how much he needs her.

The action of *Picnic* (1953) takes place in a small Kansas town. Flora Owens, a widow in her forties, is the mother of Madge, the 'pretty one' aged 18, and Millie, 16, the 'brain'. Helen Potts, a neighbour, is also a widow; she lives with her aged and invalid mother, and, soft-hearted, often takes in passing tramps. One of these, a handsome boy Hal Carter, claims to be an old school chum of Alan Seymour, the rich boy who has been dating with Madge. Flo would like Madge to marry Alan, but Madge is not interested. It is decided that Hal will be Millie's date for the picnic the next day. Hal confesses to Alan that he has never gone out with 'good girls' and doesn't know how to act. An old schoolteacher, Rosemary, insists on dancing with Hal while he is waiting for Alan to go on the picnic. Rosemary is drunk and demanding and begins to shout and humiliate Hal, calling him a tramp. Hal is so stunned that he gets ready to leave and Madge stays behind with him, trying to comfort him and soon he confides in her. They do not go to the picnic, but he takes her upstairs. The next day Hal has disappeared; later he comes out of hiding and is accused of stealing Alan's father's car. He came back because he had to say goodbye to Madge. In the last scene Madge goes off with him despite her mother's pleas and protestations.

*Bus Stop* (1955) is again set in a small Kansas town, in a restaurant which occasionally serves as a rest stop for the bus lines. The sheriff, Will Masters, announces that the bus that's due will probably be stranded and that the phones are cut. When the bus arrives, Cherie, an attractive blonde, runs in upset. She has been kidnapped by a young cowboy Bo Decker, who wants to marry her. He is still asleep in the bus and she wants to get away before he awakes. When Bo enters with Virgil, his buddy, he is altogether boisterous, and impertinent. He grabs Cherie very hard and kisses her; she asks to be left alone. First he shouts, then he sulks. Virgil tries to explain to him that you can't treat a woman so roughly. Bo is also taught a bit of humility by the sheriff; Virgil apologises and tries to explain to Cherie that Bo didn't mean any harm. She is touched and decides to go with Bo after all.

*The Dark at the Top of the Stairs* (1957) was developed out of the first play Inge wrote, *Farther Off from Heaven*, written in 1947. In rewriting it he says that it is formed from nostalgic memories of childhood, without being very autobiographical. In a typical Middletown setting Reenie, aged 16, shy, nervous, and frightened to death of parties makes a blind date with a Jewish boy Sam Goldenbaum, who has come all the way from California. Reenie is also worried because she does not know what a Jewish boy may be like. When Reenie comes down Sammy tells her how nice it is of her to let him take her to the party. He then goes on to say that although he loves parties every time he has to go to one he has to convince himself that the whole world isn't against him. It turns out that Reenie leaves the party early because after having danced three dances with Sammy without anybody cutting in she was too humiliated to stay on. Then comes the terrible news that Sammy has committed suicide. Before Reenie left she told Sammy to dance with Peg Ralston, but Peg's mother intervened and announced that she hadn't given the party for Jews and didn't want her daughter dancing with one.

In *A Loss of Roses* there is an attempted suicide when Lila Green slashes her wrists when she finds that Kenny, who has slept with her and whom she believes can save her and is truly in love with her, has only feelings of guilt. As in his other plays the story is slight, it is the hidden fears facing the Middletown American citizen which Inge explores, and the motivations which we readily overlook. *A Loss of Roses* was produced in 1959 and represents, with *Natural Affection* (1963), and *Where's Daddy* (1966) a decline in his handling of dramatic unities. He remains a dramatist in a minor key, but with a feeling for the characters and locality which is genuine, if at the same time sentimental.

Described as "a pseudoclassical tragifarce in a bastard French Tradition" by the author, Arthur L. Kopit's *Oh Dad, Poor Dad, Mamma's hung you in the Closet and I'm feelin' so Sad* (1960) is a devastatingly wicked parody of the American psychoanalysts; in fact it says *con brio* everything there is to be said about the mysogynist complex, the apron strings of "Mommy". How could poor Jonathan have a chance with his possessive dominating Mamma, Madame Rosepettle, around? He was lucky in fact to escape being killed and stuffed like his dear dad, which was done, we are assured, in order that she could possess him better. Anyway, the proof is that Jonathan's alive and Dad's hung in the closet, dead. Outside temptations will come to neither, not if Madame Rosepettle can help it; she is anti-sex, and even when Commodore Roseabove comes to win her heart she sends him away to enter his world again, "the sex-driven, dirt-washed waste of cannibals eating each other up while they pretend they're kissing". "My son shall have the light", she exclaims, but Jonathan has already had another and different kind of light; while Madame Rosepettle is spying out loving couples on the beach Rosalie enters, the picture of innocence, but not too innocent to seduce Jonathan. She enters the forbidden room of her mother where Jonathan has never set foot; already she is in control of Jonathan better than Mommy. Neither the stamp collection nor coins nor books, nor even Dad falling on top of her from the closet can put her off her design — but as she is ready for the embrace Jonathan strangles her. His mother returns, and sizes up the situation;

> *Robinson!* I went to lie down and I stepped on your father! I lay down and I lay on some girl. Robinson, there's a woman on my bed, and I do believe she's stopped breathing . . . I ask you Robinson. As a mother to a son I ask you. *What is the meaning of this?*

After this wild extravaganza who can take the psychoanalysts as seriously as has been done in so many Broadway and off-Broadway plays of recent years?

After a period when Kopit wrote a number of one act plays, in 1966 the idea of the slow death of the Indians came to him in the form of presenting *Indians* as "a combination of Wild West Show, Vaudeville and Circus". In 1968 Jack Gelber directed the Royal Shakespeare Company's London production, a noisy exciting hurly-burly which was not quite successful, mainly because the play divided itself .into a comic first half and a serious second. As the transition was "disconcertingly abrupt" Kopit re-arranged the trial scene, originally in the second half, into four parts, for the production at the Arena Stage, Washington D.C. in 1969.

As the audience enters there are three glass cases, one holding a larger-than-life-size effigy of Buffalo Bill, one an effigy of Sitting Bull dressed in simple buckskin; the last case contains a buffalo skull, a bloodstained Indian shirt, an old rifle, etc. There are distorted strains of Western American music. Then the music becomes more rodeo-like, then it's a Wild West Show! Buffalo Bill comes forward as the central character and go-between the Indians and the old-time President and senators. He tries hard to reason with Sitting Bull, whom he puts into his show, but in the end he is incurably of White Man's intelligence; like Mother Courage he will never understand. There is no saving the Indians from being cheated, their land taken away, their buffaloes killed, and finally, their massacre. Buffalo Bill still regrets he could not save their lives, but he still feels it his duty to "say a few words in defence of my country's Indian policy".

On the strength of one pseudoclassical tragifarce and one extravaganza of a Wild West show Kopit has been described as "a one-man factory" in the knockabout art of the theatre. His provocative *jeu d'esprit* is a truly creative force in the modern very American drama.

Two New York playwrights have made Broadway in the last few years: Murray Schisgal and Jack Richardson. The theatre of Schisgal is like a puppet one where the characters act out different changes of fortune, exchange roles and become the mouthpiece of their author's type of ventriloquistic wit. Richardson, in contrast, is serious and profound, philosophical and highly ambitious; he has yet to resolve this with the dramatic tempo.

Schisgal started with one-act plays; *The Typists* and *The Tiger,* performed in London in 1960, and also successfully staged in Paris. London also had the first productions of *Ducks and Lovers,* and *Luv,* a full-length play which on its Broadway production in 1964 made Schisgal's reputation. In *Luv* there are only three characters, Harry Berlin, Milt Manville and his wife Ellen. Harry is about to commit suicide by jumping off a bridge when he is rescued by his old college friend Milt. Milt suggests he finds new hope in life by marrying his wife

Ellen, from whom he is seeking a divorce. The play turns full circle until Milt and his wife are again reunited and Harry jumps off the bridge only to come up again, wet through and ridiculous.

Richardson turned to the Orestes legend for his first play *The Prodigal*, produced in 1960. His second play *Gallows Humour* consists of two one act plays; in the first a man in the death cell is offered the comfort of a prostitute for his last hour on earth; he seeks order instead of passion, while the prostitute offers passion and acceptance of death through indulgence. In the second play the executioner faces a similar problem, he wishing adventure and disorder while his wife brings him back to reality, domesticity and work. Richardson's third play, *Lorenzo*, was an over-ambitious failure, but in the present state of the theatre there is much need of the talents of so adventurous a playwright.

Elmer Rice (1892-1967), produced his most successful work during the inter-war years, when his plays *The Adding Machine* (1923) and *Judgment Day* (1934) proved him to have a fine sense of rhetoric and debate which he made good use of in the theatre. Rice graduated from New York Law School in 1912 and for a while he practised at the Bar, but the success of his first play *On Trial* (1914) made him desert law for the theatre. His decision was more than justified when in *The Adding Machine* he introduced to American audiences the expressionistic technique which Toller and Kaiser were working on in Germany. Rice brought consummate skill to his innovations of the technique. The following year came his exciting melodrama *Street Scene*, which gained him a Pulitzer Prize. The entire action of this play takes place in front of a New York tenement. Rice's growing interest in social problems is also reflected in *We, the People*, where the theatre was turned into a meeting hall. *Judgment Day* was a topical reminder for American audiences of what had just happened when the Nazis burned the Reichstag.

Unfortunately Rice did not succeed in any of his later plays in rising to this level, and plays such as *Flight to the West* — really little more than an anti-Nazi debate — *A New Life* or *Dream Girl* have been but a pale pastiche of his earlier work. He will be remembered for his interest in the social-purpose play, and his desire to win his argument with credit to his legal training.

Robert Sherwood (1896-1955) was attracted by the so-called play of ideas, the desire to impart a message in his plays, which often deal with the fears let loose in the morning papers. The subjects discussed are vital as long as they remain topical, and in his plays we have a considerable variation in the solution of the problem according

M

344 NEW TRENDS IN 20TH CENTURY DRAMA

to how his own conscience reacted to each new crisis in an age of crises. Returning gassed and wounded from the first world war, Sherwood turned pacifist, which lasted up to his writing of *Idiot's Delight* in 1936. *Idiot's Delight*, however, was not only a protest against war, but also against Fascism, and this protest led eventually to his own abandonment of pacifism. Faced with the evils of dictatorship, pacifism was no longer valid, for it was more important to safeguard freedom. Thus his mood changes and in *There Shall Be No Night*, written at the time of the Russian invasion of Finland, he takes for his theme that of a scientist who believes in pacifism, but who in the end decides to fight. It was an ironic comment that the country he wrote it for soon found itself on the enemy side, and for the London production Sherwood changed the country from Finland to Greece. The change did not really matter, for the theme was applicable to any small nation invaded by the crushing power of a military dictatorship, and Sherwood had very great sympathy for a little nation fighting for its freedom. He helped America to realise that she could no longer stand by and watch while the tyrant was triumphant.

*There Shall Be No Night*, together with *Idiot's Delight*, is Sherwood's great theatrical success, but he is also known for *The Road to Rome* (1927), *Reunion in Vienna* (1931), *The Petrified Forest* (1935), *Abe Lincoln in Illinois* (1938) and *The Rugged Path* (1945). Of these others, *The Petrified Forest* is perhaps the most interesting, introducing us to characters who symbolise the disillusionment of an age, but who at the same time seem real people. A greatly depressing play, it is nevertheless expert in its theatrical tension. These plays have earned Sherwood a place in the history of the American theatre, for his success as a playwright lay in the fact that he was a first-rate theatrical journalist in the very best sense, and he wrote with the zeal of a man who had a mission to fulfil.

The idea that our actions are governed by our economic circumstances is stressed in all the plays of Clifford Odets (1906-1963), a Left-wing social writer discovered by the Group Theatre who became a playwright of vitality, conviction and passion. His dialogue knocks hard and achieves its aim without resort to clichés; his characters are complex individuals caught up in the system, and not merely cardboard puppets with a system to present or defend. Odets' plays are gloriously partisan and biased, but propaganda is not substituted for good theatre.

His first attempt at playwriting was an out-and-out political piece which nevertheless showed that here was a playwright in the making.

In *Waiting for Lefty* (1935) Odets turned the theatre into a hall and assumed that the audience were strikers listening to their leaders on the platform debating whether the taxicab drivers should strike or not. The same year Odets wrote his first full-length play *Awake and Sing*, which portrayed a Jewish family circle at the time of the depression. It is a study of each member of the family, who meet their own disillusionment, but the bitterness of the mood and the revolutionary nature of its intent is made moving by the warmth of the humanity in his characters. Odets' next important play was *Golden Boy*, where the struggle of a man's soul between ambition and material wealth becomes the decision that Joe Bonaparte, a young American of Italian origin, has to make between his ambition to be a violinist and the prize purse of the ring. He chooses the ring and wins his riches, but he also kills a man there and can no longer continue fighting. His hands are now ruined; his life has been frustrated through his thirst for money; he ends up by meeting death in a motor accident.

For a while Odets left Broadway for Hollywood, and did not return until 1949, when his play *The Big Knife* was produced. This is a savage picture of the inhuman set-up in Hollywood which makes slaves even of its leading stars and where frustration is everywhere. The play has been severely attacked by such American critics as John Gassner who, writing in *Theatre Arts*, complains that it is "a plain case of misty motivation and misplaced sympathy". Gassner goes on to suggest that "the unemployed on Broadway must find it curious that Odets should suffer for an actor who has a fourteen-year contract and 3,500,000 dollars thrust upon him". But surely this is to miss the whole point of Odets' protest. It might be curious, but it is true. In her anthropological study of *Hollywood, the Dream Factory*, Miss Hortense Powdermaker emphasises that it is the social system under which film stars have to work that makes for such a high degree of frustration, and which, incidentally, it also passes on in the false glitter of so many Hollywood products. *The Big Knife* may be unpleasant, it may seem excessive, but I am sure that for Odets it is an honest view of the way he felt in Hollywood. So his return to Broadway is celebrated in *The Country Girl* (produced in London under the title "Winter Journey") where Odets makes amends to the theatre by writing a success story for Broadway. All is forgiven. Taking for his leading character a once famous actor now gone to seed through drink, Odets says that he "wanted to accomplish something in particular". (I quote his own words) "I wanted to take simple elements and make something sharp and theatrical out of them. I stated a fact, the story of these people, rather than speculated about the fact". This is an Odets far removed from the playwright we knew as critic of society; the dramatic instinct is still there but much of the purpose is missing.

If we turn to *The Flowering Peach* (1954) Odets retells his version of Noah and family in the contemporary idiom. Odets, very much at home in portraying the dissensions of Jewish family life in the Bronx, fails completely to come to terms with the biblical theme, a theme which he recognises with all its deadly seriousness — concerned as it is with the relationship between man, God, and the extinction of the world as a punishment for allowing sin to run riot. When disaster happens, Noah cannot understand why God has chosen him to be saved, for his house, rather his ark, is witness to the same sins that brought about the floods on earth — adultery, greed, drunkenness. Yet they have been spared to rebuild the world, the future is in their hands and is their responsibility, they have been spared but they have not been redeemed, for neither they nor Odets are any nearer to understanding what they ought to believe. And the confusion in the writing is a match for the confusion in the thinking.

Odets was attracted by themes which were too ambitious; but within his limitations he was undoubtedly one of the most forceful American writers of his generation.

Like O'Neill, Maxwell Anderson (1886-1959) approached the theatre with a roaming eye for expression and with ambitions which would have required genius and not talent, however gifted. But at least he aimed high, and his efforts to discover a harmony between modern poetry and ordinary conversation have produced a style which, though hardly what the blank verse was to the audience of Shakespeare, can be described as a twentieth-century exposition suited to the drama. Maxwell Anderson was not a poet like Eliot, nor did he even have the fluency with words that Fry possesses, but he liked the sound of words and his plays are always pleasant to the ear. A prolific writer, his successes included *Elizabeth, the Queen, Mary of Scotland, The Masque of Kings, Key Largo, The Eve of St. Mark, Joan of Lorraine* and more recently, *The Bad Seed*. But better than any of these is his gangster tragedy *Winterset* (1935) where his theme is one of injustice. A son believes his condemned father is innocent and sacrifices his own life to prove it. There are passages where the verse rises to deep imaginative insight, and the atmosphere of squalor and frustration is enlarged through the emptiness of Maxwell Anderson's own spiritual power. The lack of faith seems to make the tragic concept of the play fall short in what should have been its moment of greatness. Neither O'Neill nor Maxwell Anderson (nor, for that matter, Arthur Miller) has found the answer for modern tragedy, but both attempted its creation. They wished to make traditions of permanent values available to the shifting and sophisticated audiences on Broadway.

Highly regarded as a writer of light comedy, Philip Barry (1896-1949) made several unconventional ventures into fantasy and plays of more serious purpose, including *Here Come the Clowns*, *The Joyous Season* and *Hotel Universe*. This latter is his most ambitious work, and as can be seen from the title, it unfolds itself on a symbolic plane. It is a rendezvous where several souls, brought together in anguish, undergo a kind of expiation for their sins in such veiled significance that the play baffled its audience. Barry was really a writer of comedy, and it is in plays such as *The Philadelphia Story* and *The Animal Kingdom* that he reached his public.

Another playwright who has attempted innovations from the normal is William Saroyan; indeed, with his work experiment seems to become too often an end in itself. His plays present a hymn of optimism in ordinary people, "the beautiful people", to quote the title of one of his plays. Saroyan caused an immediate stir when the Group Theatre produced his first play *My Heart's in the Highlands* in 1939. The play may be described loosely as a fantasy, or perhaps as Brooks Atkinson has so aptly worded it: "A prose poem in ragtime with a humorous and lovable point of view." The play gained the Critics' Circle Award in New York and the Pulitzer Prize the following year. His experiments, which included *Love's Old Sweet Song*, *The Beautiful People*, *Across the Board on To-morrow Morning* continued until the production of *Get Away OldMan* in 1943.

Saroyan is a convinced and sometimes facile optimist (which is at least a change from the dismal jimmies) but his experiments do not result in clarity, and he certainly has not fulfilled the promise of his first play.

## OTHER AMERICAN PLAYWRIGHTS

Even more than in the British theatre, it is impossible to mention the numerous playwrights in the American theatre who have had success, and in a survey which attempts to place modern world drama in perspective, it is increasingly difficult with minor writers to decide whether they should be included or not. America has produced many competent craftsmen (and the schools of playwriting in American universities have had their results here) but if the standard of Broadway is technically efficient, the content of so many of her plays is banal. After all, Broadway is the longest boulevard of them all.

There are a number of playwrights, however, who might have been included here, were not we forced to restrict our company. Lillian Hellman, for example, has produced several impressive works, including *The Little Foxes* and *The Children's Hour*, *Watch on the Rhine*, and more recently, *Toys in the Attic*. Other playwrights might have included George S. Kaufmann and Moss Hart, Sidney Kingsley and the late Sidney Howard, author of *The Knew What They Wanted* and *The Silver Cord*.

### SOME OTHER WRITERS

Of the younger school the name of Paul Zindel has attracted attention for his Off-Broadway play *The Effect of Gamma Rays on Man-in-the-Moon Marigolds* (1971) which won a Pulitzer prize, while if the box office never lies, it is Neil Simon who should head our list with nine Broadway hits in nine years.

It was Elia Kazan who suggested to the American Negro writer James Baldwin that he should write for the theatre. Baldwin has now given us two plays, *Blues for Mr. Charlie* (1964) and *The Amen Corner* (1965); neither merit a reputation as a dramatist.

*Blues for Mr. Charlie* is based on the case of Emmett Till, the Negro youth who was murdered in Mississippi in 1955; following his acquittal the murderer recounted the facts. The play takes place in Plaguetown, U.S.A. "now". Baldwin has written "the plague is race, the plague is our conception of Christianity; and this raging plague has the power to destroy every human relationship". The play is not a very subtle one, although Baldwin has tried to prevent the absolute division into whites bad, Negroes good, by introducing in the character of the local newspaper editor a white sympathetic to the Negro; in the courtroom however he also lets down the Negroes. Baldwin everywhere shows the apprentice's hand in construction; his cardboard characters in the end offend our sensitivities. It is the type of imitation of the social play written in the thirties, and to-day it risks doing its cause more harm than good. It was kept artificially alive on Broadway through donations, and the "Method" production of the Actors' Studio which I saw in London was bad even by amateur standards.

Baldwin's second play *The Amen Corner* is a slight improvement;

he has a good plot but again the dramatic treatment is wrong. Sister Margaret presides as pastor over one of the Harlem Churches; she is respected until her flock grow mutinous and her spiritual authority disintegrated. Her husband returns from the Jazz cellars and her son leaves her. At least Sister Margaret is a well-drawn part. Much, however, as I would like to champion his cause, I cannot champion the claims of Baldwin as a dramatist. Baldwin is an outstanding polemical writer, and perhaps the old saying is true that cobblers should stick to their last.

The death of Lorraine Hansberry so soon after her winning the New York Drama Critics award in 1959 for her powerful exposition of the Negro cause and dream *A Raisin in the Sun* has robbed the American theatre of a playwright of above-average promise. The play concerns the poverty, humiliation and the ultimate triumph of Negro dignity. At the exciting climax the dream wavers, dignity almost capitulates to bitterness, but the Negro spirit calls on its reserve of age-old hardiness and survives. The atmosphere of Negro family life against the background of a Chicago neighbourhood is authentic.

Among Miss Hansberry's unfinished works are *The Sign in Sidney Brustein's Window* and *Les Blancs*, both of which were subsequently completed by her former husband Robert Nemiroff. The former play is about an editor of a weekly newspaper which resembles the *Village Voice* who has both lost faith in reform and in himself. The play centres on his troubles with his wife, who has undergone psychoanalysis and is lacking in principles; his younger sister is a prostitute without his knowing it and is supposed to be marrying a Negro; characters and situations pile up along with principles which are flung to the wind in a long tale of woe.

*Les Blancs* was suggested by Genet's *Les Nègres*. Tschembe, a black who has been educated in England, returns to his native Africa with a white wife. His country is in a period at the end of colonialism, yet Tschembe is not ready to throw in his lot with the militants. His real hatred in the play is reserved for a European liberal who comes on a fact finding mission. In the end his European wife persuades him to lead the blacks in their uprising, in which she is herself killed.

In both Miss Hansberry's plays, and the plays of LeRoi Jones such as *Dutchman*, *The Slave* it is the white liberal for whom the Negro reserves his greatest distaste. Assimiliation seems to have become a word of contempt. *The Slave* is less articulate than *Dutchman* and less deadly. Perhaps Jones says here less than he means because he tries to express more than he knows. Certainly his making his protagonist drunk throughout betrays a lack of confidence in his message or meaning. *Dutchman* is strong stuff: the pride and unabashed hatred of the American Negro is given the dimension of fable; it is the total repudiation of Uncle Tom. Black boy and white woman meet in a subway-train. She starts to make up to him and asks him to take her to his party; she derides him for his white man's clothes, his white man's words, the murder she sees in his heart. He is attracted to her, at first slightly awed. When she suggests he joins her in a belly dance in the aisle the Negro is first embarrassed, then angry, finally slaps her, scorns her conceit in thinking she knows all about the Negro. The theme is old but the expression is forceful. The black boy doesn't kill the white woman: the denouement is that she stabs him. His body is thrown out of the train and nobody 'notices'.

*Home on the Range* (1966) shows how the white population with their tales have become so identified with materialism that they begin to react and think like puppets, whereas the Negro, in spite of circumstances which forces him to crime, is real, full of vitality and joy. They are the new race. "Black is Beautiful" and we have the superiority of black man's instinct over white man's media which leads to self destruction.

LeRoi Jones has become one of the strongest personalities in the Black Power movement. In 1964 he opened at Harlem the Black Arts Repertory Theatre School, where as well as his plays, concerts, lectures and poetry readings were given. The white public was forbidden. In March 1966 the theatre was closed when police discovered an arms dump there. LeRoi Jones now directs the Black Theatre Spirit House at Newark, New Jersey, which has become one of the leading cultural centres of the Black Power movement.

There are also both professional and semi-professional groups in most cities in the States where there is a sizeable Negro population. At New York there is the Negro Ensemble Company, which is part of the Group Theatre Workshop of Robert Hooks. The New Lafayette at Harlem was destroyed by fire in January 1968. It had among its playwrights Ed Bullins of the Black Panthers, whose play *The Electronic Nigger* proved an immense success.

It has become apparent, as the Drama Review from Tulane University noted in its special issue of the Negro Theatre (No. 40, Summer 1968) that such things as happenings, regional theatre, actors formation and other items of interest find no support in the Negro Theatre.

There is no possible dialogue between the two theatres, as there is with the African theatre groups, where through Presence Africaine the works of French speaking playwrights (and French continues to be the language in Senegal, the Cote d'Ivoire and elsewhere in the former French colonies of West Africa) are printed and all information concerning cultural manifestations is available. The African theatre may well achieve more because it is free, and hence as the mother country it may well offer a bridge for the American Negroes to realise that memories of Satchmo will linger long after the embers of hatred have died, for art, whether of Jazz or in the theatre, does not belong to any one continent, but to the world. You do not have to live in the States to know that Armstrong's trumpet is able to tumble down not only the walls of Jericho, Berlin walls or bamboo curtains, but make us realise like the late Lord Keynes once said that politics and economics are only a means towards what is really important in life, the arts.

# TWENTY

# FRANCE

ANTOINE: The theatre is nothing more than a situation, characters and talk! And at the end of an hour or so you have an interval to sell sweets. . . . The rest is literature, as you know!

ACTOR: My dear master! Some works, all the same, have a message

ANTOINE: So! If you have one, make use of it for us. That's the avant-garde theatre. . . .

JEAN ANOUILH, *Cher Antoine*

THE history of culture seems to move in cycles; after the First World War, Paris became the international capital of the arts; after the Second there was again a cultural resurgence which had in fact started during the occupation. We have already considered at length the contributions of Claudel, Giraudoux, Cocteau, Jean-Paul Sartre, Salacrou and Anouilh. From the last decade, in spite of the fact that Paris is a city for playgoing, there are few new names to add, and no important ones. The Algerian war brought about the downfall of the Fourth Republic and President De Gaulle re-established France's prestige in the world; in his Minister of Culture, André Malraux, he could not have made a better choice for cultural prestige. And yet hopes were disappointed. Malraux started with the best of intentions, he handed over one of the theatres of the Comédie Française to Jean-Louis Barrault and Madeleine Renaud, and enabled them to establish the Theatre de France; he had intended giving Albert Camus the directorship of an experimental theatre (brought to an end with Camus' death in a road accident). The six dramatic centres in the French provinces have had a greater success, and Malraux was anxious to extend the formation of *Maisons de la Culture* around the centres and throughout provincial towns. Twenty centres are envisaged, and one of the new ones is to be entrusted to Roger Planchon, director of the Théâtre de la Cité at Villeurbanne, near Lyons. If this scheme of decentralisation succeeds Malraux will have attracted young talent away from the capital and brought the theatre into closer touch with the French people, no longer confined to the cultural ghetto of Paris and the dictates of intellectual avant-gardism, which does not seem to meet the need of the times.

Unfortunately these schemes will inevitably take time, and bureaucracy in practice is a rather different "angel" than one in theory. The death of Jean Vilar is a further loss for the French theatre. The annual assessment at the end of each theatrical season in papers like *Le Monde* do not offer either hope or confidence for the future. True Barrault has been re-instated at the Odéon, Théâtre de France, from which he was dismissed in May 1968, but state employed or not, Barrault would always find the means to continue, witness his admirable production of *Rabelais* (1968). As for the playwrights, Anouilh brilliantly continues the race on his own. Excluding Arrabal and Billetdoux, whose plays we shall consider in this chapter, there remain but an indifferent bunch of "would be's", Françoise Sagan, for example, writes a passable sophisticated boulevard comedy with smart dialogue in the vein of second-rate Coward. Marguerite Duras, much more literary in her approach, is better known for her film script of *Hiroshima, mon amour*; of her plays *Des Journées entiéres dans les Arbres* (Days in the Trees, 1965) will be remembered mainly for Madeleine Renaud's performance in Paris, and that of Dame Peggy Ashcroft, who played the mother in the Royal Shakespeare Company's London production. Finally, in the political arena we should note Armand Gatti, whose most important work to date was the Theatre National Populaire's production of *Chant publique devant deux chaises electriques* (Public Song for Two Electric Chairs 1966) which dealt with the electrocution of two Italian immigrant anarchists, Nicola Sacco and Bartolomeo Vanzetti, who were condemned to death in Boston in 1927 without any serious proof of their guilt. In 1969 the T.N.P. had to cancel its plans for the production of Gatti's *La Passion du General Franco*, for obvious political reasons.

Torn between a choice of *theatre engagé* or virtually the left-overs of the boulevard playwrights, there remain the importations from London and New York. The poor old Vieux-Colombier has now become a cinema, and many other famous theatres are in danger of closing down. The French theatre cannot look forward to the seventies with anything like the confidence that is the case in London. It is caught in a vicious circle of rising prices, and, because it is no longer sure of public taste, timidity. The older playgoers, used to the theatre of the thirties, the war years, up to the fifties, can now find little consolation in the Paris playboards, except for Anouilh, revivals or, the visiting foreign companies in the summer theatre festival. Among the student and young playgoers, it is the "gauchistes" who have been the most volatile and have succeeded in imposing their order of the day, the political diatribe, which the public is intelligent enough to reject. Perhaps they, more than anybody, are largely to blame for the present *impasse*. Only now and again, generally at a festival, or in the odd production by Planchon or Robert Wilson, there comes a reminder that the French theatre still has life in it, and revive our hope that the pendulum must once again revive theatrical experiment. It is impossible that Paris, which since 1402 when its first professional theatre opened, has been in the mainstream of European drama, is going to become a provincial city internationally speaking. Ironically it would be the inverse of what Malraux had intended with his decentralisation and the setting up of dramatic centres in the provinces. Such a *reductio ad absurdum* belongs indeed to an age of the theatre of the absurd.

### HENRY DE MONTHERLANT

If so many contemporary French dramatists are slaves of their time, Henry de Montherlant is in opposition; he wishes to have nothing to do with his time. He has been described as a 'man of the Renaissance', which is perhaps as misleading as suggesting that Fry is a 'modern Elizabethan', but it is true that Montherlant inherits the great French classical tradition and the eloquence and rhetoric of the masters of the French language. No modern writer is nearer the style of Corneille or Racine, no writer so recaptures a tradition which had been considered lost. Montherlant is not concerned with the great *débâcle* in the modern world, or ephemeral politics; neither does he serve the cause of philosophy or religion. If Montherlant chooses a religious subject, such as that of *Le Maître de Santiago*, he does so that he might explore the inner drama of the human soul, in other words, he chooses to portray a holy ascetic as he might a murderer. He would claim that he was not a Christian but an artist. His is a study not of creeds, dogmas or manifestoes, but of character and conflict. The character must not be cut to shape, and the conflict must not make a character coherent for the sake of dramatic unity. Here we have Montherlant's first quarrel with the theatre, for he believes that "the theatre, like the novel, has only importance to the extent it penetrates the study of man, that is, the study of some being who is neither 'determined' nor 'well drawn' . . ." He protests against the idea that the theatre obeys laws different from other literary forms; for him — he goes so far as to confess — it is the theatre which interests him least. Do you, he asks, think of theatre when reading Shakespeare and Racine?

The argument has quite a few flaws, and the literary value of Racine and his attachment to the French language may well be the reason why Racine does not take the side of Shakespeare outside France. Montherlant's own literary approach will prevent his works finding a large public in English-speaking countries, where audiences are less disciplined than in France to listen to the flow of language which takes the place of dramatic action. Nevertheless, in spite of himself, or perhaps because of his classical heritage, Montherlant does conceive his conflict in dramatic terms, and the force and vehemence of his language suit the intensity of the situation. His fine prose style is far removed from the banalities of every-day conversation, and this presents difficulty in translation, though Montherlant has been more widely and more successfully translated than Claudel or Giraudoux.

The plays of Montherlant are original and in striking contrast to the narrow horizons of the spirit of the age. For they are concerned with eternal problems of the human soul which present the sweep of human aspirations and reveal the dignity of the inner man. There is a pause for reflection, and an appeal is made to our intelligence to applaud the valour of his characters, however much we may detest the principles they represent. Montherlant does not present the uncertainties and *inquiétude* of other modern writers; he is a satisfied man. In 1930, he tells us, he found what he calls his equilibrium. "Since 1930 I have been happy . . . This happiness did not fall from heaven: it is my work and, besides, it is my acquisition since I have paid for it."

Montherlant is first and foremost an aristocrat, and seeks in his work to convey the nobility which is his possession. His own pride is the least appealing aspect of his work, and at the same time the most important motive in all his writings. His ancestors came from Catalonia and settled in Picardy in the sixteenth century. It is perhaps the great Spanish pride which explains Montherlant's own passion. As an aristocrat he is removed from the world in which he lives, and the temptation to infuse his works more and more with the egoism of character is his most serious danger. Montherlant's Spanish ancestry, however, has no doubt led to the inspiration of his two outstanding plays, *La Reine morte* and *Le Maître de Santiago,* set in the Spain of the Middle Ages and the Golden Age respectively. The severity of these plays, the violence of their conflict and the power of their conception are the very tones of the Spanish temperament.

The life of Montherlant presents some curious asides, such as his addiction to bull fighting (until in 1925 he was tossed by a bull and had a horn thrust into his side), his enthusiasm for running the 100 metres and for playing association football, in. spite of having been severely wounded in the war. Among his many novels he wrote in 1930 *La Rose de Sable,* which because of its anti-colonialism he refused to publish for fear of hurting French prestige. Montherlant has also gained many celebrated prizes: in 1934 he received the Grand Prix de Littérature de l'Académie Française and sent the prize money to the Moroccan Red Cross, stipulating that it was to be divided between French soldiers and the conquered Moroccan rebels. When he won the Northcliffe prize, Montherlant presented it to the hospitals of London, and the Grand Prix Colonial he refused in order to safeguard his independence as a writer on the colonial question.

It was in 1942 that Montherlant turned to the theatre (if we exclude a piece written when he was eighteen called *L'Exil*) when Jean-Louis Vaudouer, the *administrateur* of the Comédie Française at that time, suggested a subject which he thought Montherlant might make into a play for his players. *La Reine morte* was the result, and must be one of the few commissioned plays which have found a place in literature as well as theatre. Since then Montherlant has written several other plays, including *Fils de Personne* (1943), *Le Maître de Santiago* (1945), *Malatesta* (1946) *Demain il fera Jour* (1949), *Celles qu'on prend dans ses Bras* (1950), *La Ville dont le Prince est un Enfant* (1951), *Port Royal* (1954) and *Don Juan* (1958). His two most important (and successful) works are *La Reine morte* and *Le Maître de Santiago* which illustrate admirably Montherlant's rôle in the theatre.

The idea of *La Reine morte,* set in the Portugal of the Middle Ages, immediately appealed to Montherlant, though he took great liberties in his interpretation of the historical facts relating to Alphonso IV and Inès de Castro, and in order to have freedom to make his king an individual he changed his name to Ferrante. The plot is a simple one: King Ferrante is anxious to marry his son Pedro to the Spanish Princess of Navarre for political reasons. But, unknown to him, Pedro has already secretly married one of the young ladies of the Court, Inès de Castro, with whom it was known he was in love. The King is perfectly willing to let Pedro have Inès as his mistress, but when Pedro does not co-operate he askes Inès to help him in his task. But Inès then confesses her marriage to Pedro. One of the King's ministers, Egas Coelho, urges the King to kill Inès, but the King hesitates. He eventually decides on killing her, not because he wants to, but to demonstrate to his ministers that he is hard and not weak, and because some power compels him to do so. No sooner has he given the order than he himself dies. There are, then, four characters in conflict with each other, and out of the clash of their convictions comes tragedy. King Ferrante represents order, the safeguarding of public interest, and the terrible necessity that he must see done. Pedro, his son, represents the right of the individual to make his own choice. Inès represents fidelity, she is Montherlant's happiest female creation. She has done no harm, she will not run away or save herself by being unfaithful to her husband and sacrificing her unborn child. She is caught up in events she has no experience of. Finally there is Egas Coelho, the political realist, who sees for political necessity only one possible action. Thus in his characters Montherlant has the opposition of character which leads incisively to the final tragic scene which has the full grandeur of the classical style, with the brush strokes that are the characteristics of great Spanish artists, such as Velazquez.

Compared with *La Reine morte*, it may be suggested that *Le Maître de Santiago* resembles more a painting by El Greco, harsh and mystical in its effect, simple and overpowering in its design. Here we have a portrait of a man who has rejected the world. It is a short, intense drama which turns in its closing scene to a ritualistic chant of religious fervour — and yet a religious inspiration by a man who is himself without faith! We are in Spain, the Spain of the period of the development of the colonies; the idea of the play came to Montherlant during his first visit to Barcelona in 1933 when he read the sentence: "Some years after the discovery of America, there were a number of old Spaniards who believed this discovery was a disaster for Spain." So the character of the Master of Santiago, Don Alvaro Dabo, was born, a man who in his religious exactitude demands the total renunciation of the world, not only for himself, but also that his daughter, who is in love, should sacrifice herself for him. No wealth in the New World for him, no marriage and happiness for her; it is a total refusal, urged on by a kind of sadistic romanticism for purity. He is not a king who must kill his daughter-in-law out of necessity; he is a man aspiring to his idea of the good life who is determined to shut the outside world out of his vision and make his daughter renounce the world as a supreme sacrifice with him.

The Master, as Montherlant stresses, is not an example of a model Christian, for his egoism, cruelty, and all his actions have a dreadful inhumanity. Mariana does not follow her father because of the love of God. And the Master delights in making her suffer, as, for instance, on the renunciation of life by his daughter he asks her, "And yet no tears? Wrestle and suffer more. Where there is no fight there is no redemption." Tempting her with the picture of her lover, she betrays herself when she replies, "Because of him I know the full force of sacrifice. How else would I have been able to have loved him for it for ever?" There is in the religion of the Master that curious Spanish fanaticism. Consider how Alvaro gloats over his victory and rejection of life:

ALVARO With our blood no other blood shall mingle. No other man shall turn and turn you again in his arms. And no children, nobody shall besmirch me, nobody shall betray me; with you my race ends clean through and through. The last! We shall be the last! What power in that word, the last — opening out on to the void sublime.[1]

The love of Alvaro is a love of extermination, he has a hardness which is only explained by his pride. (The French word 'dur' rhymes with 'pur' and Montherlant here equates the two.)

Has one the right to choose a Christian theme when one does not believe in the theme? Montherlant defended himself against critics (Julien Green in his *Journal*, in particular) when in an article which appeared in *Combat* he pleaded his case on artistic grounds. If you can invent·a king, a queen, a mother or a murderer, why not a man who believes? He concluded that whereas for Green "sympathy and respect do not replace faith", for Montherlant they could do so.

Numerous critics have found contemporary allusions in *Le Maître de Santiago*, but apart from an unintentional one against colonialism (we recall the novel Montherlant never published on this subject) it would be wrong to imagine that Montherlant saw the play in a contemporary framework. He seems highly amused that some have found the play belonging to the literature of the Resistance and others have named it belonging to the literature of opposition (to the Resistance),

See original on p. 389.

while yet a third has found a Communist thesis therein. Montherlant's
character in this respect is not unlike his hero, Don Alvaro, turning
his back on the lesser men.

The third part of the Catholic trilogy, which started with *La Ville
dont le Prince est un Enfant* and *La Reine morte*, is *Port Royal* (1954),
a study of the Port Royal nuns who were in 1664 accused of Jansenist
heresies and isolated in different convents and deprived of the sacra-
ments by the Archbishop in an effort to make them change their
beliefs. Yet this play, written in Montherlant's fine style, is only half a
success, and perhaps only half a play, it being almost uncompromis-
ingly undramatic. His *Don Juan* (1958) proved a lamentable failure.

It seemed as if after *Don Juan* Montherlant was no longer in touch
with the dramatic form; however, in *Le Cardinal d'Espagne* ("The
Spanish Cardinal", 1960) he offers a theme not without contemporary
relevance, that of old age and power. Cardinal Cisneros is a grand old
man, utterly detached from life, but convinced that he should still
pursue his duties actively for a few more years. The Cardinal has two
characteristics of a man in his eighties, that of an unbending heart and
the tragic recognition that he can no longer return to a past. He has
other things to do, to struggle for, than die.

The contemporary parallel is also possible in *La Guerre Civile*
("The Civil War", 1964) where history gives us an example in the time
of Pompey how the Romans, corrupted morally and politically, were
prepared to sleep in the arms of a tyrant. In the second act there is an
interminably long and verbose conference with Cato, and it is not
until the final act, when Pompey appears as an old man face to face with
the last enemy that the play has dramatic force and we are reminded
of the beauty of Montherlant's language, as his powerful vision
combats the disaster of old age. Here, as in all his dramatic work,
Montherlant may hardly be a man of the theatre, but his revival of
genuine tragedy in the classical tradition, drawing on the resources of
human qualities, has a very positive value, especially at a time when
the French theatre has lost its greatness; Montherlant has his place in
the great tradition.

### OTHER WRITERS

Fernando Arrabal was born in 1932 at Lelilla in Spanish Morocco of
Spanish parents. If he deserves a place among French writers (he writes
in French and lives in Paris) nobody could be more Spanish in temperament, not even Goya, Bunuel, Dali or Lorca have been more haunted

by everything Spain represents. Arrabal is a man of obsessions, in love-hate for Church, family and country. His two characters, the Architect and the Emperor of Assyria, in his play of that title, unite the uncompromising division of the same Spanish Ego. To use Michel de Castillo's title, Arrabal is a child of our times, of the civil war. At the age of four his father, a Republican officer, was arrested in the early days of Franco's putsch. While being tortured he tried unsuccessfully to commit suicide. Sentenced to 30 years imprisonment (after having a death sentence reprieved) in 1942 he disappeared in mysterious circumstances from a psychiatric hospital he had been confined to never to be seen or heard of again. Some years later Arrabal discovered in a trunk letters relating to his father which revealed, that although his mother did not actually denounce her husband, she did nothing to comfort him in his suffering, on the contrary, her letters were so cruel that even the prison director had to remonstrate with her. Henceforth for Arrabal everything that Spain stood for was rejected. He left his country hitch-hiking to Paris in 1954. He returned on short visits, and in 1967 he was arrested for autographing a copy of one of his books with an obscene remark towards God and country. Although sentenced to 16 months imprisonment, his fame as a playwright assured his release, with the official excuse that Arrabal was "suffering from temporary mental derangement".

Arrabal arrived in the wake of Beckett and Ionesco. His own contribution to the theatre was the label "panic"; few playwrights have provoked greater controversy. Nothing in Arrabal's work is easy; he remains a child born in a Freudian nightmare, waiting for the thunderbolts to fall and punish him for his blasphemies. "I am convinced," he said in a recent interview, "that there are not two separate worlds, one real, the other imaginary." That is the schizophrenic vision, true to the times. On the contrary, the two universes are complementary and even end up by merging completely.

Arrabal started writing plays before he left Spain. Among his early works written in Spanish is *Lòs Soldadhs* (1950) written four years before he left for Paris, and eventually produced there in 1959 under the title *Pique-nique en Campagne* (Pic-nic on the Battlefield). Here the gullibilities of ordinary people towards war are explored. The parents of a soldier Zapo, Mr. and Mrs. Tepan, visit their son at the front and pic-nic in no-man's-land. Through Mr. Tepan's arguments we realise that all men are brothers and all wars are ridiculous, and that we all know it, except the enemy on both sides.

*Fando and Lis* (1955) was the first play of Arrabal's to attract attention. In this sad farce, certainly influenced by Beckett, Fando and Lis
are two adolescents. Fando leads Lis, who is paralysed, in a pram.
In a mixture of compulsive cruelty and idealism Lis is eventually
annihilated.

*Le Cimtière des voitures* (The Car Cemetery, 1957) was the play
which led Arrabal to find in a young Argentinian director Victor
Garcia a veritable driving force in theatrical style. Through his work
Arrabal was to venture further towards the Theatre of Panic proper.
In a car junk yard, Victor Garcia had eight old cars arranged in a U-
shape; the cars became places for making love, or torture, while a
metal decor is rattled throughout so that Arrabal's text has to be
shouted. The theme is that of a Christ-like musician, innocent of what
is happening, who has to suffer a similar calvary.

For his most important play to date, *l'Architecte et l'Empereur
d'Assyrie* Arrabal found another Latin American director, Jorge
Lavelli, for its Paris production in 1967, while Victor Garcia directed
the London one. The setting is a tropical island, but Garcia used
only lighting on a naked stage, while the two actors were as naked
except for the parachute which the survivor of the plane accident
used. The climaxes are punctuated by roars of thunder and lightning to maintain a sense of panic. The theme is that of an architect,
whose basic characteristics are innocence and love of nature, who
parachutes from a plane crash onto a desert island where he meets the
Emperor, highly civilised and older, and who aspires to be God. The
two men act out their fancies and inter-change roles; it is in human
nature for the natural man to kill the civilised one, by devouring him. A
new storm rages in the heavens and the situation repeats itself, a new
natural man parachutes down to find the other natural man now turned
into the Emperor. In other words, he meets up with his other self.
Yet far from being a dialogue between levels of the subconscious he
extends his meaning to cover all mankind. The sub-title is a reminder
of Kafka: "Joseph K. tenté par la mégalomanie" (Joseph K. tempted
by Megalomania).

Arrabal, like Kafka, is an example of the disinherited mind. He is
an exile from the Church, yet his blasphemy itself would be irrelevant
if one (including Arrabal) did not attach importance to Catholicism.
Arrabal's orgasms of panic have power, but I feel it is difficult to
sustain a full length evening of panic. Even panic when continuous
becomes normality. There is also something in Arrabal like his com-

patriot Dali, of the exhibitionist; one feels he is capitalising on his obsessions and just as you either like or dislike Dali's realistic surrealism, so I think you react to Arrabal's post-Freudian hallucinations. At any rate you cannot remain indifferent.

At the time of the Liberation of France, when the existentionalism of Sartre reached its zenith, the name of Albert Camus was associated with his new French school. Very soon, however, we were able to revise such arbitrary pigeon-holing of his work, for not only was Camus an independent thinker, but a writer who was quite capable of taking over from Sartre. As a philosopher his works *The Myth of Sisyphus* and *L'Homme revolté* established him in his own right, while the novels *L'Etranger* and *La Peste* would be among any half dozen titles of outstanding post-war fiction. Although also a dedicated *homme de théâtre*, Camus never achieved the same distinction in this medium. More recently he seemed a better adapter, of Faulkner's *Requiem for a Nun*, for example, than an original playwright, if we compare this to *Le Malentendu, Caligula, L'Etat de Siège* or *Les Justes*.

It is possible to see in his novels a kind of signposting which could lead to an exit from the existentialist gloom, whereas his plays appear too much like skeletons to make this road seem worth while. Through very obvious symbolism and painstaking abstraction they are contrived to represent philosophical ideas, no matter how artificial and lifeless may be the result. Yet they do remind us of the loneliness of man and the misunderstanding that seems incurable between man and the very nature of existence. This is the absurd reality which man meets in the theme of *Le Malentendu* ("Cross Purpose"). It is founded on the misunderstanding of an old lady and her daughter who murder a wealthy traveller who comes to their inn, only to discover that he is in fact their son and brother, returning home after making his fortune. This slick little magazine-story plot is the starting point for an angry and despairing question mark for man's relation to the universe, and in the last act all pretence at being a murder story — or any kind of illusory fiction — is dropped. Martha, the accomplice in her brother's murder, confronts her brother's wife with these revealing words:

MARTHA  Realise that neither for him nor for us, neither in life nor in death, is there fatherland or peace. (*Laughing scornfully*) For you can hardly call it a fatherland, can you, this heavy earth deprived of light, where you go about feeding sightless animals . . . That great call of the human being, that awaken-

ing of souls, what's the good of it? Why cry out to the sea
or to love? It is laughable ... Remember that your sorrow will
never equal the injustice done to man.[1]

The play has a certain dramatic drive which compensates to some
extent for the plot which is too slender to sustain a full-length play,
even when used as an illustration of philosophical intentions. But
neither in *Le Malentendu* nor in his best-known play *Caligula* has
Camus expounded his philosophy as successfully as Sartre has done in
his plays such as *Les Mouches* or *Huis Clos*. The figure of Caligula,
the model emperor turned tyrant, committed to wickedness and his
own isolation, should have admirably served Camus in search for a
theme to express the maladjustment of the communion between man
and the world we live in, but while there are many notable passages in
the dialogue, the play hardly survives as a unity. The observations,
such as "Men die and still they are not happy", or "Everything around
me is lies, and I want to live in the truth", or Caligula's realisation after
killing his mistress that "killing isn't the solution" and his question
"Who would dare in this world to condemn me without a judge, where
no one is innocent?" compel our attention, even though they lead to
the cul-de-sac of nihilism. Caligula cannot understand, and his own
humility is the saving grace of Camus, which, even when he leads the
race towards pessimism, makes his company far preferable to the dog-
matism of Sartre. "What matters is truth. And I call truth everything
that is matter", Camus wrote in *Noces* at the beginning of his career.
His death came suddenly in a road accident on 4 January 1960, a loss
of a great writer and potential dramatist.

Few playwrights of any importance have appeared in France in
recent years; it is almost as if the death of the small Left-bank theatres
of the Fifties has been catastrophic for playwrights, while the good
intentions of Malraux has not had effect; is it that there are no playwrights, or is it the lack of small theatres? It cannot be said that the
principle aim of the different and flourishing French Dramatic Centres
is to encourage new experiments; rather their task is to offer what is
best from the past and contemporary repertories.

François Billetdoux (born 1927) is the only playwright of any
stature to appear. He first attracted attention with his ironic study of
two opposites drawn together through drink in *Tchin-tchin* (1959) but
it was the production of *Va Donc Chez Torpe* in the Studio des
Champs-Elysées (1961) which established him as a writer to watch.

[1] See original on p. 409.

Here we meet the beautiful Madame Torpe in her Central European pensione where recently five of her clients have committed suicide. A police inspector arrives to investigate, only to discover that all her clients are hovering on the precipice of self-destruction, and that Madame is doing nothing about it. It is left to the inspector to argue the case for life.

In *Comment va le Monde, Môssieur? Il tourne, Môssieur* Billetdoux allies Brechtian Epic technique with French lightness of touch. "The text consists of a single dialogue of the two heroes, to which is added as a counterpoint the words of the songs. These must not be recited, but should be taken beyond that" Billetdoux writes in his notes. The theme deals with the friendship of Hubert Schulz with Job, an American, between 1944 and 1945. Starting in a concentration camp Schulz follows Job to the States, thus enabling a contrast to be drawn between to achieve effects, and the result is somewhat pretentious. Real achievement in art is simplicity; with *Silence, l'arbre remue encore* (1967) and even more so with *Rintru pa trou tar, hin!* (1971) Billetdoux seems to have fallen into confusion, and risks ending up with a coterie, impressed by his incoherence, rather than a public who cannot be fooled all the time; better to join the two solitary drinkers of *Tchin-tchin*. the European's impressions and an American way of doing things.

*Il Faut Passer par les Nuages* was produced by Jean-Louis Barrault in the Théâtre de France, 1964. Billetdoux describes this as an *épopée bourgeoise* in five movements. The action takes place in the south-west of France, where the heroine, Claire Verduret-Balade, in the course of the play moves from being rich to the dispossession of her fortune and absolute poverty. It is a highly ambitious play, but the author has an excessive overflow of language and obscurity, and the play lacks, it seems to me, the precision of *Va Donc chez Torpe*; he is trying too hard

Just as once upon a time we were all socialists (if Sir William Harcourt's observation was true), so the modern French theatre assumes that we are all philosophers now. All plays, of course, have presented some kind of a philosophy even though it was no more than the expression of the author's temperament, a kind of philosophy of the theatre — to use Cocteau's terminology — whereas the modern French theatre introduces the philosopher into the theatre. We have already seen in the case of Sartre how a philosopher has found a large public by becoming *un homme de théâtre,* a public which is willing to accept that existentialism rather than the play is the thing — even though they would never dream of studying existentialism in *L'Etre et le*

*Néant.*

Gabriel Marcel, unlike Sartre, can hardly be described as a man of the theatre, for although he has always from childhood been attracted by the theatre, he has remained strictly a philosopher. His plays, so rich in philosophical content, are often stimulating and profound, but they can also appear contrived, artificial and, alas, monotonous. They are not, heaven forbid, the type of *pièce à thèse* which Marcel also detests, but somehow his attempt to expound complex philosophical conflicts in terms of commonplace character types and every-day conversational dialogue just cannot ring true. His plays have a dimension which requires some kind of symbolism and stylisation to simplify for the audience the reality of the conflict, but Marcel rules out these devices and relies on natural dialogue. The plays are of interest more for their ideas than as good theatre, and it is for this reason that Marcel — in spite of the moderate success he has achieved in France — is never likely to find the wider and international public that Sartre (much less a philosopher, but much more a playwright) enjoys. We shall not, therefore, attempt in this outline a study of the theatre of Marcel and the development of the philosophical background, since such a task would be out of all proportion to his status in the modern drama. The theatre for him is a subsidiary interest, as is music, and although he recognises the importance of the drama as second to none in the arts, he approaches it like a surgeon does a patient, not as an artist does life.

Gabriel Marcel is a philosopher, not a prophet, and consequently he is honoured in his own country. His plays are philosophical conflicts, they do not present ready-made solutions and they are never dogmatic.

Nothing could be further from his intentions than the existentialist drama of Sartre or Camus, with which his name is so often carelessly associated. It has been convenient for French critics to pigeon-hole Marcel as the leader of the Christian wing of the existentialist school (which has led Sartre to emphasise that his atheistic type of existentialism is the only coherent and logical analysis), which Marcel himself denies. In a talk given at the Institut Français in London in July, 1950, (and subsequently translated by Rosalind Heywood and published in the introduction to *Three Plays* by Gabriel Marcel) he defines his plays as the drama of the soul in exile: "For me, the soul in exile is the soul who has become a stranger to itself, who can no longer understand itself, who has lost its way. . . . But we are *not* alone, and only too often our uncertainty takes the virulent form of misunderstanding our own intentions and our own behaviour to other people. Once this happens, our misunderstanding inevitably becomes contagious and tends to spread misery and bewilderment." For his drama of the soul in exile Marcel takes ordinary characters and leaves them to fight out their situation in ordinary conversation; they do not fully understand themselves, nor do others their situation. His conflict becomes an intellectual challenge, running through all his works from *Le Seui. invisible,* written in 1914, up to the present. Among his best known works are *La Chapelle ardente* ("The Funeral Pyre") produced in 1925, *Un Homme de Dieu* from the same year, and *Le Monde cassé* (1933). No satisfactory account can be given in a few lines of the ideas implicit in these plays, the *angoisse* provoked by their inner conflict. Perhaps a suggestion of these features may be found if we recall the theme of *Rome n'est plus dans Rome,* produced at the Théâtre Hébertot in 1951, and one of the most actable of Marcel's plays.

In *Rome n'est plus dans Rome* Marcel confronts a problem which is one of the most disturbing anxieties for all Europeans, and especially those who have suffered German occupation: whether when threatened with Russian occupation and the dictatorship of the Communist Party, one should escape while the going is good, or stay and fight. Can the flight to freedom, like those who escaped to London in the last war, be the solution for the next war? Should those who know that they are on the extermination list dare to stay? It should be remembered that at the time the play was produced it was a known fact that Russia could have overrun Europe in a few days had the cold war turned hot.

So the stage is set. A French professor is known to be on the Communist black list, and his wife, thinking of their children, has secured for him — against his wishes — a chair in French literature in a South American Dominican university. We also meet the professor's nephew, Marc-André, who having left school asks his uncle whether he should flee to a job he has heard about in Equatorial Africa, or stay. If he stays Marc-André fears that he must become a Communist in order to save himself, although he does not believe in Communism. The professor gives in to his wife's wishes, and they all sail for South America. But it turns out to be a reactionary university where the professors must be actively engaged in turning their subjects to suit the ends of propaganda. Too late the professor realises his mistake: the duty of Frenchmen is to remain in France. When asked to speak over the radio and give a message to those who remain in France, he denounces the lines of Corneille:

Et, comme autour de moi j'ai tous les vrais appuis,
Rome n'est plus dans Rome, elle est toute où je suis.

"That is false", he exclaims through the microphone, Rome must remain in Rome: "We were wrong to leave; we should have stayed and struggled on the spot. The illusion that you can take your country with you is only the origin of pride and foolish presumption. You who are perhaps hesitating before the threat of to-morrow, remain, I implore you, and if you do not feel able . . . if you have not the strength . . ."

His speech ends uncompleted, but we know his message is complete. Faith is the only way to fight the menace.

Such is the type of 'lounge-suit' tragedy which Gabriel Marcel describes in the tragedy of the soul in exile. He would offer a promising evening's debate for those theatre-goers who are more interested in the argument than in the importance for a play to reveal an imaginative vision of life.

From time to time the French take a holiday away from classical and philosophical texts and enable us to enjoy the unsophisticated and good-humoured way of life under the Midi sun. For a portrait of Provence we have but to turn to Jean Giono whose *La Femme du Boulanger* has so admirably captured the mood of the region, while Marcel Pagnol holds the mirror to the comings and goings in the old port of Marseilles (before it was destroyed) in his *Marius* trilogy. In both Giono and Pagnol we have the different generations, the old cronies gossiping in the bistro drinking their pernod, the schoolmaster determined to get the better of Monsieur le Curé, the Lyonnais gentlemen trying to convince César that Paris is larger than Marseilles, while the young Marius is torn between the desire for adventure and his love for Fanny. These plays come gloriously alive, there is a down-to-earth humanity which makes us feel the characters exist and we know them out of the theatre. The part of César was created by the late Raimu in the original production of *Marius,* and his performance has been magnificently recorded in the film version — how seldom can such acting be enjoyed these days. How can we ever forget the tender affection he shows for his son when he reminds Marius of his duty to marry Fanny: "Honour, Marius, is like matches: it is only any good once."

Emmanuel Roblès (born 1914) is remembered for his prize-winning play *Montserrat* (1948). Montserrat is an officer in the Spanish army which is fighting the Venezuelan insurrection led by Simon Bolivar.

Montserrat is led to disgust with his own side by the excess of cruelty they inflict on the rebels, and secretly he warns Bolivar that he must flee before capture. His treachery is discovered by his own side, and Izquierdo, who commands the garrison, has him and six innocent passers-by in the street arrested. These six innocent victims will be held as hostages and shot unless Montserrat discloses the hiding-place of Bolivar. One by one the innocent characters are dragged to their execution, to the horror of Montserrat. The repetition of this scene six times does not lead to monotony, but such is the dramatic skill of Roblès that the terror increases death by death. When Montserrat faces his own, it is with final relief that we know the revolution will succeed, and that the sacrifice has not been in vain. Roblès wrote one other play *La Verité est morte* (1953) which proved a failure. Since then: nothing.

# TWENTY-ONE

# OTHER EUROPEAN COUNTRIES

"A man enters a shop and asks for some reading spectacles. As none of the pairs of glasses enable him to read,
after turning the shop half upside down, the optician
becomes impatient and asks him:
" 'Now tell me, are you sure you can read?' "

PIRANDELLO

"The craft of playwrighting is an optical illusion.

DÜRRENMATT

PARIS, London, New York — but theatre and playgoing are
not, we hope, to be restricted to the big three. Many of the
masters of the modern theatre would be excluded were plays
only produced in these cities — in fact, the modern theatre would
probably not exist at all. Ibsen was a Norwegian, Strindberg a Swede,
Pirandello an Italian. And a theatre-going public is to be found in most
of the European capitals, often more enlightened than those who consider themselves the élite among playgoers on the boulevards, Broadway,
or Shaftesbury Avenue. Moscow, of course, is a great theatre city, and
many of the capitals of her satellites have also a flourishing theatre,
so far as the theatre can be said to flourish under the yoke of 'socialist
realism' (or should we say 'Soviet realism'?). The Polish theatre outwardly seems prosperous, and to have escaped the worst dictates of
the Commissars; but between two camps it is influenced either by the
nihilist plays of the West, or the lip-service it must pay to the Soviet
Commissars of the East, though it has in writers like Slawomir Mrozek
established an identity of its own.

In the last ten years the West German theatre has made important
advances, and Berlin is once again a theatre-going capital, with the
Schiller Theatre among the most active and adventurous in any city.
And of course, in East Berlin there is the famous Berliner Ensemble

which Brecht established, and which continues to flourish and make frequent tours in the West.

The strong municipal theatres throughout West Germany, with each contending with the other for the works of local and foreign talent (Düsseldorf has secured the world premieres of Ionesco, for example), have added hope to the revival of the German drama. Finally there is a flourishing theatre in Zurich which rose to fame during the war when it was able to speak for the German-speaking nations by producing Brecht, just as to-day it is able to produce the foremost dramatist in the German language, Friedrich Dürrenmatt, and also plays by his compatriot, Max Frisch. Dürrenmatt is now director of the Basle theatre.

## MARTIN WALSER

A playwright who has come to the forefront in the recent stirrings of the theatre in Germany is Martin Walser (born 1927) whose dramatic method closely resembles that of Dürrenmatt or Frisch. Walser is working on a German trilogy, the first part of which *Eiche und Angora* "Oaktree and Angora", produced at the Schiller Theatre, Berlin, 1962 and translated and presented at the Edinburgh Festival as *The Rabbit Race*), is a caustic and pessimistic parable on modern man in general, and German guilt in particular. In a darkening world there is little cause left for hope; man trims his conscience to whichever wind of creed is blowing. First we see a representative group of German soldiers preparing the defence of a town against the oncoming French at the end of the war (but really they are getting out of harm's way). Then we see the same men as civilians shortly after the war is over; finally we see them ten years later. Their creeds change with the changing times, their consciences dance to the new tunes, but their hearts remain the same. The ugly hypocrisy of these ever-respectable men is unconsciously put into focus by the play's chief protagonist, a political innocent called Alois. Alois's great interests are rabbits and getting in to a choral society; but since he also likes to be a good German he has taken pains to imbibe Nazi doctrine and furthermore has submitted his body to sinister medical experiment (the result of which is that he has become a matchless counter-tenor). Alois cannot understand how what is right one moment can be wrong the next. First he is a traitor because he was the inadvertant cause of the town's surrender, then immediately after the war he is hailed as its deliverer and admitted into the choral society as a patriot in the cause of German science, and then, as the spirit of German militarism revives, he is obliged to leave the society because he is an embarrassing reminder of the past. The grim climax comes when Alois, utterly bewildered and certain only that he should never more try and do what is right, affixes the skins of his rabbits to the flags of many nations that flutter over a festival scene. He doesn't know himself why he commits this act and puts it down to come unconscious prompting. The audience however are in no doubt as to the author's meaning: the skins say that once more blood is in the wind — for each rabbit bore a Jewish name. Finally Alois goes voluntarily into an asylum, happy in the thought that he will be getting better and better while the world outside is getting worse and worse.

*Eiche und Angora* is a powerful play that derives its strength from the economy of its writing and the harrowing force of its argument. The second play of the German trilogy, *Der Schwarze Schwan* ("The Black Swan") was given its première at the Staatstheater, Stuttgart. Whereas Alois was sent to an asylum, in this play the hero, a young student called Rudi Goothein, is already in one. Rudi's father (like the father of the German boy in Peter Shaffer's *Five Finger Exercise*) is a war criminal, in this case a doctor guilty of genocide. When his son finds out the truth, his mind breaks. The question arises how to cure Rudi's illness. Walser offers a contemporary parallel to Hamlet; Rudi stages a play within a play performed by the inmates, to move the conscience of the guilty.

In *The Detour* (1961) Walser portrays a pompous, shallow bully type of company director who decides to make a detour on his way to Munich in order to pay a visit to an old flame who lives at Ulm. The reception he gets from Frieda, however, takes the wind out of his sails for she is more than a little cold. Hubert it appears had in the past failed to desert his wife for Frieda, and Frieda has not forgotten this. She describes the manner in which she killed her husband Erich; Hubert is puzzled whether he should believe this when Erich comes in. Frieda and Erich proceed to quiz Hubert with double-edged questions until suddenly, fastening him to a chair and putting his bare feet in water, they prepare to electrocute him. Frieda is for summary execution but Erich insists on a trial — and if possible a confession. The charges are: that Hubert murdered Frieda as a woman' by his faithless conduct and in doing so ruined Erich's life as well. Hubert confesses to part of the charge and worms his way out of the rest in a manner that wins the respect of Erich as it excites the anger of Frieda. Hubert is now released and he and Erich go off for a drink.

Like so many Germans of his generation, Walser finds himself between two ages, the past discredited, and the present, which Walser portrays as a satirist. Walser is certainly the most promising German playwright to emerge, and as the outline of these themes suggest, he has a deep concern for the society in which he finds himself. Yet although he has undoubted dramatic sense, he has not the dark overwhelming strength of Dürrenmatt, nor does he observe with the sensitivity of Frisch; his characters are in danger of becoming caricatures at times. But he is a writer of great promise, a white hope for the years to come.

### FRITZ HOCHWÄLDER

The name of the Austrian dramatist Fritz Hochwälder first attracted attention in 1952, when his play *Das Heilige Experiment* was presented in Paris under the title *Sur la Terre comme au Ciel*, and caused an immediate stir through the relationship of its theme with that of the worker-priest controversy then topical. The play was subsequently presented in London and New York under the title *The Strong are Lonely*, which assured him of an international reputation, and not merely as an author of a controversial play. *Das Heilige Experiment* was in fact written in 1943, and Hochwälder is now the author of eight other plays, including *Donnerstag*, a modern miracle play written in 1959 for the Salzburg Festival in the hope that it might replace *Jedermann*. Born in Vienna in 1911, Hochwälder went into exile in Switzerland in 1938, and has lived there since, thus taking his place alongside the two Swiss dramatists Frisch and Dürrenmatt.

*Das Heilige Experiment* is an experiment carried out in a Jesuit college at Buenos Aires in the year 1767. The Jesuit fathers are building in Paraguay a kingdom of Heaven on earth. With the arrival of the King of Spain, and as it turns out, the Pope's representative, they have to decide between abandoning their work in Paraguay and defying their instructions and following their individual consciences "for the greater glory of God". It is a case of submission or open rebellion. One of the fathers refuses to submit, suggesting that perhaps for a long time they had all ceased to be Jesuits. The same father, when later brought to face a Spanish firing squad, submits and receives absolution. Duty demands obedience, but in their hearts the question remains unanswered "what shall it profit a man to gain the universe if he should lose his soul . . . ?"

Hochwälder's second play *Der Flüchtling* ("The Fugitive", 1945) is taken from a scenario by Georg Kaiser, is set in a German-occupied country. A fugitive seeks refuge in the house of a frontier guard and his wife; the guard accepts the beliefs of the fugitive. The twist of *Der äffentliche Ankläger* "The Public Prosecutor," 1949) is that the prosecutor Fouquier-Tinville at the time of the French Revolution conducts a case against an unknown person who turns out to be himself. It is a theme which would certainly have interested Dürren-matt, from whose work the public prosecutor and executioner are seldom absent.

After a further play on a religious theme *Donadieu* (1953) set in the period of the French Huguenot wars, Hochwälder presents the moral aspects of the theft of a bag of gold in *Die Herberge* (1956). His next play *Der Unschuldige* ("The Innocent", 1958) has for its theme the prospect of a respected "Biedermann' who is suspected of murder when a corpse is unearthed in his garden; the body is that of a Napoleonic soldier, but the establishment of his innocence does not comfort the citizen whose guilt complexes have been awakened and whose views on moral certainties been changed.

*Donnerstag*, the modern miracle play written for the Salzburg Festival is a variation on the Faust theme. A salesman employed by "Beliac Inc" is commissioned by the "Grossingenieur" (the devil) to find a man dead, though physically alive. A famous architect Pomfrit, who has lost his faith, hope and charity, is engaged as candidate. He is promised bourgeois comfort, space travel, and the most beautiful blonde in the world — in return for his own soul. There is a time limit of three days — until Thursday. The pact is in the end violated by Pomfrit, who prays to a God he does not believe in, so that "man in his final hour has freedom of choice". Like Cocteau's *Bacchus* Hochwälder would seem to use a religious theme as providing the drama between opposing forces of good and evil, a conflict of ideas without himself taking sides.

There are only two characters in *1003* (1963) — the author and his imagination. Here the author is in process of losing his creation, who seems more alive than himself. Once again as so often in the modern theatre since Pirandello we have an experiment in form and the elimination of the frontiers between imagination and reality.

Hochwälder's *The Raspberry Picker* (1965) may be described as an Austrian farcical variation on the more austere black comedy themes we have come to expect from Dürrenmatt. A notorious mass murderer, the Raspberry picker who is thus nicknamed because he used to send his victims to gather berries in the woods, where he shot 8,000 of them with his telescopic-sighted rifle, is given shelter by the disreputable councillors of an Austrian town, partly out of political sympathy, partly out of fear of being exposed "for what they really are". Once again we have Hochwälder's obsession of the fugitive walking into our midst. But who is this fugitive? The irony comes when he is none other than a petty thief they have chosen the wrong man. In a rewritten ending for the Zurich production Hochwälder provided a further twist by making the petty thief a Jew, and thus restoring the self-assurance of the neo-Nazi councillors.

The development of Hochwälder and his constant experiment both in ideas and form makes him not only an important dramatist for the German-speaking theatre, but together with Dürrenmatt and Frisch, also living in Switzerland, and Peter Weiss, another "exile" living in Sweden, it may be said that the most interesting living dramatists anywhere to-day are to be found in these representatives of the German language.

## ROLF HOCHHUTH

Until the production in 1965 of *The Investigation* by Peter Weiss the most forceful documentation on the horrors of Auschwitz had come from a young German writer Rolf Hochhuth (born 1931) whose controversial play *Der Stellvertreter* ("The Representative" in London, "The Deputy" in New York), caused a storm of protests from Catholics following its production in Berlin in 1962, and in Paris in 1964. Hochhuth accuses the Vatican of having kept silent during the mass extermination of the Jews, although even the Pope himself was fully aware of what was happening in the concentration camps. In the course of an eight hour script Hochhuth has martialled his documentary evidence, but much less effectively than the cold impressive statement of facts without comment to which Weiss bears witness. There is something tendentious in Hochhuth's dramatic treatment; only two of his scenes come alive, the audience with Pope Pius XII himself, and the dialogue between the Jesuit priest and the Mephistophelian S.S. doctor who is a lapsed priest and has turned to the orgies of the gassings as a means of provoking God to prove his existence. The theme itself follows the Jesuit priest, Riccardo Fontana, from the time he meets with the cool indifference of the Pope and the refusal to commit the Vatican to intervention, to his taking it upon himself to wear the yellow star of David and join a transportation of Jews from the gates of the Vatican to their end in the gas chambers of Auschwitz.

The present Pope Paul, when he was still Cardinal Montini, protested in a letter to *The Tablet* that according to his reports (he had not himself read the play) the portrait of Pope Pius was that of a man "inspired by a calculating political opportunism"; this is in fact not so, for Hochhuth's portrayal was not far from Pope Paul's own description of Pius as having an "exquisite sensibility and the most delicate human sympathies". Judged by artistic standards Hochhuth has much to learn on the art of the theatre; the play seems flat and poorly constructed. One has the feeling this is more of a thesis which has to be studied on paper before you can decide on the rights and wrongs of the facts presented; as theatre it is certainly less effective propaganda than a play like *The Diary of Anne Frank*.

In *Die Soldaten* (The Soldiers, 1967) Hochhuth sees in Churchill the incarnation of all that is Machiavellian and perfidious; Churchill is accused not only of duplicity, but in ordering personally the murder of General Sikorsky, leader of the Polish Government in exile, who died in a plane crash at Gibraltar before Yalta. This is not the place to take up political cudgels with Hochhuth; Churchill was certainly no angel and was responsible for many foolish adventures in his life, but never such a crazy concept as getting rid of Sikorsky (to hand Poland as an offering to Stalin?). It was completely against Churchill's strategy. On the other hand it should be noted that the Russian agent for Spain at that time was a man named Philby, supposedly carrying out the orders of His Majesty. In the face of such facts the documentary evidence of Hochhuth's play collapses, and nothing else remains.

GÜNTER GRASS

Where Hochhuth was pretentious in his attacks on Pope Pius XII and Churchill was in claiming the authenticity of historical facts, Günter Grass (born 1927) does not fall into this trap. He succeeds in his play *Die Plebejer proben den Aufstand* (The Plebeians rehearse the Uprising, 1966), because in making his play one of speculation he is not so much concerned with destroying the reputation of a hero as with capturing in the ethos of the Berlin tragedy a statement for our times. Just as in his savage mockery of the Third Reich in his novel "*The Tin Drum*", so we watch Brecht's reaction to the East Berlin Worker's rebellion in June 1955, during those critical 24 hours when the future of Communism was in the balance. What did Brecht do? Certainly he was no hero, for Brecht never believed in heroics. He went on rehearsing his company in his famous Marxist re-interpretation of Shakespeare's "Coriolanus". Momentarily he hesitates, he sits on the fence, and in the end, too late, he sends his guarded letter of support, adding as a post script his continuing affirmation of loyalty to the party and regime. Only the last was published and used against the workers. So Brecht, like other Germans during the Nazi period, preferred "safety first". Abstract Marxism was more important than convictions. Hypocrisy, said la Rochfoucauld, is the homage paid by vice to virtue.

Grass is also the author of a number of earlier plays, including *Hochwasser* (High Tide, 1957), *Noch zehn minuten bis Buffalo* (Ten Minutes from Buffalo, 1959) and *Die bösen Köche* (The Wicked Cooks, 1961).

## ITALY

In Italy, where the theatre has such a fierce struggle against the material superiority of the Italian cinema, there are a number of playwrights of interest, though only Ugo Betti has achieved eminence and had success beyond Italy's frontiers. The other playwrights have yet to suggest that the theatre in Italy has the vitality (however much it may lack the prosperity) of the cinema.

We have left out in this survey Eduardo de Filippo, born 1900, because his work in his native Naples is unrelated to the modern trends in drama. De Filippo is in his humour, humanity and pathos, pure Neopolitan gold. While still young he played in the company of the famous Eduardo Scarpetta (1853-1925) and then joined a dialect theatre group. Since 1925 de Filippo has written prolifically. His genius is in the ordinary business of living, his heroes seem to be reconstructions of himself face to face with the noise, gaiety and sadness of life around him. He is one of the few great personalities in the modern theatre; he would be unique in any age, but without Naples De Filippo would surely die. For the Neopolitans forget neither their kings nor those who wear the mask or assume the heritage of Pucinella.

## UGO BETTI

Inevitably after the death of a great dramatist the mantle of his fame is assumed to fall on a playwright of the younger generation, as for a time Ibsen's was said to have fallen on Helge Krog. Pirandello's mantle has not fallen on Ugo Betti, for this is a dramatist with his own vision of a world on trial, a vision which avoids the innate pessimism of the great Italian master. Ugo Betti (1892–1953) was a High Court judge, and an acute observer of the reaction of those condemned. As a philosopher of man, Betti realises the transcending quality of human courage and the need for Christian charity in a world where social conditions and upheavals make us all in some degree condemned, and even the best of us incompetent to judge other men. His characters long for a reconciliation with God, so that they can reveal the nobility of their souls. Betti is not a dramatist of pessimism, far from it, but living through an era of Fascism and disaster for Italy, Betti could not help being a wiser and a sadder man than others.

His first play *La Padrona*, produced in 1927, attracted attention by the force and even violence of his theme and writing. Twenty-five plays have followed, as well as short stories and a novel. Among his plays are *Frana allo Scalo Nord* (1935), *Notte in Casa del Rico* (1942) and *Ispezione* (1947), the last one having affinities with Priestley's *An Inspector Calls*. But we shall consider here three more recent works, *Corruzione al Palazzo di Giustizia* ("Corruption at the Palace of Justice" — broadcast by the B.B.C. under the title "The Sacred Scales") produced in 1949, *Delitto all'Isola delle Capre* ("Goat's Island") produced in 1950, and his last play *La Regina e gli Insorti* ("The Queen and the Rebels") produced 1953.

In *Corruption at the Palace of Justice* Betti contemplates the possibilities of the discovery of corruption in high places, and the miscarriage of justice which could be worse than the corruption. Ludvi-Pol, a man of great power and evil repute, commits suicide in the law chambers, and the scandal of his death causes consternation among the judges, since nearly all have been involved in corruption to suit Ludvi-Pol's intents. The guilty party is known to one man who, mortally sick, takes the guilt upon himself, and leaves the guilty member to seek his own salvation in the knowledge of his rival's gesture, and in the suicide of a young girl caused through the case.

*Goat's Island* is a very different type of play, wild and pagan in its tempo, for it is set in that part of Italy beyond the Eboli Christ stopped at. The action takes place in an isolated farmhouse in the midst of marshland and far from the nearest town. Here Agata with her daughter Silvia and her sister-in-law Pía have gone to live after Agata's husband has left her. Life there is like the title of the play, for they are cut off as it were on an island living with their goats. The life is dreary, for the three women are not peasants, until one day a stranger arrives carrying a sack and announcing that he was an intimate friend of Agata's husband. It is soon obvious that he has come to stay and take the place of the husband who had once said to him "Angelo, go to my home and find my wife. Take my place, and you'll be night and day the master of the house." So he sits down with the three women to dinner. He is at home and helps himself to wine:

> Drink then, my friends. Ah! You were a little flock without a shepherd: just notice how a man's voice livens things up! What excellent cheese! And what nice goats! Do you know what people say about goats and shepherds in my country? A tall story but true . . . they say that shepherds, because they have to remain alone for such a long time with the company of their beasts, forget the language and customs of men . . . when they believe no one is present, they bleat "beeh" . . . they don't boast about it, but they have been caught out . . . and then you can guess the rest without difficulty. . . . That is why in the villages of my country the best guardian of goats is a devil. . . . Come on, all of you, why aren't you drinking?

Angelo stays, an absolute parasite, but a passionate lover of Pía and Agata, much to Silvia's disgust. She is driven to desperation and attempts to kill him, but Agata warns him just in time. Angelo realises that he has to make her happy like the other two.

The final act is an act of fate. Angelo goes down the well one day where Agata's husband used to store his wine (the well has dried up) and the ladder falls, imprisoning him there. Gradually he realises that the women don't intend to rescue him. There is an unknown power which prevents Silvia and Pía from doing so. They leave for the town, and Agata remains behind, so as to be beside the memory of Angelo "until the beginning of eternity".

In his last play Betti returns to a Christian theme which we can all accept, the dignity of the human soul in face of martyrdom. In *The Queen and the Rebels* we are in a world of rebellion, a world where ordinary people all try to be on the side of the law but where always the unfortunate and innocent are convicted. Argia, a prostitute, is taken captive along with other travellers during a period of internal revolution, on the pretext that the ex-Queen is in the neighbourhood. Argia discovers the identity of the ex-Queen among the travellers and discusses with one of the guards (who has been her lover) how they can sell her to the authorities. But on meeting the ex-Queen alone, Argia takes pity on the poor girl who is terrified of everyone and only wants to be allowed to live in peace:

ARGIA     What do you want?
THE QUEEN To be left alive. Nothing else. Unknown, far away. And
          to sleep, night after night, in peace.

To be Queen is Argia's desire, to be what she never can be, because she is so common. But soon the tables are turned, the Queen dies and Argia is accused of being the Queen. She appeals to the guard, her lover, to save her, but he no longer comes to her aid. There is no way out for Argia but to be Queen:

> Now every eye shall look to the ground. There shall still be
> someone to stand before you. Yes, I am the Queen!

Her courage is equal to her rôle, a prostitute can be queen, for the object of life is to be lived regally.

Two years after his death the plays of Ugo Betti had been discovered, and in the autumn of 1955 three of his plays were running in the West End. Introduced by the B.B.C. Third programme, *L'Aiuola Bruciata* was presented by the Arts Theatre Club, *The Queen and the Rebels* offered Irene Worth a chance in an actress's lifetime at the Haymarket, while *Summertime* was a reminder that Betti was a versatile playwright and could laugh as well as be a philosopher in the theatre. *Summertime* is an unimportant piece, the mildest of light comedies, but sharing with the serious works that unique sense of theatre which was Betti's great understanding. His death is a serious blow for the modern theatre, for his work brought to the theatre the outlook of a philosopher and a humanist, to say nothing about the Italian love of all that is dramatic in life.

★

The contemporary Italian theatre is better known for names of directors like Paolo Grassi, Giorgio Strehler, and Luca Ronconi rather than dramatists. Only Diego Fabbri (born 1911) and Dino Buzzati (born 1906) attract attention among the playwrights. Fabbri has written *Inquisizione* ("Inquest", 1950") which concerns the spiritual crisis of a priest, and *Il seduttore* ("The Seducer", 1951) which examines man's attraction and different approaches to love in different women. Dino Buzzatti is the author of a very compelling play in *Un caso clinico* ("A Hospital Case", 1953), which is an astringent satire on an ultra modern hospital. Patients who are not really ill are accommodated on the top floor of a skyscraper building, and according to the gravity of the case they descend downwards until those on the ground floor have already virtually ceased to live. We follow the terrifying sequences of events which threaten Giovanni Corte, a formidable tyrannical business executive who unintentionally finds himself a patient in the hospital, where he had merely gone for a consultation; as his spirit becomes more depressed, he is moved downwards from floor to floor although everyone in the hospital reassures him that there is a very good reason, and that he is behaving in his protests "like a big baby". In the end his descent is complete, to the ground floor. With no hope there is no alternative but to die. In this play Buzzatti has brilliantly portrayed not merely the case of an ordinary individual caught in the machinery of hospital efficiency, but the image of every man ageing and dying like cogs in a machine it cannot understand.

### POLAND: SLAWOMIR MROZEK

The October rising in 1956 had more fortunate consequences in Poland than in Hungary. Even allowing for the fact that the censors have since tried to curb intellectual freedom, the Polish theatre had already reflected Western influences. In Beckett's Godot Poles recognised a symbol of their own impossible situation; Jan Kott in *Shakespeare our Contemporary* had offered an existential interpretation of Shakespeare. A young school of Polish playwrights was gradually emerging; of these Slawomir Mrozek (born near Cracow, 1930) is the most promising and outspoken.

Mrozek first came to notice as a satirist when "The Elephant" was published in 1957. The following year his first one act play *The Police* was produced. He has written numerous other short plays, but it was his full-length play *Tango* which was to win him recognition following its productions in Poland, Germany, and, in 1966, by the Royal Shakespeare Company in London.

*Tango* is a play concerned with three generations, but only the young generation has the say. Arthur is an idealist, searching in vain for an answer to the generation of his parents. He is disgusted at their rejection of the principles of grandma's generation; in their free and easy non-conformism he sees the consequence of the contemporary chaos. The time has come for a further revolution, the return to discipline. Arthur first tries the past and stages a real old-fashioned wedding; but he realises this is impractical. Confused, he endeavours to assert his authority and impose his ideals but alas, he is not a superman. He is himself killed by his mother's lover, Eddie, who as a servant had been up till now in the background. Intellect is not enough, brute force takes over. Eddie now dictates to the entire family and forces the reactionary granduncle to dance a tango, which brings the play to a stylish and precise climax.

So *Tango* is acted out like the dance itself, with three forward steps corresponding to each generation, and a reversal. It is the drama not only of Mrozek's own generation in his native Poland, but of us all in the Western world. We are also witnesses of a parody of our innate tragedy in his earlier play *The Police*. The last prisoner in a Ruritanian country is ready to sign his confession after ten years of interrogation. This places the Chief of Police in a highly iniquitous situation, for there is nobody left in his prisons or for him to arrest. If he is to keep his job, there must be at least one prisoner; there is no alternative for his sergeant to play the role of prisoner as he has been doing already that of *agent-provocateur*. The prisoner becomes the *aide* to the general he tried to throw a bomb at when he was anarchist. Before the end of the play the general, the aide and the chief of police have arrested each other, giving work to the police at last, while the sergeant becomes the rebel with the famous cry: Long live Freedom.

Mrozek has also written a number of highly amusing one acters, but his other full length play *Second Service,* which consists of three rather bizarre nightmares, lacks the humour of *Tango*. At first sight Mrozek, who now lives in Italy near Genoa, seems to be a follower of Ionesco, but gradually he emerges as a powerful and original mind; in *Tango* he has written the masterpiece of the decade which far transcends national boundaries or thoughts.

### JERZY GROTOWSKI

If it is in spite of Communist Commissars that Mrozek has achieved international fame, even more so is the case of Jerzy Grotowski (born 1933) who has become the Stanislavski of our times. Grotowski, in fact has taken over many of the rough ideas suggested by Stanislavski and developed them first in his Theatre Laboratory at Opole and since

1965 in his Institute on the art of the Actor at Wroclaw, Poland. Wroclaw has become for the theatre what the Film Institute at Lodz was for the cinema a decade or two ago. Among those who have been influenced by his theories are Peter Brook, and his theories are evident in such productions as The Living Theatre.

In the Institute Grotowski presents his productions in small halls where actors (never more than a dozen) intermix with audience (never exceeding 80). Taking subjects of a mythical nature Grotowski returns us to the very basis of theatre by enabling the actor to redefine legends for us, to express his sub-consciousness *vis-à-vis* our civilisation. None of the acting is improvised, on the contrary, his actors must respond to a severe methodology. The actor is himself, and the text of the play is used as a wall. The actor, by attempting the impossible, extending himself to the limits of his physical and mental endurance, is literally making an offering. As Grotowski puts it, the art of the theatre is very close to prostitution, "he repeats the gesture of redemption . . . and finds out where the theatre is irreplaceable". The gift of one self has to be confidently delivered, through discipline; the actor has to free himself of his complexes, like in psychoanalysis.

Hence the use of myths as confrontations rather than the desire to seek identification. The actors have an amazing physical dexterity and endurance; he has to know himself completely, to be ready to give, perform, his public confession. Everything that is not essential is extraneous; the stage is as bare as possible.

Perhaps Grotowski is more remarkable, like the early Corbusier, for his theories rather than his achievements. His production at the Edinburgh Festival of the *Akropolis* of Wyspianski, also seen in Paris, was not as exciting as his blue-prints. Set in a crematorium at Auschwitz, rather than in Cracow Cathedral like in the play by Wyspianski in 1904, we watch his inmates building a funeral pyre while we the audience are all dead. In the end I am forced back to the belief that the text, far from being a board to play against, must be the creation and the truth which the director, actor and finally the audience will interpret and experience. Otherwise we might as well accept the words of Orson Welles: "We only have theatres because actors have to act in them."

## HUNGARY AND CZECHOSLOVAKIA

The Hungarian Rising of 1956 revealed momentarily a number of potential dramatists: Tibor Déry, for example, better known as a novelist, who started writing plays only after the last war; Laszlo Németh, whose *Galilei* was actually produced at the time of the Rising. Alas, any hopes for a theatrical renaissance were as short lived as the rising. We witness another glimmer of hope just before the Prague "Spring" twelve years later. The Czech theatre, which in the twenties had given us such writers as the Capek brothers and Frantisek Langer, lay dormant under the Nazi and Stalinist years of oppression. It was not until the early sixties, later than most of the other satellite countries, that a visible thaw enabled a number of young playwrights to come forward and enable the Czechs one again to relax, laugh at their bureaucracy and the nightmares of a Kafkian reality. The best known is Václav Havel (born 1936) who in spirit is close to Mrozek in Poland; there is much of the theatre of the Absurd in Havel's work. In *Zahradni Slavnost* (The Garden Party, 1963), we have a study of the mind and vocabulary of bureaucrats, their meaningless ramifications of planifications, their outworn stereotyped vocabulary, their endless slogans and labyrinthine clichés of Communist party jargon. "To-day," Hugo explains to his parents, "we are no longer at the period of static and unalterable categories where A was only A and B never anything but B. For to-day we know that A can at the same time be A and B, and B can perhaps be A and C, and not only C, but A, B and D; in certain circumstances it can even happen that F can be OQY and even R!" After which his poor father has to admit that his son has in his blood "the sane philosophy of the middle classes". He gathers his daring and his courage, and risks it as he shouts his belief: "the Czech people are immortal and survive all misfortune!" Perhaps the last word we should remember from Havel; a second play of his Vyrozumeni (The Memorandum) was produced in 1965, three years before the Russian tanks brought down again the iron curtain.

SPAIN: JACINTO BENAVENTE

In the theatre Spain has given us, as well as García Lorca, her only Nobel Prize winner Jacinto Benavente. Benavente had the fecundity of the great Spanish dramatists, though he did not capture their spirit half so successfully as did Lorca. For Benavente was not only a Spaniard, but also a European; he had translated into Spanish Shakespeare and Molière, was a student of Ibsen and had read Freud, and had a general admiration for and understanding of the ways of the West. All this he introduced in his volumes of plays, produced over a period of more than sixty years, and which ranged from satire and comedy of manners to the drama of ideas and the philosophy of sceptism; from realism to fantasy there seemed no end to Benavente's industry to cover the whole field of modern dramatic experiment. His theatre is consequently too diverse to attempt any satisfactory short study, and all his plays together do not seem to this critic to have anything like the merit of Lorca's half-dozen folk dramas. Europe and Spain is somehow an unsatisfactory hybrid, and while all of us must admire the civilised intellect of a man like Benavente, his plays do not come across to us as fresh and powerful in their interpretation of the Spanish soul as might have been hoped. It is almost as if Benavente was concerned in introducing from abroad the attitude of mind to enable Spain to become part of the West; he was not caught up, as, for example, Pirandello was, in the creation of his own imagination; for Benavente (unlike Pirandello) passion did not need to be brought to bear on intellect — ideas could walk perfectly well by themselves. Benavente has had one success in translation, his famous *Los Intereses Creados* ("The Bonds of Interest") written in 1907, but it is questionable whether his plays will ever be widely known abroad. Far more likely that he will be remembered in histories of the drama as a Spaniard who let loose modern European movements in Spain, delighted in exposing the foibles of Spanish society and survived his satires to find himself a national hero, worshipped by all.

Since Benavente's death in 1953 the Spanish theatre continues with what might be called 'caretaker playwrights', if this term may be used to suggest those who carry the theatre on until such time as an important new dramatist arrives.

## SCANDINAVIA

The Danish playwright Kaj Munk (1898-1944) was, like Lorca, one day suddenly snatched from his home and family, driven away secretly, and his bullet-riddled body thrown into a wayside ditch. Munk was a Lutheran pastor, in fact priest, politician and playwright. He wrote some twenty plays, among which the best known are *An Idealist, The Word, Cant,* and *The Elect.* Had he lived there is reason to believe that he would have become a considerable figure in European drama, but his work up to the time of his martyrdom in 1944 was a powerful attack on dictatorship and a trumpet call to action, perhaps too *engagé* to have permanent value. One of his last works was *Niels Ebbeson,* based on the life of Denmark's national hero who himself resisted the invaders of his day. No wonder the Nazis were after Munk's blood, for he could not be silenced any other way and in his plays there is the testament of a man who suffered for his faith, for truth and freedom, and who knew that he had defeated his murderers.

Another victim of the war was the Norwegian playwright and poet Nordahl Grieg (1902-1943). His most important work was *Nederlaget* (The Defeat) set in the Paris Commune, but very definitely featuring contemporary society in its implications. The conviction of right and the ardour of faith in face of the darkness of defeat is the theme, and the result is a political drama of white heat. Again we have the death of a young dramatist who would almost certainly have developed had he lived.

JAPAN: YUKIO MISHIMA (1925-1970)

Tokyo has, in recent years, joined the ranks of London, New York and Paris as a major theatre centre. Like so much in modern Japan, a technetronic civilisation is surplanting traditional structures and culture. The younger Japanese are little interested in their past; they are as likely as never not to have been to a Noh play or a Kabuki performance. The gloss of Western civilisation may not have changed their insularity, their politesse, but it has forced them into their own schizophrenic world. You have only to look through the advertisements in popular Japanese magazines and newspapers, where the influence of Maddison Avenue surplants the tea ceremonies and Buddhist temples of the tourist posters.

Nobody was more aware of the discrepancies between traditional values and present materialism than Yukio Mishima. In his writing Mishima seemed to belong to both the West and the Orient; perhaps that is why he was the best known Japanese writer in the West. Yet Mishima has all the fanaticism of the Japanese mentality; he had tried in the theatre to help the Noh play tradition to continue by writing new plays dealing with contemporary themes. In the end his dramatic hara-kiri was the final act of an obsession, a final protest to cling to Japanese standards and principles which the example of his death would revive. A gesture of a romantic idealist to some, and a criminal act to other Japanese, which perhaps demonstrates their profound divisions.

Mishima's best known and most successful play was *Sado Koshaku Fujin* (Madame de Sade, 1965). He had found, in reading a biography of de Sade, that the figure of de Sade's wife was the key to her husband. De Sade, then, seen through a woman's eyes is the theme, or altogether five women's eyes, for her mother, Madame de Montreuil, represents law and society; the younger sister Anne, proves her feminine guilessness by having an affair with the marquis. There is Madame de Saint Fond who thinks she understands de Sade's behaviour best of all because she knew that he "was the bloodstained abortion of God who could become himself only by escaping from himself, and that whoever there was beside Alphonse — the woman he tormented and the woman who lashed him — were Alphonse too". Another woman puts the religious viewpoint, the servant the workers, but it is his wife who remains the enigma. Why, having demonstrated such absolute fidelity during all the years the Marquis was in prison, did she leave her husband when he was freed. The riddle is explained when his wife came across de Sade's book *Justine* where she recognised herself:

> The poor heroine of the book! . . . It is just as if Alphonse had portrayed me as a girl, when I knew nothing. I realised that it may have been for my sake that he wrote this story about a woman who suffers repeated indignities on account of her virtue.

Whereas she had believed Alphone her husband and her were one, suddenly she saw herself as his Justine. The play ends with her turning de Sade away: "The marquise will never see him again."

With this play Mishima had crossed into a foreign culture; the bridge between East and West proved too much in everyday life. His loss was one neither culture could afford.

# TWENTY-TWO

# THEATRE AND MASS MEDIA

"The theatre has become for the most different types of
public a kind of Esperanto, a language within a language."

CAMILLE BOURNIQUEL

OURS is an age of miracles in science and mediocrity in the
arts; the miracles of science have been and are being put to
evil uses and their destruction of man is reflected for man in
the arts. Man has surpassed his own imagination, discoveries are made
faster than intelligence can appreciate their significance; yet far from
living in an age of great adventure, watching new horizons opening up
before us as they must have done in the days of the Renaissance, our
eyes are turned inwards towards the terror and confusion which surround the modern tempo. What should have been the greatest adventure of all turns to criminal disillusionment; the pace has made us lose
control and instead of nations uniting to rise together on the synthesis
of human achievement they turn on one another, dog eats dog, and in
their madness threaten the extinction of existence. What a fiasco! No
wonder artists cannot reveal the hopes when man has not the courage
to realise them. The spirit of the age is something completely alien to
the delight of discovery of the Renaissance or Elizabethan man, who
celebrated the crescendo of his excitement in poetry, drama and the
arts. To-day we all know that the individual no longer exists — as
one wit once noted, there is even a society of individualists — and man
has been replaced by machines which operate without thinking. The
spirit of the age is anxiety, confusion, despair, and a desire to escape
from the responsibilities of man's genius and folly without being able
to do so. For the easy solution of the Twenties 'to eat, drink and be
merry' is no longer possible to-day; the artist is committed to intervene
directly in the lives of the people and prick their conscience by holding

a mirror to the turmoil. We enter here a maze from which there is no escape.

The drama, more than the other arts, is influenced most directly by the spirit of the age and the intellectual level of the playgoer. The theatre does not exist for plays meant only to be read, and a play which does not immediately communicate with an audience and hold their interest while in performance ceases to be a play, or to belong to the drama. The novelist can write for an individual reader and invite him to enter alone his world of imagination; the artist can paint for an individual viewer and even the pianist can perform as well in rehearsal as in recital. The theatre, on the other hand, is quite different, for it is a collective whole. The audience, the actors and the playwrights are its three essential creators, and they cannot be separated. Anyone who believes television drama can be a substitute ignores the vital rôle and meaning of theatre; television plays may in their own right be a medium of expression and a craft, but if a dramatic experience is anticipated you may as well look through the wrong end of a telescope. The personality that comes from a close up of a face momentarily captures the small screen — but you cannot hold a close up. Television does not, cannot present a whole. It is an impatient medium, the point must be made immediately to be effective and dialogue must be rationed if it is to have the maximum visual effect. For the television viewer in his arm-chair does not listen, he watches. Language as such becomes mere signposting.

There is little doubt that for many people deprived, for various reasons, of the chance of visiting the live theatre, television drama fills a need; the magic box is clearly better than no theatre at all. But it can never replace the magic that comes from audience participation. A member of the audience knows that his support, which becomes the collective will of an audience, determines the performance. Television can be turned off with a switch, while a play is live and the magnetism between actor and audience has a communicative power unknown to television watchers. The conventions in the drawing-room are not those of the auditorium.

It has often been said that a play always finds the audience it deserves (though in the long run), and so why should not the reverse be true, that audiences find the play *they* deserve (and in the short run)? I think that the mediocrity of so much of the contemporary theatre is to be explained through the confusion which has resulted from the arrival of the mass media. We have taken the new media like mechanical toys without being aware of their potential harm (and good); we have become the servants of our inventions rather than the masters because we have not troubled to learn how to live with them. Just as instant culture has replaced culture (and for that matter pop art risks being mistaken for art) so in the theatre instant drama replaces drama. We have embraced the new media without keeping a sense of perspective; the old truth of Gresham's law remains, yet we have not realised the meaning of mass or what Ortega y Gasset foresaw long ago, "the revolt of the masses". If mediocrity drives out the best, it can at least be claimed at the other end that it ensures technical standards of efficiency. We reach, like society, the level of the common denominator which may, economically speaking, have never been so good for so many, but from the cultural viewpoint, produces products rather than works of art.

We have seen in the course of this study of modern drama how great dramatists have risen above the spirit of their times and entered the living traditions of the drama. On the whole, however, the serious theatre to-day is not one of illumination, and if we divide dramatists, to use Bernard Berenson's definition of "life-enhancers" and "life-diminishers", we realise that the modern dramatist, with the notable exceptions, is increasingly falling on the side of the "life-diminishers". The life diminisher sees no further than a claustrophobic maelstrom of confusion, he does not perceive the levels of reality, he eschews the dimension of illusion. He is at once negative, destructive, and prefers the alienation of materialism to screen his inability to come to terms with life and the mysteries of creation. The life diminishers have succeeded so well in their task that they have almost wrecked the aesthetics of drama and have so blinded audiences that they threaten to overthrow the continuation of dramatic values as we have always known them.

This is not an argument against the mass media, nor is it a swan song for the living theatre; the media are a *fait accompli*, we cannot ignore them; what we have to ensure is that they do not usurp the place of the theatre or drive it into a cultural cul-de-sac. The public viewing a television play at a normal viewing hour in any Western country is to be counted in millions; the most successful box-office successes in major theatrical capitals can hardly muster more than a few hundred thousand. There is however an overlap, witness the theatrical managements who are only too anxious to preview an act of their productions on the small screens to entice viewers to visit the live production;

television drama itself makes frequent use of its drawings from the commercial theatre, and here lies the danger, for the theatre should not be regarded as having a complementary identity with television. Rather the theatre must offer something different, an experience which television does not nor ever can rival.

Television is like an evening paper, it lives on topicality and information; theatre on the other hand is just theatre. The one is a craft like journalism, the other an art. Television then cannot kill the drama, for it is a new form of daily journalism. If the drama dies — and it is often forgotten that it is mortal — it will be through its failure to give the public what television cannot provide, a theatrical experience. Plays which can only be understood on careful reading and mean nothing at first performance, plays which interpret life in the chaos of Orwellian "doublethink", where ambiguity becomes a kind of crossword for the author's own enjoyment, such fancies and fashions can no longer be afforded if the theatre is to keep open in an age of mechanical entertainments. No more can the slick, tailor-made, triangular light comedy be allowed to monopolise the boards, for rather than see a second-rate play the public will remain by their T.V. sets. If the theatre tries to fight T.V. by imitating it, it is lost. The theatre must offer something different and continue its traditions if it is to continue its existence.

Never have our theatrical entrepeneurs been so bewildered about the fickleness of public taste. Until 1956 or thereabouts they believed implicitly that this was best served by flights of escapist fancy; now the wheel has almost turned full circle, and managements can claim to have tried everything from kitchen comedy to the frontiers of obscurist drama and the wilder absurdities of morbidity. In vain they have sought for the gimmick, unconvinced that good theatre is in itself sufficient. Why, we may ask, should this age with its infinite possibilities require gimmicks; why indeed should the life of the ordinary citizen whether of say Birmingham, Milwaukee or Lyons seem dull must remain questions which could only be answered outside of the canvas of this book. Because our average citizen to-day is protected from the cradle to death by the Welfare State, and insurance schemes, it seems a bitter irony that all this should seem dull. The popular press try to make this appear otherwise in an effort to take the public out of themselves, while evading their more serious responsibilities. The community prospers, with more time than ever before for leisure and the arts. Not only in Britain and North America, but in every industrialised country a large percentage of the population sit by their television sets every night; as such they are better informed as a mass than ever before, but against this, a surfeit of non-stop T.V. is as good a way as any to blunt the desire to be taken out of oneself. To repeat Claudel's definition of the theatre:

> Man grows bored and the ignorance he was, born with sticks to him. And not knowing a thing about how it begins or ends, that's what makes him go to the theatre.

For the theatre is an art, and neither television or the evening paper can offer a coherent view of life. If the drama dies, it will not be the fault of television, but through its own failure to give the public what television cannot provide, a theatrical experience. This is a danger also in obscurist drama which can only be understood on careful reading and explanation of the symbols. Such assaults on the human brain no longer meet the needs of the times.

In *Cahiers Renaud-Barrault* a number has been devoted to *La Télévision, une dramaturgie nouvelle*. Jean-Louis Barrault insists that "television, as an art, is happenings, or the projection of happenings, or the reconstruction of happenings, even in time . . . the climate of the cinema is . . . *romanesque*. That of theatre is the presence in the present: the physical presence." Television, he claims, is a combination of presence with the *romanesque*, in other words, happenings.

Perhaps this is the place to dismiss any consideration of so-called "Happenings" which end up by being little more than practical jokes; such experiments belong to the world of culture-mongers whose senses have been blunted by pop-art, op-art or whatever peg the latest gimmick electronically dictates. Happenings, however, in another sense can take the form of improvisations which can be traced back to the *Commedia del'Arte* tradition. Group improvisation and setting about the writing of a collective script on a given theme is to be found in Peter Brook's production of *U.S.* (1967). I think the fault in this type of production is that Brook is playing to an audience he has chosen: the leftist intellectuals of Chelsea or Hampstead, London, the typical readers of the Sunday *Observer*, who deplore American action in Vietnam without doing anything about it. Brook presents *U.S.* in the form of a living newspaper, we are given the facts about Vietnam, a man is painted different colours to represent the two Vietnams and then pushed against a canvas to leave his imprint; the result is unfortunately more like playing clever games, talking to no point about

o

Vietnam and in the end doing nothing about it either, other than burn a butterfly on stage. The audience is left to return to their cosy existence with their books and piles of gramophone records and welfare state domesticity.

The actual theme of the American tribal love-rock musical *Hair* (1967) even less than *U.S.*, is not for export; after all, the burning of a draft card on stage cannot mean the same to others as it does to citizens of the United States. The danger was evident, that when produced outside the States, as happened in its Paris production, *Hair* risked becoming an anti-American musical. Several months too late, the Paris production had to be drastically modified on the insistence of those who had launched *Hair*. What is important, however, is not that *Hair* is just a hippie musical, but the so-called tribal liberation belongs to a long American tradition of using the stage as a means to protest about what is going on in their own free country. Back in 1925 John Howard Lawson attempted a "Jazz Symphony of American Life" in *Processional*, which, although it failed in the Theatre Guild production, nevertheless proved that jazz was to be the rhythm of American life. Another forerunner of *Hair* may be said to be Olson and Johnson's wild extravaganza *Hellʒ-a -Poppin'* produced in 1939; a number of the "spontaneous" ideas of *Hair*, those who stroll round the audience, have their 100 per cent American origin back in *Hellʒ-a-Poppin'* — but there is a difference. Never before *Hair* had an American generation had to assert its "liberation" by its rejection of basic assumptions. For the first time American youth were taking over those European qualities of being negative. This trend, however, would seem to be transitory; already the rock opera successor to *Hair*, *Jesus Christ Superstar*, is a return to the Bible, not so much a challenge to the Billy Grahams as a compliment, in the best American evangelist tradition.

There is no room here for us to be side-tracked by the so-called Theatre in the Nude, the cult of which was not started by *Hair*, but Kenneth Tynan's revue *Oh! Calcutta!* which without the gimmick of nudity would hardly have fitted the bill for a fourth rate student's charity show. We are a long way from the Aristophanic tradition, with his devastating satire worthy of a great mind.

Present trends in the theatre seem to be away from the playwright's theatre: to-day the playwright is neither thinker nor creator in the productions of Grotowski, Peter Brook, The Living Theatre, and elsewhere. Max Frisch, in a recent interview in *Le Monde*, has already accepted the disappearance of the written text. As a result, he has decided not to continue with playwrighting. The traditional theatre, he feels, is already doomed. Replying to a question as to what function he sees for a theatre without playwrights or text, Frisch replied: "A very important and short future. The eclipse of literature would be like the removal of pictures from churches at the time of the Reformation, which were later replaced by others." Frisch likewise feels that the Epic theatre of Brecht is doomed, for the theatre can only stir the forces of revolt in an erotic way, such as torture. He does not believe that dramatic art can "any longer represent social structures which have become too complex and underground to appear on the stage".

I would agree with Frisch that momentarily the new deviations of the drama could correspond to Marshall McLuhan's "the medium is the Message" and that the Gutenberg revolution is here and cannot be ignored. Nor, on the other hand, can we ignore the public and the risk that in a relatively short space of time the theatres will themselves be empty. Only then will the living traditions of the great masterpieces assert themselves, and the theatre will continue as an art, with playwrights, new trends, but it will be a theatre without labels.

The theatre never will be a mass medium. There must however be a sufficiently large minority public to support the living theatre, and according to their demands and rejects, the theatre will survive. If we are content with the inferior, the second-rate will give way to the third-rate until the theatre of compromise becomes the theatre of the lowest common denominator, an ersatz theatre.

In the last decade, however, the contemporary drama has shown a new restlessness and rebellion against "safe box-office propositions"; in Britain even the star system has taken a knock with the magnificent team work achieved by the two major London companies, the National Theatre and the Royal Shakespeare Company. In New York the Lincoln Centre is equally ambitious. It is easier to end a book on the contemporary theatre to-day more optimistically than I did in the first edition in 1956. In Britain at least the theatre has again attached itself to a living tradition, and augurs well for a theatre for tomorrow. This, however, does not mean that all is well; the artist in any modern epoch has so often been rejected in his life, to be discovered by posterity. Likewise, there are many second-rate talents who are vastly overpraised and because they run after fashions are "with it".

The question remains, from Pirandello to whom? Who, indeed, of the living dramatists are the 'life-enhancers', among whom we may include Pirandello, Claudel, Giraudoux, Lorca from yesterday. Alas, so many writers to-day are 'life-diminishers'. Will they continue in fashion, or is there already a stir which promises to be a prelude to a revival in the life-force of the arts, and indeed a new hope for the world? Are we beginning to build up from the debris, to reconsider our definitions and beliefs? The very concept of good and evil, so upset by our existentialist moralists and our great dictators, continues to play its rôle with certain modern dramatists as it has done, unchanging in its laws, throughout the centuries of dramatic history.

We want to know about this place man occupies in the universe. We want the theatre to be our revealer and to be able to approach, at the frontiers of theatre, the great unknown. For in the supreme moments of theatre there is a collective communion which can give life itself a meaning. The theatre in the living tradition of the drama gives man hope, faith and courage in fellow-man. The world in any age is as exciting or as terrible as man makes it, and according to the spiritual level at which man wishes to live — for since the beginnings of drama the theatre has been associated with religion. "Who shoots at the midday sun, though he be sure he shall never hit the mark, yet as sure he is he shall shoot higher than he who aims at a bush", wrote Sir Philip Sidney in the true spirit of the Elizabethan age. Have we the courage to aim likewise? Making the theatre live means making the theatre part of our existence and an expression of the continuity of the life-force.

# ACKNOWLEDGMENTS

THOSE critics who have become part of dramatic history appear to the young critic like the giant Atlas himself; they are our inheritance (though not responsible for our views) and yet it is not the done thing to canonise them in a list of acknowledgments. I do, however, acknowledge the debt I owe to contemporary critics and writers, and even here a list of all the sources of information collected over the years from reading about the theatre in newspapers, magazines, books and in conversation would be impossible. I have given a selected bibliography of those books which cover some of the subjects discussed in this volume and which may help to fill in the background.

For permission to include quotations from plays discussed (and the translations where these have been used) I would like to thank the following:

Signor Enzo Scipioni and *Amministrazione degli eredi di L. Pirandello*, and E. P. Dutton, New York; the Office Artistique International for quotations from the plays of Jean Giraudoux; Librairie Gallimard, Paris, for extracts from Paul Claudel and Jean-Paul Sartre (Copyright by Librairie Gallimard); Messrs. Faber & Faber for T. S. Eliot quotations and for the quotation from *Casida de la. Hinda*, published in Arturo Barea's *Lorca, the Poet and his People;* Mr. Roy Campbell and Miss Karin Alin, Stockholm (representing Trustees of the Garcia Lorca estate) for the passage from *Blood Wedding;* New Directions, New York, for the passage from *The House of Bernarda Alba* published in *Three Tragedies;* Messrs. Methuen for passage from Jean Anouilh's *Colombe;* Messrs. Secker & Warburg for quotation from *Three Plays by Gabriel Marcel*, introduced and translated by Rosalind Heywood; Messrs. Calder & Boyars for quotations from *Marat* by Peter Weiss, English version and verse adaptation by Adrian Mitchell; Messrs. Methuen for quotation from *Count Oederland* by Max Frisch, translated by Michael Bullock; Messrs. Jonathan

Cape for quotation from *Theaterprobleme* by Friedrich Dürrenmatt, translated by Gerhard Nellhaus; Messrs. Faber & Faber for quotations from the works of John Osborne.

I would like to thank Mr. Iain Hamilton who originally encouraged me to write this book, Mr. Richard O. Paterson for his suggestions and Mr. Lothian Small, who has provided me with translations of Claudel and Giraudoux. Mr. Small's translations are those marked with an asterisk. Where translations are taken from other sources I have indicated the translator; those where no translator is named are my own responsibility.

In this new completely revised and enlarged edition I would like to thank in particular Mr. Peter Gardener for all his assistance in notes, synopsis and editorial help while I was working against the calendar; also to his wife Leah. Finally to Mr. Michael Stapleton and Miss Paula Davies.

I do not, of course, ask friends to share my views; I stand to be judged alone.

F.L.
*London, 1 March, 1966.*


For the revised edition I would like to acknowledge the following for permission to include quotations from plays discussed.

Adam International Review and translators Mary Mayer and Bernard Seal for the extracts from Jean-Paul Sartre's *Bariona*;

The Oxford University Press for the quotation from *A Yard of Sun* by Christopher Fry;

Grove Press Inc. for the quotation from *Madame de Sade* by Yukio Mishima, translated by Donald Keene.

F.L.

# SELECTED BOOK LIST

The following selected books are those most likely to be of interest and help to readers of the present volume; the list does not aim at being exhaustive. Ibsen and Shaw are not included, and the choice of other works has been restricted to those easily obtainable in libraries and bookshops. Fuller bibliographies will be found in those volumes marked with an asterisk.

## I REFERENCE BOOKS

*The Oxford Companion to the Theatre*, Edited by Phyllis Hartnoll. (Oxford University Press. Second edition 1957.)

*World Drama*, by Allardyce Nicoll (Harrap, 1949).

*Who's Who in the Theatre*, Edited by John Parker (Pitman, 10th ed., 1957).

*European Theories of the Drama*, by Barrett H. Clark (editor) (New York, 1918. Revised 1947).

*Masters of the Drama*, by John Gassner (New York, 1940. New ed., 1954).

*The Reader's Encyclopedia of World Drama*, Edited by John Gassner and Edward Quinn (New York, 1969).

*Storia universale del teatro drammatico*, by Vito Randolfi (UTET, Turin, 1969).

*The Rise and Fall of the Well-Made Play*, by John Russell Taylor (London, 1967).

## II THE WORLD'S A STAGE

*Le théâtre Moderne — hommes et tendances* (ed. Jean Jacquot: Centre national de la récherche scientifique, Paris, 1958).

*Théâtre et collectivité*, A symposium edited by André Villiers (Paris, 1953).

*Frontières du théâtre*, by Paul Arnold (Paris, 1946).

*Playgoing*, by James Agate (Jarrolds, 1927).

*Le théâtre et son double* by Antonin Artaud (Paris, 1944).

*Réflexions sur le théâtre*, by Jean-Louis Barrault (Paris, 1949. Translated and published by Rockliff, 1951)

*The Playwright as Thinker*, by Eric Bentley (Published in London under the title *The Modern Theatre*, 1948).

*In Search of Theatre,* by Eric Bentley. Collected essays. (New York, 1953. London, Dobson, 1954).

*Métamorphose de la littérature (de Proust à Sartre)* Volume 2, by Pierre de Boisdeffre. Essays on Cocteau, Anouilh, Sartre and Camus (Paris, 1952).

*Animateurs de théâtre,* by Robert Brasillach (Paris 1936. Revised ed., 1954).

*On the Art of the Theatre,* by Edward Gordon Craig (London, 1911. New edition as *Dramatic Scene,* 1923).

*Edward Gordon Craig — Designs for the Theatre,* by Janet Leeper (Penguin Books, 1948).

*A Study of the Modern Drama,* by Barrett H. Clark (New York, 1934. Revised ed., 1938).

*The Actor and his Audience,* by W. A. Darlington (Phoenix House, 1949).

*Drama and Life,* by Roger Dataller (Nelson, 1938).*

*Tragedy,* by W. Macneile Dixon (Edward Arnold, 1924).

*Souvenirs et notes de travail d'un acteur,* by Charles Dullin (Paris).

*Drama,* by Ashley Dukes (London, 1926. Revised ed., Home University Library, 1936).*

*The Organised Theatre,* by St. John Ervine (Allen & Unwin, 1924).

*Poetry and Drama,* by T. S. Eliot (Faber and Faber, 1951).

*The Three Voices of Poetry,* by T. S. Eliot (National Book League, 1953).

*Selected Prose,* by T. S. Eliot (Penguin Books, 1953).

*The Idea of a Theatre,* by Francis Fergusson (Princeton University Press, 1949).

*L'art du théâtre,* by Henri Ghéon (Montreal, 1944).

*New Theatres for Old,* by Mordecai Gorelik (New York, 1940. London, Dobson, 1947).

*L'essence du théâtre,* by Henri Gouhier (Paris, 1943).

*The Use of the Drama,* by Harley Granville-Barker (London, 1946).

*The Theatre in our Times,* by John Gassner (New York, 1954).

*Life and the Theatre,* by Lynton Hudson (Harrap, 1949).

*Théâtre et vie intérieure,* by Georges Jamati (Paris, 1952).

*Témoignages sur le théâtre,* by Louis Jouvet (Paris, 1952).

*The Theatre of To-morrow,* Kenneth Macgowan (New York, 1922).

*Continental Stagecraft,* by Kenneth Macgowan and Robert Edmund Jones (New York, 1922).

*Dramatic Values*, by C. E. Montague (Chatto & Windus).
*The Poet in the Theatre*, by Ronald Peacock (Routledge, 1946).
*Les deux cent mille situations dramatiques*, by Etienne Souriau (Paris, 1950).
*La mise en scène théâtrale et sa condition esthétique*, by André Veinstein (Paris, 1955).
*The Stage is Set*, by Lee Simons (New York, 1932).
*My Life in Art*, by Constantin Stanislavsky (London & New York, 1938).
*Notes sur un tragique et une tragédie*, by Paul Valéry (Paris, 1946).
*La psychologie de l'art dramatique*, by André Villiers (Paris, 1951).
*Drama from Ibsen to Eliot*, by Raymond Williams (Chatto & Windus, 1952).
*European Drama*, by N. Scarlyn Wilson (London, 1937).
*The Art of Drama*, by Ronald Peacock (Routledge & Kegan Paul, 1957).
*The Producer and the Play*, by Norman Marshall (Macdonald, 1957).
*Index to the Story of My Days*, by Gordon Craig (Hulton, 1957).
*Life of the Drama*, by Eric Bentley (London, 1965).
*Anatomy of Drama*, by M. Boulton (1960).
*Theatre of Revolt*, by Robert Brustein (London, 1965).
*Drama Essays*, by N. F. Dennis (London 1962).
*Nature of Plot in Drama*, by U. M. Ellis-Fermor (London, 1960).
*Encore Reader*, chronicle of the new drama. Edited by Charles Marowitz (London, 1965).
*Theatre of the Absurd*, by Martin Esslin (London, 1962).
*Twentieth Century Drama*, by Bamber Gascoigne (London, 1962).
*Four Playwrights and a Postscript*, (Brecht, Ionesco, Beckett and Genet), by D. I. Grossvogel (1962).
*The Live Theatre*, by H. Hunt (London, 1962).
*Mid-Century Drama*, by Laurence Kitchin (London, 1960; 1962).
*Sights and Spectacles*, 1937-58, by Mary McCarthy (1959).
*Producer and the Play*, by Norman Marshall (London, 1962).
*The Theatre and dramatic theory*, by Allardyce Nicoll (London, 1962).
*Living Theatre*, by E. L. Rice (London, 1960).
*Theatre, Rediscovery of Style*, by Michel Saint-Denis (1960).
*Dramatic Experience*, by J. L. Styen (London, 1965).
*Elements of Drama*, by J. L. Styen (London, 1960).
*Curtains, 1950-1960*, by Kenneth Tynan (London, 1961).
*Anger and After*, by John Russell Taylor (London, 1962).

*Landmarks in Contemporary Drama*, by Joseph Chiari (London, 1965).

III THE DRAMATISTS

### LUIGI PIRANDELLO

*Luigi Pirandello*, 1867–1936, by Walter Starkie (London, 1926. Revised 1936).
*The Drama of Luigi Pirandello*, by Domenico Vittorini (Philadelphia, 1935).
*Pirandello* by Guy Dumur (Collection "les grands dramaturges", Paris, 1955).

### JEAN GIRAUDOUX

*Le théâtre de Jean Giraudoux, technique et style*, by H. Sörensen (Denmark, 1950).
*L'oeuvre de Jean Giraudoux*, by Gunnan Host (Oslo, 1942).
*Giraudoux par lui-même* (Pictures and texts presented by Christian Marker. Paris, 1952).
*Jean Giraudoux et "Pour Lucrèce"* (Cahiers de la Compagnie Madeleine Renaud — Jean Louis Barrault, 1953).
*Le théâtre de Giraudoux et la condition humaine*, by Marianne Mercier-Compiche (Paris, 1954).
*The Making of a Dramatist, Jean Giraudoux*, by Donald P. Inskip (Oxford, 1958.)
*Louis Jouvet, Man of the Theatre*, by Bettina Knapp (Columbia, 1957).

### PAUL CLAUDEL

*Le drame de Paul Claudel*, by Jacques Madaule (Paris, 1947).
*Introduction à l'oeuvre de Paul Claudel*, by Sainte-Marie-Perrin.
*Paul Claudel*, by Georges Duhamel.
*Paul Claudel and "The Tidings Brought to Mary"*, by Kathleen O'Flaherty.
*Paul Claudel et "Christophe Colomb"* (Cahiers de la Compagnie Madeleine Renaud — Jean-Louis Barrault).
*The Poetic Drama of Paul Claudel*, by Joseph Chiari (The Harvill Press, 1954).
*The Theme of Beatrice in the Plays of Claudel*, by Ernest Beaumont (Rockliff, 1954).
*Paul Claudel* by Jacques Madaule (Collection "les grands dramaturges" Paris).

*Claudel, aujourd'hui* (Cahiers de la compagnie Madeleine Renaud — Jean-Louis Barrault, Dec. 1958).

## T. S. ELIOT

For the development of Eliot's dramatic style, nothing could be more revealing than Mr. Eliot's own self-criticism in *Poetry and Drama* (Faber & Faber). The British Council pamphlet on T. S. Eliot by M. C. Bradbrook (revised 1951) gives the essential background to Eliot's writing.

*The Plays of T. S. Eliot*, by D. E. Jones (1960).

*T. S. Eliot's Dramatic Theory and Practice*, by Carol H. Smith (1963).

## BRECHT

*Brecht* by Geneviève Serreau (Collection "les grands dramaturges" Paris, 1955).

*The Theatre of Bertolt Brecht* by John Willet (Methuen, 1958).

*Theaterarbeit* (Berliner Ensemble productions. 1954 Dresdner Verlag).

*Parables for the Theatre* (two plays, "The Caucausian Chalk Circle", and "The Good Women of Setzuan", New York, Evergeern).

*Brecht: A Choice of Evils*, by Martin Esslin (Eyre & Spottiswoode, 1959)

## GARCIA LORCA

*Lorca, the Poet and his People*, by Arturo Barea (Faber, 1944).

*Lorca, An Appreciation of his Poetry*, by Roy Campbell (Bowes & Bowes).

*García Lorca*, by Edwin Henig (London, 1944).

*Three Tragedies of Lorca translated with introduction* (New Directions, New York).

*Lorca* by François Nourissier (Paris, 1955).

*The Theatre of Garcia Lorca*, by Robert Lema (1963).

## JEAN COCTEAU

*Jean Cocteau*, by Margaret Crosland (Peter Nevill, 1954).

*Dramaturgie de Jean Cocteau*, by Pierre Dubourg (Paris, 1954).

## EUGENE O'NEILL

*The Plays of Eugene O'Neill*, by John H. Raleigh (1965).

*O'Neill: A Collection of Critical Essays*, Edited by John Gassner (1964).

*Eugene O'Neill, the Man and his Plays,* by Barret H. Clark (New York, 1926. New ed. and revised, 1947).

*The Haunted Heroes of Eugene O'Neill,* by Edwin Engel, (Harvard 1953).

*Eugene O'Neill and the tragic vision,* by Doris V. Falk (Rutgens Univ. Press, 1958).

### JEAN-PAUL SARTRE

*Jean-Paul Sartre,* by Maurice W. Cranston (1962).
*L'homme Sartre,* by Marc Beigbeder (Paris, 1947).

### ARMAND SALACROU

*Armand Salacrou,* by José van den Esch (Paris, 1947).

### JEAN ANOUILH

*Jean Anouilh,* by Hubert Gignoux (Paris, 1946).
*A la rencontre de Jean Anouilh,* by Jean Didier (Brussels, 1946).
*Jean Anouilh, Poet of Pierrot and Pantaloon,* by Edward Owen Marsh (W. H. Allen, 1953).

### EUGENE IONESCO

*Ionesco and the Comic Absurdity,* by J. S. Doubrousky.
*Notes et contre-notes,* by Eugène Ionesco (London, 1962).
Special number devoted to Ionesco of "Cahiers des Saisons" (Paris, Winter, 1959).

### JEAN GENET

*The Imagination of Jean Genet,* by Joseph H. McMahon (Yale Univ. Press, 1963).

### HENRY DE MONTHERLANT

*Notes sur mon théâtre* (Paris, 1950).
*Le théâtre de Montherlant,* by Jacques de Laprade (Paris, 1950).

#### IV NATIONAL DRAMA

### THE BRITISH THEATRE

*Dobson's Theatre Year Book,* 1948, Edited by John Andrews & Ossia Trilling (London, 1949).
*No Star Nonsense,* by Peter Cotes (Rockliff, 1949).
*The Unholy Trade,* by Richard Findlater (Gollancz, 1952).

*Christopher Fry*, by Derek Stanford (Longmans, 1954).

*James Bridie and his Theatre*, by Winifred Bannister (Rockliff, 1955).

*The Other Theatre*, by Norman Marshall (John Lehmann, 1947).

*British Theatre*, by Peter Noble (British Yearbooks, 1946).

*Theatre Outlook*, by J. B. Priestley (Nicholson & Watson, 1947).

*Theatrical Cavalcade*, by Ernest Short (Eyre & Spottiswoode, 1942).

*Modern English Drama*, by Ernest Reynolds (1949).

*Drama since 1939*, by Robert Speaight (The Arts in Britain series, London, 1947).

*Theatre of Two Decades*, by Audrey Williamson (Rockliff, 1951).

*The Fugitive Art*, by T. C. Worsley (John Lehmann, 1952).

*Le théâtre contemporain en Grande-Bretagne et aux Etats-Unis* (Etudes Anglaises Paris, October-December, 1957).

*Actress*, by Yvonne Mitchell (Routledge, 1957).

*Experimental Drama*, edited by William A. Armstrong (London, 1963).

*Anger and After*, by John Russell Taylor (London 1962).

*Mid-Century Drama*, by Laurence Kitchen (London, 1960; 1962).


## THE AMERICAN THEATRE

*The Fervent Years*, The story of the Group Theatre and the 'thirties, by Harold Clurman (Dobson, 1946).

*American Playwrights 1918–1938, the Theatre Retreats from Reality*, by Eleanor Flexner (New York, 1938).

*The American Drama since 1918*, by Joseph Wood Krutch (New York, 1939).

*'Modernism' in Modern Drama*, by Joseph Wood Krutch (New York, 1952).

*Modern American Drama and Stage*, by Boyd Martin (Pilot Press, 1943).

*The Theatre Guild Anthology* (New York, 1936).

*Best Plays of the Modern American Theatre*, Edited and introduced by John Gassner (Two volumes, New York, 1947).

*The Off-Broadway Theatre*, by Julia S. Price (1962).


## THE FRENCH THEATRE

*Le théâtre des années folles*, by Pierre Brisson (Geneva, 1943).

*The French Theatre of To-day — An English View*, by Harold Hobson (Harrap, 1953).

*Le théâtre en France depuis* 1900, by René Lalou (Paris, 1951).

*La galerie dramatique*, by Francis Ambrière (Paris, 1949).

*Anthologie du théâtre français contemporain*, Edited by G. Pillement. (Three volumes, Paris, 1945–1948).

*Le théâtre français contemporain*, by Edmond Sée (Paris, 1931. New ed., 1951).

*The Contemporary French Theatre*, by Joseph Chiari (Rockliff, 1958).

*Dictionnaire du théatre français contemporain*, Edited by Alfred Simon (Paris, 1970).

## THE GERMAN THEATRE

*Modern German Drama*, by H. F. Garten (London, 1959; 1964).

*German Men of Letters*, Vol. III, edited by Alex. Natan (London, 1964) — see essays on Dürrenmatt by Professor H. M. Waidson, and Frisch by Martin Esslin.

*Theater-schriften und Reden*, by Friedrich Dürrenmatt (Zurich, 1966).

### v THEATRE JOURNALS

*The Stage* (London, the theatrical profession's weekly newspaper).

*Plays and Players* (A monthly illustrated magazine published in London).

*Drama* (The quarterly published by the British Drama League).

*L'Avant-scene* (Paris, bi-monthly with text of current productions).

*The Drama Revue*, T.D.R. (Tulane Univ., New Orleans) Quarterly.

*Il Drammo* (Milan).

# ORIGINAL TEXT OF PASSAGES
## QUOTED IN THE BOOK

(The translations from the following passages have been made by Lothian Small)

*Quotation A: Siegfried,* by Jean Giraudoux

ROBINEAU ... Qu'as-tu fait pourtant depuis ces douze ans, Zelten? Toi qui aimais le printemps, la musique, la joie, la paix, qu'as-tu-fait?

ZELTEN La guerre! La guerre contre trente-cinq nations. Le combat contre une seule.... Et toi, le porte-lunettes, le démocrate paisible des bibliothèques royales et impériales, toi, mon ami le plus cher, depuis douze ans, qu'as-tu-fait?

ROBINEAU La guerre, contre toi ..

*Quotation B: Siegfried,* by Jean Giraudoux

LEDINGER Revenez avec nous, mon ami. Vous souffrez. Vous avez maigri. Revenez.

SIEGFRIED Oui, j'ai maigri, Ledinger. Mais, autant que de la grandeur de la perte, c'est de la grandeur du cadeau que j'ai souffert ces nuits dernières. Un convalescent, comme moi, aurait plutôt besoin en effet d'une patrie minuscule. Celui qu'on ampute subitement de l'Allemagne et sur lequel on charge la France, il faudrait que les lois de l'équilibre fussent vraiment bouleversées pour qu'il n'en éprouvât aucun trouble. Je vous dirai que j'ai songé, avant-hier, à disparaître, à chercher un asile dans un troisième pays, dans un pays que j'aurais choisi autant que possible sans voisins, sans ennemis, sans inaugurations de monuments aux morts, sans morts. Un pays sans guerre passée, sans guerre future. . . . Mais plus je le cherchais sur la carte, plus les liens au contraire qui m'attachent aux nations qui souffrent et pâtissent se reserraient, et plus je voyais clairement ma mission.

*Quotation C: Siegfried,* by Jean Giraudoux

SIEGFRIED Je vivrai, simplement. Siegfried et Forestier vivront côte à côte. Je tâcherai de porter, honorablement, les deux noms et les deux sorts que m'a donnés le hasard. Une vie humaine n'est pas un ver. Il ne suffit pas de la trancher en deux pour que chaque part devienne une parfaite existence. Il n'est pas de souffrances si contraires, d'expériences si ennemies qu'elles ne puissent se fondre un jour en une seule vie, car le coeur de l'homme est encore le plus puissant creuset. Peut-être, avant longtemps, cette mémoire échappée, ces patries trouvées et perdues, cette inconscience et cette conscience dont je souffre et jouis également, formeront un tissu logique et une existence simple. Il serait excessif que dans une âme humaine, où cohabitent les vices et les vertus des plus contraires, seuls le mot "allemand" et le mot "français" se refusent à composer. Je me refuse, moi, à creuser des tranchées à l'intérieur de moi même. Je ne rentrerai pas en France comme le dernier prisonnier relâché des prisons allemandes, mais comme le premier bénéficiaire d'une science nouvelle, ou d'un coeur nouveau . . . Adieu. Votre train siffle. Siegfried et Forestier vous disent adieu.

*Quotation D: Pour Lucrèce,* by Jean Giraudoux

LUCILE    Sans recours? Quelle erreur! Il est là, dans ma main, mon recours. Je riais de vous tout à l'heure, quand vous m'appeliez vaincue, car il y était déjà. Je le tiens d'une petite fille, qui avait mon nom,´ mon âge, et qui s'est juré, quand elle avait dix ans, de ne pas admettre le mal, qui s'est juré de prouver par la mort s'il le fallait, · que le monde était noble, les humains purs. Cette terre est devenue pour elle vide et vile, cette vie n'est plus pour elle que déchéance, cela n'importe pas, cela n'est pas vrai, puisqu'elle tient son serment!

*Quotation E: Pour Lucrèce,* by Jean Giraudoux

BARBETTE  Tu as bien été violée. Pas par Marcellus, cela on en guérit, cinquante en ont guéri. Tu le sentais bien toi-même. Tu t'en serais remise. Mais par la bêtise des hommes, la grossièreté des hommes, la méchanceté des hommes. Elle t'est apparue d'un coup. C'était trop. Douce comme toi, on en meurt.

*Quotation F: L'Echange,* by Paul Claudel

Le théâtre. Vous ne savez pas ce que c'est? — Non — Il y a la scène et la salle.
Tout étant clos, les gens viennent là le soir et ils sont assis par rangées les uns derrière les autres, regardant,
. . . Ils regardent le rideau de la scène.
Et ce qu'il y a derrière quand il est levé.
Et il arrive quelque chose sur la scène comme si c'était vrai.
. . . Je les regarde, et la salle n'est rien que de la chair vivante et habillée.
Et ils garnissent les murs comme des mouches jusqu'au plafond.
Et je vois ces centaines de visages blancs.

L'homme s'ennuie et l'ignorance lui est attachée depuis sa nais-
sance.
Et ne sachant de rien comment cela commence ou finit, c'est pour
cela qu'il va au théâtre.
Et il se regarde lui-même, les mains posées sur les genoux.
Et il pleure et il rit, et il n'a point envie de s'en aller.
Et je les regarde aussi et je sais qu'il y a là le caissier qui sait que
demain
On vérifiera les livres, et la mère adultère dont l'enfant vient de
tomber malade,
Et celui qui vient de voler pour la première fois et celui qui n'a
rien fait de tout le jour.
Et ils regardent et écoutent comme s'ils dormaient.

(Théâtre, III, pp. 195-196).

*Quotation G: Partage de Midi,* by Paul Claudel
YSÉ      Non, non, il ne faut point m'aimer. Non,
Mesa, il ne faut point m'aimer.
Cela ne serait point bon.
Vous savez que je suis une pauvre femme.
Restez le Mesa dont j'ai besoin.

        .     .     .     .

Dites que vous ne m'aimerez pas. Ysé, je ne vous aimerai pas.

*Quotation H: Partage de Midi,* by Paul Claudel
YSÉ      Et que nous font les autres? mais tu es unique et je suis unique.
Et j'entends ta voix dans mes entrailles comme un cri qui ne peut
être souffert,
Et je me lève vers toi avec difficulté comme une chose énorme et
massive et aveugle et désirante et taciturne.
Mais ce que nous désirons, ce n'est point de créer, mais de détruire,
et que ah!
Il n'y ait plus rien d'autre que toi et moi, et en toi que moi, et en
moi que ta possession, et la rage, et la tendresse, et de te détruire
et de n'être plus gêné
Détestablement par ces vêtements de chair, et ces cruelles dents
dans mon coeur,
Non point cruelle!
Ah, ce n'est point le bonheur que je t'apporte, mais ta mort, et la
mienne avec elle.

*Quotation I: Partage de Midi,* by Paul Claudel
MESA     Dis, Ysé, ce n'est plus le grand soleil de midi. Tu te rapelle
notre Océan?

Mais la lampe sépulcrale colore ta joue, et l'oreille, et le coin de
    votre tempe,
Et se reflète dans vos yeux, vos yeux dans le miroir . . .
                                            *Il souffle la lampe*
La petite lampe est éteinte. Et il est éteint en même temps,
Ce dernier soleil de notre amour, ce grand soleil de midi d'août
Dans lequel nous nous disions adieu dans la lumière dévorante,
    nous séparant, faisant de l'un à l'autre désespérément
Un signe au travers de la distance élargie.
Adieu, Ysé, tu ne m'as point connu! Ce grand trésor que je porte
    en moi,
Tu n'as point pu le déraciner,
Le prendre, je n'ai pas su le donner. Ce n'est pas ma faute.
Ou si! c'est notre faute et notre châtiment.
    Il fallait tout donner,
Et c'est cela que tu n'as pas pardonné.
                                                    *Silence*

Quotation *J: Le Soulier de Satin*, by Paul Claudel
Et crois-tu donc que ce soit le corps seul qui soit capable d'allumer
    dans le mien un tel désir?
Ce que j'aime, ce n'est point ce qui en elle est capable de se
    dissoudre et de m'échapper et d'être absent, et de cesser une
    fois de m'aimer, c'est ce qui est la cause d'elle même, ce qui
    produit la vie sous mes baisers et non la mort!
Si je lui apprends qu'elle n'est pas née pour mourir, si je lui
    demande son immortalité, cette étoile sans le savoir au fond
    d'elle-même qu'elle est,
Ah, comment pourrait-elle me refuser?
Ce n'est point ce qu'il y a en elle de trouble et de mêler et d'in-
    certain que je demande, ce qu'il y a d'inerte et de neutre et de
    périssable,
C'est l'être tout nu, la vie pure,
C'est cet amour aussi fort que moi sous mon désir comme une
    grande flamme crue, comme un rire dans ma face!
Ah, me le donnât-elle (je défaille et la nuit vient sur mes yeux!)
Me le donnât-elle et il ne faut pas qu'elle me le donne,
Ce n'est point son corps chéri jamais qui réussirait à me contenter!
Jamais autrement que l'un par l'autre nous ne réussirons à nous
    débarrasser de la mort,
Comme le violet s'il fond avec l'orange dégage le rouge tout pûr!

Quotation *K: Le Soulier de Satin*, by Paul Claudel
PROUHÈZE Eh quoi, noble Rodrigue, aurais-tu donc voulu que je remette
    entre tes bras une adultère?

Et plus tard quand Don Pélage est mort que je t'ai jeté cet appel
à toi,
Oui, peut-être il vaut mieux qu'il ne t'ait pas atteint.
Je n'aurais été qu'une femme bientôt mourante sur ton coeur et
non pas cette étoile éternelle dont tu as soif.

*Quotation L: Le Malentendu* by Albert Camus
MARTHA  Comprenez que ni pour lui ni pour nous, ni dans la vie ni dans la
mort, il n'est de patrie ni de paix. (*Avec un rire méprisant*) Car on
ne peut appeler patrie, n'est-ce pas, cette terre épaisse, privée de
lumière, où l'on s'en va nourrir des animaux aveugles. . . . A quoi
bon ce grand appel de l'être, cette alerte des âmes? Pourquoi crier
vers la mer ou vers l'amour? Cela est dérisoire. . . . Comprenez
que votre douleur ne s'égalera jamais à l'injustice qu'on fait à
l'homme.

*Quotation M: Les Mouches,* by Jean-Paul Sartre
JUPITER  Imaginez qu'il se présente un jour aux portes de cette ville. . . .
Je dirais donc: "Jeune homme, allez-vous-en! Que cherchez-
vous ici? Vous voulez faire valoir vos droits? Eh! vous êtes ardent
et fort, vous feriez un brave capitaine dans une armée bien batail-
leuse, vous avez mieux à faire qu'à régner sur une ville à demi
morte, une charogne de ville tourmentée par les mouches. Les gens
d'ici sont de grands pécheurs, mais voici qu'ils se sont engagés
dans la voie du rachat. Laissez-les, jeune homme, laissez-les,
respectez leur douloureuse entreprise, éloignez-vous sur la pointe
des pieds. . . . Bon voyage, jeune homme, bon voyage; l'ordre
d'une cité et l'ordre des âmes sont instables: si vous y touchez,
vous provoquerez une catastrophe (*Le regardant dans les yeux*)
Une terrible catastrophe qui retombera sur vous.

*Quotation N: Les Mouches,* by Jean-Paul Sartre
ELECTRE  Il faut que j'éclaire ton visage, car la nuit s'épaissit et je ne te vois
plus bien. J'ai besoin de te voir: quand je ne te vois plus, j'ai peur
de toi; il ne faut pas que je te quitte des yeux. Je t'aime. Il faut que
je pense que je t'aime. Comme tu as l'air étrange!
ORESTE  Je suis libre, Electre; la liberté a fondu sur moi comme la foudre.

*Quotation O: Le Maître de Santiago,* by Henry de Montherlant
ALVARO  A notre sang nul sang ne viendra se mêler. Il n'y aura pas d'homme
qui te tournera et te retournera dans ses bras. Et pas d'enfants,
personne pour me salir, personne pour me trahir: avec toi je
m'éteins dans toute ma propreté. Les derniers! Nous serons les
derniers! Quelle force dans ce mot de *derniers,* qui s'ouvre sur le
néant sublime.

# INDEX